Hebrew
Primer
and
Grammar

Hebrew
Primer
and
Grammar

A. B. Davidson

Sovereign Grace Publishers, Inc.
P.O. Box 4998
Lafayette, IN 47903
2001

*Printed In the United States of America
By Lightning Source, Inc.*

PUBLISHER'S PREFACE

Nothing is more needed today than a deeper study of the Bible, and for this one needs a knowledge of the original languages of Scripture. Many are able to study the Greek of the New Testament, but Hebrew and the Old Testament are somewhat neglected. Because God in His wisdom prepared for His Son by the revelation of the Old Testament, a full understanding of Christ depends upon understanding its message and the language in which it is expressed.

To that end, two beginning grammars of the Hebrew language are offered in one volume as books of proven worth. Whether the student is a layman studying on his own, a pastor reviewing what he studied once before, or a beginning student taking a class in the subject, they will be of great help. Of special interest is the direct approach and exercises, designed for self study, in Fagnani's *A Primer of Hebrew*. McFadyen's revision of Davidson's *An Introductory Hebrew Grammar* is of special value in giving very readable background information and many examples of grammatical points. The books also present the material with a very similar approach but from differing points of view and somewhat different terminology. This allows the student to compare, aiding his understanding by finding that one throws light on the subject where he may have found the other unclear. Thus, the books are completely complementary to each other and give the student a combination that will answer the questions that arise in his study.

It is the publisher's hope that God will bless this book in helping His children learn Hebrew so that they will have a more complete understanding of His Word.

A PRIMER OF HEBREW

BY

CHARLES PROSPERO FAGNANI

Third Edition

INTRODUCTION

The following manual is not put forth as a Hebrew grammar, but simply as a primer of the Hebrew language. Its object is to give a general survey of the principal phenomena of the language, with a view to putting the student, in the shortest possible time and with the minimum of arduousness, in position to begin reading and translating with the use of lexicon and grammar. The standpoint is not that of a contribution to Hebrew philology, but purely practical and empirical. The material has been at times forcibly systematized and some current definitions modified, but only for the sake of simplicity and ease of acquisition; subsequent study will very easily furnish the few readjustments thus made necessary.

The work is a growth; it has been the slow result of ten years of experience in teaching elementary Hebrew. During the first six of these, the author used Davidson's "Introductory Hebrew Grammar" as a text-book, but he gradually was obliged to rearrange and modify the material until, four years ago, he gave up the use of Davidson's Grammar and substituted dictated notes of his own. For four years these notes have been used, tested, revised, corrected, simplified, until they have attained their present form. The chief motive in printing is to save the seminary students the labor of copying some fifty foolscap pages of hektographed material, but the hope is entertained that the Primer may prove useful to a larger circle. The book can be used without an instructor. The attempt has been made (with but partial success, necessarily) to anticipate every possible question a student would be likely to ask (and which students actually have asked) and to guard against all conceivable aberrations from the path marked out, which path will inevitably lead the patient learner in time (say about two months, at the rate of a lesson a day) to the goal proposed; to wit, a sufficient equipment for beginning the study of the original text of the Old Testament with the standard helps, lexical and grammatical.

It is hoped that ministers who have forgotten their Hebrew may find in this little work an inducement to start over again from the beginning; the difficulties of Hebrew are chiefly at the outset, and it is here that simplification and gradatim arrangement can be of most service. Perhaps Sunday-school teachers and other students of the Bible may be tempted to explore a field whose difficulties are not so insuperable as they are traditionally supposed to be.

C. P. F.

Union Theological Seminary,
New York City,
June, 1903.

CONTENTS

LESSON I

                    THE ALPHABET

ORDER	FORM	EQUIVALENT	NAME	PRONUNCIATION OF NAME *
1	א	ʾ	ʾắleφ	áh-leph
2	ב	β / b	Bêθ	bayth
3	ג	γ / g	Gímel	† geé-mel
4	ד	δ / d	Dắleθ	dáh-leth
5	ה	h	Hê	hay
6	ו	w	Wāw	oo-ah-oo
7	ז	z	Záyin	zá-yin
8	ח	ḥ	Ḥêθ	hhayth
9	ט	ṭ	Ṭêθ	tayth
10	י	y	Yôδ	yōdh
11	כ ך	χ / k	Kaφ	kaph
12	ל	l	Lắmeδ	láh-medh
13	מ ם	m	Mêm	maym
14	נ ן	n	Nûn	noon
15	ס	s	Sắmeχ	sáh-mekh
16	ע	ʿ	ʿáyin	ghá-yin
17	פ ף	φ / p	Pê	pay
18	צ ץ	ṣ	Ṣāδê	ssah-dhay
19	ק	q	Qôφ	kōph
20	ר	r	Rêš	raysh
21	שׂ שׁ	ś / š	Śîn / Šîn	seen / sheen
22	ת	θ / t	Tāw	tāh-oo

---

* This column guides only in the matter of pronunciation; the spelling of the names of the letters is found in the preceding column.   † *g* hard.

b.   **REMARKS ON THE ALPHABET**

1. These letters are all consonants.

2. Five letters, Nos. 11, 13, 14, 17, 18, have final forms ך, ם,* ן, ף, ץ, which are used when this letter comes at the end of a word.

3. Six letters, Nos. 2, 3, 4, 11, 17, 22, when written without a dot inside, are aspirated in sound thus: ב, ג, ד, כ, פ, ת.

              bh, gh, dh, kh, ph, th

The equivalents for transliteration are respectively β, γ, δ, χ, ϕ, θ, Greek letters with their modern Greek pronunciation (in order to avoid representing one Hebrew letter by two English letters).

β is sounded like *v.*

γ is difficult to distinguish from *g.*

δ is sounded like *th* in *thus.*

χ is sounded like *ch* in the German *ich.*

ϕ is sounded like *f.*

θ is sounded like *th* in *thin.*

4. No. 1, א (ì,** ìáleφ) stands for a light emission of the breath like that which precedes the utterance of any vowel. It is represented by the sign for the smooth breathing in Greek, with a vertical line added beneath to make it level with the other letters and to show that it is a constituent part of the word.

5. No. 6, ו (w, Wāw) is pronounced like *w* in *water.*

6. No. 8, ח (ḥ, Ḥêθ) is a guttural *h* like *j* in Spanish or *ch* in the German *Sache.*

7. No. 16, ע (ì,** ìáyin) stands for a strong guttural sound with various modifications difficult to reproduce. The Greek rough breathing is a sufficient approximation to it, written like No. 1 with a vertical line beneath as a support.

8. No. 18, צ (ṣ, Ṣāδê) is a hissing palatal *s.*

9. No. 19, ק (q, Qôφ) is a guttural *k.*

10. No. 9, ט (ṭ, Ṭêθ) is a palatal *t.*

11. No. 20, ר (r, Rêš) is pronounced with rolling of the tongue

12. No. 21, שׂ (ś, Śîn) is sounded like No. 15 *s.*

     שׁ (š, Šîn) is pronounced *sh.*

---

* Contrast No. 15, ם.   ** In writing use one continuous stroke.

13. In pronouncing Hebrew words (as indicated in the last column), the continental sound of the vowels is to be used.

The mark ^ or ‾ over a vowel indicates that it is long.

The mark ′ over a vowel indicates the accented syllable, when that syllable does not happen to be, as usual, the final one.

For facility in memorizing, the alphabet may be divided into five groups containing 4, 5, 5, 4, 4 letters respectively, as indicated in the table.

c. SUGGESTIONS FOR WRITING

<h2 style="text-align:center">A PRIMER OF HEBREW</h2>

1. Two strokes at the most suffice to form any Hebrew letter, as shown on p. 3.

2. Notice that the top of the ל (No. 12) extends above the other letters, and the bottom of the ק (No. 19) extends below, thus: קול, לא.

3. Distinguish in writing between ע (No. 16) and צ (No. 18).

4. Note the difference between

ר and ד (Nos. 20 and 4),

ו and ן (Nos. 6 and 14, final form),

ך and ן (Nos. 11 and 14, final forms),

ם and ס (Nos. 13, final form, and 15).

Exercise

Learn the alphabet as a whole and in its five groups backward and forward.

Write the English equivalents of (*i.e.* transliterate) the following Hebrew words.

NOTE. — Hebrew is written from right to left, hence the word at the *right*-hand end of the first line below is the *first* word, etc.

In writing put the Hebrew words in a column one under the other and place the English equivalents alongside to the right,* forming two regular columns.

Write only on every other line.

← אב, אדם, בין, דבר, גם, ויקטל, זהב, תוך, קדש

צדק, פר, אף, עבד, נם, לב, נשא, ארץ.

Write the Hebrew equivalents of (*i.e.* transliterate) the following groups of letters.

NOTE. — Hebrew words must never be divided, as for instance, at the end of a line.

Write the English forms in a column one under the other, beginning with the *left*-hand word of course, and place the Hebrew equivalents alongside to the right with a space between, forming two regular columns.

Write only on every other line.

→ iḥ, drχ, khn, qδš, šm, nφš, irṣ, mzbḥ, bθ, iṣ, śr, kφ, sin, rši, 1ββ, byδ, lḥm, mwθ, mym.

NOTE. — Write final form when required.

---

* In all the exercises the given matter in the book, whether Hebrew or English, must be placed on the left, and the work required done on the right.

Oral Exercise

שכרך, הדברים, האלה, דבר, טפסר, במחזה, אל ,תורה, אנכי,
טפף, ציץ, מאד, ויאמר, אדני, גזם, צבע, ובן, משק, ביתי;

LESSON II

THE VOWEL SIGNS

a. The Vowels are indicated by means of dots and dashes written below the consonants, with two exceptions (1 and 2 below).

1. A single dot written above the left-hand side of the consonant
   = long *o*, thus בֹ = bō.
2. A single dot in the bosom of ו
   = long *u*, thus רוּ = rû (roo).
   The wāw is now no longer a consonant, but merely part of the sign for the vowel.
3. A single dot below   = short *i*, thus לִ = li (lĕĕ).
4. Two dots horizontally below
   = long *e*, thus מֵ = mē (may).
5. Two dots below vertically
   = a faint vowel sound, thus שְ = š˙.
   This sound is like that of *e* in the first syllable of "believe"; it is represented in English transliteration by a dot above, to the right.
6. Three dots below slantingly   = short *u*, thus הֻ = hu (hŏŏ).
7. Three dots below triangularly
   = short *e*, thus אֶ = ie (aȳ), as *e* in "met."
8. Two dashes below forming a ָ
   = long *a*, thus רָ = rā (rah);
   or = short *o*, thus רָ = ro.

NOTE. — Assume that ָ in any given case = *ā* until certain that it = *o*. (Cf. Less. X, *o*.)

9. A horizontal dash below

$\qquad$ = short *a*, thus ﬡ = ka (*a* as in "cat").

10. No. 9 with two dots vertically to the right

$\qquad$ = shortest *a*, thus ֽ = yᵃ.

11. No. 7 with two dots vertically to the right

$\qquad$ = shortest *e*, thus ֽ = yᵉ.

12. No. 8 with two dots vertically to the right

$\qquad$ = shortest *o*, thus ֽ = yᵒ.

NOTE. — Nos. 10, 11, and 12 in English are written above the line. In pronunciation they are a trifle clearer than No. 5.

Summary

(‐̇) = ō (long)	(⸗) = · (extra short)	(⸗) = a (short)
(וּ) = û (long)	(⸗) = e (short)	(⸗) = ᵃ (extra-short)
(⸗) = i (short)	(⸗) = u (short)	(⸗) = ᵉ (extra-short)
(⸗) = ē (long)	(⸗) = ā (long) or o (short)	(⸗) = ᵒ (extra-short)

b. NOTE. — Vowel No. 1 (‐̇)

following ל, is written ל.

preceding א, is written over the right-hand side of the א, if the א does not begin the next syllable, thus לֹא lōı̄, רֹאשׁ rōı̄š, but otherwise בֹאָם bō-iām.

preceding שׁ, coincides with the dot of the consonant, thus בֹשׁ bōš.

following שׁ, is written regularly, thus שֹׁם šōm.

preceding שׂ, is written over the right-hand side of the consonant, thus, פֹּשׂ pōś.

following שׂ, coincides with the dot of the שׂ, thus שֹׂן śōn.

Written Exercise

I

Write in columns first the Hebrew words, then the English equivalents of consonants and vowels, separating syllables by hyphens.

A syllable must always begin with a consonant, and can contain but one vowel. Thus:

אֶרֶץ lé-reṣ.

אָב, אָדָם, אֶחָד, בִּין, בְּהֶן, בֵּית, חָ
מֶלֶךְ, מְאֹד, חוּץ, נְאָם, זְקַן, תָּי, לִי, בְּ

II

Write in columns first the English forms, then the Hebrew equivalents. Do not separate the Hebrew into syllables.

iᵃ-lē-hem, lōī, hā-iá-reṣ, w·-lōī, šé-βer, tā-mú-θû, íim, dā-βār.

Oral Exercise

שְׁמַע עֹבֵר לְבֹא לְרֶשֶׁת גְּדֹלֹת וְרָם אֲשֶׁר עָנָק אֹכְלָה מַחֵר לָךְ אֵל
תֹּאמַר בַּהֲדֹף נָתַן עֹרֶף זָכֹר לְמֵן מֵאֶרֶץ בְּחֹרֶב

LESSON III

a. **THE NAMES OF THE VOWEL SIGNS**

(◌ֹ) ō = Ḥólem (long)	(◌ֻ) u = *Qibbûṣ (short)
(וֹ) û = Šúreq (long)	(◌ָ) ā = Qámeṣ (long)
(◌ִ) i = Ḥíreq (short)	(◌ָ) o = Qámeṣ Ḥātûφ (short)
(◌ֵ) ē = Ṣērê (long)	(◌ַ) a = Páθah (short)
(◌ְ) · = Š·wā (extra-short)	(◌ֲ) ᵃ = Ḥāṭēφ Páθah (extra-short)
(◌ֶ) e = S·γôl (short)	(◌ֱ) ᵉ = Ḥāṭēφ S·γôl (extra-short)
	(◌ֳ) ° = Ḥāṭēφ Qámeṣ Ḥātûφ (extra-short)

NOTE. — The *h* in these names is always hard (ḥ), the *t* likewise is always dotted (ṭ).

---

* *Q* pronounced like *k*.

b. There are three classes of vowels :

Long, Short, and Extra-short.

The long vowels are indicated in English by ˘ or ˄ placed above.

Note. — The distinction in the use of these will be indicated later (see Less. V).

The short vowels have no mark.
The extra-short vowels are written above the line ª, ᵉ, º, ∵.

Written Exercise

Write the following words one under the other and to the right the spelling of each, writing in English the names of consonants and vowels, and finally the English transliteration or equivalent of the word.   Thus :

אֶרֶץ, ἄleφ, s·γôl, rēš, s·γôl, ṣāδê = ìé-reṣ

עָוֹן, מְאֹד, נַעַר, יֵשׁ, בֵּין, אֱמֶר, חוּץ.

LESSON IV

SYLLABLES AND SILENT Š·WĀ

SYLLABLES

a. A syllable is a combination of one or two consonants and one vowel.
b. A syllable must always begin with a consonant.*
c. There are two kinds of syllables, open and closed.
An open syllable is one that ends with a vowel.

---

* וֹ at the beginning of words forms the only exception ; cf, Less. XVII, *l, m.*

A closed syllable is one that ends with a consonant.

Thus גָּדַל gā-δal, the first syllable is open, the second closed.

d. The vowel of an open syllable may be long or extra-short*; it cannot be short unless the syllable is accented (exception Less. X, *j*).

e. The vowel of a closed syllable must be short unless the syllable is accented, when it may be long.

It can never be extra-short. Thus:

יְעַמֵּד yē-ĩa-mēδ   זֶרַע zé-raĩ

קָטְלוּ qā-ṭ·-lû   דָּבָר dā-βār

f. As a rule the final syllable is the accented one; this admits of the vowel being long though the syllable be closed.

Silent Š·wā

g. When a syllable not final is closed, two dots are placed vertically under the consonant that closes the syllable. This sign is called *Silent Š·wā*.

h. Silent Š·wā is not placed under the last consonant of a word (hence מִדְבָּר not מִדְבָּר) except in the case of final ךְ (to distinguish it from final ן, Nûn), thus: מֶלֶךְ " king."

i. Though identical in form with vocal Š·wā, the two must be carefully distinguished.

Vocal Š·wā indicates an extra-short vowel.

Silent Š·wā is merely a sign denoting the absence of a vowel, and hence the close of a syllable.

---

* The sound of the extra-short vowels is not by most grammarians considered to be sufficient to form an independent syllable. It will be found advantageous, however, for the purposes of this Primer, to depart from the common practice in this respect.

j. When two Š·wās are found in succession, the first is silent, the second vocal.

Written Exercise

I

Transliterate the following words, separating the syllables in English by hyphens. Apply carefully *d* and *e* above. An extra-short vowel is always in an open syllable. A short vowel unaccented is in a closed syllable. A long vowel unaccented is in an open syllable.

מָקְרָב, תָּחְדַּל, הֲלָהֶן, אָמַרְתָּ, יְשׁוּעָתֶךָ.

Note. — Silent Š·wā is not specially represented in English.

II

Transliterate:

miz-mōr, šā-maṭ, mam-lā-χā, šā-má-yim, yiś-rā-ʾēl, nil-ḥam.

Note. — When the final syllable of a word is Kaφ and Qåmeṣ, the final form of Kaφ is used and the Qåmeṣ is written in its bosom, thus: ךָ, χā.

Oral Exercise

לְיַחְצְאֵל מִשְׁפַּחַת שְׁנַיִם תְּרוּמַת לְאֶלְעָזָר נְשָׂאֶךָ הֲלַכְתֶּם בְּאָכֶם
וִירֵאתֶךָ בָּאֵשׁ הָאָרֶץ דָּרַךְ יַעַן הָעֹמֵד יָבֹא הָחֵל וְהִתְנַגֵּר פְּחָדְךָ

LESSON V

THE QUIESCENTS AND MAPPÎQ

a. The four letters א, ה, ו, י may lose their consonantal force and be merged into vowels.

This can only take place when a suitable vowel precedes in the same syllable (hence never the beginning of a word).

The consonant is then said to quiesce in the vowel.

b. A quiescent no longer being a consonant cannot close a syllable, and therefore does not take silent Š·wā.

The absence with one of these four letters of succeeding vowel or of silent Š·wā is indication that it quiesces.

c. א may quiesce in any vowel in any position, even within a syllable, thus: מָצָא mā-sā(î),   זֹאת zō(î)θ.

NOTE. — It always quiesces at the end of a word.

d. ה quiesces only at the end of a word and generally in (ָ) or (ֶ) or (ֵ) and sometimes (ֹ), thus:

בְּהֵמָה b·-hē-mā(h),   יִגְלֶה yiγ-le(h),   שִׁילֹה šî-lō(h).

e. NOTE. — When ה at the end of a word does not quiesce, a dot called *Mappîq* ("sounder") is inserted in it to indicate that it remains a consonant, thus לָהּ lāh.

f. ו quiesces in Hólem.

The two together form the vowel *large* Ḥólem וֹ = ô, thus:

גָּדוֹל gā-δôl "great."

g. י quiesces in Híreq, Sērê, and S·γôl.

With Híreq it forms the vowel *large* Híreq,
      יִ = î, thus כְּלִי k·-lî.
With Sērê it forms the vowel *large* Sērê,
      יֵ = ê, thus בֵּין bên.
With S·γôl it forms the vowel *large* S·γôl,
      יֶ = ẽ, thus תִּגְלֶינָה tiγ-lẽ-nā(h).

h. The combination יו at the end of a word is pronounced *āw* (ah-oo) and is transliterated ā(y)w, the י quiesces by exception.

i. Šúreq, וּ, belongs to the class of large vowels, that is, those written with a consonant and a vowel sign.

It is transliterated therefore û (not ū).

j. The quiescents that do not form part of large vowels are to be inclosed in parentheses in transliterating, thus:

נְבֵלָה n·-βē-lā(h),   יֹאמֶר yō(î)-mar.

k. The marks ^ and ˜ in English indicate large vowels.

l. א quiesces even in large vowels, thus:

הִמְצִיא him-ṣî (î).

Written Exercise

Transliterate:

I

נוֹלְדוּ, לֹא, אַל, חֵיטִיב, קְרוּאָיו,
צְבָאוֹת, כָּאוּ, בָּרָא, גֵּיא, לוּא, קָלְיא, אֶרְאָה.

II

liq-ra(î)θ, yiš-mā-iēl, mā(î)-θá-yim, šā-iû-nî,
ṣ·-βō-îîm, lô, b·-yā-mā(y)w, kā-sûy, iᵃ-δō-nāy, šā-lēw.

Oral Exercise

אֲדֹנָי הִשְׁלִיךְ שְׁמֵי זֹאת שׁוֹאֲפִים אֶבְיוֹן לֵאמֹר מָתַי וְנִשְׁבִּירָה
וְנִפְתְּחָה לְהַקְטִין מֹאזְנֵי נִשְׁבַּע כָּאַר שִׁירֵיכֶם וְשַׂמְתִּיהָ קְטַלְתָּה מַלְכָּה

LESSON VI

DĀɣĒŠ FORTE AND LENE

a. A letter doubled in English is not written twice in Hebrew, but a dot is placed in it called *Dāɣēš forte* ("strong D.").

Dāɣēš forte may occur in any consonant except the four gutturals, cf. Less. IX.

One of the two letters indicated by Dāɣēš forte closes the preceding syllable, the other begins the following one, thus:

קִטֵּל qiṭ-ṭēl.

b. Š·wā under a doubled letter is always vocal, thus:

מִלְּאוּ mil-l·-iû.

c. NOTE.—Dāɣēš forte is often omitted (though implied) in certain consonants when simple vocal Š·wā follows, thus:

וַיְהִי for וַיְּהִי way-y·-hî.

(This practice is not to be followed in writing exercises.)

d. The dot placed in the six letters ב, ג, ד, כ, פ, ת (cf. Less. I) to indicate that they have the hard sound, *i.e.* are not aspirated, is called *Dāγēš lene* ("light D.").

Dāγēš lene can occur only in these six letters, and only when they are *not* preceded by a vowel.

e. To tell whether the dot in one of these six letters is meant for Dāγēš forte, or Dāγēš lene, *i.e.* whether the letter is doubled or not, notice whether the preceding consonant has a vowel under it; if it has, the Dāγēš is *forte* and the letter is doubled.

The same rule applies in distinguishing Šúreq from Wāw with Dāγēš forte, thus:

צַוָּה = ṣiw-wā(h).

f. When one of the six letters that may be aspirated takes Dāγēš forte, the aspiration is lost for the doubled letter; thus:

לִבּוֹ = lib-bô, not liβ-βô.

g. Dāγēš lene must be placed in the six letters with which it is used whenever no vowel sound immediately precedes.

Written Exercise

Transliterate:

I

מְבַקְשִׁים, מְדַבֵּר, דִּבֶּר, מְקַטֵּל, יִתְּנוּ

II

bad-dām, lim-maδ-t, ham-má-yim, l·-βad-dô, mib-b·-nê,
hab-b·-liy-yá-ial, iat-tem, haz-ze(h), ṣuw-wô-θā(h).

Oral Exercise

NOTE. — Pronounce doubled letters distinctly, with a pause between.

וְאָוֶן, עֵינָיו, יִצְפֹּנוּ, כְּאַרְיֵה, בְּסֻכָּה, תַּבִּיט, גּוֹיִם, לְבָם, הַמֶּלֶךְ, לְחַלּוֹת,
הַצִּילוּ, הַטֹּבָה, בַּשֻּׁקִים, וַיִּתְּנוּ, הַפַּסִּים, לְעָבְדְךָ, אֲקַבְּצֶךָ, גְּמַלְיךָ,
כְּתַבְתָּם, וַיִּכְתֹּב.

LESSON VII

GENERAL VIEW OF THE VOWELS

a.

TABLE

Long		Short	Extra-Short
Unchangeable	Changeable		
Qấmeṣ (⳨) â	Qấmeṣ (⳨) ā	Páθaḥ (⳨) a	Ḥāṭēφ Páθaḥ (⳨) ᵃ
Large Ṣērê (ʼ⳨) ê	Ṣērê (⳨) ē	S·γôl (⳨) e	Ḥāṭēφ S·γôl (⳨) ᵉ
		Ḥíreq (⳨) i	
Large S·γôl (ʼ⳨) ẽ			
Large Ḥíreq (ʼ⳨) î			
Large Ḥólem (ʼ) ô	Ḥólem (⳨) ō	Qấmeṣ Ḥāṭûφ (⳨) o	Ḥāṭēφ Qấmeṣ Ḥāṭûφ (⳨) °
		Qibbûṣ (⳨) u	
Šúreq (ʼ) û			
			Simple Vocal Š·wā (⳨) ·

b. There are three kinds of Vowels: Long, Short, and Extra-Short.

c. The Long vowels are of two kinds:

(1) Those that cannot be shortened by inflection, *six* in number. They are all, with the exception of Qắmeṣ, written with a quiescent, that is, they are *large* vowels; they are distinguished in English by the circumflex sign ^ or ~, with five of them written ^, with one ~.

Note. — Unchangeable Qắmeṣ is so rare that changeable Qắmeṣ is to be assumed in lack of knowledge to the contrary.

d. (2) Those that may be shortened when the word is inflected, *three* in number.

They are distinguished in Hebrew by not being written with quiescents, and in English by a dash above.

e. As a matter of fact unchangeably long vowels are often written without quiescents ("defective writing"), and, more rarely, changeably long vowels are written with quiescents. Confusion therefore arises in distinguishing changeable and unchangeable long vowels by the orthography alone; in such cases etymology must decide.

Note. — Large vowels written defectively should be transliterated thus: (^) (~).

f. Short vowels in closed syllables not final are unchangeable; in final syllables, though closed, they may be changeable.

g. Short vowels not in closed syllables and extra-short vowels are changeable; that is, short vowels may be lengthened or short-ened as the result of inflection, and extra-short vowels may be lengthened.

h. The four extra-short vowels are called *vocal* Š·wās, as distin-guished from silent Š·wā.

The first three are also called *composite* Š·wās **or Ḥăṭēφs, and** the fourth, simple Š·wā *vocal.*

Written Exercise

Transliterate:

I

כָּנָה: מְלֵאתָיו: לַחְמְךָ: וַיִּזְכֹּר: מִבְּשָׂרֶיךָ:

II

baṣ-ṣā-φôn, b·-χul-lām, w·-hig-gî-íû, hā-íᵉ-lŏ-hîm, tim-ṣā-íén-nû.

Reading Exercise

בְּרֵאשִׁית בָּרָא אֱלֹהִים אֵת הַשָּׁמַיִם וְאֵת הָאָרֶץ: וְהָאָרֶץ הָיְתָה
תֹהוּ וָבֹהוּ וְחֹשֶׁךְ עַל פְּנֵי תְהוֹם: וַיֹּאמֶר אֱלֹהִים יְהִי אוֹר וַיְהִי אוֹר:
וַיַּרְא אֱלֹהִים אֶת הָאוֹר כִּי טוֹב:

LESSON VIII

LENGTHENING AND SHORTENING OF VOWELS

a. (⟋) Qā́meṣ (changeable) may be ⎰ (⟋) Pátheah,
         shortened to   ⎱ (⟋) Ḥāṭēφ Pátheah,
                  or (⟋) Simple Š·wā.
   (⟋) Ṣērê may be shortened to   (⟋) Ḥíreq,
                            (⟋) S·γôl,
                            (⟋) Ḥāṭēφ S·γôl,
                  or (⟋) Simple Š·wā.
   (⟋) Ḥólem may be shortened to   (⟋) Qibbûṣ,
                            (⟋) Qā́meṣ Ḥāṭûφ,
                            (⟋) Ḥāṭēφ Qā́meṣ Ḥāṭûφ
                  or (⟋) Simple Ŝ·wā.

b. So, conversely, the extra-short and the short vowels may be lengthened, and the short vowels may be shortened:

(⌄) may be lengthened to (⌄) and shortened to (⌄) or (⌄).
(⌄) and (⌄) may be lengthened to (⌄) and shortened to (⌄) or (⌄).
(⌄) and (⌄) may be lengthened to (⌄) and shortened to (⌄) or (⌄).

c. In shortening Ṣērê give the preference to Ḥíreq rather than to Sᵉγôl (save under gutturals, cf. Less. IX).

In shortening Ḥólem give the preference to Qắmeṣ Ḥāṭûφ rather than to Qibbûṣ.

d. Ḥíreq (⌄), when lengthened, does not become large Ḥíreq (ᵉ⌄) î; it becomes Ṣērê (⌄).

Qibbûṣ (⌄), when lengthened, does not become Šûreq (ו) û; it becomes (⌄) Ḥólem.

e. When, as the result of inflection, *two vocal Š·wās* come together, if they are both *simple*, the first one is lengthened to Ḥíreq; if one is composite, the first is lengthened to the same short vowel that is in the composite Š·wā; in either case the second remains vocal. Thus:

$$ דְּבַר + לְ = לִדְבַר \quad \text{li*-δ·-βar,} $$
$$ חֲמֹר + לְ = לַחֲמֹר \quad \text{la*-hᵃ·-mōr.} $$

LESSON IX

THE GUTTURALS

The four letters א, ה, ח, ע are gutturals. Their peculiarities are of great importance.

1. These letters take vowels of the *a* class before and after in preference to the other vowels.

A final guttural must be preceded by a vowel of the *a* class.

Hence when a final guttural would be preceded by a long vowel other than Qắmeṣ, a Páθaḥ is inserted between that vowel and the final guttural.

---

* For the short vowel in an open unaccented syllable, cf. Less. X, *i. r.*

This Páθaḥ is called *Páθaḥ Furtive* and is written under the final guttural, but pronounced before it. Thus:

רוּחַ rûaḥ,   יַגְבִּיהַ yaγ-bîah.

NOTE.—הַ at the end of a word without Mappîq is of course a quiescent and not a guttural.

This Páθaḥ furtive is not a constituent part of the word, but only a help to pronunciation and disappears when any suffix is added, thus: רוּחַ + וֹ = רוּחוֹ rû-ḥô.

2. A guttural cannot be doubled, therefore cannot take Dāγēš forte.

Hence if a guttural occurs as one of the letters of a word which the laws of inflection would require to be doubled and take Dāγēš forte, this is not done, but, instead, the preceding vowel is lengthened, thus: דִּבֵּר but שָׁאֵל not שָׁאֵּל.

Dāγēš forte is said to be implied in a guttural to explain the occurrence of a short vowel in a preceding open unaccented syllable, thus: נִחַם ni[ḥ]-ḥam.

Rēš ר shares with gutturals the peculiarity that it cannot be doubled and take Dāγēš forte, hence: בֵּרֵךְ not בֵּרֵּךְ.

3. Gutturals as a rule take *composite* Š·wā instead of *simple* Š·wā, whether vocal or silent. Thus:

קְטֹל but יֶעֱטֹד,   מַלְכִּי but נַעֲרִי na-iᵃ-rî.

The composite Š·wā most usual with gutturals is (ֱ) but א in the pretone* generally takes (ֲ), thus: אָמֹר.

From the above peculiarities it follows that a guttural unless at the end of a word cannot (as a rule) close a syllable.

Written Exercise

Correct the following words wherever necessary by

1. Inserting Páθaḥ furtive.
2. Substituting composite for simple Š·wā (usually ֱ when no other is indicated).
3. Removing Dāγēš forte and lengthening the preceding vowel.
4. Making the appropriate change when two vocal Š·wās come together (cf. Less. VIII, *e*).

---

* Cf. p. 20, *g*.

שָׁמַע ׃ עָבַד ׃ יִשְׁחֲטוּ ׃ שָׁלוֹחַ ׃ בָּרַךְ ׃ יַהֲפֹךְ ׃ שָׁרִים ׃ טָעֲמוּ ׃

לְחָלִי ׃ בָּרֵךְ ׃ יֹאמֵר ׃ מָשִׁיחַ ׃ מְשַׁלֵּחַ ׃ נִשְׁלֹחַ ׃ גָּאַל ׃

———◆———

LESSON X

THE ACCENTS, MÉΘΕΓ, MAQQĒΦ, AND RĀΦE(H)

I. The Accents

a. The syllable on which falls the stress of the voice, the tone
syllable, is indicated in the Hebrew text by means of an accent.

This syllable is usually the last syllable; it may be less frequently the next to the last (the penult); very rarely the ante-
penult.

The accents are written some above and some below the word.

Some that must be placed at the very end of a word are called
postpositive, thus: וַרְקָא; some that must come at the very beginning, *prepositive,* thus: יְתִיב.

Accents are either *Disjunctive,* separating words in sense, or
Conjunctive, connecting them.

b.　　　　TABLE OF THE PROSE ACCENTS

Disjunctive

1.　(⟨̱⟩) Sillūq, only at the end
　　of the verse with (׃)
　　the verse divider.

2.　(⟨̱⟩) Aθnāḥ, at the principal
　　division of the verse.

3 *a.* (⟨̱⟩) S·γôltā, postpositive.

3 *b.* (⟨̱⟩) Šalšéleθ.

4 *a.* (⟨̱⟩) Zāqēφ Qāṭôn.

4 *b.* (⟨̱⟩) Zāqēφ Gāδôl.

5.　(⟨̱⟩) Tiφḥā.

6.　(⟨̱⟩) R·βîaÍ.

7.　(⟨̱⟩) Zarqā, postpositive.

8 *a.* (⟨̱⟩) Paštā, postpositive.

8 *b.* (⟨̱⟩) Y·θîβ, prepositive.

9.　(⟨̱⟩) T·βîr.

10 *a.* (⟨̱⟩) Géreš.

10 *b.* (⟨̱⟩) G·rāšáyim.

11 *a.* (⟨̱⟩) or (⟨̱⟩) Pāzēr.

11 *b.* (⟨̱⟩) Pāzēr Gāδôl.

12.　(⟨̱⟩) T·lîšā G·δôlā, preposi-
　　tive.

CONJUNCTIVE

1. (֯) Múnāḥ.   5. (֯) Íazlā.
2. (֯) M·huppáχ.   6. (֯) T·líšā Q·ṭannā.
3 a. (֯) Mēr·χā.   7. (֯) Galgal or Yérah.
3 b. (֯) Mēr·χā K·φûlā.   8. (֯) Máy·lā.
4. (֯) Dargā.

c. Postpositive accents may be repeated to indicate the tone syllable, thus:

אֲהַבְתָּ֫ Ía-hắβ-tā.

d. The effect of several of the disjunctive accents especially at the end and at the middle of the verse is to lengthen the vowel of the tone syllable, or to shift the tone backward one syllable, lengthening the vowel in that syllable. The word is then said to be in *Pause*. Thus:

מֵ֫יִם, in pause מָ֫יִם; שָׁכְנָ֫ה, in pause שָׁכֵ֫נָה.

קְטַלְתְּ, in pause קָטָ֫לְתְּ qā-ṭal-tā.

II. MÉΘEΓ

e. Méθeγ is a vertical line written to the left of a vowel.
When the vowel is Šûreq or Ḥólem, Méθeγ is written under the preceding consonant, thus:

הָאָדָם hā-Íā-δām,   יְשׁוּפֶךָ y·-šû-φ·-χā.

f. Méθeγ marks the secondary tone of a word. (It also has other uses not here considered.)

g. Méθeγ is used with the *first open* syllable,* counting from (*i.e.* not including) the pretonic syllable. (The pretonic syllable is the one before the accented syllable.)

This open syllable with Méθeγ may have a long or a short vowel (cf. Less. IV, d, Méθeγ serving as a secondary accent) but not an extra-short one.

The presence of Méθeγ therefore shows that the syllable is open. Thus:

---

* That by rule admits of it. For exceptious cf. *j*, below.

יַעֲמֹד yạ-îᵃ-mōδ,   קְטָלָה qā̆-ṭ·-lā(h),

אָנֹכִי lā̆-nô·ֹχî,   הָאַרְבָּעִים hā̆-ìar-bā-ìîm.

h. Μέθεγ may be repeated if the word is long enough by
treating the syllable with Μέθεγ as the accented syllable, and
starting from it to apply the rule again, thus:

וּמֵהַתִּיכוֹנוֹת û-mē̆-hat-tî-χô-nôθ.

i. The rule for using Μέθεγ applies uniformly to long vowels.

j. It applies also to short vowels (*i.e.* short vowels will have
Μέθεγ) unless the vowel is followed by a simple vocal Š·wā,
thus:

יֶחֱזַק yẹ-hᵉ-zaq,   יַעַמְדוּ yạ-ìa-m·-δû,

but מַלְכֵי (not מָלְכֵי) ma-l·-χê,   לְבָבֵי (not לִבְבֵי) li-β·-βê.

k. 1. A syllable with a short vowel is known to be open when
   the short vowel has arisen by the coming together of
   two vocal Š·wās (see Less. VIII, *e,* and below Inflection
   of Nouns, Less. XXI).
   2. That this is the case is often apparent from the fact
   that the Š·wā following is shown to be vocal by the
   absence of Dáγeš lene in the succeeding consonant (see
   Less. VI, *g*). Thus:

מַלְכֵי, לְבְבֵי.

l. In the absence of knowledge, or of evidence in the form of
the word itself, a doubtful syllable should be assumed to be
closed.

Hence חָכְמָה = họχ-mā(h). If the first ָ were ā, Μέθεγ would
be required (see *i,* above).

m. Μέθεγ helps in a measure to differentiate ָ = ā from ָ = o.
Thus:

חָכְמָה = hā̆-χ·-mā(h) in accordance with *i* and *j* above.

חָכְמָה = họχ-mā(h) in accordance with *l* above.

n. Hence ֱ usually = *ǎ,* unless it is followed by an *o* vowel, *i.e.* ָ֫ or ָ = *o,* thus:

פָּרָשִׁים = pā-rā-šîm, but יַעֲמֹד = yǫ-ǐ°-maδ, פָּעֳלְכֶם = pǫ-ǐo-l·χem. (For the second *o* see *k,* 2 above.)

o. ָ followed by ֳ is *o,* it cannot be *ā* (see *i* above). Whether the syllable is open or closed depends on *k.* Thus:

קָדְשִׁי = qo-δ·-šê, but קָדְשִׁי = qoδ-šî.

Only knowledge of inflection can determine that *k,* 1, applies to the former and not to the latter, and thus withdraw it from the application of *l.*

p. ָ in a final accented syllable whether open or closed, in an open accented syllable not final, and in an open pretone is always *ā.*

q. In accordance with *l* יִרְאוּ = yir-ǐû, "they will see," but in accordance with *i* and *j,*

יִרְאוּ = yî·r·-ǐû, "they will be afraid,"

defective writing (see Less. VII, *e*) for יִירְאוּ.

r. Méθeγ is always used with the vowel preceding a composite Š·wā.

s. Méθeγ must not be used in closed syllables.

NOTE. — Decide first in any given case whether ָ = *ā* or = *o ;* if the latter, whether the syllable is open or closed.

III. MAQQĒΦ

t. Maqqēφ is a hyphen connecting two or more words which as a consequence lose their accents save the last, thus: עַל־בֵּיתוֹ. Changeably long vowels in closed syllables must be shortened when they thus lose their accent, thus:

כֹּל הָעָם but כָּל־הָעָם (kol).

The rule for Méθeγ applies as though the combination were one word, thus: כִּי־עַל־כֵּן.

IV. Rāɸe(h)

u. Rāɸe(h) is a horizontal stroke placed over a letter to call attention to the fact that Dāɣēš forte, or lene, or Mappîq is absent. Thus:

מַלְכָּה, יְקְחוּ yi[q]-q·ḥû.

Written Exercise

I

Insert Méθeɣ where required:

אָנֹכִי: הַמֶּלֶךְ: הֶחָכָם: הַמְדַבֵּר: קְטָלִים: מָרְדְכַי:

גְּחֹנְךָ: הָאָרֶץ: נִדְכַּת: דִּבְרֵי:

II

Transliterate:

אֶכְלָה, אָכְלָה, קָטְלִי, קָטְלִי, עָבְדָה, אֲכַלְכֶם, וַתֹּרֶץ.

Oral Exercise

אֲנִי: כְּתָב־לִי: שָׁמָּה: שָׁמְרֵנִי: גָּפְרִית: אֹהֶל: כָּל־אָדָם:

יַעַרְם: אָרְכוּ: יְחָנֵּנִי: מַלְכֵי: יְשׁוּפְךָ: שָׁמְרָה: אֲהָלִי: מָתְנַיִם:

וַיֵּשֶׁב: קָדְשְׁךָ: בְּהִבָּרְאָם: יָרָבְעָם: שֹׁמְרוֹן: קָרְבָּן: תּוֹלְדוֹת:

יִרְאוּ: מַלְכִי: יְכָנְיָהוּ: *גֻּנַּבְתִּי: וָאֲבָרְכָה:

LESSON XI

THE ARTICLE

a. There is no indefinite article in Hebrew.

b. The definite article consists of the particle הַ prefixed to a

---

* ו defectively written is represented by ֻ.

word together with the insertion of Dā𝛾ēš forte in the first consonant of the word, thus:

מֶלֶךְ "king,"　　הַמֶּלֶךְ "the king."

Hence the article properly consists of three parts, (ה), (-), and (·)

c. If the first letter of the word has Dā𝛾ēš lene, when the article is prefixed Dā𝛾ēš forte takes the place of Dā𝛾ēš lene, thus:

הַ + כֹּהֵן = הַכֹּהֵן hak-kō-hēn.

d. If the word begins with a guttural or ר, the Pá𝜃aḥ of the article is lengthened to Qắmeṣ to compensate for the omission of Dā𝛾ēš forte, for the open syllable must have a long vowel, thus:

אָב "father,"　　הָאָב "the father."

e. EXCEPTIONS. — Before a word beginning with הָ, עָ *not accented*, חָ whether accented or not, and חֳ, the article is written with S·𝛾ôl, thus:

הֶעָפָר "the dust," but הָעָם "the people."

f. NOTE. — This S·𝛾ôl which takes the place of Qắmeṣ is considered long, and is to be transliterated ẹ.

g. Before ח or ה with some other vowel than Qắmeṣ, the article is written הַ, thus:

הַחֹשֶׁךְ ha[ḥ]-ḥō-šeχ "the darkness."

NOTE. — The guttural, in such cases, is said to be implicitly or virtually doubled; the first syllable is not, properly speaking, open, yet is treated as such, and can take Mé𝜃e𝛾; thus:

הַהֵיכָל "the palace."

Summary I

h. The article is written:

הַ· before all letters but gutturals and ר;

הָ before א, הָ, ע, עָ, ר;

הֶ before הֶ, חֶ, חָ, חֳ, עֶ;

הַ before ה, ח.

Summary II

Before **א** the article is written הָ.

Before { עֳ / אֳ / עֲ } the article is written הָ.

Before עָ the article is written הֶ.

Before { ה / הָ / הָ } the article is written הַ / הָ / הֶ.

Before { הֳ / הֳ / הָ } the article is written הֶ.

Before ח the article is written הַ.

NOTICE. — Words beginning with ח never have the article pointed with Qámeṣ.

i. RULE 1. — An adjective qualifying is placed after the noun it qualifies.

RULE 2. — If the word qualified has the article, all its qualifiers must have the article; thus: "The good man" הָאִישׁ הַטּוֹב (literally "The man the good").

RULE 3. — The copula (*is, are,* etc.) will not be expressed in translating from English to Hebrew.

RULE 4. — The predicate precedes the subject (unless the latter is a pronoun or is emphatic).

RULE 5. — An adjective when predicate does not take the article.

j. The conjunction *and* is expressed by וֹ prefixed,* thus:

"The man and the woman" הָאִישׁ וְהָאִשָּׁה.

Written Exercise

I

Complete the writing of the following words by supplying the vowel that belongs to the article, also Dāγēš forte and Méθeγ, where required.

------

* See further Less. XVII, *l, m.*

הַצְּרִי, הָעֶרֶב, הָעֲבָדִים, הַיֶּלֶד, הָאָרֶץ, הֶחָכָם,
הָאֶחָד, הָהָר, הַזָּקֵן, הַחֹדֶשׁ, הַהִיא, הֶהָרִים.

II

Translate: The morning [41]. The man [14]. The dust [169]. The light [7] (is) good [88]. A great [47] day [91]. The word [53]. The hand [89]. The day (is) good. The good day. A good day. The man and the day.

Note. — The numbers refer to the vocabulary at the back of the Primer where the corresponding Hebrew words may be found.

The Hebrew equivalent of the words in the English Exercise should be memorized from now on.

———◆———

LESSON XII

THE PERSONAL PRONOUNS

		Singular		*Plural*	
a.	1st *pers. com. gender,*	אָנֹכִי *or* אֲנִי	I	אֲנַחְנוּ (i[a]-náh-nû)	we
	2d *pers. masc.*	אַתָּה	thou	אַתֶּם	ye
	2d *pers. fem.*	אַתְּ (iatt)	thou	אַתֵּן	ye
	3d *pers. masc.*	הוּא	he	הֵם *or* הֵמָּה	they
	3d *pers. fem.*	הִיא	she	הֵן *or* הֵנָּה	they

b. Rule 6. — Five words, אֶרֶץ "land," "earth" (fem.), פַּר "bull" (masc.), חַג "feast" (masc.), עַם "people" (masc.), הַר "mountain" (masc.), when the article is prefixed, lengthen the first vowel to Qámes; thus:

הָעָם, הָאָרֶץ.

Written Exercise

Translate:

I

The mountain [64] (is) very [123] great [47]. The man [14] (is) wise [81]. The good [88] and [65] the wise people [167]

II

הָעֶרֶב הַטּוֹב: הַשָּׁמַיִם וְהָאָרֶץ: טוֹב הָאִישׁ: הָעָם אַתֶּם:
אֶת־הָאִשָּׁה: חָכָם מְאֹד הָאִישׁ:

Oral Exercise

הַבֹּקֶר: הָאִישׁ: הֶעָפָר: הָאוֹר: הַיּוֹם הַגָּדוֹל: הַיָּד וְהַדָּבָר:
טוֹב הַדָּבָר: הַמֶּלֶךְ הַטּוֹב וְהָאִשָּׁה: הָאִשָּׁה וְהֶעָפָר: גָּדוֹל מְאֹד
הָהָר: הָעָם הַטּוֹב וְהֶחָכָם: הוּא וְאָנֹכִי: אַתֶּם הָעָם: הָאִישׁ אַתָּה:
הַפָּר הַגָּדוֹל: טוֹב הָאָרֶץ:

———◆———

LESSON XIII

DEMONSTRATIVE AND OTHER PRONOUNS

a. The Demonstratives:

	Singular		*Plural*	
Masc.	זֶה this	אֵלֶּה		these
Fem.	זֹאת this	אֵלֶּה		these
Masc.	הוּא that	הֵמָּה *or* הֵם		those
Fem.	הִיא that	הֵנָּה *or* הֵן		those

NOTE. — With the article by exception הָהֵמָּה, הָהֵם (and so the feminines),
not הַ.

b. The Relative: אֲשֶׁר "who," "which," indeclinable.

c. The Interrogative: מִי "who?" indeclinable, referring to
persons. מַה־ "what," prefixed with Maqqēφ, indeclinable, referring to things.

It is pointed, like the article, with Páθaḥ and Dāγēš
forte in the first consonant of the following word, unless
the word begins with a guttural, in which case מַה־ is
pointed as the article would be before a guttural (cf.
Less. XI).

d. RULE 7. — The interrogatives come first in the sentence, as in English. The demonstratives, when predicates, come first, as in English.

e. RULE 8. — The demonstratives, when used as qualifiers, make the noun definite, take the article also themselves, and are placed after any other qualifier, thus:

"This good man" הָאִישׁ הַטּוֹב הַזֶּה.

Written Exercise

Translate:

I

Who (are) these? That day[91]. I (am) the great[47] king[131] who[27] (is) upon[164] the land[25]. This good[88] head[191]. This (is) the good boy[95].

II

הַיּוֹם הַזֶּה: זֶה הָרֹאשׁ הַטּוֹב: הַחֶרֶב הַהִיא: מָה־אַתָּה:

LESSON XIV

THE INSEPARABLE PREPOSITIONS AND THE INTERROGATIVE PARTICLE

a. Three of the inseparable prepositions are:

בְּ "in," כְּ "as," לְ "to" or "for."

They are prefixed to the words they govern.

NOTE. — In prefixing apply Less. VIII, *e.*

b. These prepositions before the accented syllable frequently lengthen their Šʾwā to Qā́meṣ (called pretonic Qā́meṣ). Thus:

$$לָלֶדֶת = לְ + לֶדֶת.$$

(Do not use pretonic Qā́meṣ in the Exercises.)

c. When the word to which the preposition is prefixed has the article, the consonant of the preposition is substituted for the ה of the article; thus:

הַמֶּלֶךְ "the king," לַמֶּלֶךְ "for the king."

d. Another inseparable preposition is מִן "from."
It is prefixed as follows:
(1) It may be connected by Maqqēφ, thus:

מִן־הַחֶרֶב "from the sword."

(2) It may be attached to the word by assimilating the נ to the first consonant of the word.

If the initial consonant be a guttural and therefore cannot be doubled as the result of the assimilation, the Ḥíreq under the מ is lengthened to Ṣērê, thus:

מֵהָאִישׁ = מִן + הָאִישׁ "from the man."

If the initial consonant be not a guttural, it takes Dāγēš forte and the Ḥíreq remains, thus:

מִיּוֹם = מִן + יוֹם "from a day."

(Compare in-remediable = irremediable.)

e. RULE 9. — The object of a verb when definite usually has the particle אֵת (or אֶת־) before it. This does not affect the translation.

(Use this particle regularly in the exercises whenever permissible.)

f. RULE 10. — The verb usually comes first, then the subject, then the object.

NOTE. — The root of the verb is not its infinitive as in English, but its third person, singular, masculine, past. Hence the verb "to see" is רָאָה, literally "he saw."

g. RULE 11. — The subject of a verb when a personal pronoun is not expressed unless emphatic.

h. RULE 12. — The negative לֹא "not," when used, precedes the verb, thus:

לֹא רָאָה "he saw not."

i.   THE INTERROGATIVE PARTICLE

To express questions a particle is used called Hê Interrogative. It is prefixed to the first word of the interrogative clause.

Before non-gutturals (including ר), the ה is pointed with Ḥāṭē𝜙 Pá𝜃aḥ, thus: הֲשָׁמֵר.

Before a vocal S̆·wā, simple or composite, and gutturals, ה is pointed with Pá𝜃aḥ, thus:

הֲאֵלֶךְ,   הַמְעַט ha-ın·-iaṭ.

Before gutturals pointed with Qāmeṣ or Ḥāṭē𝜙 Qāmeṣ Ḥāṭûφ, ה is pointed with s·ɣôl, הֶאָנֹכִי "(Is) it I?"

Written Exercise

Translate:

I

To the slave[160]. In the water[128]. As gold[68]. (He) took[122] the head[191] from the dust[169]. (He) heard[210] not[114] the name[208].

II

רָאָה הָעֶבֶד אֶת־הַוָּהָב : בַּבֹּקֶר : בַּמַּיִם הָאֵלֶּה : לָקַח הַיֶּלֶד
מֵהַוָּהָב אֲשֶׁר רָאָה בָּאָרֶץ : נָתַן הַמֶּלֶךְ אֶת־הָעֶבֶד אֶל־יֶלֶד :

Oral Exercise

לַמַּיִם : לְמַיִם : כַּיֶּלֶד : כְּיֶלֶד : לָעֶבֶד : מְמֶּלֶךְ : מֵהַמֶּלֶךְ :
לְאִישׁ : לְ + אָכַל : לְ + חֲמוֹר : לְ + הָאוֹר : לְ + הַחֹשֶׁךְ : בְּ + הָעָם :
בְּ + רָקִיעַ : לְ + מָשׁוֹל : כְּ + דְּמוּתֵנוּ : לְ + עָבַד : בְּ + חֳרִי : לְ + חֳלִי :
מֵהָאָרֶץ : בְּ + הַסּוּף : מֵאִישׁ : מִן־הָאָרֶץ : מְיֶלֶד : הֶאָנֹכִי : הֲקֹטֵל
אָנִי :

LESSON XV

a.   **THE VERB : THE PERFECT**

NOTE. — The verbal forms in their order are to be memorized.

	Singular			*Plural*	
3d *p. m.*	קָטַל	he killed	3d *p. c.*	קָטְלוּ	they killed
3d *p. f.*	קָטְלָה	she killed			
2d *p. m.*	קָטַלְתָּ	thou killedst	2d *p. m.*	קְטַלְתֶּם	ye killed
2d *p. f.*	קָטַלְתְּ*	*thou killedst	2d *p. f.*	קְטַלְתֶּן	ye killed
1st *p. c.*	קָטַלְתִּי	I killed	1st *p. c.*	קָטַלְנוּ	we killed

b. These different persons and numbers are formed from the
root by means of affixes that are fragments of personal pronouns.

	Singular		*Plural*	
3 *p. m.*	——	3 *p. c.*	וּ
3 *p. f.*	ָה		
2 *p. m.*	תָּ		תֶּם
2 *p. f.*	תְּ		תֶּן
1 *p. c.*	תִּי		נוּ

All these affixes begin with a consonant save ָה and וּ.

c. Before affixes beginning with a vowel (vocalic affixes) the
preceding (second) vowel of the root is reduced to Š·wā.

This may be called the *Verbal Law*. Note the Méθeγ in the
antepretone.

d. The vocalic affixes, and the consonantal affixes תֶּם and תֶּן,
take the accent.

e. The first radical (that is, letter, consonant) of the root has
Qấmeṣ throughout, save in the two forms with the accented consonantal affixes.

Written Exercise

Translate: I

Ye (fem.) weaned [49]. We remembered [69]. Thou (masc.) went-
est [100] down. They went down. I fell [150]. She sat [102]. The man [14]
fell in the water [128].

---

* The final Š·wā in the 2d pers. fem. sing. is vocal (Less. IV, *k*) and the word has
three syllables with the accent on the penult.   But in conformity with prevalent
usage hereafter the accent will be omitted, as though the word had but two syllables.

II

יָשַׁב הַמֶּלֶךְ בֶּעָפָר ׃ יָשַׁבְתָּ ׃ נְפַלְתֶּם ׃
כָּרַתְנוּ ׃ זָכְרָה ׃ יָלְדָה הָאִשָּׁה יֶלֶד ׃

Oral Exercise

קָטַל "to kill,"　　מָשַׁל "to rule,"　　גָּנַב "to steal."

קָטַלְתָּ ׃ גָּנַבְתִּי ׃ מְשַׁלְתֶּם ׃ קְטַלוּ ׃ קָטְלָה ׃ מְשַׁלְתָּ ׃ משלתן ׃
גָּנְבָה ׃ משלת ׃ משלה ׃ גָּנַבְנוּ ׃ קְטַלְתִּי ׃ משלו ׃ גנבו ׃ גנבנו ׃
משל ׃ גנבתי ׃ קטלתם ׃ גנבה ׃ גנבתן ׃ קטלת ׃ גנבת ׃ משלנו ׃

◆

LESSON XVI

a.　　**THE VERB: THE IMPERFECT**

	Singular			*Plural*	
3 *p. m.*	יִקְטֹל	(yiq*-ṭōl) he will kill		יִקְטְלוּ	they will kill
3 *p. f.*	תִּקְטֹל	she will kill		תִּקְטֹלְנָה	they will kill
2 *p. m.*	תִּקְטֹל	thou wilt kill		תִּקְטְלוּ	ye will kill
2 *p. f.*	תִּקְטְלִי	thou wilt kill		תִּקְטֹלְנָה	ye will kill
1 *p. c.*	אֶקְטֹל	I will kill		נִקְטֹל	we will kill

b. These different persons and numbers of the Imperfect are
formed from the root by means of prefixes and affixes, fragments
of the personal pronouns.

	Singular	*Plural*
3 *p. m.*	יְ——	יְ——וּ
3 *p. f.*	תְּ——	תְּ——נָה
2 *p. m.*	תְּ——	תְּ——וּ
2 *p. f.*	תְּ——	תְּ——נָה
1 *p. c.*	אֶ——	נְ——

---

* The first syllable throughout the Imperfect is closed.

c. In the singular only one form has an affix. In the plural only one form is without an affix.

d. The ending וּ indicates a plural masculine.

e. Notice the *Verbal Law* (Less. XV, *c*) in forms with vocalic affixes.

f. Only two forms are not accented on the final syllable, those ending in נָה.

g. The forms called *Perfect* (Less. XV) describe actions or states conceived as completed; the forms called *Imperfect* describe actions or states conceived as in process, incomplete. These Tenses (?) therefore have no direct reference to time as past, present, or future; but, for practical purposes, the perfect may be rendered by the English past, and the imperfect by the English future (or present).

Written Exercise

Translate:

I

He will write [112]. We will write. She will steal [50]. They (f.) will steal. Thou (m.) wilt reign [130].

II

תִּכְתְּבוּ׃ תִּגְנֹבְנָה׃ אֶמְלֹךְ׃ יִמְכְּרוּ׃ תִּלְכֹּד׃ יִזְכֹּר׃ נִכְרֹת׃

Note. — Dāγēš lene, in the first letter of גָּנַב, כָּתַב, etc., of course is removed when, after a prefix, the letter no longer begins, but closes, a syllable. The letter that begins the second syllable of the imperfect takes Dāγēš lene when admissible because the first syllable is closed.

Oral Exercise

יִקְטֹל׃ תִּקְטְלִי׃ אֶקְטֹל׃ נִמְשֹׁל׃ נקטל׃ יַקְטְלוּ׃ כתבו׃ ימשלו׃

יגנב׃ תִּכְתֹּבְנָה׃ אכתב׃ תכתב׃ ימשלו׃ נכתב׃ תגנבו׃

תמשלנה׃ תכתבי׃ כֶּתְבָה׃ כתבתם׃

LESSON XVII

THE JUSSIVE, WĀW CONSECUTIVE, ETC.

a. The 3d and 2d persons of the Imperfect may express not only incomplete action historically, but also a desired action, a command, or a wish.

The form with this jussive or desiderative meaning does not differ from the ordinary Imperfect.

.(This statement will need to be completed later on.)

Thus:

יִקְטֹל = " he will kill " or " let him kill."

b. The negative that is used with the Jussive and the Cohortatives is always אַל־, not לֹא. Thus:

לֹא יִקְטֹל " he will not kill,"   אַל־יִקְטֹל " let him not kill."

c. The ending ה, added to the 1st person singular or plural of the Imperfect forms the *Cohortative.* It expresses desire or intention. Thus:

אֶקְטְלָה " I must kill," " let me kill."

(Notice the Verbal Law, Less. XV, *c.*)

d. The conjunction ְו prefixed to the *Perfect* gives to the form the force of the Imperfect, and throws the accent forward on the last syllable (except in the case of the 1st person plural). Thus:

וְקָטַלְתָּ " and thou wilt kill," not " and thou hast killed."

This ְו is called *Wāw Consecutive of the Perfect.*

e. The conjunction ְו pointed like the article ַו, when prefixed to the Imperfect (to the Jussive form when that differs from the ordinary Imperfect [see Less. XXXI, *b*, 3]), gives to the form the force of the Perfect. The accent is drawn back on the penult if the penult is an open syllable. Thus:

וַיִּקְטֹל " and he killed," not " and he will kill," וַיֹּאמֶר " and he said."

Before a guttural ·וַ = וָ; thus:

וָאֶקְטֹל "and I killed."

This ·וַ is called *Wāw Consecutive of the Imperfect.*

f. These uses of the conjunction are peculiar to the Hebrew, and form one of the most important features of its Syntax.

g. ·וַ is never used with the Perfect.

h. The conjunction וְ prefixed to the Jussive or Cohortative, especially if a Jussive or Imperative precedes, expresses purpose or design. It is called *Wāw Subordinate.* Thus:

וְאֶקְטְלָה "that I may kill."

i. The conjunction וְ prefixed to the ordinary Imperfect does not affect the force of the verb; it is merely Wāw connective or conjunctive.

j. The conjunction וְ "and" is also used before other parts of speech, as has been seen.

k. It is sometimes pointed with Qâmeṣ when in the syllable before the accented one; thus:

וָרָע "and evil."

(Cf. Less. XIV, *b.*)

l. Before the labials (פ, מ, ב) and before simple Š·wā vocal, it becomes וּ (Šûreq). This is true of Wāw Consecutive of the Perfect also. Thus:

וּמֶלֶךְ "and a king," וּלְכֹל "and to all," וּמָכַר "and he will sell."

m. NOTE. — This is the only exception to the rule that a syllable cannot begin with a vowel.

n. This Šûreq does not follow the rule for Méθeɣ (Less. X, *g*), hence וּבָנִים not וּּבָנִים, unless a *composite* Š·wā follow.

Summary

Perf.   + וְ = Wāw Consec. = "and he will ..."
Imperf. + ·וַ = Wāw Consec. = "and he did ..."
Imperf. + וְ = Wāw Connect. = "and he will ..."
Juss. }
Cohort. } + וְ = Wāw Subord. = "that he (I) may ..."

Written Exercise

Translate:

I

וַתִּקְטֹלְנָה: וָאֶזְכְּרָה: וּמְבָרְנוּ: וְלָקַחְתָּ: וַיִּזְכֹּר: אֶשְׁפְּטָה:

II

And he judged [215]. Let him judge. That I may watch [212]. And he will burn [201]. Let him not burn. Do not thou (m.) watch. And thou wilt cut [111].

Oral Exercise

וַיִּקְטֹל: וָאֶמְשֹׁל: וְכָתַב: וַנִּקְטֹל: וְאֶקְטְלָה: וַתִּמְשֹׁל: וּמָשַׁלְתָּ:
וְקָטַלְנוּ: וְקָטְלָה: וַנִּמְשֹׁל: וְיִקְטֹל: אַל־יִמְשֹׁל: לֹא תִכְתֹּב:
וַתִּקְטֹלְנָה: וכתבתם: ניכתבו: וְאמשלה: ומשלתם: ומשלנו:
וכתבתָ:

LESSON XVIII

THE VERB: THE IMPERATIVE, THE INFINITIVE, AND THE PARTICIPLES

a.   THE IMPERATIVE

	Singular		*Plural*	
2 *p. m.*	קְטֹל	kill thou	קִטְלוּ (qi-ṭ·-lû)	kill ye
2 *p. f.*	קִטְלִי (qi-ṭ·-lî) kill thou		קְטֹלְנָה	kill ye

b. These forms are obtained from the corresponding forms of the Imperfect by removing the prefixes.

$$\text{קְטֹל} = \text{תִּקְטֹל}, \quad \text{קִטְלִי} = \text{קְטֹלִי} = \text{תִּקְטְלִי}.$$

c. There is no Méθeɣ in the open syllable preceding vocal Š·wa pretonic according to Less. X,*j*.

d. The Imperative cannot be used with a negative; the Jussive is used instead. Thus:

" Do not (thou) kill " = אַל־תִּקְטֹל, not לֹא קְטֹל or אַל־קְטֹל.

e. Additional emphasis is given to the masculine singular by adding the ending הָ‎, thus:

קְטֹל‎ + הָ‎ = קָטְלָה‎ (verbal law) = קָטְלָה‎ qo-ṭ·-lā(h) "O kill thou!"

(*o* because of influence of vowel of second syllable.)

f.　　　　　　　THE INFINITIVES

Infinitive Construct　　　　　　*Infinitive Absolute*

קְטֹל‎ q·-ṭōl "to kill"　　　קָטֹל‎ or קָטוֹל‎ qā-ṭôl "to kill"

g. The Infinitive Construct may have prefixes and suffixes. The Infinitive Absolute does not.

h. The Infinitive Construct is generally used with the preposition לְ‎ "to." Thus:

קְטֹל‎ + לְ‎ = לִקְטֹל‎ liq-ṭōl.

i. NOTE. — In such cases by exception to Less. VIII, *e*, the second S̆·wā becomes silent.

THE PARTICIPLES

Active　　　　　　　　　　*Passive*

קֹטֵל‎ q'ô·-ṭēl "killing"　　קָטוּל‎ "killed"

These are inflected as nouns.

NOTE. — The entire verb קָטַל‎ will be found on p. 40, 1st col.

Written Exercise

I

Transliterate and translate:

שָׁמְרוּ ׃ שָׁמְרוּ ׃ שָׁמֵר ׃ שְׁמֹר ׃ לִשְׁמֹר ׃ שָׁמֵר ׃ כָּרוֹת ׃ וְנִבְנָה ׃
אַל־תִּלְכֹּד ׃ כָּתוּב ׃ לִמְכֹּר ׃

II

Translate:

Steal[50] (thou, *m.*).   Do not (thou, *m.*) steal.   O keep[212] (thou, *m.*). (He) will not steal.   Writing[112] (partic.).   Stolen.   Judge[215] (ye, *f.*). To bury[181] (inf. cons. with לְ‎).   Watch[212] (thou, *f.*).

For the Oral Exercise see at end of Less. XIX.

LESSON XIX

STATIVE OR INTRANSITIVE VERBS

a. Stative verbs are so called because they usually describe the state or condition of the subject.   They are also called intransitive, which means that they do not take objects.

b. While the root of the active (or transitive) verb has Páθaḥ in the second syllable, stative verbs usually have Ṣērê or Ḥólem, thus :   כָּבֵד "to be heavy,"   קָטֹן "to be little."

(These are the type verbs for Intransitives; their forms are to be committed to memory.)

NOTE. — There are more verbs in Ṣērê than in Ḥólem.

c.   PECULIARITIES OF STATIVE VERBS

Perfect. — Verbs in Ṣērê: The Ṣērê appears only in the third person, masculine, singular, the other forms are pointed like קָטֵל.

Verbs in Ḥólem: The Ḥólem is retained before consonantal affixes save those that are accented, when it becomes Qámeṣ Ḥāṭûφ. Thus :   קָטֹנְתָּ,   קְטָנְתֶּם q·-ṭon-tem.

d. NOTE. — The Perfect of Intransitive verbs may be rendered by the English present, but the past will be employed as usual in the exercises to avoid ambiguity.

e. Imperfect. — Verbs in Ṣērê and Ḥólem both take Páθaḥ in the second syllable instead of Ḥólem, thus :

יִקְטַן, יִכְבַּד.

Imperative. — Follows the Imperfect, taking Páθaḥ.

f. Infinitive Construct. — Follows the Imperfect (or more usually takes Ḥólem like the active verb), thus :

קְטֹן, כְּבֹד.

g. The Participle. — There is but one and it is like the root, כָּבֵד, קָטֹן.

Written Exercise

Translate:

I

And he was holy [182]. And he will be holy. Ye (m.) were little [185]. We were able [93]. I am old [73]. Let them (f.) draw near [184]. Let them (m.) not draw near. And the woman [26] wrote [112] in the great [47] book [158]. And the king [131] will descend [100] to the water [128].

NOTE. — The verb comes first with Wāw Consecutive, then the subject.

II

קִבְרוּ ׃ וְקָבַרְתִּי ׃ וַיִּזְקַן ׃ וַיְקַדְּשׁוּ ׃ קָדְשׁוּ ׃ וְכָלִתָ ׃

Oral Exercise, Less. XVIII and XIX.

מָשְׁלוּ ׃ יִכְתֹּב ׃ קָטְלִי ׃ מְשֹׁל ׃ כָּתֵב ׃ מָשׁוּל ׃ קָטֹלְנָה ׃ תִּקְטֹל ׃

תמשלי ׃ אכתב ׃ נמשלה ׃ מְשְׁלוּ ׃ כתוב ׃ משלתם ׃ וַתמשל ׃

אל־יקטל ׃ לא נמשל ׃ ואקטלה ׃ תקטלו ׃

יכבדו ׃ נכבַּד ׃ כבדה ׃ וַיקטן ׃ קטנתם ׃ קטנתי ׃ קטנה ׃

כבדתָ ׃ יקטנו ׃ כְּבדי ׃ כבדנו ׃ נקטנה ׃ וָאכבד ׃ וְאקטנה ׃

תכבדנה ׃ כָּבֵד ׃ קָטֹן ׃

Paradigm of Verbs: Active and Stative

			he killed		he is heavy		he is little
Perfect	Sg. 3 p. m.		קָטַל	כָּבֵד		קָטֹן	
	3 p. f.		קָטְלָה	כָּבְדָה		קָטְנָה	
	2 p. m.		קָטַלְתָּ	כָּבַדְתָּ		קָטֹנְתָּ	
	2 p. f.		קָטַלְתְּ	כָּבַדְתְּ		קָטֹנְתְּ	
	1 p. c.		קָטַלְתִּי	כָּבַדְתִּי		קָטֹנְתִּי	
	Pl. 3 p. c.		קָטְלוּ	כָּבְדוּ		קָטְנוּ	
	2 p. m.		קְטַלְתֶּם	כְּבַדְתֶּם		קְטָנְתֶּם	
	2 p. f.		קְטַלְתֶּן	כְּבַדְתֶּן		קְטָנְתֶּן	
	1 p. c.		קָטַלְנוּ	כָּבַדְנוּ		קָטֹנּוּ	
Imperfect	Sg. 3 p. m.		יִקְטֹל	he will kill	יִכְבַּד	he will be heavy	יִקְטֹן	he will be little
	3 p. f.		תִּקְטֹל	תִּכְבַּד		תִּקְטֹן	
	2 p. m.		תִּקְטֹל	תִּכְבַּד		תִּקְטֹן	
	2 p. f.		תִּקְטְלִי	תִּכְבְּדִי		תִּקְטְנִי	
	1 p. c.	_coh._ אֶקְטְלָה	אֶקְטֹל	_coh._ אֶכְבְּדָה אֶכְבַּד	_coh._ אֶקְטְנָה אֶקְטֹן	
	Pl. 3 p. m.		יִקְטְלוּ	יִכְבְּדוּ		יִקְטְנוּ	
	3 p. f.		תִּקְטֹלְנָה	תִּכְבַּדְנָה		תִּקְטֹנָּה	
	2 p. m.		תִּקְטְלוּ	תִּכְבְּדוּ		תִּקְטְנוּ	
	2 p. f.		תִּקְטֹלְנָה	תִּכְבַּדְנָה		תִּקְטֹנָּה	
	1 p. c.	_coh._ נִקְטְלָה	נִקְטֹל	_coh._ נִכְבְּדָה נִכְבַּד	_coh._ נִקְטְנָה נִקְטֹן	
Imperative	Sg. 2 p. m.	_emph._ קָטְלָה	קְטֹל	_emph._ כָּבְדָה כְּבַד	_emph._ קָטְנָה קְטַן	
	2 p. f.	קְטְלִי	(qi-ṭ·-li)	כִּבְדִי	(ki-β·-δi)	קִטְנִי	(qi-ṭ·-ni)
	Pl. 2 p. m.	קִטְלוּ	(qi-ṭ·-lû)	כִּבְדוּ	(ki-β·-δû)	קִטְנוּ	(qi-ṭ·-nû)
	2 p. f.		קְטֹלְנָה	כְּבַדְנָה		קְטַנָּה	
Infinitives	Constr.	קְטֹל	(q·-ṭōl)	כְּבַד		קְטַן	
	Absol.	קָטוֹל	(qā-ṭôl)				
Participles	Active,		קֹטֵל	כָּבֵד		קָטֹן	
	Passive,		קָטוּל				

LESSON XX

INFLECTION

a.   I. INFLECTION IN GENERAL

By inflection is meant the changes that words undergo to express number, gender, syntactical relations, etc.

These changes are effected chiefly by the addition of affixes and prefixes, and by modifications in the length of changeable vowels.

An understanding of the laws of the tone is of prime importance in this connection. These laws of course apply only to changeable vowels.

b.   **The Laws of the Tone**

The Verbal Law (Less. XV, *c*) requires the vowel of the pre-tone, if open, to be extra-short, and that of the antepretone, if open, to be long, thus:

קֳטְלָה qā̆-ṭ·-lā(h).

The Nominal Law requires the vowel of the pretone, if open, to be long, and the vowel of the antepretone, if open (or of the syllable preceding when the antepretone is unchangeable), to be extra-short, thus:

זְקֵנִים z·-qē-nîm.

NOTE. — It will be seen that these laws apply only to open syllables.

c. REMARKS. — The vowel of the tone syllable is usually long whether open or closed, both in verbs and in nouns.

d. The pretone, if open, may be long or extra-short.

e. The antepretone, if open, is long when the pretone is extra-short, and extra-short when the pretone is long.

f. The extra-short pretone is found more frequently in verbs, hence the expression, *Verbal Law*.

g. The long pretone is found more frequently in nouns, hence the expression, *Nominal Law*.

h. Closed syllables other than final being unchangeable (Less. VII, *f*) are not affected by inflection.

II. The Four Classes of Nouns

NOTE. — Under the term *nouns* throughout are also included adjectives, participles, etc. The description following refers to the Absolute Singular (see *o*, below).

i. CLASS I. — Nouns containing at least one changeable Qámeṣ, thus:

זָקֵן "old,"   גָּדוֹל "great,"   דָּבָר "word."

This includes all nouns having the feminine ending ה, no matter to what class their masculines may belong.

מַלְכָּה "queen,"   קְטֻלָה   זְקֵנָה

j. CLASS II. — Nouns accented on the Penult (except מַיִם and שָׁמַיִם). Thus:

מֶלֶךְ "king,"   נַעַר "lad."

k. CLASS III. — Nouns whose last vowel is Ṣērê with pretone unchangeable. Thus:

קֹטֵל q̊ô'ṭēl "killer,"   מִסְפֵּד "mourning."

l. CLASS IV. — Nouns ending in ה; these may also belong to the first class. Thus:

שָׂדֶה "field."

m. Besides the nouns that fall under one of these four classes there are those containing no changeable vowels, which therefore undergo no internal changes when inflected, nouns that double the final letter before suffixes and some others.

III. The Absolute and the Construct States

n. The genitive and similar relations are expressed as a rule not by connecting the two terms by a preposition, but by placing the noun expressing the thing possessed immediately in front of the noun expressing the possessor and putting the former in the *Construct State*.

o. A noun not in the Construct State is said to be in the *Absolute State.* The Absolute is the usual state of the noun, as found in the Lexicon, etc.

Rules for Forming the Construct of Singular Nouns

p. Class II and III. — The Construct is the same as the Absolute.

q. Class IV. — Change S·ɣôl of last syllable to Ṣērê.

r. Class I. — Begin at the right hand and shorten the vowels as much as possible. (See Less. VIII.)

Note. — The Nominal Law (Less. XX, *b*) applies only to the Absolute. The law for the Construct is pretone extra-short, antepretone short.

These two laws apply as a rule only to nouns of Class I and plurals of Class II.

Thus: דָּבָר, construct דְּבַר. The first Qámeṣ is shortened as much as possible, to Š·wā; the second Qámeṣ can only be shortened to Páθaḥ, for the closed syllable must contain at least a short vowel.

Examples

גָּדוֹל, construct גְּדוֹל, ו is unchangeable.

מִדְבָּר,   "   מִדְבַּר, first syllable unchangeable.

שָׂדֶה,   "   שְׂדֵה, belongs to Cl. I and IV.

לֵבָב,   "   לְבַב.

זָכָר,   "   זְכַר.

זָקֵן,   "   זְקַן, not זְקֵן or זְקָן, and so with other words having Qámeṣ and Ṣērê.

s. Rule 13. — The noun in the construct though definite must *never* take the article, thus:

"The word of the man," דְּבַר הָאִישׁ.

t. Rule 14. — No word or particle must come between the construct and the word governing it. Hence an adjective qualifying the construct must come *after* the governing word and its modifiers (if any), agreeing with the construct in gender and number but *not in state.* Thus:

"The good word of the woman," הַטּוֹב הָאִשָּׁה דְּבַר.

u. RULE 15. — Qualifiers of a word in the absolute agree with it in number, gender, and state.

v. The presence or absence of the article with the governing noun decides whether the construct is to be regarded as definite or not. Thus:

סוּס מֶלֶךְ "A horse of a king," סוּס הַמֶּלֶךְ "The horse of the king."

Written Exercise

I

Write the following words in columns, and in parallel columns state the class to which they belong and give the constructs:

מַצָּב: כֹּהֵן (k'ô'-hēn) : בֹּקֶר: מָקוֹם: נָדִיב: סוּס:
צַדִּיק: טוֹב: קוֹנֶה: כּוֹכָב: מִקְנֶה: מוֹשֵׁל:

II

Translate:

The place[138] of the star[106]. The flock[140] of the righteous[180] man[14]. The good[88] horse[156] of the woman[26].

For Oral Exercise, see close of Less. XXII.

———◆———

LESSON XXI

AFFIXES OF NUMBER AND GENDER

INFLECTION OF NOUNS OF THE FIRST CLASS

a. There are three numbers, Singular, Plural, and Dual.

b. There are two genders, Masculine and Feminine.

c. The numbers, plural and dual, and the gender, feminine, are indicated by means of affixes which differ in the absolute and the construct.

Table of Affixes for Number and Gender for All Kinds of Nouns

	Singular		*Plural*	
	Masculine	Feminine	Masculine	Feminine
Absolute	——	(הָ) ā(h)	(ים) îm	(וֹת) ôθ
Construct	——	(ת) aθ	(י) ê	(וֹת) ôθ

	Dual	
	Masculine	Feminine
Absolute	(יִם) á-yim	(תַיִם) ā-θá-yim
Construct	(י) ê	(תַי) ·-θê

NOTE. — Nouns found with the ending הָ are shown by that ending to be feminine singular absolute.

d. To form any particular number, gender, etc., it is not sufficient to provide the appropriate affix; certain changes in the word are rendered necessary by the new syllable that is attached. These changes vary for each of the four classes.

General Directions for Inflection

e. 1. Determine the class to which the word belongs.

2. Mark the gutturals, if any, by a cross above, thus: כָּכֶם. This is simply to call attention to them.

3. If the word belongs to class II, III, or IV *prepare it* for the reception of an affix by following the rules given for each class.

4. To form an Absolute:
   (*a*) Add the appropriate affix.
   (*b*) Shorten the antepretone if possible.   (Nominal Law.)

5. To form a Construct:
   (*a*) Substitute the appropriate affix.
   (*b*) Shorten the vowels as much as possible, beginning at the right.

46 A PRIMER OF HEBREW

Inflection of Nouns of Class I

f. Rule for the Absolute. — Add to the masculine singular the appropriate affix, then apply the *Nominal Law* (Less. XX, *b*), that is, reduce the vowel of an open antepretone to Š·wā.

g. Rule for the Construct. — Change the affix (if any) of the absolute form to the corresponding affix for the construct, then apply the rule for forming the construct (Less. XX, *r*), that is, begin at the right and shorten the vowels as much as possible.

In both cases (*f* and *g*) apply the rule for two contiguous vocal Š·wās (Less. VIII, *e*).

Example

h.	Singular		Plural		Dual	
	m.	**f.**	**m.**	**f.**	**m.**	**f.**
Abs.	דָּבָר	(דְּבָרָה) דְּבָרָה	(דְּבָרִים) דְּבָרִים	(דְּבָרוֹת) דְּבָרוֹת	(דְּבָרַיִם) דְּבָרַיִם	(שְׂפָתַיִם) שְׂפָתַיִם
Const.	דְּבַר	(דְּבָרַת) (דְּבָרַת) דְּבָרַת di-β·raθ	(דְּבָרֵי) (דְּבָרֵי) דְּבָרֵי di-β·rê	(דְּבָרוֹת) דְּבָרוֹת di-β·rôθ	(דְּבָרֵי) (דְּבָרֵי) דְּבָרֵי di-β·rê	(שְׂפָתֵי) שְׂפָתֵי śi-φ·θê

Note. — The forms in parentheses are merely intermediate steps.

Observe in the Absolute the long vowel of the pretone.

Written Exercise

Inflect after the same manner but omitting the dual feminine.

זָכָר, נָדִיב, מַצָּב.

For Oral Exercise, see close of Less. XXII.

LESSON XXII

INFLECTION OF NOUNS OF CLASS I CONTAINING GUTTURALS

NOTE. — Review Less. IX on the Gutturals.

Nouns containing gutturals are inflected after the manner indicated in the preceding section save for such differences as the peculiarities of gutturals require.

Inflection of חָכָם "wise." First Consonant a Guttural

	Singular		*Plural*		*Dual*	
	m.	f.	m.	f.	m.	f.
Abs.	חָכָם	חֲכָמָה	חֲכָמִים	חֲכָמוֹת	חֲכָמַֽיִם	
Const.	חֲכַם (חֲכַמַת)	(חֲכָמֵי) (חֲכָמוֹת)	(חֲכָמֵי)			
	(חֲכְמַת)	(חֲכְמֵי) חַכְמוֹת	(חֲכְמֵי)			
	חַכְמַת	חַכְמֵי	חַכְמֵי			
	ḥa-χ·-maθ	ḥa-χ·-mê ḥa-χ·-môθ	ḥa-χ·-mê			

Inflection of רָעָב "hunger." Second Consonant a Guttural

	Singular		*Plural*		*Dual*	
	m.	f.	m.	f.	m.	f.
Abs.	רָעָב	רְעָבָה	רְעָבִים	רְעָבוֹת	רְעָבַֽיִם	
Const.	רְעַב (רְעָבַת)	(רְעָבֵי) (רְעָבוֹת)	(רְעָבֵי)			
	(רְעֲבַת)	(רְעֲבֵי) רַעֲבוֹת	(רְעֲבֵי)			
	רַעֲבַת	רַעֲבֵי	רַעֲבֵי			

Inflection of רָשָׁע "wicked." Third Consonant a Guttural

The inflection of words of this type differs in no respect from that of words without gutturals.

Written Exercise

I

Inflect, after the same manner and arrangement:

חָזָק "strong,"   נָחָשׁ "serpent,"   רָשָׁע "wicked."

II

Translate: He wrote [112] in [32] the book [158] of the prophets [146]. The two hands [89] (dual) of the great [47] king [131]. Do not (thou, *m.*) kill [184] the good [88] boy [95] of the woman [26].

Oral Exercise, Less. XX, XXI, and XXII

זָכָר ׃ זָכַר ׃ חֹדֶשׁ ׃ חָכָם ׃ חֵלֶק ׃ יָד ׃ יוֹבֵל ׃ נָּדוֹל ׃ גְּדוֹל ׃

עֹלֶם ׃ צַדִּיק ׃ בַּעַל ׃ שֹׁפֵט ׃ שֹׁרֶשׁ ׃ רֹעֶה ׃ זְכָרִים ׃

זִכְרִי ׃ דְבָרָה ׃ דִּבְרַת ׃ דְּבָרוֹת ׃ רֹעֲבֵי ׃ מַצָּבִים ׃ כּוֹכְבֵי ׃

חָכְמָה ׃ חָכְמַת ׃ חָכְמוֹת ׃ רְשָׁעִים ׃ רִשְׁעֵי ׃ רִשְׁעַת ׃ רְשָׁעוֹת ׃

חֲזָקִים ׃ חָזְקִי ׃ חֻזְקַת ׃ נְחֹשֶׁת ׃ נְחֻשִׁי ׃ נָחָשׁ ׃ חָזָק ׃ עָפָר ׃ נְבִיאֵי ׃

הָאָרֶץ ׃ אֲדָמָה ׃ אַדְמַת ׃ בִּרְכַּת ׃ בְּרָכוֹת ׃

LESSON XXIII

INFLECTION OF NOUNS OF CLASS II

a. Nouns of Class II comprise all those accented on the penult (the next to the last syllable) no matter what their vowels.

They are of three kinds, after the three types:

מֶלֶךְ "king,"   סֵפֶר "book,"   בֹּקֶר "morning."

b. Nouns of Class II are also called *Segholates* because of the S·γôl usually found in the second syllable.

---

* Words with gutturals may have different vowels, cf. Less. XXIV.

c. Nouns of the first type are called Segholates in *a* (Pá𝜃aḥ), because the first S·γôl is derived from an original Pá𝜃aḥ.

Nouns of the second type are called Segholates in *i* (Híreq), because the Ṣērê is derived from an original Híreq.

Nouns of the third type are called Segholates in *o* (Qámeṣ Hāṭû𝜙), because the Hólem is derived from an original Qámeṣ Hāṭû𝜙.

d. In each case the final S·γôl is a helping S·γôl; that is, it is not a constituent part of the original root (which is supposed to have had but one vowel), but is inserted to help the pronunciation.

Hence this helping S·γôl disappears before affixes.

(Cf. Pá𝜃aḥ furtive, Less. IX, *b.*)

Note. — Some nouns with S·γôl in the first syllable belong to the *i* class. When this is the case, attention will be called to it.

Inflection of Nouns of Class II

e. 1. The construct of the singular is the same as the absolute.

f. 2. In the singular, before receiving an affix, the word is to be prepared as follows :

The helping S·γôl is replaced by silent Š·wā, and the vowel of the first syllable (‑̤), (‑̤), (‑̇) gives place to the type (the original) vowel (‑̤), (‑̤), (‑̤). The first syllable, therefore, is now closed. Thus:

מֶלֶךְ becomes מַלְךּ		mal-k
סֵפֶר becomes סִפְר		si𝜙-r
בֹּקֶר becomes בָּקְר		boq-r

g. It is to these monovocalic prepared forms that the affix is appended and the penult then is no longer the accented syllable, thus :

$$הָ + מֶלֶךְ = מַלְכָּה \quad \text{mal-kā(h) “queen.”}$$

h. 3. To form the *plurals absolute*, both masculine and feminine, remove all the vowels of the singular (this includes the quiescent ה of the feminine, and Dāγēš lene if there is one in the third radical), then place vocal Š·wā under the first consonant, Qắmeṣ under the second, and add the plural affix (that is, follow the analogy of nouns of Class I). Thus:

בְּקָרִים, סְפָרִים, מְלָכִים, מְלָכוֹת.

i. To form the *plurals construct* treat the plurals absolute as in Class I. (Less. XXI, *g.*)

j. 4. The *dual* (masculine and feminine) is formed from the prepared root of the *singular* by adding the appropriate dual suffix, thus:

מַלְכָּתַיִם, מַלְכַּיִם.

k. 5. When two vocal Š·wās come together, and a short vowel must take the place of the first one, the vowel of the *type* to which the word belongs is used, thus:

מֶלֶךְ, m. pl. abs. מְלָכִים, const. (מַלְכֵי) מַלְכֵי ma-l·-χê, not מִלְכֵי.

בֹּקֶר, m. pl. abs. בְּקָרִים, const. (בִּקְרֵי) בָּקְרֵי bo-q·-rê, not בִּקְרֵי.

Examples

l. INFLECTION OF NOUNS OF THE *a* TYPE: מֶלֶךְ "king"

	Singular		Plural		Dual	
	m.	f.	m.	f.	m.	f.
Abs.	מֶלֶךְ	מַלְכָּה	מְלָכִים	מְלָכוֹת	מַלְכַּיִם	מַלְכָּתַיִם
Const.	מֶלֶךְ / מַלְכַּת mal-kaθ		(מְלָכִי) מַלְכֵי / (מְלָכֵי) מַלְכֵי ma-l·-χê	(מְלָכוֹת) / מַלְכוֹת ma-l·-χôθ	מַלְכֵי mal-kê	מַלְכְּתֵי mal-k·-θê

Note the presence of *Dāγēš lene* in the third radical letter of the singular and dual forms with affixes, and its absence in the plurals, because, in the singular and dual forms, the first syllable is closed, and, in the plural, it is open.

m.   INFLECTION OF NOUNS OF THE *i* TYPE: סֵפֶר "book"

	Singular		Plural		Dual	
	m.	f.	m.	f.	m.	f.
Abs.	סֵפֶר	סִפְרָה	סְפָרִים	סְפָרוֹת	סִפְרָתַיִם	סִפְרָתַיִם
Const.	סֵפֶר סִפְרַת siφ-raθ	(סִפְרֵי) (סִפְרֵי) סִפְרֵי si-φ·-rê	(סִפְרוֹת) סִפְרוֹת si-φ·-rôθ	סִפְרֵי סִפְרָתַי siφ-rê	si-φ-r·-θê

n.   INFLECTION OF NOUNS OF THE *o* TYPE: בֹּקֶר "morning"

	Singular		Plural		Dual	
Abs.	בֹּקֶר בָּקְרָה	בְּקָרִים	בְּקָרוֹת	בָּקְרָתַיִם בְּקָרַיִם		
Const.	בֹּקֶר בָּקְרַת boq-raθ	(בְּקָרֵי) (בְּקָרֵי) בְּקָרֵי bo-q·-rê	(בְּקָרוֹת) בְּקָרוֹת bo-q·-rôθ	בְּקָרֵי בְּקָרָתַי boq-rê	boq-r·-θê

Written Exercise

Inflect, after the same manner:

יֶלֶד "boy,"   פֵּשֶׁת "flax,"   שֹׁרֶשׁ "root."

For Oral Exercise, see close of Less. XXIV.

LESSON XXIV

INFLECTION OF NOUNS OF CLASS II CONTAINING GUTTURALS

(Review Less. IX on Gutturals.)

NOTE. — When the guttural takes a Š·wā, the composite Š·wā of the *type*
to which the word belongs must be used (cf. Less. XXIII, *c*).

a. INFLECTION OF NOUNS HAVING AS *FIRST* LETTER A GUTTURAL

(1) *a* type: אֶבֶן "stone," like מֶלֶךְ save in plu. abs. אֲבָנִים, אֲבָנוֹת.

(2) *i* type: עֵשֶׂב "grass":

	Singular		Plural		Dual	
	m.	f.	m.	f.	m.	f.
Abs.	עֵשֶׂב	עֶשְׂבָּה	עֲשָׂבִים	עֲשָׂבוֹת	עֲשָׂבַּיִם	עֲשָׂבָתַיִם
Const.	עֵשֶׂב	עֶשְׂבַּת	עֲשָׂבֵי	עֲשָׂבוֹת	עֲשָׂבֵי	עֲשָׂבְתֵי

Note that the guttural prefers (ֲ) to (ְ), but (ֱ) to (ֶ).

(3) *o* type: חֹדֶשׁ "month," like בֹּקֶר save in plu. abs. חֳדָשִׁים, חֳדָשׁוֹת.

b. INFLECTION OF NOUNS HAVING AS *SECOND* LETTER A GUTTURAL

(Particular attention is to be paid to these.)

Note the helping Páθaḥ instead of S·γôl in the second syllable of בַּעַל and פֹּעַל and the retention of the original Páθaḥ in the first syllable of בַּעַל.

(1) *a* type: בַּעַל "master":

	Singular		Plural		Dual	
	m.	f.	m.	f.	m.	f.
Abs.	בַּעַל	בַּעֲלָה	בְּעָלִים	בְּעָלוֹת	בְּעָלַיִם	——
Const.	בַּעַל	בַּעֲלַת	בַּעֲלֵי	בַּעֲלוֹת	בַּעֲלֵי	——

(2) *i* type. There are no examples.

(3) *o* type: פֹּעַל "work":

	Singular		Plural		Dual	
	m.	f.	m.	f.	m.	f.
Abs.	פֹּעַל	פָּעֳלָה	פְּעָלִים	פְּעָלוֹת	פְּעָלִים	——
Const.	פֹּעַל	פָּעֳלַת	פָּעֳלֵי	פָּעֳלוֹת	פָּעֳלֵי	——
		pǫ-íᵒ-laθ	po-íᵒ-lê	pǫ-íᵒ-lôθ	pǫ-íᵒ-lê	

Note the composite Š·wā of the *o* type. This is used with words of this type under the first or the second radical letters (if guttural), but not under the third where the usual Ḥātéϕ Páθaḥ is preferred.

c. INFLECTION OF NOUNS HAVING AS *Third* LETTER A GUTTURAL

(1) *a* type: זֶרַע "seed," like מֶלֶךְ save in dual fem. const. זַרְעָתִי.

(2) *i* type: שֵׁמַע "report," like סֵפֶר save in dual fem. const. שִׁמְעָתִי.

(3) *o* type: רֹמַח "spear," like בֹּקֶר save in dual fem. const. רָמְחָתִי.

Written Exercise

I. Inflect: נַעַר "lad," חֵלֶק "portion," אֹכֶל "food."

II. Translate: Thou (m.) shalt not judge[215] the righteous[180] kings[131] of the earth[25]. O let me[184] kill the wicked[196] prophet[146] with the good[88] sword[87].

Oral Exercise, Lessons XXIII and XXIV

כֶּסֶף ׃ נַעַר ׃ אֹכֶל ׃ אכלה ׃ אכלת ׃ כספים ׃ כספֵי ׃ דָּרֶךְ ׃

דרכֵים ׃ דרכי ׃ דרכי ׃ אֲרצות ׃ ארצות ׃ פֹּעַל ׃ פעלים ׃

פֹּעלי ׃ נערה ׃ פֶּשֶׁת ׃ פשתה ׃ חֹרֶשׁ ׃ חדשה ׃ חדשת ׃ מלכֵי ׃

מלכֵים ׃ מלכֵי ׃ מלכים ׃ מלכה ׃ מלכות ׃ ילדה ׃ ילדות ׃

ילדים ׃ ידי ׃ כְּפָרים ׃ נפשות ׃ עשבה ׃ עשבת ׃ עשבים ׃

עשבֵים ׃ מלכות ׃

LESSON XXV

INFLECTION OF NOUNS OF CLASS III

a. Nouns of Class III have Ṣērê in the final syllable and an unchangeable vowel in the pretone.

Peculiarities of Inflection

1. The construct singular is (usually) the same as the absolute.

2. When affixes are added Ṣērê is shortened to Š·wā. Under a guttural the Š·wā will be ‑ː as usual.

3. When this brings two vocal Š·wās together the first is lengthened to S·γôl (not Ḥíreq nor Páθaḥ), thus:

$$ \text{קְטֶלְךָ} + \text{ד} = (\text{קְטְלְךָ}) = \text{קְטְלְךָ} \quad \text{q'ọ̆'-te-l·χā.} $$

Example

מַקֵּל " staff "

	Singular		*Plural*		*Dual*	
	m.	**f.**	**m.**	**f.**	**m.**	**f.**
Abs.	מַקֵּל מַקְּלָה	מַקְּלִים מַקְּלוֹת			מַקְּלַיִם	——
Const.	מַקֵּל מַקְּלַת	מַקְּלֵי מַקְּלוֹת			מַקְּלֵי	——

Written Exercise

I. Inflect (being careful to insert Méθeγ when necessary):

יוֹבֵל "trumpet," כֹּהֵן k'ô'-hēn "priest," שֹׁמֵעַ "hearer."

(Note the guttural in the last two words.)

II. Translate: And the good [88] priests shall go down [100] to the water [128]. The judges [216] of the people [167] have fallen [150].

———◆———

LESSON XXVI

INFLECTION OF NOUNS OF CLASS IV

a. Words of Class IV end in הָ‑, they may contain a change-able Qắmeṣ which brings them also under Class I.

PECULIARITIES OF INFLECTION

b. 1. In the construct singular the ending הָ is changed to הֶ.

2. Before an affix the final הָ is removed altogether and the affix is substituted.

Examples

	Singular		Plural		Dual		
	m.	f.	m.	f.	m.	f.	
Abs.	מִקְנֶה flock מִקְנָה		מִקְנִים מִקְנוֹת		מִקְנַיִם מִקְנָתַיִם		
Const.	מִקְנֵה מִקְנַת		מִקְנֵי מִקְנוֹת		מִקְנֵי מִקְנְתֵי		
Abs.	שָׂדֶה field שָׂדָה		שָׂדִים שָׂדוֹת		שָׂדַיִם שָׂדָתַיִם		
Const.	שָׂדֵה שָׂדַת		שָׂדֵי שָׂדוֹת		שָׂדֵי שָׂדָתֵי		śi-δ·-θê
Abs.	עָלֶה leaf עָלָה		עָלִים עָלוֹת		עָלַיִם עָלָתַיִם		
Const.	עָלֵה עָלַת		עָלֵי עָלוֹת		עָלֵי עָלָתֵי		ʿa-l·-θê

c. NOTE. — Nouns with the feminine ending הָ belong to Class I even though their masculines belong to one of the other classes.

Written Exercise

I. Inflect: יָפֶה "fair," מַעֲשֶׂה "work," רֹעֶה r'ô-ʼie(h) "shepherd."

II. Translate: And the good [88] shepherds [195] will give [154] (verb first with "and") the leaves [165] to [113] the lads [149]. Those [60] old [74] prophets [146] and these [19] wicked [196] judges [216].

Oral Exercise

THE FOUR CLASSES OF NOUNS

(The numbers indicate the class to which the words belong, the letters show the type in the case of nouns of Class II.)

[4]רֹעֶה : [4]רֹעִי : [1,4]עָלִים : [1,4]עָלַת : [4]מִקְנַיִם : [1,4]שָׂדוֹת : [1,4]עָלֶה :

[3]מַקְּלִים : [20]אֹרַח : [3]מַקְלִי : [1]אֲדָמָת : [1]בְּרָכוֹת : [20]אָכְלָה :

נִצְרִי[2a] : נֹעַר[2a] : זֶרַע[2a] : שְׁמָעוֹת[2i] : רִמְחַת[20] : חֶלְקָה[2i]

וְרִעֲתִי[2a] : פָּעַל[20] : פָּעֳלִי[20] : פָּעֳלָה[20] : אָרְחוֹת[20] : פְּעָלִים[20]

פְּעֻלַּת[20] : נַחְשִׁי[1] : חֻזְקוֹת[1] : עֻלִּי[1,4] : עֻלַּת[1,4] : עָלָה[1,4] : שָׁדַיִם[1,4]

עִשְׂבִּים[2i] : עֶשְׂבָּה[2a] : מַלְכִּי[2a] : בִּקַּרְתִּי[20] : פֵּשֶׁת[2i] : יַלְדִּי[2a]

יַלְדוּת[2a] : שֹׁרֶשׁ[20] : מַלְכוּת[2a] : מַלְכֻתִים[2a] : נַעֲרָה[2a] : וְנָתְנוּ

הָרֹעִים הַטּוֹבִים[20] : אֶת־רֻמְחִי הַמֶּלֶךְ[2a] : לַנְּעָרִים

LESSON XXVII

PRONOMINAL SUFFIXES OF NOUNS

a. The Personal Pronouns in an abbreviated form are affixed
to nouns, prepositions, etc., to express the genitive and objective
cases, thus:

$$\text{סוּס} + \text{ִי} = \text{סוּסִי}\quad\text{``my horse,''}\qquad \text{ל} + \text{ְךָ} = \text{לְךָ}\quad\text{``to thee.''}$$

b. The rules to be followed in affixing pronominal suffixes are
the same as those for other affixes (cf. Less. XXI, *e*) with three
additions (*e, f, g* below).

The addition of these pronominal suffixes affects nouns (according to the classes to which the noun belongs) in the same way that
the affixes for gender, number, and state do.

c.　　TABLE OF THE PRONOMINAL SUFFIXES FOR NOUNS

		Singular *Suffixes of* Singular Nouns			Singular *Suffixes of* Plural Nouns	
1 *p. c.*	my	יִ	î	my	יַ	ay
2 *p. m.*	thy	ךָ	-χā	thy	יךָ	ĕ-χā
2 *p. f.*	thy	ךְ	ĕχ	thy	יִךְ	á-yiχ
3 *p. m.*	his	ו	ô	his	יו	ā(y)w
3 *p. f.*	her	הָ	āh	her	יהָ	ĕ-hā

---

* This is simply a combination of noun and suffix in which the noun is really in
the construct governed by the suffix, so that *My horse* is literally *The horse of me*.

		Plural *Suffixes of* Singular Nouns				Plural *Suffixes of* Plural Nouns		
1 *p. c.*	our	נוּ֫	é-nû		our	ינוּ֫	é-nû
2 *p. m.*	your	כֶם	·χem		your	יכֶם	ê-χem
2 *p. f.*	your	כֶן	·χen		your	יכֶן	ê-χen
3 *p. m.*	their	ם	ām		their	יהֶם	ê-hem
3 *p. f.*	their	ן	ān		their	יהֶן	ê-hen

d. These suffixes are divided into *light and heavy.*

All are light save the six that have S·γôl in the last syllable.

e. The two heavy suffixes כֶם and כֶן require that the word to which they are affixed be put in the same shortened form which it would have in the construct.

This must be done *before* the suffix is attached.

f. The other four heavy suffixes require that the word be shortened as much as possible after adding the suffix; *e.g.*

$$ \text{בְּרָכוֹת} + \text{יכֶם} = \text{בִּרְכוֹתֵיכֶם} $$

g. Segholates masculine singular are not affected by *e* above, which applies only to nouns of Class I.

h. REMARKS. —

1. It will be seen that there are 20 suffixes: 10 for singular nouns, and 10 for plural nouns.

2. All the suffixes of plural nouns contain י, and none of the suffixes of singular nouns contain י save י "my."

3. The first syllable of the suffixes for plural nouns is really the termination of the masculine plural construct of nouns. This termination, as contained in the *plural* suffixes, is pointed regularly י, but not so in the case of the *singular* suffixes, namely, twice י, twice י, once י.

4. Hence, to add pronominal suffixes to *plural masculine* nouns, the plural ending ים must first be removed, and then the suffix, as given in the table, which is provided with the necessary י of the masculine plural, is affixed.

By a strange anomaly, feminine plural nouns retain their feminine ending (וֹת), and also take the masculine plural construct ending as part of the pronominal suffix, thus:

$$\text{נוּ} + \text{ַ֫יִ} + \text{בְּרְכוֹת} = \text{בִּרְכוֹתֵ֫ינוּ},\ \ \text{``our blessings.''}$$

5. Dual nouns take the suffixes of plural nouns.

6. The ending ה of feminine singular nouns must be removed and ת substituted whenever a pronominal suffix is added.

7. The first person suffix of plural nouns (ַ֫י) is the masculine plural construct ending (ֵ֫י) with the original Páθaḥ instead of Ṣērê, plus the pronominal suffix of the first person (ִ֫י) which has been absorbed in the י of ַ֫י, and therefore does not appear, thus:

$$\text{ַ֫י} + \text{ִ֫י} = \text{ַ֫י}.$$

i.   Points to be observed in appending Pronominal Suffixes

1. Determine to which of the four classes the word belongs.
2. Mark gutturals and unchangeable vowels.
3. Note whether the *word* is singular or plural.
4. Note whether the *suffix* is to be singular or plural.
5. Note whether the suffix is כֶם֖ or כֶן֖.
6. Note whether the word has the ending ָה.

Then apply the rules for inflection of the four classes of nouns respectively.

j.   TABLE OF NOUNS WITH PRONOMINAL SUFFIXES

	UNCHANGEABLE	Class I	Class I, fem.	Class II	Class II, gutt.	Class III	Class IV
	סוּס	דָּבָר	בְּרָכָה	מֶלֶךְ	פֹּעַל	כֹּהֵן	רֹעֶה
	"horse"	"word"	"blessing"	"king"	"work"	"priest"	"shepherd"
my horse	סוּסִי	דְּבָרִי	בִּרְכָתִי	מַלְכִּי	פָּעֳלִי	כֹּהֲנִי	רֹעִי
thy (m.) horse	סוּסְךָ	*דְּבָרְךָ	*בִּרְכָתְךָ	מַלְכְּךָ	†פָּעָלְךָ	כֹּהֶנְךָ	רֹעֲךָ
thy (f.) horse	סוּסֵךְ	דְּבָרֵךְ	בִּרְכָתֵךְ	מַלְכֵּךְ	פָּעָלֵךְ	כֹּהֲנֵךְ	רֹעֵךְ
his horse	סוּסוֹ	דְּבָרוֹ	בִּרְכָתוֹ	מַלְכּוֹ	פָּעֳלוֹ	כֹּהֲנוֹ	רֹעוֹ
her horse	סוּסָהּ	דְּבָרָהּ	בִּרְכָתָהּ	מַלְכָּהּ	פָּעֳלָהּ	כֹּהֲנָהּ	רֹעָהּ
our horse	סוּסֵנוּ	דְּבָרֵנוּ	בִּרְכָתֵנוּ	מַלְכֵּנוּ	פָּעֳלֵנוּ	כֹּהֲנֵנוּ	רֹעֵנוּ
your (m.) horse	סוּסְכֶם	דְּבַרְכֶם	בִּרְכַתְכֶם	מַלְכְּכֶם	פָּעָלְכֶם	כֹּהֶנְכֶם	רֹעֲכֶם
your (f.) horse	סוּסְכֶן	דְּבַרְכֶן	בִּרְכַתְכֶן	מַלְכְּכֶן	פָּעָלְכֶן	כֹּהֶנְכֶן	רֹעֲכֶן
their (m.) horse	סוּסָם	דְּבָרָם	בִּרְכָתָם	מַלְכָּם	פָּעֳלָם	כֹּהֲנָם	רֹעָם
their (f.) horse	סוּסָן	דְּבָרָן	בִּרְכָתָן	מַלְכָּן	פָּעֳלָן	כֹּהֲנָן	רֹעָן
my horses	סוּסַי	דְּבָרַי	בִּרְכוֹתַי	מְלָכַי	פְּעָלַי	כֹּהֲנַי	רֹעַי
thy (m.) horses	סוּסֶיךָ	דְּבָרֶיךָ	בִּרְכוֹתֶיךָ	מְלָכֶיךָ	פְּעָלֶיךָ	כֹּהֲנֶיךָ	רֹעֶיךָ
thy (f.) horses	סוּסַיִךְ	דְּבָרַיִךְ	בִּרְכוֹתַיִךְ	מְלָכַיִךְ	פְּעָלַיִךְ	כֹּהֲנַיִךְ	רֹעַיִךְ
his horses	סוּסָיו	דְּבָרָיו	בִּרְכוֹתָיו	מְלָכָיו	פְּעָלָיו	כֹּהֲנָיו	רֹעָיו
her horses	סוּסֶיהָ	דְּבָרֶיהָ	בִּרְכוֹתֶיהָ	מְלָכֶיהָ	פְּעָלֶיהָ	כֹּהֲנֶיהָ	רֹעֶיהָ
our horses	סוּסֵינוּ	דְּבָרֵינוּ	בִּרְכוֹתֵינוּ	מְלָכֵינוּ	פְּעָלֵינוּ	כֹּהֲנֵינוּ	רֹעֵינוּ
your (m.) horses	סוּסֵיכֶם	דִּבְרֵיכֶם	בִּרְכוֹתֵיכֶם	מַלְכֵיכֶם	פְּעָלֵיכֶם	כֹּהֲנֵיכֶם	רֹעֵיכֶם
your (f.) horses	סוּסֵיכֶן	דִּבְרֵיכֶן	בִּרְכוֹתֵיכֶן	מַלְכֵיכֶן	פְּעָלֵיכֶן	כֹּהֲנֵיכֶן	רֹעֵיכֶן
their (m.) horses	סוּסֵיהֶם	דִּבְרֵיהֶם	בִּרְכוֹתֵיהֶם	מַלְכֵיהֶם	פְּעָלֵיהֶם	כֹּהֲנֵיהֶם	רֹעֵיהֶם
their (f.) horses	סוּסֵיהֶן	דִּבְרֵיהֶן	בִּרְכוֹתֵיהֶן	מַלְכֵיהֶן	פְּעָלֵיהֶן	כֹּהֲנֵיהֶן	רֹעֵיהֶן

---

* The suffix ךָ has two syllables, but in adding it to nouns of Class I it is treated as though it was but one syllable until the shortening of the antepretone has been effected. This having been done, Méθeɣ is inserted in the new antepretone formed by reckoning two syllables to ךָ.

Written Exercise

I. Inflect, with pronominal suffixes:

אֲדָמָה "ground,"   בַּעַל "lord,"   מַטֶּה "staff."

II. Translate:

A

בְּשַׂרְכֶם ׃ יָדַי ׃ שְׂפָתָיו ׃ יְדֵיהֶן ׃ לְבָבֵנוּ ׃ מִבְּשָׂרִי ׃ בִּרְכָתֶךָ ׃

דִּבְּרוּ ׃ דִּבְרֵיכֶם ׃ בִּרְכוֹתֵינוּ ׃ אַרְצָם ׃ זַרְעֶךָ ׃ עֲשָׂבַי ׃ מַלְכָּה ׃

סִפְרוּ ׃ סִפְרֵיהֶם ׃ שָׁרָשַׁי ׃ שָׁרָשֶׁיךָ ׃ פִּשְׁתֵּנוּ ׃ נַעֲרוֹ ׃ מַקֶּלְךָ ׃

פְּנֵיהֶם ׃ נַעַרְכֶם ׃ אַרְצֵךְ ׃ בִּרְכַתְכֶן ׃ נַעֲלַיִךְ ׃

B

NOTE. — Nouns with pronominal suffixes do not take the article.

My book [158]. Your (m.) heart [116]. My prophets [146]. His king [131]. His kings. Your queen [131 fem.]. Your queens. Her lad [149]. Her lads. Our boy [95]. Our boys. Their land [25]. His flax [178]. To my horse [156]. He gave [154] my staff [139] to his servant [160]. I shall write [112] his words [53] in [32] my books [158]. Who [127] killed [184] their kings. His kindness [86] (is) great [47].

Oral Exercise

PRONOMINAL SUFFIXES OF NOUNS

[2a]מלכה ׃ [2i]ספרן ׃ [2i]ספריהם ׃ [2o]שרשי ׃ [2o]שרשיך ׃ [2i]עשבי ׃

[2i]פשתנו ׃ [2a]נערו ׃ [3]מקלך ׃ [1]פניהם ׃ [2a]נערכם ׃ [2a]ארצך ׃ [1]ברכתכן ׃

[2a]נעריך ׃ אלהינו ׃ לי ׃ בך ׃ בם ׃ [1]לבבכם ׃ [1]לבבותיכם ׃

[2o]חכמתכם ׃ [1]בשרכם ׃ [1]מקומה ׃ [1]שפתיך ׃ [1]לבבנו ׃ [3]איבכם ׃

[1]מדברו ׃ [1]מדברכם ׃ [2a]נפשותיהן ׃ [2a]נפשם ׃ [2a]דרכיך ׃ [2i]חלביהם ׃

[1]ברכתה ׃ [1]דברכן ׃ [1]דברו ׃ [1]דברינו ׃ [1]דבריכם ׃ [2a]מלכך ׃

[2a]מלכיך ׃ [2o]פעלך ׃ [2o]פעלו ׃ [1.4]שדה ׃ [1.4]שדך ׃ [4]מקנו ׃ [1.4]עליה ׃

[2o]פעליהם ׃ [2a]נעריך ׃

LESSON XXVIII

THE PRONOMINAL SUFFIXES OF VERBS

a.
Singular Suffixes

		With the Perfect			With the Imperfect and Imperative	
1 *p. c.*	נִי ‎	á-nî	me	נִי ‎	é-nî	me
2 *p. m.*	ךָ ‎	-χā	thee	ךָ ‎	-χā	thee
2 *p. f.*	ךְ ‎	ēχ	thee	ךְ ‎	ēχ	thee
3 *p. m.*	וֹ *or* הוּ ‎	ô *or* á-hû	him	הוּ ‎	é-hû	him
3 *p. f.*	הָ ‎	āh	her	הָ ‎	é-hā	her

Plural Suffixes

1 *p. c.*	נוּ ‎	á-nû	us	נוּ ‎	é-nû	us
2 *p. m.*	כֶם ‎	-χem	you	כֶם ‎	-χem	you
2 *p. f.*	כֶן ‎	-χen	you	כֶן ‎	-χen	you
3 *p. m.*	ם ‎	ām	them	ם ‎	ēm	them
3 *p. f.*	ן ‎	ān	them	ן ‎	ēn	them

NOTE. — The first vowel of a suffix is lost when the verb ends in a vowel, thus:

קְטָלוּם ‎ "they killed them."

One exception:

קָטַלְתָּ ‎ + נִי ‎ = קְטַלְתַּנִי‎, not קְטַלְתָּנִי‎.

b. These suffixes express the object of the verb.

c. The object, when pronominal, may also (less usually) be expressed by means of a nominal suffix added to the sign of the definite accusative אֵת‎, which, with a suffix, becomes אֹת‎, thus:

אֹתִי‎, אֹתְךָ ‎ "me," "thee."

d. General Rules for adding Verbal Pronominal Suffixes

1. The Perfect of active verbs and the Perfect, Imperfect, and Imperative of stative verbs (*i.e.* verbs that have Páθaḥ as the vowel of the second syllable of the Imperfect) follow the analogy of nouns of Class I, that is, pretone long, antepretone extra-short, thus:

$$ \text{קְטָל} + \text{ו} = \text{קְטָלוֹ} \quad \text{"he killed him."} $$

2. The Imperfect of active verbs and those forms of the derived stems which have Ṣērê in the last syllable follow the analogy of words of Class III, shortening the vowel of the final syllable to Š·wā; when this brings two vocal Š·wās together, and the shortened vowel was Ḥólem, the first Š·wā becomes Qámeṣ Ḥāṭûφ. Thus:

$$ \text{יִקְטֹל} + \text{ם} = \text{יִקְטְלֵם} \qquad \text{he will kill them,} $$

$$ \text{יִשְׁמֹר} + \text{ךָ} = \text{יִשְׁמָרְךָ} \quad \text{yiš-mo-r·-χā he will keep thee.} $$

3. The Imperative second singular masculine of active verbs and the Infinitives construct of both active and stative verbs follow the analogy of nouns of Class II, a short vowel appearing under the first radical and Š·wā under the second radical. This vowel is *o* for Infinitives in *ō*, and *i* for Infinitives in *a*.

   Unlike Segholates, the first syllable is generally *open* (except in the case of the *Infinitive* with the suffixes ךָ, כֶם, כֶן). Thus:

קָטְלֵנִי	qo-ṭ·-lē-nî	kill (thou) me.
בְּכָתְבוֹ	b·-χo-θ·-βô	in his writing (*inf. const.*).

but

בְּכָתְבְךָ	b·-χoθ-b·-χā	in thy writing.

4. The Infinitive construct takes the pronominal suffixes that are used with nouns, not those used with verbs, save in the

case of the suffix of the first person ; this will be *nominal* (‎ִי)
to express the *subject,* and *verbal* to express the *object,* thus :

שָׁמְרִי	šo-m·-rî	my watching
שָׁמְרֵנִי	šo-m·-rĕ-nî	to watch me

e. The following scheme embodies the above rules (*d*) :

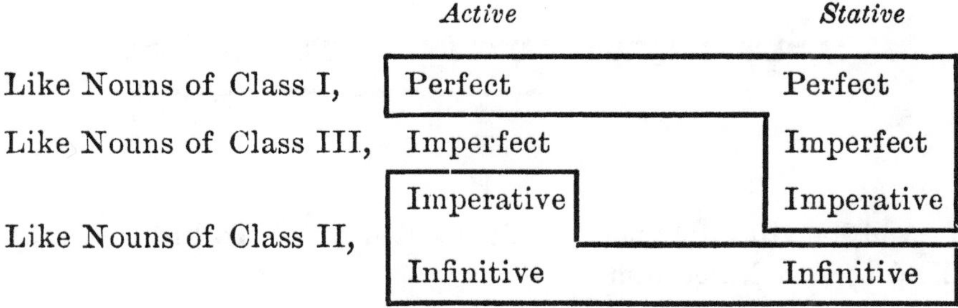

f. REMARKS. —

1. קָטְלָה "she killed," before any suffix, changes ה to ת, as in
   feminine nouns.
2. קָטַלְתְּ "thou (f.) killedst," before it can take a suffix, must be
   changed to קְטַלְתִּי, the final Š·wā becoming ‎ִי, which is the
   original final vowel of this form.
3. קְטַלְתֶּן, קְטַלְתֶּם "ye killed," before they can take a suffix,
   must be changed to קְטַלְתּוּ.
4. The Imperfect, in certain cases, inserts a syllable, ‎ֶן "en,"
   between the verb and the suffix. This is called the *energetic*
   nûn, but has no special significance. The Nûn is generally
   assimilated to the consonant of the suffix, thus :

יִקְטְלֶנּוּ	(from יִקְטְלֶנְהוּ)	he will kill him
יִקְטְלֶךָ	(-lek-kā)	he will kill thee

5 תִּקְטֹלְנָה cannot take a suffix ; the masculine תִּקְטְלוּ must be
   used instead.

6. The Infinitive construct, with the suffixes קְ֫ךָ, כֶם֫, or כֶן֫,
may follow the analogy either of Class II or Class III in
nouns, thus:

קָטְלְךָ qoṭ-l·-χā   *or*   קְטָלְךָ q·-ṭo-l·-χā.

Written Exercise

Translate:

I

שְׁמַרְתִּ֫יךָ ׃ וּשְׁמָרוּ ׃ וַיִּשְׁמְרֵ֫נִי ׃ שְׁמַרְתַּ֫נִי ׃ שָׁמְרֵ֫נִי ׃
וּלְשָׁמְרָהּ ׃ לְשָׁמְרְךָ ׃ וְאֶשְׁמְרֶ֫נּוּ ׃

II

And he will kill [184] me.   And he killed him.   To kill thee (m.).
Ye (m.) have killed him.

Oral Exercise

Pronominal Suffixes of Verbs

קְטַלְתַּ֫נִי ׃ קְטָלַ֫נִי ׃ קְטָלִי ׃ קְטָלֵ֫נִי ׃ כְּתָבְךָ ׃ קְטָלֵךְ ׃ קְטָלֵךְ ׃ קְטָלְךָ ׃
קְטָלוּ ׃ קְטָלַ֫תְנִי ׃ קְטַלְתָּ֫נוּ ׃ קְטַלְתֶּם ׃ קְטַלְתִּ֫ינוּ ׃ קְטָלַ֫תָּה ׃ קְטָלַ֫תּוּ ׃
קְטַלְתִּיכֶם ׃ קְטָלֹ֫ונוּ ׃ קְטַלְתִּים ׃ קְטָלֹ֫נוּהָ ׃ קְטַלְתּ֫וּנִי ׃ קְטָלְךָ ׃
קָטְלוּ ׃ קְטָלֵ֫הוּ ׃ קָטְלֵם ׃ יִלְבָּשֵׁ֫נִי ׃ יִקְטָלֵ֫נִי ׃ יִקְטָלֵךְ ׃ יִלְבָּשְׁךָ ׃
יִקְטְלֵם ׃ יִקְטָלְכֶם ׃ קְטַלְתּ֫וּהוּ ׃ יִקְטְלוּ֫נִי ׃ יִקְטְלוּהָ ׃ יִקְטָלֵךְ ׃
יִקְטְלֵ֫נוּ ׃ יִקְטָלֶ֫נָּה ׃ קָטְלְכֶם ׃

LESSON XXIX

THE STEMS OF THE VERB

a. There are seven Stems to the Verb (not so correctly called
conjugations).

<table>
<tr><td>I The Ground Stem,
active or stative.</td><td>III The Intensive Stem,
active.</td><td>VI The Causative
Stem, active.</td></tr>
<tr><td>. . . . . . .</td><td>IV The Intensive Stem,
passive.</td><td>VII The Causative
Stem, passive.</td></tr>
<tr><td>II The Reflexive (or
Passive) of the
Ground Stem.</td><td>V The Intensive Stem,
reflexive.</td><td>. . . . . . .</td></tr>
</table>

b. The ground stem (cf. Less. XV–XVIII) is called *Qal* (*i.e.* "light") because it presents the verb in its simplest form.

The other stems are derived from the ground stem, and may be designated either by number, as above, or by the corresponding forms of the verb פָּעַל "to do" (which was used as a paradigm by the older grammarians), or by the corresponding forms of the verb קָטַל "to kill" (the verb now generally used as a paradigm).

c.

TABLE

Stems	Name from Verb פָּעַל	Name from Verb קָטַל	Characteristic Marks
I The Ground Stem (Qal).			
II The Reflexive (or Passive) of the Ground Stem,	נִפְעַל Niφ-ial	נִקְטַל Niq-ṭal	Prefix נ and הִנ.
III The Intensive Stem, Active,	פִּעֵל Pi[i]-iēl	קִטֵּל Qiṭ-ṭēl	Doubling 2d Radical.
IV The Intensive Stem, Passive,	פֻּעַל Pu[i]-ial	קֻטַּל Quṭ-ṭal	Doubling 2d Radical.
V The Intensive Stem, Reflexive,	הִתְפַּעֵל Hiθ-pa[i]-iēl	הִתְקַטֵּל Hiθ-qaṭ-ṭēl	Doubling 2d Radical. Prefix הִת.
VI The Causative Stem, Active,	הִפְעִיל Hiφ-iil	הִקְטִיל Hiq-ṭîl	Prefix ה.
VII The Causative Stem, Passive,	הָפְעַל Hoφ-ial	הָקְטַל Hoq-ṭal	Prefix ה.

REMARKS. —

d. The meaning of any stem in relation to the ground stem must be ascertained from the lexicon, but, in general:

The Niqtal (II) = passive or reflexive of the Qal.

The Qiṭṭēl (III) = to do often or intensely the act expressed by the Qal.

The Hiqṭîl (VI) = to cause to do the act expressed by the Qal.

e. Since the first letter of פָּעַל is פ (Pê), the second ע (iáyin), the third ל (Lámeδ), it is the custom to call the first letter of any verb its Pê, the second its iáyin, and the third its Lámeδ. Thus:

אָמַר is called a Pê iáleϕ verb (written פ"א), *i.e.* a verb whose first letter is an iáleϕ.

שָׁלַח is a Lámeδ guttural verb, *i.e.* one whose last letter is a guttural, etc.

f. Stem II: NiϕiAL or Niqtal: The Reflexive or Passive of the Ground Stem

Note. — The Niqtal and all the derived stems take the same afformatives and preformatives to express tense, person, number, and gender as the Qal.

Hence, when the Qal is known by heart, it is necessary only to learn the distinctive or clue forms of a given derived stem in order to be able to form the entire stem.

g. The clue forms of a stem comprise the first or top form of the Perfect, Imperfect, and Imperative, together with the first form in each case that has a vocalic affix, and the first that has a consonantal affix, also the two Infinitives and the Participle, — about twelve in all. These will be found marked with * in the Tables of Paradigms.

h.   CHARACTERISTIC OR CLUE FORMS OF STEM II

Pf. sg. 3 *m.*	נִקְטַל	*Impf. sg.* 3 *m.*	יִקָּטֵל	*Imperat. sg. m.*	הִקָּטֵל
3 *f.*	נִקְטְלָה	3 *f.*	ת——	*f.*	הִקָּטְלִי
2 *m.*	נִקְטַלְתָּ	2 *m.*	ת——	*pl. m.*	ה——וּ
2 *f.*	——תְּ	2 *f.*	תִּקָּטְלִי	*f.*	הִקָּטַלְנָה
1 *c.*	——תִּי	1 *c.*	א——		

Pf. pl. 3 c.	נוּ——	*Impf. pl.* 3 m.	יִ——וּ	*Inf. const.*	הִקָּטֵל
2 m.	——תֶּם	3 f.	תִּקָּטֵלְנָה	*abs.*	הִקָּטֹל
2 f.	——תֶּן	2 m.	תִּ——וּ		נִקְטֹל
1 c.	——נוּ	2 f.	תִּ——נָה		
		1 c.	נִ——	*Partic.*	נִקְטָל

i. REMARKS. —

1. The Perfect and the Participle and one form of the Infinitive Absolute prefix נ, which forms a closed syllable with the first radical.
2. The Infinitive Construct, one form of the Infinitive Absolute, and the Imperative prefix הִ, and double the first radical (really הִן with נ assimilated).
3. The Imperfect doubles the first radical. (This is due to loss of ה and assimilation of נ: יִקָּטֵל = יִהְנְקָטֵל.)
4. The vowels of the clue forms, so far as they differ from those of the Qal, must be carefully noted.

Written Exercise

Translate:

I

יִלָּחֵם ׃ נִגְמַל ׃ הִשָּׁמֵר ׃ הִלָּחֲמוּ ׃ אֶשָּׁמְרָה ׃ נִשְׁפַּט ׃ נִשְׁפַּטְתִּי ׃

II

They (m.) will be counted [157]. Thou (m.) wilt take heed [212]. Take ye (m.) heed. O let me be killed [184].

LESSON XXX

STEMS III, IV, V: QIṬṬÊL, QUṬṬAL, HIΘQAṬṬÊL: THE INTENSIVES — ACTIVE, PASSIVE, AND REFLEXIVE

a.   CLUE FORMS

			Qiṭṭēl	Quṭṭal	Hiθqaṭṭēl
Pf.	*sg.*	3 *m.*	קִטֵּל	קֻטַּל	הִתְקַטֵּל
		3 *f.*	קִטְּלָה	קֻטְּלָה	הִתְקַטְּלָה
		2 *m.*	קִטַּלְתָּ	קֻטַּלְתָּ	הִתְקַטַּלְתָּ
Impf.	*sg.*	3 *m.*	יְקַטֵּל	יְקֻטַּל	יִתְקַטֵּל
		3 *f.*			
		2 *m.*			
		2 *f.*	תְּקַטְּלִי	תְּקֻטְּלִי	תִּתְקַטְּלִי
		1 *c.*			
	pl.	3 *m.*			
		3 *f.*	תְּקַטֵּלְנָה	תְּקֻטַּלְנָה	תִּתְקַטֵּלְנָה
		2 *m.*			
		2 *f.*			
		1 *c.*			
Imperat.	*sg.*	*m.*	קַטֵּל	wanting	הִתְקַטֵּל
		f.	קַטְּלִי		הִתְקַטְּלִי
	pl.	*m.*			
		f.	קַטֵּלְנָה		הִתְקַטֵּלְנָה
Inf. const.			קַטֵּל	wanting	הִתְקַטֵּל
abs.			קַטֹּל / קַטֵּל	קֻטַּל	הִתְקַטֵּל
Partic.			מְקַטֵּל	מְקֻטָּל	מִתְקַטֵּל

b. REMARKS. —

1. The distinguishing characteristic of all intensive forms is the doubling of the middle radical.
2. In the Imperfects III and IV, the Š·wā in the first syllable is to be noted.
3. In V, when the verb begins with one of the sibilants ס, שׁ, שׂ, the ת of the preformative הִתְ changes place with the sibilant, thus:

הִשְׁתַּמֵּר, not הִתְשַׁמֵּר.

If the verb begin with צ, the ת changes place with it, and becomes ט, thus:

הִצְטַדֵּק, not הִתְצַדֵּק.

If the verb begin with ד, ט, or ת, the ת of the preformative is assimilated, thus:

הִדַּבֵּר, not הִתְדַּבֵּר,   הִטַּמֵּא, not הִתְטַמֵּא.

Written Exercise

Translate: Tell [157] thou (m.). Consecrating [182]–oneself. I have walked [59]. Ye (f.) will consecrate them (m.). They told. We will break-in-pieces [204]. Seek [42] ye (f.) We will make-atonement [110]. Let them consecrate. O let me seek.

LESSON XXXI

STEMS VI AND VII: HIQTÎL AND HOQTAL: THE CAUSATIVES —ACTIVE AND PASSIVE

CLUE FORMS

		Hiqtîl	Hoqtal
Pf.	*sg.* 3 *m.*	הִקְטִיל	הֻקְטַל
	3 *f.*	הִקְטִילָה	הֻקְטְלָה
	2 *m.*	הִקְטַלְתָּ	הֻקְטַלְתָּ

			Hiqtîl	Hoqtal
Impf.	*sg.*	3 *m.*	יַקְטִיל	יָקְטַל
		3 *f.*		
		2 *m.*		
		2 *f.*	תַּקְטִילִי	תָּקְטְלִי
		1 *c.*		
	pl.	3 *m.*		
		3 *f.*	תַּקְטֵלְנָה	תָּקְטַלְנָה
		2 *m.*		
		2 *f.*		
		1 *c.*	*Cohort.* אַקְטִילָה	
Imperat. sg.		*m.*	הַקְטֵל	wanting
		f.	הַקְטִילִי	
	pl.	*m.*		
		f.	הַקְטֵלְנָה	
Inf. const.			הַקְטִיל	wanting
	abs.		הַקְטֵל	הָקְטֵל
Partic.			מַקְטִיל	מָקְטָל

b. REMARKS. —

1. In the Imperfect, the characteristic ה of the stem is merged in the tense preformative, יַקְטִיל shortened from יְהַקְטִיל (cf. the Niqtal Imperfect, Less. XXIX, *i*, 3).

2. The Jussive of the Hiqtîl differs from the ordinary Imperfect in the forms without afformatives, the *î* of the last syllable being changed to *ē*; thus:

יַקְטֵל "let him cause to kill,"   תַּקְטֵל "let her cause to kill."

With a suffix the *î* reappears, thus:

יַקְדִּישֵׁם "let him consecrate them." (Contrast Less. XXVIII, *d*, 2.)

The same is true, in the Imperative singular masculine, with a suffix, thus:

הַקְדִּישֵׁהוּ "consecrate him." Emphatic הַקְטִילָה (Less. XVIII, *e*).

3. When Wāw Consecutive is used with the Hiqtîl, it is prefixed to the Jussive form (see Less. XVII, *e*); thus:

וַיַּקְטֵל "and he caused to kill."

Written Exercise

Translate: He will divide[33] the earth[25]. Let him divide it (masc.). Divide (thou, *m.*). Do not (thou, *m.*) divide. O let me divide. And he divided. And they caused him to be king[130] (hiφ.).

Oral Exercise

The Stems of קָטַל.

קָטַלְתֶּן תְּקַטְּלִי קַטְּלֶנָה הֻקְטְלוּ הֻקְטַלְתֶּם נִקְטַלְתֶּם הָקְטְלוּ יְקַטֵּל הִתְקַטַּלְנָה
הִתְקַטַּלְנוּ הִתְקַטַּלְתְּ קָטוֹל הֻקְטְלָה אַקְטִיל הָקְטַלְתֶּם הֻקְטַלְתֶּם יִתְקַטֵּל
יַקְטִילוּ הֻקְטִילָה הֻקְטְלִי תְּקַטַּלְנָה קַטְּלֵנוּ תְּקַטֵּל מְקַטֵּל הֻקְטִילוּ
הִתְקַטַּלְנָה נִקְטַל תִּתְקַטֵּל תִּתְקַטְּלוּ מַקְטִיל נִקְטַל נִקְטְלָה קָטְלוּ
אֲקַטֵּל אֶתְקַטֵּל תְּקַטִּילִי נִקְטַלְתִּי תְּקַטְּלוּ נִתְקַטֵּל מִתְקַטֵּל הִתְקַטַּלְתֶּם
הֻקְטְלָנָה נִקְטְלוּ קָטַלְתִּי יִקְטַל נִקְטַל הָקְטְלוּ נִקְטַלְנוּ קַטְּלִי נִקְטַלְתֶּם
קָטַלְתְּ יִקְטְלוּ יְקַטְּלוּ יִקְטְלוּ הֻקְטַלְתֶּם קָטַל קָטְלָה קָטַל נִקְטַלְנוּ הֻקְטַלְתִּי
תִּתְקַטְּלִי תַּקְטִיל יֻקְטַל

Note. — In describing a verbal form use the following order:

1. The Root, *i.e.* the Lexicon Form.	4. Number.
2. Stem.	5. Person.
3. Tense.	6. Gender.

LESSON XXXII

THE IRREGULAR VERBS

Pê Guttural Verbs

a. By irregular verbs are meant such as differ in inflection from the strong or regular verbs, such as קָטַל, either because of the presence of gutturals and weak letters, or because of containing two radicals only instead of three.

b.　　　　　TABLE OF IRREGULAR VERBS

A. Guttural Verbs.	*A* 1.	Pê Guttural	עָמַד to stand
	A 2.	Íáyin Guttural	שָׁחַט to slay
			בֵּרֵךְ to bless (Qittēl)
	A 3.	Lámeδ Guttural	שָׁלַח to send
B. Biliteral Verbs.	*B* 1.	Double Íáyin (ע״ע)	סָב to go around
	B 2.	Íáyin û (ע״ו)	קוּם to stand
	B 3.	Íáyin î (ע״. ״י)	בִּין to understand
C. Weak Verbs.	*C* 1.	Pê Íáleφ (פ״א)	אָכַל to eat
	C 2.	Pê Wāw (פ״ו)	יָשַׁב to sit
	C 3.	Pê Yôδ (פ״י)	יָטַב to be good
	C 4.	Pê Nûn (פ״ן)	נָגַשׁ to approach
	C 5.	Lámeδ Íáleφ (ל״א)	מָצָא to find
	C 6.	Lámeδ Hê (ל״ה)	גָּלָה to uncover

NOTE.—Verbs פ״ו are always פ״י in the Qal perfect.

c.   *A*1. Pê Guttural Verbs
               Type: עָמַד "to stand"
                      CLUE FORMS

(Namely, the forms whose pointing differs from that of the corresponding
forms of קָטַל. When there are more than one exhibiting the same characteristic only the first is given. Thus the Qal perfect plural עֲמַדְתֶּם is given; it is
understood that the following form, the second feminine, is pointed in the
same way עֲמַדְתֶּן.)

		Qal	Niφ.	Hiφ.	Hoφ.
Pf.	sg. 3		נֶעֱמַד	הֶעֱמִיד	הָעֳמַד
	3		נֶעֶמְדָה		
	2		ne̞-ie-m·-δā(h)		
	2				
	1				
	pl. 3				
	2	עֲמַדְתֶּם			
	2				
	1				
Impf.	sg. 3	יַעֲמֹד	יֵעָמֵד	יַעֲמִיד	יָעֳמַד
	3				
	2				
	2	תַּעַמְדִי			
	1	אֶעֱמֹד			
Imperat. sg. m.		עֲמֹד	הֵעָמֵד	הַעֲמֵד	
	f.	עִמְדִי			
	pl. m.				
	f.				
Inf. const.			הֵעָמֵד		
	abs.		נַעֲמֹד, הֵעָמֵד		
Partic.			נֶעֱמָד	מַעֲמִיד	מָעֳמָד

74   A PRIMER OF HEBREW

d. REMARKS. —

1. Gutturals take composite rather than simple Š·wā; hence עֲמַדְתֶּם, not עְמדתם; נֶעֱמַד not נְעֱמַד (the ֱ under נ, in place of ְ, is due to the vicinity of the guttural, cf. the Hiφîl Perfect).
2. Gutturals cannot be doubled; hence יֵעָמֵד, not יְעָמֵד.
3. Notice the result of the coming together of two vocal Š·wās, thus: תַּעֲמְדִי, from נֶעֶמְדָה, so נֶעֱמְדָה.
4. In most פ״ח verbs, the ח, though a guttural, takes silent Š·wā, thus:

    יַחְתֹּם "he will seal,"   נֶחְתַּם Niφial Perfect.
5. With stative verbs, פ״ח, like חָכַם "to be wise," חָזַק "to be strong," the Qal Imperfects are יֶחֱכַם, יֶחֱזַק.
6. The Intensive stems are regular.

Written Exercise

Translate: The wise[81] man[14] will stand[168]. And the boys[95] stood on[164] the ground[5]. And the wicked[196] kings[131] of the earth[25] dreamed[84]. The queens[131 fem.] of the earth will be strong[78] in[32] my ways[54].

------◆------

LESSON XXXIII

A 2. ῾Áyin Guttural Verbs

Types: שָׁחַט "to slay," בֵּרֵךְ "to bless"

a.   CLUE FORMS

		Qal	Niq.	Qiṭ.	Quṭ.	Hiθqaṭ.
Pf.	*sg.* 3			בֵּרֵךְ	בֹּרַךְ	הִתְבָּרֵךְ
	3	שָׁחֲטָה	נִשְׁחֲטָה			
	2			בֵּרַ֫כְתָּ		
	2					
	1					

			Qal	Niq.	Qiṭ.	Quṭ.	Hiθqat.
Pf.	*pl.*	3	שָׁחֲטוּ				
		2			הִתְבָּרַכְתֶּם	בֵּרַכְתֶּם	בֵּרַכְתֶּם
		2					
		1					
Impf.	*sg.*	3	יִשְׁחַט		יְבָרֵךְ	יְבֹרַךְ	
		3					יִתְבָּרֵךְ
		2					
		2	תִּשֲׁחֲטִי	תִּשֶּׁחֲטִי			
		1					
Imperat. sg. m.			שְׁחַט		בָּרֵךְ	wanting	הִתְבָּרֵךְ
	f.		שַׁחֲטִי	הִשָּׁחֲטִי			
	pl. m.						
	f.						
Inf. const.			שְׁחֹט		בָּרֵךְ } wanting		
abs.							
Partic.					מְבָרֵךְ	מְבֹרָךְ	מִתְבָּרֵךְ

b. REMARKS.—

1. The guttural prefers compound Š·wâ, hence שָׁחֲטוּ, not שְׁחְטוּ.
2. The guttural prefers the sound of *a*; hence יִשְׁחַט, not יִשְׁחֹט.
   So in the Imperative, שְׁחַט, not שְׁחֹט; the feminine שַׁחֲטִי is
   from שְׁחֲטִי, just as קִטְלִי is from קְטְלִי (cf. Less. VIII, *e*).
3. Gutturals and ר cannot be doubled; hence בָּרֵךְ, not בִּרֵךְ;
   בֹּרַךְ, not בֻּרַךְ. (The reason בָרַךְ is used as type in the
   intensive stems is that, in verbs ע״ח and ע״ה, the Dāγēš
   forte is implied, and the preceding vowel, therefore, is not
   lengthened; thus: שִׁחַט ši[ḥ]-ḥēt, שֻׁחַט šu[ḥ]-ḥaṭ.)
   The Qiṭṭēl of נָחַם is נִחַם ni[ḥ]-ham "to comfort," with *a*
   instead of *ē* in the last syllable because of the preceding
   guttural. The Niqṭal of נחם is also נֻחַם (for נֻנְחַם).

Written Exercise

Translate: And the good [88] priests [107] blessed [44] the boys [95] of the people [167].   And they cried [71] to [113] him, saying (לֵאמֹר lit. "to say"), Drive [51] out our enemies [13].   The kings [131] will serve [218] your Baals [40].

———◆———

LESSON XXXIV

A 3. Lāmedh Guttural Verbs

a.   Type: שָׁלַח "to send"

Perfect

	Qal	Niq.	Qit.	Qut.	Hiθqat.	Hiq.	Hoq.
Sg. 3			שִׁלַּח		הִשְׁתַּלַּח	הִשְׁלִיחַ	
3							
2							
2	שָׁלַחְתָּ שָׁלַחַתְּ	נִשְׁלַחַתְּ	שִׁלַּחַתְּ	שֻׁלַּחַתְּ	הִשְׁתַּלַּחַתְּ	הִשְׁלַחַתְּ	הָשְׁלַחַתְּ
1							
Pl. 3							
2							
2							
1							

Imperfect

	Qal	Niq.	Qit.	Qut.	Hiθqat.	Hiq.	Hoq.
Sg. 3	יִשְׁלַח	יִשָּׁלַח	יְשַׁלַּח		יִשְׁתַּלַּח	יַשְׁלִיחַ	
3							
2							
2							
1							
Pl. 3							
3	תִּשְׁלַחְנָה		תְּשַׁלַּחְנָה		תִּשְׁתַּלַּחְנָה	תַּשְׁלַחְנָה	
2							
2							
1							

		Qal	Niq.	Qiṭ.	Quṭ.	Hiθqaṭ.	Hiq.	Hoq.
Imperative	Sg. m.	שְׁלַח	הִשָּׁלַח	שֻׁלַּח	wanting	הִשְׁתַּלַּח	הַשְׁלַח	wanting
	f.						הַשְׁלִיחִי	
	Pl. m.							
	f.			שַׁלַּחְנָה				
Infinitive	const.	שְׁלֹחַ	הִשָּׁלַח	שַׁלַּח	שֻׁלַּח	הִשְׁתַּלַּח	הַשְׁלִיחַ	
	abs.	שָׁלוֹחַ	נִשְׁלוֹחַ	שַׁלֵּחַ	שֻׁלַּח		הַשְׁלֵחַ	הָשְׁלֵחַ
Participle		שֹׁלֵחַ	מְשֻׁלָּח	מְשֻׁלָּח	מִשְׁתַּלֵּחַ	מַשְׁלִיחַ		
		שָׁלוּחַ						

b. REMARKS. —

1. Páθaḥ furtive must intervene between a final guttural and any
other preceding long vowel save Qắmeṣ; hence מְשַׁלֵּחַ, not
מְשַׁלֵּח; הַשְׁלִיחַ, not הַשְׁלִיח.

2. The final guttural prefers Páθaḥ to Ḥólem or Ṣērê; hence
יִשְׁלַח, not יִשְׁלֹח; שָׁלַח, not שָׁלֵח, etc. Note, therefore, that
the clue form of the Imperfects of all stems, except Hiqṭîl,
has Páθaḥ as the vowel of second radical.

3. The guttural, by exception, takes simple Š·wā (thus, שָׁלַחְתְּ),
save in the Perfect singular second person feminine of all
the stems, in these a helping Páθaḥ is found instead. This
does not cause the removal of the Dāγēš lene in the final ת;
hence שָׁלַחַתְּ šā-lá-ḥ(a)t for שָׁלַחְתְּ.

Written Exercise

Translate: Thy word [53] shall not be forgotten [206]. In the day [91]
of his being anointed [142] (niq. inf. c.). He caused thee to hear [210] his
words, and caused thee to write [112] them in thy books [158]. And he
fought [119] all [108] that day [91] that (Wāw sub. Less. XVII, *h*) I might
send [207] thee.

Oral Exercise

THE GUTTURAL VERBS

הַעֲמִיד הָעֳמַד עָמֹד הֶעֱמַד נֶעֱמַד תַעֲמִדִי אֶעֱמַד נֶעֱמַד עָמְדִי נֶעֱמַד
נֶעֱמַד יַעֲמְדוּ יֶחֱזַק נֶחֱזַק הָעֳמַדְתָּ שַׁחֵט שֹׁחֵט שַׁחֵט נִשְׁחֲטוּ יִשָּׁחֵט
יְבֹרַךְ נְבֹרַךְ הִתְבָּרְכִי אֲבָרְכִי שַׁחֲטוּ שֹׁחֵט נִשְׁחַט מְבֹרָךְ שִׁלַּחְתָּ שִׁלְּחוּ
נְשֻׁלַּח יְשֻׁלַּח תְּשֻׁלְּחִי אֶשְׁתַּלַּח מִשְׁתַּלֵּח מְשֻׁלָּח מְשֻׁלָּח הִשְׁלִיחַ
הִשְׁלַחְתָּ נְשַׁלַּח תְּשַׁלַּחְנָה נְשַׁלַּח הִשְׁתַּלַּח הֻשְׁלַח שֻׁלְּחָנָה אֶשְׁלַח שָׁלַח
שָׁלֹחַ שָׁלוּחַ מַשְׁלִיחַ

LESSON XXXV

BILITERAL VERBS: *B* 1. DOUBLE ʿÁYIN (ע״ע)

Type: סַב (סָבַב) "to go around"

NOTE. — These verbs are called "double ʿáyin" because the **second radical** (originally final) is repeated.

a.   **CLUE FORMS**

Perfect

		Qal	Niq.	Qit.	Qut.	Hiq.	Hoq.
Sg.	3	סָבַב or סַב	נָסַב	סוֹבֵב	סוֹבַב	הֵסַב	הוּסַב
	3	סָבְבָה or סֵבָּה	נָסַבָּה	סוֹבְבָה		הֵסַבָּה	הוּסַבָּה
	2	סַבּוֹת	נְסַבּוֹת	סוֹבַבְתָּ		הֲסִבּוֹת	הוּסַבּוֹת
	2						
	1						
Pl.	3	סָבְבוּ or סַבּוּ					
	2	סַבּוֹתֶם					
	2						
	1						

		Qal	Niq.	Qit.	Qut.	Hiq.	Hoq.
Imperfect	*Sg.* 3	יָסֹב יִסֹב	יַסֵּב	יְסוֹבֵב	יְסוֹבַב	יָסֵב	יוּסַב
	3						
	2					תָּסֵבִּי	
	2	תָּסֵבִּי תָּסֹבִּי	תִּסֵּבִּי				
	1	אָסֹב אֶסֹב					
	Pl. 3						
	3	תִּסֹבְנָה תְּסֻבֶּינָה	תִּסַּבֶּינָה				תּוּסַבֶּינָה תְּסֻבֶּינָה
	2						
	2						
	1						
Imperative	*Sg. m.*	סֹב		סוֹבֵב	wanting	הָסֵב	wanting
	f.	סֹבִּי					
	Pl. m.						
	f.	סֻבֶּינָה					
Participle		סֹבֵב סָבוּב	נָסָב	מְסוֹבֵב	מְסוֹבָב	מֵסֵב	מוּסָב

b. Remarks. —

1. With any affix the second (final radical) is always doubled (but see 3 below).
2. In the Perfects throughout before consonantal affixes large Ḥôlem is inserted; in the Imperfects under the same circumstances large Ṣᵉγôl is inserted.
3. The Intensive stems and often the third person forms of the Qal Perfect follow the analogy of triliteral stems, the second radical being repeated to supply a third radical.
4. The Qal Imperfect has two forms, the second doubles the first radical instead of the second; it is called the Aramaic Imperfect.

Written Exercise

Translate: We have surrounded [155] the enemies [13] of the king [131]. Let him go around [155] that he may take [122]. He caused the man [14] to go around the flock [140] of the lad [149]. We will surround this place [138] and we will take it.

———◆———

LESSON XXXVI

Biliteral Verbs: *B* 2. ïáyin û (ע״ו)

Type: קוּם "to arise"

a.   CLUE FORMS

			Qal	Niq.	Qiṭ.	Quṭ.	Hiq.	Hoq.
Perf.	sg.	3	קָם	נָקוֹם	קוֹמֵם	קוֹמַם	הֵקִים	הוּקַם
		3	קָ֫מָה	נָק֫וֹמָה	קוֹמְמָה		הֵ֫קִימָה	הוּקְמָה
		2	קַ֫מְתָּ	נְקוֹמ֫וֹת	קוֹמַ֫מְתָּ		הֲקִימ֫וֹת	הוּקַ֫מְתָּ
	pl.	3						
		2						
		2						
		1						
Impf.	sg.	3	יָקוּם	יִקּוֹם	יְקוֹמֵם		יָקִים	יוּקַם
		3						
		2						
		2	תָּק֫וּמִי	תִּקּ֫וֹמִי	תְּקוֹמְמִי	2 *pl.* תָּקֵ֫מְנָה		
		1						
Imperat.	sg. *m.*		קוּם	הִקּוֹם	קוֹמֵם	wanting	הָקֵם	wanting
		f.	ק֫וּמִי				הָקִ֫ימִי	
	pl.	*m.*						
		f.	ק֫וֹמֶמְנָה	הִקּ֫וֹמְנָה	קוֹמֵ֫מְנָה		הָקֵ֫מְנָה	

	Qal	Niq.	Qiṭ.	Quṭ.	Hiq.	Hoq.
Inf. const.	קוּם	הִקּוֹם	קוֹמֵם		הָקִים	הוּקַם
abs.	קוֹם	{ הִקּוֹם נָקוֹם			הָקֵם	
Partic. act.	קָם	נָקוֹם	מְקוֹמֵם		מֵקִים	מוּקָם
pass.	קוּם					

b. Remarks. —

1. ע"ו verbs are quoted not, as usual, by the form of the Qal Perfect singular third person masculine, but by the Infinitive construct, which exhibits the characteristic middle *û*.

2. The Qal Perfect singular third person feminine and the feminine of the Participle active are distinguished from each other by the place of the accent, thus:

$$\text{קָ֫מָה} \quad \text{``she arose''} \qquad\qquad \text{קָמָ֫ה} \quad \text{``arisen''}$$

3. The Qal Jussive is יָקֹם and with the Wāw Consecutive וַיָּקָם (way-yá-qom), (see Less. XVII, *e*), the accent being drawn back to the open penult and the vowel of the last syllable consequently shortened.

4. The Perfects Niqṭal and Hiqṭîl in the forms having a consonantal afformative insert Hólem before the afformative (cf. ע"ע verbs).

5. The Intensives are formed like those of verbs ע"ע, the final radical being reduplicated.

6. The Jussive of the Hiqṭîl is יָקֵם, with Wāw Consecutive וַיָּקֶם.

Written Exercise

Translate: And he arose [183] and went [59]. Let God [20] arise. The queen [131 fem.] will arise. And I will cause to return [205]. Do not (thou, m.) cause to return. O cause (sing. m.) to return (Emph. Imper., Less. XVIII, *e*).

B 3. ʿÁyin î (ע״י)

Type : בִּין "to understand"

c.   CLUE FORMS

			Qal	Niq.			Qal	Niq.
Perf.	*sg.*	3	בָּן	נָבוֹן		*pl.* 3		
		3	בָּנָה	נָבוֹנָה		2		
		2	בַּנְתָּ	נְבוּנוֹתָ		2		
		2				1	בַּנּוּ	
		1						
Impf.	*sg.*	3	יָבִין	יִבּוֹן		*pl.* 3		
		3				3	תְּבִינֶינָה	
		2				2		
		2				2		
		1				1		
Imperat.	*sg. m.*		בִּין		*pl. m.*			
	f.				*f.*		בֵּנָה	
Inf. const.			בִּין		*abs.*		בּוֹן	

d. REMARKS. —

1. The Qal Jussive is יָבֵן, with Wāw Consecutive וַיָּבֶן.
2. Compare in general verbs ע״ו.

Oral Exercise

THE BILITERAL VERBS

סבות סובב סובכתם יסובב תסובבנה מסובב הוסבה תוסבינה

מוסב הסבותי הסבו הסבו יסבו הסב מסב נסב נסבותם סב יסב

יסב הסב נסבו נסב נסב נסב סבב סבוב סבוב תסבי הוסבותם

קוּמֶם יָבִין נָבוֹן הוּקַם הֲקִימוֹתָ הֲקִימִי תְקוּמֵם בֵּין בְּנֶת תְּקֻמְנָה
תְקוּמֶינָה מְקִים הֻקַם נְקוּמוֹנוּ יָקוּם הָקוּם קוּם קָם קֹמָה
קֹמָה יָקוּם יָקֹם וַיָּקָם נְקוּמוּ יָקֻם וַיָּקָם בְּנתם

LESSON XXXVII

Weak Verbs: *C* 1. Pê iÁlɛᴘ (פ״א)

Type: אָכַל "to eat"

a.

CLUE FORMS

	Qal	Niq.	Hiq.	Hoq.
Pf.		נֶאֱכַל	הֶאֱכִיל	הָאֳכַל
Impf. sg. 3	יֹאכַל			
3				
2				
2	תֹּאכְלִי			
1	אֹכַל			
pl. 3				
3	תֹּאכַלְנָה			
2				
2				
1				
Imperat. sg. *m.*	אֱכֹל			
f.	אִכְלִי			
pl. *m.*				
f.	אֱכֹלְנָה			
Inf. const.	אֲכֹל			
abs.				
Partic.				

b. REMARKS. —

1. פ״א verbs are Pê guttural verbs in all respects save in the Qal Imperfect where א quiesces in preceding Páθaḥ and the resultant Qắmeṣ is transmuted into Ḥólem, thus:

$$\text{יֹאכַל} = \text{יָאכַל} = \text{יַאֲכַל}$$

Notice the Páθaḥ in the second syllable instead of the regular Ḥólem.

2. In pause יֹאכַל becomes יֹאכֵל.

3. In Qal Imperfect singular first person אֹכַל is for אַאֲכַל, the quiescent first radical is not written.

4. There are only five פ״א verbs; the one most common is אָמַר "to say," Qal Imperfect יֹאמַר, with Wâw Consecutive וַיֹּאמֶר (but first person וָאֹמַר); Qal Infinitive Construct אֱמֹר, with ל it becomes לֵאמֹר (from לֶאֱמֹר).

Written Exercise

Translate: And he said[21] to the man[4], From the tree[170] thou mayest eat[15]. I will make thee eat (Hiφ.) the flesh[46] of great[47] kings[131]. O let us not perish[2]. And I said, Draw[189] near (pl. fem.) that (Wâw sub.) we may eat.

LESSON XXXVIII

C 2. Pê Wâw (פ״ו) Verbs

Type: יָשַׁב "to dwell," "sit," יָרַשׁ "to take possession of"

a. CLUE FORMS

		Qal	Niq.	Hiq.	Hoq.
Pf.	*sg.* 3		נוֹשַׁב	הוֹשִׁיב	הוּשַׁב
	3			הוֹשִׁיבָה	
	2			הוֹשַׁבְתָּ	
	2				
	1				

		Qal	Niq.	Hiq.	Hoq.
Pf.	*pl.* 3				
	2		נוֹשַׁבְתֶּם		
	2				
	1				
Impf.	*sg.* 3	יִרַשׁ יֵשֵׁב	יִנָּשֵׁב	יוֹשִׁיב	יוּשַׁב
	3				
	2				
	2				
	1				
	pl. 3				
	3		תִּנָּשַׁבְנָה		
	2				
	2				
	1				
Imperat. sg. m.		יְרַשׁ שֵׁב	הִנָּשֵׁב	הוֹשֵׁב	
f.		שְׁבִי			
pl. m.		שְׁבוּ			
f.		שֵׁבְנָה			
Inf. const.		שֶׁבֶת	הִנָּשֵׁב	הוֹשִׁיב	
abs.		יָשׁוֹב			
Partic.			נוֹשָׁב	מוֹשִׁיב	מוּשָׁב

b. REMARKS. —

1. Verbs פ״ו appear as פ״י in the Qal Perfect.
   In the Qal Imperfect the original ו disappears altogether; thus יֵשֵׁב (and so in seven other verbs), or is changed to י and quiesces; thus יִירַשׁ.
2. The Qal Imperfect with Wāw Consecutive is וַיֵּשֶׁב, וַיִּירַשׁ.
3. In the Qal Imperative and in the Infinitive, the ו(י) is usually dropped.

In the Infinitive Construct this loss is compensated for by adding the feminine ending ת; thus שֶׁבֶת, which with a suffix is שִׁבְתִּי "my sitting."

4. In the Niqtal the Wāw appears throughout.

In the Perfect and in the Participle it coalesces with Páθaḥ to form Ḥólem; thus נַוְשַׁב naw-šaβ = nau-šaβ = nô-šaβ = נוֹשַׁב (cf. the Hiqtîl throughout).

5. In the Hoqtal ו uniting with Qibbûṣ forms Šûreq.

6. The verb הָלַךְ "to go" forms its Qal Imperfect (and the entire Hiφîîl) like a פ"ו verb, יֵלֵךְ, וַיֵּלֶךְ, הוֹלִיךְ.

Written Exercise

Translate: And he sat [102] on the ground [5] all [108] day [91]. O come down [100] (emphatic imperat.) with [166] thy sword [87]. And he went down that he might know [90] the words [53]: They shall possess [101] them. My seed [75] shall know their flocks [140]. And he said [21], Sit down [102] that I may take [122] them.

C 3. Pê Yôᴅ (פ"י) Verbs

c.   Type: יָטֵב "to be good"

CLUE FORMS

	Qal	Hiq.		Qal	Hiq.
Pf.		הֵיטִיב	*Imperat.*		הֵיטֵב
		הֵיטַבְתֶּם	*Inf.*	יְטֹב	
Impf.	יִיטַב	יֵיטִיב	*Partic.*		מֵיטִיב

d. REMARKS. —

1. Qal Imperfect with Wāw Consecutive וַיִּיטַב.
2. In these verbs Yôδ is the original first radical.

In the Qal Imperfect it quiesces in Ḥíreq, and in the Hiqtîl, it combines with Páθaḥ to form large Ṣērê.

3. There are but six or seven of these verbs.

LESSON XXXIX

C 4. Pê Nûn (פ״ן) Verbs

Types: נָגַשׁ "to approach," נָפַל "to fall," נָתַן "to give"

a. CLUE FORMS

	Qal			Niq.	Hiq.	Hoq.
Pf.	נָגַשׁ	נָפַל	נָתַן	נִגַּשׁ	הִגִּישׁ	הֻגַּשׁ
			נָתַתָּ			
Impf.	יִגַּשׁ	יִפֹּל	יִתֵּן	יִנָּגֵשׁ	יַגִּישׁ	יֻגַּשׁ
Imperat.	גַּשׁ	נְפֹל	תֵּן			
	גְּשִׁי	נִפְלִי				
	גַּשְׁנָה	נְפֹלְנָה				
Inf. const.	גֶּשֶׁת	נְפֹל	תֵּת			
abs.						

b. REMARKS. —

1. Pê Nûn verbs are divided into two classes, those that have the vowel Ḥólem in the Qal Imperfect and those that have the vowel Páθaḥ.

2. All Pê Nûn verbs assimilate the Nûn with the second radical (which is consequently doubled) when this Nûn would regularly close the first syllable; thus יִגַּשׁ from יִנְגַּשׁ, נִגַּשׁ from נִנְגַּשׁ.

3. In the Imperative and the Infinitive Construct of verbs with Ḥólem in the Qal Imperfect, the נ remains; in verbs with Páθaḥ, the נ is dropped.

   In the case of the Infinitive Construct, the נ being dropped, ת is added to lengthen the form (cf. verbs פ״י).

4. The verb נָתַן has special peculiarities.

   (1) The final Nûn is assimilated with the consonant of consonantal affixes.

   (2) The Qal Imperfect has Ṣērê in the second syllable.

(3) The Qal Infinitive Construct תֵּת arises from תִּנְתְּ by
assimilation of Nûn with the affixed ת; hence with a
suffix תִּתִּי "my giving."

5. The verb לָקַח "to take," in the Qal Imperfect, assimilates the
ל like a פ״ן verb, thus:

יִקַּח "he will take."

Imperative קַח, Infinitive Construct קַחַת.

6. Some פ״י verbs assimilate the Yôδ like פ״ן verbs, thus:

יָצַת "to burn"   יִצַּת "it will burn."

7. Notice the Qibbûṣ in place of Qấmeṣ Ḥāṭûφ in the Hoφial.

Written Exercise

Translate: Give [154] to me the books [158] of the prophets [146]. And
he gave to me all [108] that gold [68]. Take [122] ye my sword [87]. I will
cause you to fall [150] (Hiq.) in that day [91]. Deliver [152] me from the
swords of the wicked [196] pl..

Oral Exercise

Verbs פ״ן, פ״וי, פ״א

יאכל אכל אכל יאכל אכל אכלי תאכלי ישׁב שׁבת יושׁב נושׁב
הושׁיב הושׁב היטיב היטב ויּשׁב נושׁבו גשׁ יגּשׁ יגּשׁ גּשׁת נגשׁ יִנגּשׁ
הגישׁ תגּשׁנה הגּשׁ הגישׁי הנגשׁ נגּשׁ יפּל נפל

———◆———

LESSON XL

C 5. Lấmeδ ʾấleφ (ל״א)

Type: מָצָא "to find," מָלֵא "to be full"

Remarks. — (See the Paradigm, p. 108 f).

1. א quiesces whenever it is final.
2. It quiesces also before consonantal affixes.

(1) In all the Perfects save the Qal, and in the Qal as well of
stative verbs (מָלֵא), א quiesces in Ṣērê.
(2) In the Qal Perfect of the active verb it quiesces in Qắmeṣ.
(3) In the Imperfects and Imperatives it quiesces in S·γôl.
3. It is a consonant only before vocalic affixes.
4. When א quiesces in Páθaḥ, the vowel is lengthened to Qắmeṣ.

Written Exercise

Translate: God created [43] the heavens [209] and the earth [25] with [166]
the breath [192] of his lips [200] (dual).   We found [136] the good [88] sword [87]
and we will find the wise [81] man [14].   And the king [131] said [21], I
hate [199] him for (כִּי) he does not prophesy [145] good.

------◆------

LESSON XLI

C 6. Lámeᴅ Hê (לי״ה) Verbs

Type: גָּלָה "to uncover," "reveal"

Remarks. — (See the Paradigm, p. 110 f).

1. The Perfect singular third person masculine of all stems ends
   in הָ.
   The Perfect singular third person feminine of all stems ends
   in תָה.
   The Imperfect singular third person masculine of all stems
   ends in ה֔ (also the Participles).
   The Imperative singular masculine of all stems ends in ה֔.
   The Infinitive Construct cf all stems end in וֹת.
2. Lámeδ Hê verbs are properly לי״.
   This original third radical י appears only in the Qal passive
   Participle (where it is a consonant), and, as a quiescent, in
   all forms with consonantal affixes.
   In the Perfects active it quiesces in Ḥíreq (usually); in the
   Perfects passive it quiesces in Sērê (usually); in the Imperfects it quiesces in large S·γôl.
3. Before vocalic affixes the Yôδ disappears and the affixes come
   therefore directly after the second radical.

4. Jussive forms are made by removing (apocopating) the ending ־ֶה.

יִגְלֶה becomes יִגֶל or יֶגֶל from יִגֶל

יִגָּלֶה becomes יִגָּל

יִגָּלֶה becomes יִגָּל

יַגְלֶה becomes יֶגֶל from יַגֶל

יִתְגַּלֶּה becomes יִתְגַּל

5. ל״ה verbs are very numerous.

6. הָיָה "to become," "to be," is doubly weak, being ל״ה and Pê guttural. It has certain peculiarities. Qal Imperfect clue form is יִהְיֶה yih-ye(h) with *silent* Š·wā under the initial guttural. The Méθεγ merely serves to call attention to this peculiarity.

    יִהְיֶה apocopated becomes יְהִי from יִהִי, the Ḥíreq passing over to the second letter; with Wāw Consecutive וַיְהִי wa(y)-y·hî, with Dāγēš forte omitted from the Yôδ because of the vocal Š·wā following (see Less. VI, c). The verb חָיָה "to live," has the same peculiarities.

Written Exercise

Translate: And he revealed [48] the good [88] words [53] which [27] (were) in the great book [158]. And the king [131] shall build [39] in these places [138]. The prophet [146] commanded [179] to reveal it to her. I will redeem [173] thy seed [75] in the land [25] which thou seest [190].

Oral Exercise

Verbs ל״א and ל״ה

מָצָאה מָצָאתָ יִמְצָא תִּמְצָאנָה מֹצֵא מָצָא נִמְצָאת אֶמְצָא מְצָאנוּ

יִמָּצְאוּ הַמְצָאתֶם הַמְצָא תַּמְצִיאִי הִתְמַצָּאוּ נִתְמַצָּא מָמְצָא נָמְצָא

גָּלְתָה גָּלִיתָן גָּלֹה גָּלוּי אֶגְלֶה אַגְלֶה נִגְלִיתָ הָגְלִית הִתְגַּלִּיתָ גָּלִיתִי

גָּלִיתִי יִגְלֶה מְגַלֶּה הִגְלֹונוּ יִגָּל יֶגֶל יִגְלֹ יִתְגַּל תַּגְלֶינָה תַּגֲלוּ תַּגְלוּ

נִגְלָה נִגְלָה הֻגְלוּ גָּלוּ הֻגְלֵינָה גָּלִיתֶם יֶגְלֶךָ יַגְלֵךָ יַגְלֶנוּ גָּלִינָה גָּלִינוּ

הֻגְלֵיתֶן

VOCABULARY

ABBREVIATIONS

<table>
<tr><td>n. = noun.</td><td>v. = verb.</td><td>adj. = adjective.</td><td>intr. = intransitive.</td></tr>
<tr><td>m. = masculine.</td><td>adv. = adverb.</td><td>pr. = pronoun.</td><td>irr. = irregular.</td></tr>
<tr><td>f. = feminine.</td><td>prep. = preposition.</td><td>c. = common.</td><td>part. = particle.</td></tr>
</table>

1. אָב n. m. irr. father.
2. אָבַד v. פ״א to perish.
3. אֶבֶן n. f. stone.
4. אָדָם n. indeclin. man, Adam.
5. אֲדָמָה n. f. ground.
6. אֹהֶל n. f. tent.
7. אוֹר n. light.
8. אָז adv. then.
9. אֹזֶן n. f. ear.
10. אָח n. m. irr. brother.
11. אֶחָד adj. m. אַחַת f. one.
12. אַחֲרֵי, אַחַר prep. after.
13. אוֹיֵב participle, enemy.
14. אִישׁ pl. אֲנָשִׁים n. m. man, husband.
15. אָכַל v. פ״א to eat.
16. אֹכֶל n. food.
17. אַל־ negative used with Jussive.
18. אֶל־ prep. to.
19. אֵלֶּה pr. dem. pl. c. these.
20. אֱלֹהִים n. pl. gods, God.

21. אָמַר v. פ״א to say. וַיֹּאמֶר.
22. אֲנִי pr. pers. 1 c. I.
23. אֲנַחְנוּ pr. pers. 1 c. we.
24. אָנֹכִי = אֲנִי.
25. אֶרֶץ n. f. earth, land, with art. הָאָרֶץ.
26. אִשָּׁה n. f. woman, wife, const. אֵשֶׁת, w. suff. אִשְׁתִּי, pl. נָשִׁים.
27. אֲשֶׁר relat. part. who, which, conj. that.
28. אַתְּ pr. pers. 2 f. thou.
29. אֵת, אֶת־ sign of def. accus., w. suff. אֹת.
30. אֵת, אֶת־ prep. with.
31. אַתָּה pr. pers. 2 m. thou.

32. בְּ prep. in, by.
33. בָּדַל v. hiqt. to divide.
34. בְּהֵמָה n. f. cattle, beast.
35. בּוֹא v. to come, qal pft. בָּא, impf. יָבוֹא.

36. בֵּין *prep.* between.

37. בַּיִת *n.* house, *const.* בֵּית, *pl.* בָּתִּים (bāt-).

38. בֵּן *n. m.* son, *const.* בֶּן, בֶּן־, בָּן, בָּן־, *w. suff.* בְּנִי, *pl.* בָּנִים.

39. בָּנָה *v.* to build.

40. בַּעַל *n.* master, lord.

41. בֹּקֶר *n.* morning.

42. בקש *v. qit.* בִּקֵּשׁ, to seek.

43. בָּרָא *v.* to create.

44. ברך *v. qit.* בֵּרֵךְ to bless.

45. בְּרָכָה *n. f.* blessing.

46. בָּשָׂר *n.* flesh.

47. גָּדוֹל *adj.* great.

48. גָּלָה *v.* to reveal.

49. גָּמַל *v.* to wean.

50. גָּנַב *v.* to steal.

51. גרש *v. qit.* גֵּרֵשׁ to drive out.

52. דבר *v. qit.* דִּבֵּר to speak.

53. דָּבָר *n.* word, thing.

54. דֶּרֶךְ *n.* way.

55. הֲ *interrog. prefix.*

56. הוּא *pr. pers.* 3 *m.* he, *pr. dem. m.* that.

57. הִיא *pr. pers.* 3 *f.* she, *pr. demonstr. f.* that.

58. הָיָה *v.* to come to pass, be, *impf.* יִהְיֶה (yih-), *apoc.* יְהִי, וַיְהִי.

59. הָלַךְ *v.* to go, *impf.* יֵלֵךְ, וַיֵּלֶךְ *hiθq.* to walk.

60. הֵם *pr. pers.* 3 *m. pl.* they, *pr. dem.* 3 *m. pl.* those.

61. הֵמָּה (*longer form of preceding*).

62. הֵן *pr. pers.* 3 *pl. f.* they, *pr. dem.* 3 *pl. f.* those.

63. הֵנָּה (*longer form of* הֵן).

64. הַר *n.* mountain, *with art.* הָהָר.

65. וְ, וּ *conj.* and.

66. זֹאת *pr. dem.* 3 *f. s.* this.

67. זֶה *pr. dem.* 3 *m. s.* this.

68. זָהָב *n.* gold.

69. זָכַר *v.* to remember.

70. זָכָר *n.* a male.

71. זָעַק *v.* to cry out.

72. זְעָקָה *n. f.* cry.

73. זָקֵן *v. intr.* to be old.

74. זָקֵן *adj.* old, *const.* זְקַן.

75. זֶרַע *n.* seed.

76. חַג *n.* feast, *w. suff.* חַגִּי.

77. חֹדֶשׁ *n.* month.

78. חָזַק *v.* to be strong, *impf.* יֶחֱזַק.

79. חָיָה *v.* to live.

80. חָכַם *v.* to be wise, *impf.* יֶחְכַּם.

81. חָכָם *adj.* wise.

82. חָכְמָה *n. f.* wisdom.

83. חֳלִי *n.* sickness.

84. חָלַם *v.* to dream.

85. חֵלֶק *n.* portion.

86. חֶסֶד *n.* kindness.

87. חֶרֶב *n. f.* sword.

88. טוֹב *adj.* good.

89. יָד *n.* hand.

90. יָדַע *v.* פ״ו to know.

91. יוֹם *n.* day, *pl.* יָמִים.

92. יוֹבֵל *n.* ram's horn.

93. יָכֹל *v. intr.* to be able.

94. יָלַד *v.* פ״ו to bear a child, *hiqt.* to beget.

95. יֶלֶד *n. m.* boy.

96. יָם *n.* sea.

96ᵃ. יָנַק *v.* פ״״ to suck.

97. יָסַף *v.* פ״ו to add.

98. יָפֶה *adj.* handsome.

99. יָצָא *v.* פ״ו to go out.

100. יָרַד *v.* פ״ו *impf.* יֵרֵד to go down.

101. יָרַשׁ *v.* פ״ו to acquire, *impf.* יִירַשׁ.

102. יָשַׁב *v.* פ״ו to sit, dwell.

103. כְּ *prep.* as.

104. כָּבֵד *v. intr.* to be heavy.

105. כָּבֵד *adj.* heavy, *const.* כְּבַד.

106. כּוֹכָב *n.* star.

107. כֹּהֵן (kʻô'-) *n.* priest.

108. כָּל־, כֹּל *n.* all.

109. כֶּסֶף *n.* silver.

110. כפר *v. qit.* כִּפֶּר to atone.

111. כָּרַת *v.* to cut.

112. כָּתַב *v.* to write.

113. לְ *prep.* to, for.

114. לֹא *negat. part.* not.

115. לֵב *n.* heart, *w. suff.* לִבִּי.

116. לֵבָב *n.* = לֵב.   [ment).

117. לָבֵשׁ *v. intr.* to put on (a gar-

118. לֶחֶם *n.* bread.

119. לחם *v. niqt.* to fight.

120. לָכַד *v.* to capture.

121. לִפְנֵי *prep.* before.

122. לָקַח *v.* to take, *impf.* יִקַּח.

123. מְאֹד *adv.* very.

124. מִדְבָּר *n.* pasture, wilderness.

125. מָה *pr. interr.* what?

126. מִזְבֵּחַ *n.* altar.

127. מִי *pr. interr.* who?

128. מַיִם *n. pl.* water.

129. מָכַר *v.* to sell.

130. מָלַךְ *v.* to be king.

131. מֶלֶךְ *n.* king.

132. מָלֵא *v. intr.* to be full.

133. מִלְחָמָה *n. f.* battle.

134. מִן *prep.* from.

135. מַעֲשֶׂה *n.* work.

136. מָצָא *v.* to find.

137. מַצָּב *n.* place.

138. מָקוֹם *n.* place.

139. מַקֵּל *n.* staff.

140. מִקְנֶה *n.* flock.

141. מָשַׁל *v.* to rule.

142. מָשַׁח *v.* to anoint.

143. מִשְׁפָּט *n.* decision, judgment.

144. מָתֹק *v. intr.* to be sweet.

145. נבא *v. niq., hiθq.* to prophesy

146. נָבִיא *n.* prophet.

147. נָדִיב *n.* prince.

148. נָחָשׁ *n.* serpent.

149. נַעַר *n.* lad.

150. נָפַל *v.* to fall.
151. נֶפֶשׁ *n.* breath, living creature.
152. נצל *v. hiqt.* to deliver.
153. נָשָׂא *v.* to lift, bear.
154. נָתַן *v.* to give, *impf.* יִתֵּן.

155. סָבַב, סַב ,סבב *v.* to go around.
156. סוּם *n.* horse.
157. סָפַר *v.* to count, *qit.* to tell.
158. סֵפֶר *n.* book.

159. עָבַד *v.* to work.
160. עֶבֶד *n.* slave.
161. עָבַר *v.* to cross over.
162. עַד *prep.* to, unto.
163. עַיִן *n.* eye, fountain.
164. עַל־ *prep.* on.
165. עָלֶה *n.* leaf.
166. עִם־ *prep.* with.
167. עַם people, *w. art.* הָעָם.
168. עָמַד *v.* to stand.
169. עָפָר *n.* dust.
170. עֵץ *n.* tree.
170ᵃ. עֶרֶב *n.* evening.
171. עֵשֶׂב *n.* herb, *w. suff.* עֶשְׂבִּי.
172. עָשָׂה *v.* to do, make.

173. פָּדָה *v.* to redeem.
174. פָּנִים *n. pl.* face.
175. פָּעַל *v.* to do, work.
176. פֹּעַל *n.* work.
177. פַּר *n.* bull, *w. art.* הַפָּר.
178. בֶּשֶׁת *n.* linen.

179. צוה *v. qit.* to command.
180. צַדִּיק *adj.* righteous.

181. קָבַר *v.* to bury.
182. קָדֵשׁ *v. intr.* to be holy, *qit.* *hiqt.* to consecrate, *hiθq.* to consecrate oneself.
183. קוּם *v.* to arise.
184. קָטַל *v.* to kill.
185. קָטֹן *v. intr.* to be little.
186. קַל *adj.* light, quick.
187. קָנָה *v.* to acquire.
188. קָרָא *v.* to call.
189. קָרֵב *v. intr.* to draw near.

190. רָאָה *v.* to see.
191. ראֹשׁ *n. m. pl.* רָאשִׁים head.
192. רוּחַ *n.* wind, spirit.
193. רֹמַח *n.* spear.
194. רָעָה *v.* to shepherd.
195. רֹעֶה *participle*, shepherd.
196. רָשָׁע *adj.* wicked.

197. שָׂדֶה *n.* field.
198. שִׂים *v.* to place.
199. שָׂנֵא *v.* to hate.
200. שָׂפָה *n. f.* lip, *dual,* שְׂפָתַיִם.
201. שָׂרַף *v.* to burn.
202. שֶׁבַע *n.* seven.
203. שִׁבְעָה *n. f.* seven.
204. שָׁבַר *v.* to break, *qit.* to break in pieces.
205. שׁוּב *v.* to turn, return.
206. שָׁכַח *v.* to forget.

207. שָׁלַח *v.* to send.

208. שֵׁם *n.* name.

209. שָׁמַיִם *n. pl.* heaven.

210. שָׁמַע *v.* to hear.

211. שֵׁמַע *n.* hearing, news.

212. שָׁמַר *v.* to keep, watch, *niq.* to take heed.

213. שָׁנָה *n. f.* year.

214. שְׁנַיִם *n. dual,* two.

215. שָׁפַט *v.* to judge.

216. שׁפֵט *partic.* judge.

217. שֹׁרֶשׁ *n.* root.

218. שרת *v. qit.* שֵׁרֵת to serve.

219. תַּחַת *prep.* under, instead of.

AN INTRODUCTORY
HEBREW GRAMMAR

WITH

PROGRESSIVE EXERCISES IN READING
WRITING, AND POINTING

BY THE LATE

A. B. DAVIDSON, Litt.D., LL.D.

PROFESSOR OF HEBREW, ETC., IN THE NEW COLLEGE, EDINBURGH

(TWENTIETH EDITION)

REVISED THROUGHOUT BY

JOHN EDGAR McFADYEN, B.A.(Oxon.), M.A., D.D.

PROFESSOR OF OLD TESTAMENT LANGUAGE, LITERATURE, AND THEOLOGY
UNITED FREE CHURCH COLLEGE, GLASGOW
AUTHOR OF
"OLD TESTAMENT CRITICISM AND THE CHRISTIAN CHURCH"
"INTRODUCTION TO THE OLD TESTAMENT" ETC.

CONTENTS.

INTRODUCTION.

THE beginner should enter upon his study of Hebrew with the assurance that it is not only not more difficult, but in some important respects easier, to acquire a working knowledge of that language than of most others. With a reasonable amount of intelligent application, he will more quickly learn to read a piece of ordinary historical narrative in Hebrew than in Latin, Greek, or German.

Hebrew, of course, has difficulties of its own, which must be frankly faced. Of these the three which meet the beginner on the threshold are (i.) the strangeness of the alphabet, (ii.) the fact that the language is read from right to left, and (iii.) the unlikeness of some of the sounds to any in our own language. A little practice reduces the first two difficulties to the vanishing point: the third is more serious. There are, *e.g.*, two *k* sounds and two *t* sounds, one in either group having no equivalent in English. Thus if, for the one *k* which appears in *kōl*, the word for *all*, we substitute the other *k*, we get the word for *voice*. Unless, therefore, we learn from the beginning to make some distinction between these sounds—and this is not easy—in pronunciation, we shall be in perpetual danger of confusing totally dissimilar words. (iv.) Another difficulty is that the roots are almost entirely triliteral,[1] with the result that, at first, the verbs at any rate all look painfully alike—e.g. *malak, zakar, lamad, harag,* &c.,—thus imposing upon the

---

[1] עקרב *'qrb* may be a genuine quadriliteral; but behind most quadriliterals (cf. כרמל *krml, garden-land*) lies a triliteral root (*e.g.* כרם *krm, vineyard*). There are probably also biliteral roots (§§ 40, 43).

memory a seemingly intolerable strain. Compound verbs are impossible: there is nothing in Hebrew to correspond to the great and agreeable variety presented by Latin, Greek, or German in such verbs as *exire, inire, abire, redire*, &c.; ἐκβαίνειν, ἐμβαίνειν, ἀναβαίνειν, καταβαίνειν, &c.; *ausgehen, eingehen, aufgehen, untergehen*, &c. Every verb has to be learned separately: the verbs *to go out, to go up, to go down*, are all dissyllables of the type illustrated above, having nothing in common with each other or with the verb *to go*.

But against these difficulties have to be set facts which weigh more heavily on the other side. (i.) The working vocabulary of Hebrew is comparatively small. Many rare words occur, as we should expect, in books like Job; but the running vocabulary of average prose is meagre and simple. To know a dozen or even half a dozen chapters thoroughly is to have the key to an immensely wider area. (ii.) The noun has no case-endings, and the verb has only two tenses. What a contrast with the elaborations of Latin and Greek, especially, *e.g.*, of the Greek verb! (iii.) Hebrew syntax, though it has many subtleties of its own, is, broadly speaking, extremely simple, as a glance at any literal translation of the Old Testament, with its ever recurring *and*, will show. The clauses in a Greek or Latin sentence are built together: in Hebrew they are laid together. By the use of particles, participles, relative and other subordinate clauses, a number of thoughts are expressed in those languages in their perspective and relation to each other and presented as an artistic whole—it may be with only one principal verb. The Hebrew habit is to coordinate rather than to subordinate, and one principal verb follows another with a regularity which reminds one of the simple speech of children. A piece of idiomatic Greek, such as the introductory words of Luke's Gospel, does not readily go into Hebrew. Even simpler Greek would become simpler still in Hebrew. Take, *e.g.*, Mat. 27. 28–30: καὶ ἐκδύσαντες αὐτὸν χλαμύδα κοκκίνην περιέθηκαν αὐτῷ, καὶ πλέξαντες στέφανον . . . ἐπέθηκαν ἐπὶ τῆς κεφαλῆς αὐτοῦ . . . καὶ γονυπετήσαντες . . . ἐνέπαιξαν αὐτῷ . . . καὶ ἐμπτύσαντες εἰς αὐτὸν ἔλαβον τὸν κάλαμον, &c. These participles would in Hebrew be most naturally rendered by finite verbs, and the passage would run as follows: "and they stripped him and put a scarlet robe on him and plaited a crown . . . and put it upon his head and kneeled . . . and mocked him . . . and spat on him and took the reed," &c. Manifestly this makes for syntactical simplicity. (iv.) When the principles underlying the language—which are simple enough—are understood, it is found to be characterized by an altogether extraordinary regularity. Hebrew is methodical almost to the point of being mechanical. The so-called irregular verbs, *e.g.*, are, for the most part, strictly regular, springing no surprises, but abundantly intelligible to one who understands fundamental principles. It is therefore of the utmost importance that the learner be at pains to understand those principles from the very beginning, passing over nothing which he does not clearly see and which he has not thoroughly grasped; and if he goes forward to the study of the language with a faith in its regularity, he will find its very phonetic and grammatical principles to be instinct with something of that sweet reasonableness, that sense of fair play, we might almost say that passion for justice,[1] for which the Old Testament in the sphere of human life so persistently and eloquently pleads.

[1] Cf. the striking words in Deut. 16. 20, "Justice, justice shalt thou pursue." Illustrations of the principle of compensation will appear *passim*.

OF SOUNDS AND WRITING.

§ 1. HEBREW ALPHABET.

Name.	Form.	Final.	Sound and Sign.	Signification of the Name.	Numerical Value.
'Ā́-leph	א		'	Ox	1
Bêth	ב		b, bh	House	2
Gî́-mel	ג		g, gh	Camel	3
Dắ-leth	ד		d, dh	Door	4
Hē	ה		h	Air-hole *or* Lattice-window ?	5
Wāw	ו		w	Hook	6
Zá-yin	ז		z	Weapon	7
Ḥêth	ח		ḥ	Fence	8
Ṭêth	ט		ṭ	Snake ?	9
Yôdh	י		y	Hand	10
Kaph	כ	ך	k, kh	Bent hand	20
Lắ-medh	ל		l	Ox-goad	30
Mêm	מ	ם	m	Water	40
Nûn	נ	ן	n	Fish	50
Şắ-mekh	ס		ş	Prop	60
'Á-yin	ע		'	Eye	70
Pê	פ	ף	p, ph	Mouth	80
Çā-dhê	צ	ץ	ç	Fish hook ?	90
Qôph	ק		q	Eye of needle *or* back of head ?	100
Rêsh	ר		r	Head	200
Sîn, Shîn	שׂ שׁ		s, sh	Tooth	300
Tāw	ת		t, th	Sign or cross	400

The shapes of the letters appear originally to have roughly represented the objects denoted by their names; *e.g.* שׁ (*sh*) suggests *tooth*, for which the Hebrew word is *shēn*. These resemblances, which are often remote and obscure in the present alphabet, were frequently more obvious in the older form of the alphabet, in which, *e.g.*, the letter *'áyin*, which means *eye*, was represented by ○, and the letter *tāw*, which means *cross*, by ✕ or ✝.

1. These 22 letters are all consonants. The vowels, which were not originally written, came, in course of time, to be indicated in a manner which will be explained in §§ 2–4. The absence of vowels from the alphabet, and the consequent appearance of no letters but consonants in the original form of the Hebrew text, might be regarded as a grave misfortune, and likely to expose interpretation to ambiguity : the consonants דבר, DBR, for example, can be read to mean *speak*, or *speaking*, or *he spoke*, or *word*, or *pestilence*. In point of fact, however, these conflicting interpretations are generally little more than theoretical possibilities : the context usually puts the matter beyond doubt, just as, in an English sentence written with consonants alone, it would be tolerably easy to discover whether FR stood for *far, fare, fair, fear, fir, fire, for, fore, four, fur, fray, free, fry*, or *fro*. The proof that vowels are by no means indispensable to a rapid and accurate appreciation of meaning may be found in the fact that in Pitman's phonetic shorthand, the reporting style, which practically dispenses with vowels, can be read with perfect ease.

א is sometimes mistaken by beginners for an *a* : this it could not be, as it is a consonant. Similarly ע is mistaken for a *y*, whereas *y* (as in *yet*) must be represented by ׳ (*yôdh*).

Hebrew is written from right to left.

Observe how the following letters are distinguished : (1) ג כ נ ב. כ *k* is round, ב *b* has a "tittle" (Mat. 5. 18) at the lower right-hand corner, נ *n* is square, while ג *g* is broken at the foot ; (2) ד ר ך. ד *d* is square at the top, ר *r* is round, ך final *k* is like ד *d*, but comes below the line ; (3) ה ח ת. ה *h* is open at the top, ח *ḥ* is shut, and

ה *th* has a foot at the left; (4) י ו ז נ. י *y* does not touch the line, ו *w* does, ז *z* has a cross-stroke at the top and is wavy, while ן final *n* comes under the line; (5) ס ם. ס *s* is round, and ם final *m* is square; (6) ט מ. ט *ṭ* is open at the top and מ *m* open at the foot; (7) ע צ ץ. ע (transliterated by ') has its tail turned to the left, צ *ç* curves first to the right, ץ final *ç*, droops its tail straight down.

2. It is very important to learn from the beginning, so far as possible, the distinctive sounds of the various consonants for which we have no precise equivalent, and especially of those consonants whose sounds more or less closely resemble each other. Hebrew, *e.g.*, never confuses ט (*ṭ*) with ת (*t*), nor כ (*k*) with ק (*q*), nor ח (*ḥ*) with ה (*h*), nor ס (*s*) with צ (*ç*). The letter א (transliterated by ') expresses simply the emission of the breath. It may be well heard if in such words as *re-enter*, *co-operate*, the stream of sound of the first vowel be suddenly shut off, and the second vowel uttered with a new emission of breath. Its appearance and effect at the beginning of a Hebrew word may be roughly compared to that of the letter *h* in the word *hour*. To transliterate the English word *am*, for example, into Hebrew, we should require to begin with the *consonant* א, representing the emission of the breath; so that, ignoring the vowel (which we have not yet learned to write), the word would be אם (= '*m*, not *am*).

The letter ח is a deep guttural sound like *ch* in the Scotch word *loch* or the German *Macht*.

The letter ע had also two sounds, the one a sharp guttural sound bearing the same relation to א that ח bears to the simple ה, the other a vibratory palatal sound like the French *r*. Greek could not reproduce this consonant adequately any more than English; it transliterates it sometimes by a smooth breathing (עמלק = ’Aμαλήκ), sometimes by a rough breathing (עלי = ‘Hλί, also ’Hλει), sometimes by γ (עזה = Γάζα). Our transliteration is always ‘, and some modern pronunciations scarcely distinguish it in sound from א; but an attempt should be made to give it a guttural quality.

The *lingual* sound ט *ṭ* is produced by pressing the flat of the tongue to the top of the mouth; in ת *t* the tip of the tongue touches the teeth.

The letter ק *q* (by some transliterated *ḳ*) is much stronger than כ *k*, and is pronounced farther back—at the back of the palate.   It must not be pronounced like *qu*.

The sign שׁ *Shin* sounds *sh*; שׂ *Sin* sounds *s*, and ס is scarcely distinguishable from it: in the Old Testament they are sometimes, though rarely, interchanged, *e.g.* סכר for שׂכר *to hire*.

The letter צ *ç* is a sort of hissing *s*.   It bears the same relation to ס *s* as ט *ṭ* does to ת *t*.   The traditional *ts*, which has sometimes been retained for conveniently distinguishing צ from the other sibilants שׁ שׂ ס ז, is a quite incorrect transliteration.

3. The six letters תפכדגב have a double pronunciation, which will be explained in § 7.   Suffice it here to say that, when they have a point in their bosom, they are hard, and pronounced thus: ב *b*, ג *g* (as in *gas*, never as in *gem*), ד *d*, כ *k*, פ *p*, ת *t*; when they have no point (*e.g.* ב, ג, &c.) they are spirant and usually transliterated by the somewhat misleading *bh* (pronounced *v*), *gh* (like N. German *g* in *Tage*), *dh* (like *th* in *this*), *kh ph* (= *f*) *th*—for which some scholars prefer to adopt $\beta\,\gamma\,\delta\,\chi\,\phi\,\theta$.

4. The five letters כ מ נ פ צ are written thus : ך ם ן ף ץ, when these letters happen to be the last consonant of a word.

All the finals except ם have a tail coming below the line, and no other letter except ק comes below the line.

ל begins above the line.

EXERCISE.   WRITE THE FOLLOWING IN ENGLISH
AND HEBREW.

בית, דבר, ירד, ירך, גנב, זקן, ימט, טעם, מעט, עצה, החשׁך,
קצף, כפים, מגן, מים, רצח, כנען, אתה, אזן:

bh, b, l, lm, ml, ṣṭ, shn, lkh, gdh, dgh, qwm, rç, kph, çw, hm, mṣ, mṭ, 'ç, r', 'm, yyn, ngn, mym, 'wphph, ḥmṣ, çyç, tmm.

N.B.—The forms *bh*, *gh*, &c., represent ב, ג, &c., without the dot ; *b*, *g*, &c., the dotted letters ב, ג, &c.

§ 2. VOWEL SOUNDS.   VOWEL LETTERS.

1. The vowel system is of fundamental importance.   It can only be completely understood by watching the transformations which the vowels of a word undergo in the living

language, but the general principles can be made clear at this stage. There are in Hebrew, as in other languages, short vowels, long vowels, and diphthongs. But in Hebrew, besides the ordinary short vowels, there is a vowel so short as to be practically indistinct; the long vowels may be either pure long or tone-long; and the diphthongs have passed, for the most part, into the form of long vowels. What this means, and when these things occur, will now be explained.

2. *Vowel Sounds.*—The three primary vowel sounds are A I U (pronounced *ah ee oo*), and these may be either long or short. Though it would be scientifically more accurate to begin with the short vowels, let us begin, for convenience' sake, with the

(1) *Pure long vowels.*—The vowels of a Hebrew word are, as we shall see, capable, in certain circumstances, of great transformation: the essence of a pure (or naturally) long vowel is that it cannot, under any circumstances, be modified. For example, the *ô* in *qôṭēl* is a pure long vowel; that is, nothing that can happen to the word (*e.g.* the addition of a suffix) can in any way affect the length or quality of the *ô*, which remains, through all possible transformations of the word, unchangeable. Syllables which, etymologically, would involve the diphthongal formations *ai* (from an original *ay*) or *au* (from an original *aw*) are generally written, instead, with *ê* and *ô*. Cf. sound of *ai* and *au* in French. Thus *gul-lay-tha = gul-lai-tha = gul-lê-tha*; and *haw-shîbh = hau-shîbh = hô-shîbh*. (The vowel *ô* is not always diphthongal in origin, but may be long in its own rights, corresponding with the Arabic *â* in cognate words; *e.g.* Hebr. *shālôm* = Arab. *salâmu*; Hebr. *qôṭēl* = Arab. *qâtilu*: cf. *stone*, Old Eng. *stan.*) Thus the pure long (including the diphthongal) vowels are *â ê î ô û*, all unchangeable, and indicated in transliteration by the circumflex accent. The pure long *â* is much the least common.

(2) *Tone-long vowels.*—In contrast to the pure long vowels which, as we have seen, are long by nature and unchangeable, are the so-called tone-long vowels, which are long only because they happen to be where they are, and which, when their place shifts, no longer remain long. To under-

stand this, it is necessary to remember that by *tone* or *accent* is meant the stress of the voice, and the tone-syllable is the syllable of the word on which the stress falls—*in Hebrew, as a general rule, the last syllable.* In the noun *présent*, *e.g.*, the first syllable is the tone-syllable; in the verb *presént*, it is the last. Now the great strength of the Tone in Hebrew, besides demanding for the tone-syllable (as a very general rule) a long vowel, has the further curious effect of lengthening, where possible (this reservation will be readily understood when we reach § 6), the vowel of the preceding syllable. These vowels, thus long or lengthened, are known as *tone-long vowels.* Thus, neither of the vowels in *dābhár* (דבר *word*) is pure long, both are tone-long: the latter is long because (being in the last syllable) it bears the accent, and the former is obliged to be long because it falls immediately before the tone-syllable. The first vowel, of course, need not be *ā*; it might conceivably be *ē* or *ō*, but it must be long: a short vowel in this place would be in-conceivable. The moment, however, the word receives an addition, one or both vowels will be instantly transformed: e.g. *dibh*ᵉ*rê*, where the first vowel has changed, and the second almost vanishes (in a way to be explained in § 6). Similarly the *ē* of *qôṭēl* almost vanishes in the plur. *qôṭ*ᵉ*lîm*: this is possible only because *ē* is a tone-long (not a pure long) vowel. The *ô* and the *ē* in the word *qôṭēl* happily illustrate the difference between a pure long and a tone-long vowel.—The tone-long vowels are *ā ē ō* (but not *ī* nor *ū*), written with the long mark, to distinguish them from the pure long, which are written with the circumflex.

> Of course the vowel of the tone-syllable or the pre-tone may, etymologically, be *pure* long in its own right; *e.g.* pure long in tone *gādhôl*, *'āṣîr*; in pre-tone *qôṭēl*, *hêkhāl*.

(3) *Indistinct vowels.*—The great strength of the Tone in Hebrew has the further curious effect of reducing, where possible (this reservation will be readily understood when we reach § 6) the vowels before the pretone to a swift and somewhat indistinct sound, which approximately corresponds to the *e* in the word *the*, and which is represented by the small *ᵉ* above the line. For example, the plural of *dābhār*

is *d͡ebhārîm* : The last syllable has, as usual, the tone ; the pretonic syllable has a tone-long vowel ; and the original long vowel *ā* (long in *dābhār* because it was pretonic), now that it is two places from the tone, vanishes into the indistinct *e*. This, of course, can never happen where the first vowel is *pure* long ; e.g. *kôkhābh* could never become *k͡ekhābhîm*, but only *kôkhābhîm*, though *rōmaḥ* (with only a tone-long *ō*)[1] naturally becomes *r͡emāḥîm*. When this indistinct sound is attached to one of the four guttural letters ע ח ה א, it becomes more distinct, and definite vowels are written, less distinct than full vowels, but more distinct than the indistinct vowel which follows ordinary consonants. These vowels are transliterated by *ᵃ ᵉ ᵒ* above the line ; thus, *ḥᵃmôr, ᵉmōr, ḥᵒlî*. In spite of the identity of transliteration, there is, as we shall see in § 8, no possible confusion between this *ᵉ* (with gutturals) and the other.

(4) *Pure short vowels.*—The three primary pure short vowels are *a i u* : *a* could be deflected into *e* (cf. *a* in *many* : and *ketch* for *catch*) and even into *i* (as *instant* in careless speech becomes *instint*) ; *i* could be deflected into *e* (as *kitchen* in careless speech becomes *ketchen*), and *u* into *o*— the root *qudsh*, seen in (*el*) *quds*, the modern Arabic name for Jerusalem, becomes, with suffix, *qodshî*. But these bald statements can hardly be understood till we come to the study of actual words. The short vowels are therefore *a e i o u*, and, in transliteration, receive no accentual mark.

3. *Vocalization.*—(*a*) All the Semitic Alphabets consisted originally of consonantal signs only (§ 1. 1). In course of time the need, or at least the desirability, of expressing in some way the vowels of a word came to be felt. To meet this need, instead of adding new letters to the alphabet, three of the existing consonants, י ו ה,[2] were drawn upon to

---

[1] This word belongs to a familiar group of nouns in which, for good reasons to be afterwards explained (§ 29), the penult has the accent, while the last syllable is unaccented.

[2] א, as an indication of long *a* (*e.g.* שֵׁנָא *shēnâ, sleep*), may be here ignored, as it is rare and late. Such a form as קָאַם for *qâm* (*he arose*) is extremely rare.

represent certain vowels.[1]   As these signs, however, were not now *exclusively* reserved to represent vowels, but could still retain their full consonantal force, this device might be supposed to lead to confusion.   In point of fact this is not so: for, as every Hebrew syllable must begin with a consonant, these letters, if they appear at the beginning of a syllable, are necessarily consonantal; they will (with one or two trifling exceptions) be vocalic only at the end.   In ים, *e.g.*, the י is consonantal (*yām, sea*), in מי it is vocalic (*mî, who*). Similarly הם is *hēm* (*they*), but מה is *mâ* (*what*).

> At the end of any other syllable than the last, however, ה has its consonantal force of *h*; *e.g.* מהפכה = *mahpēkhâ* (*overthrow*). Here the last ה represents a vowel, but the first is a consonant: this, however, is perfectly natural, as the root verb, from which this noun comes, is הפך *haphakh* (*to turn*), where ה, coming first, must be a consonant.

(*b*) On account of their being used to indicate vowels, the letters י ו ה have sometimes been called *vowel letters*, or vocalic consonants (also *matres lectionis*); it is altogether reasonable that these letters should be reserved to indicate only important vowels.   Generally speaking, therefore, they are never used to indicate short vowels (in the few cases where this happens, it is considered an anomaly, and attention is called to it in a footnote to the Hebrew text): it would not be even conceivable that they should be used to indicate the indistinct vowel *ᵉ*.   They represent therefore the long vowels; and, broadly speaking, the pure unchangeably long rather than the tone-long.   This, too, is eminently reasonable, that the vowels most deserving consonantal representation are those which, like the consonants, form an integral and immovable part of the word.

(*c*) The following is the usage, when the consonants in question are used to represent vowels:

---

[1] This would occur doubtless first of all in cases where these letters had been ultimately consonantal: e.g. *a* before ו (i.e. *aw*) would pass (through *au*) into *ô*; so *uw* into *û*; *ay* (*ai*) into *ê*; and *iy* into *î*.   Thus ו would come in time to stand for long *o* and *u*, י for long *e* and *i*.

ה represents, chiefly,[1] the long *a* ;

י represents the long *i* or the long *e* ;

ו represents the long *o* or the long *u*.

Thus, independently of the special system which was later devised for the accurate representation of the vowels, we know that מה is *ma*, לי *li* or *le*, לו *lo* or *lu*, סוסי *sosi*, *sose*, *susi* or *suse*.   Only a knowledge of the language, of course, will enable us to decide between these possibilities ; but within these narrow limits words containing long vowels may be accurately read.

(*d*) But though ה represents, as a rule, long *a*, it does not follow that every long *a* should be represented by ה ; in point of fact, this distinction is reserved only for a long *a* at the end of a word.[2]   *E.g.* סוסה = *sûsâ* (*mare*), but *dābhār* = דבר (*word*), and even *qâmîm* = קמים (*arising*, plu. ptc.).

(*e*) Similarly, at the end of a word, all the other long vowels, *e*, *i*, *o*, *u*, are regularly represented by a consonant: קמי = *qâmê* or *qâmî*, קמו = *qâmô* or *qâmû*.   When any of these four long vowels, however, occurs in any other place than at the end, a distinction is usually drawn between the pure long and the tone-long vowels.   Broadly speaking, the tone-long vowels are not represented by a consonant, while the pure or naturally long vowels are : *e.g.* לבב = *lēbhābh* (*heart*), where the *ē* is only tone-long and changeable, capable of vanishing into *e* ; whereas שירה = *shîrâ* (*song*), where the *i* is pure long, and constant.   So בקר, *bōqer* (*morning*), where the *ō* is tone-long and changeable ; but כוכב, *kôkhābh* (*star*), where the *ô* is pure long and unchangeable.   Though the usage is to represent the pure long vowel consonantally, this is not invariable : e.g. *qîṭôr* קיטור (*thick smoke*), may also be written קטור or even קטר ; so *qôṭēl* = קוטל or קטל (*killing*, ptc.), *k'rûbhîm* = כרובים or כרבים (*cherubs*).   But it is an almost invariable usage that the merely tone-long vowel does not have consonantal representation : e.g. *lēbhābh* could not be ליבב.   So, for *qôṭēl* we may not write קוטיל or קטיל.

<hr>

[1] Sometimes also long *e* and *o*, but never *i* or *u*.

[2] The pronominal suffixes, however, *ka*, *ha*, *ta*, are usually written without ה ; thus ך, not כה, &c.

EXERCISE. WRITE THESE WORDS IN ENGLISH LETTERS.

מַה, מִי, מֵימֵי, לִי, לוֹ, לִין, לוּן, שִׁירוּ, קוּמָה, לוּלֵי, שִׁירוֹת,
הֵינִיק, הוֹשִׁיעָה, סוּסִים, הוֹרִיתִי, קוֹל, קוֹלוֹתֵינוּ, עוּף, הוֹבִישׁוּ,
הֵילִילִי, הוֹלִיכוּ, נָא:

Write these Hebrew words, expressing the vowels by
vowel letters :

qûm, qôm, shîr, shîrîm, ṣûṣ, ṣûṣôthênû, qôṣ, lî, lô, lû, mê,
mêshîbh, môth, hêlîl, ḥûl, ḥîlâ, hôṣî', çîph, mêqîç, ṭôbhê, nîrî.
hôshîbhû, hôlîkhû, lûlê, mênîqôthênû.

§ 3. EXTERNAL VOWEL SIGNS. THE MASSORETIC POINTS.

1. So long as Hebrew was a living language, the helps
to vocalization described in § 2. 3, though scanty, might be
found sufficient. But when the language ceased to be spoken
and became unfamiliar, fuller representation of the vowels
was needful for correct reading. The proof of this is that
the vowel-less text was frequently read in one way by the
Greek translators, and in another by the later Jewish
scholars who added the vowels. *E.g.*, Gen. 47. 31, " Jacob
bowed upon the head of the *bed*" (miṭṭâ); but in LXX,
" of the *staff*" (maṭṭe). (Cf. Heb. 11. 21.) The consonantal outline is the same for both words, הַמַּטֶּה : had the
vowels been original, the mistake could not have been
made. So in Amos 9. 12 the *Edom* of the original becomes
men (= Hebr. 'adam) in the translation (cf. Acts 15. 17);
and in Zeph. 1. 10, " the *fish*-gate," הַדָּגִים *haddāghîm* of the
original, becomes " the gate of the *slayers*," הֹרְגִים *hôrᵉghîm*,
in the translation. (This last passage also incidentally
illustrates the early confusion of ד with ר.) The necessity
for determining the exact sense, in combination with the
literary activity of the time, gave rise to the present very
complete system of vowel signs.

As the pronunciation of the language was not expressed by signs
but handed down by tradition, this tradition became an important

branch of study.   The word for "tradition" is *Massôrâ*, under which term was embraced the whole Textual Criticism of the Scriptures, including the vocalization and reading.   Hence those who employed themselves about this have been called Massoretes, and the new system of vowel signs introduced by them is named the Massoretic System of Points.

The history of this system is difficult to trace.   The names of its authors are quite unknown.   So complicated and perfect a machinery of signs could have been matured only very slowly and by successive generations of labourers.   The system probably dates from the sixth and seventh centuries ; neither Jerome (d. 420 A.D) nor the Talmud (*c.* 500 A.D.) appears to know anything of vowel *signs*.   Being the result of a formal scientific effort to express the pronunciation of the language, it is, like all systems of vowel notation arising in similar circumstances, completely phonetic ; the new signs, however, are not regarded as integral parts of the word and are not placed among the consonants, but, with rare exceptions, beneath or above them, *outside* the word.

The names given to the vowel signs probably have some reference to the action of the mouth in uttering the sounds.   These sounds are contained in the first syllable of most of the names.

2. TABLE OF EXTERNAL VOWEL SIGNS OR MASSORETIC POINTS.

	FIRST CLASS. A sound.	SECOND CLASS. I and E sounds.	THIRD CLASS. O and U sounds.
Short vowels	páthaḥ — *a* fat e.g. בַּר *badh*	ḥîreq — *i* pin e.g. מִן *min* s̤ghôl — *e* pen e.g. חֶלְקָם *ḥelqām*	qibbûç — *u* put e.g. מֻשְׁלָךְ *mushlākh* qam. ḥaṭûph — *o* on e.g. הָדְשָׁם *ḥodhshām*
Long vowels	qắmeç — *â ā* calf e.g. קָם *qâm* דָּבָר *dābhār*	ḥîreq — *î* ravine e.g. חָסִד *ḥāṣîdh* çērê — *ê ē* pain e.g. חֵק *ḥêq* כָּבֵד *kābhēdh*	shûreq qibbûç } *û* true e.g. קוּם or קֻם *qûm* ḥôlem — *ô ō* bone e.g. דֹּר *dôr* חֹק *ḥōq*
Indistinct vowels	simple shᵉwa . . . ᵉ e.g. דְּבַר *dᵉbhar* composite shᵉwas or ḥaṭephs . . . ᵃ e.g. חֲכָמִם *ḥᵃkhāmîm*	e.g. סְפָרָם *sᵉphārām* e.g. יֶחֱזַק *yeḥᵉzaq*	e.g. בְּקָרִם *bᵉqārim* e.g. הֳדָשִׁם *lᵉdhāshîm*

N.B.—In the above illustrations I have intentionally written words involving the pure long *î* without the vocalic letter י which usually accompanies them, in order to exhibit the vowel signs by themselves. The customary spelling will be explained in § 4.

(1) This vocalic system, ingenious and comprehensive as it is, has one or two disadvantages, which, however, are more apparent than real.   (*a*) It does not distinguish between long *i* and short *i*.   *E.g.* in הִשְׁמִידָם (*he destroyed them*) the first *i* (in *hish*) is short, while the second is long. But the explanation simply is that, as every Hebrew syllable must begin with a consonant, and the last syllable must therefore be *dhām*, not *ām*, consequently the second syllable is not *midh*, but *mi*: and then to the first two syllables we have simply to apply the rule that the vowel of an unaccented shut syllable (*i.e.* one ending in a consonant) is short, while the vowel of an open syllable (*i.e.* one ending in a vowel) is long.   Therefore the first *i* is short and the second long, and there is no real confusion :—*hish-mî-dhām*.

(*b*) The risk of confusion, however, would seem to be much greater with the sign ָ , which may represent two vowels not only of different classes (first *ā*, and third *o*) but even of different quantity (long *ā*, and short *o*).   Doubtless the reason for the identity of sign was the approximate similarity of sound between these two vowels ; just as *a*, in words like *small*, is pronounced like *o*, and as, in some parts of England, words like *demand*, *command*, are pronounced not quite, but almost, like *demond*, *commond*, with the *o* somewhat sustained—something like *demawnd*, &c. It is convenient, however, for us to make a rather more definite distinction between the two sounds represented by ָ , by pronouncing the one as *ā* and the other as *o*.   Here, again, there is no real confusion, as there is always some feature of the Hebrew word which puts the quality of the vowel beyond doubt ; *e.g.* in בָּקְרָם (*boqrām*, their morning) the last ָ is *ā*, because the last syllable is accented, and therefore has the tone-long vowel (therefore *ā*), while the vowel of the first syllable, being shut and unaccented, will be short (therefore *o*).   So לִשְׁפָּךְ־דָּם (two words treated as one) = *lishpokh-dām* (*to shed blood*).   The same principle essentially applies to וַיָּקָם *way-yā-qom*, " and he arose " (the dot in the י doubles it, cf. § 7. 3, hence *yy*), though, for a reason to be afterwards explained (§ 23. 3. 4), the accent falls on the penult.   This syllable is open (and accented), therefore the vowel must be long (i.e. *ā*), the last syllable is shut and unaccented, therefore its vowel must be short (i.e. *o*).   Thus this part of the word could not be *yoqom*, nor *yoqām*, nor even *yāqām*, but only *yāqom*.

(2) *Long and Short signs.*—(a) There are five short signs, viz. ⁻, ⁻ (short), ⁻, ⁻, and ⁻ ; and five long, viz. ⁻, ⁻ (long), ⁻ or ⁻ (long), ⁻ and ⁻.

The pure long and the tone-long, *â, ā,* &c., are expressed by the same sign.

(b) There is good ground for regarding ⁻, though usually short, as, in certain cases, a long vowel—sometimes tone-long, as in the first syllable of words like מֶלֶךְ *mélekh* (*king*), where it regularly takes the accent ; sometimes pure long (arising out of *ay*), *e.g.* תִּבְכֶּינָה *tibhkénâ* (*they weep*, fem.), פָּנֶיךָ *pānékhâ* (*thy face*).

(c) Short *u* is expressed by *qibbûç*, as שֻׁלְחָן *shul-ḥān* (*a table*).   Long *û* was usually already represented in the text by *waw*, in which a point was inserted, forming *shûreq*, as קוּם *qûm*, pointed קוּם (*to arise*; not קוֹם).   When *waw* was not already expressed in the text, *û* was indicated by *qibbûç*, as קם *qûm*, pointed קֻם.

(3) *Indistinct vowels.*—(a) *Sh⁽ᵉ⁾wa simple and composite.*— The name *sh⁽ᵉ⁾wa* was given to that indistinctest of all sounds resembling the swift *e* in *the*, § 2. 2. 3.   Its sign is ⁚. This *sh⁽ᵉ⁾wa* (which appears in many cases to have formerly been assimilated in sound to a neighbouring vowel: *e.g.* סדם is in Greek Σόδομα, whence comes our *Sodom*) is now so indistinct that the class of vowel to which it belongs cannot be detected, and hence it is common to the three classes.

(b) The other three indistinct vowels approached so much towards distinctness that the class of vowel sound to which they belonged could be detected, though they did not reach the rank of full vowels, § 2. 2. 3.   They thus seemed to stand midway between the simple sh⁽ᵉ⁾wa and true vowels, and are indicated by signs compounded of simple sh⁽ᵉ⁾wa and the three short vowels ⁻, ⁻, ⁻.   Hence they are often named *Composite sh⁽ᵉ⁾was.*   Being also vocalic sounds perceptibly of the nature of the short vowels they are often

2

called *swift* or *hurried* short vowels: *ḥāṭēph pathaḥ, ḥāṭēph ṣᵉghôl, ḥāṭēph qāmeç*. This peculiar degree of vowel sound was heard chiefly in connection with the consonants called *gutturals*, § 8, *e.g.* חֲמֹר *ḥᵃmôr, ass* (not חְמֹר), אֲמֹר *ᵃmôr, say* (not אְמֹר), חֳלִי *ḥᵒlî, sickness* (not חְלִי); and occasionally, though rarely, with others, *e.g.* where a letter is followed by the same letter, as עֲנֲנִי (*ʿanᵃnî, my bringing of clouds*), where עֲנְנִי (*ʿanᵉnî*) might have been expected.

(c) The sign of simple shᵉwa ּ is also put under every consonant without a vowel of its own, if it be sounded and not final, § 5. 6 b. The shᵉwa in this position is called *silent*, having no sound. *E.g.* in נִקְטָל *niqṭāl* (*killed*, ptc.), the ק has ּ under it, because, unlike נ and ט, it has no vowel of its own; on the other hand, ל, though, like ק, it has no vowel of its own, is written without ּ, because it is final.

(d) It is unfortunate that the same sign ּ should be used to indicate both sound and silence—on the one hand, an indistinct vowel, on the other, merely the end of a syllable; but, as we shall see, there is little possibility of confusion in practice. It ought to be remembered that two sounded or vocal *shᵉwas* cannot come together; *e.g.* such a form as דִּבְרֵי *dᵉbhᵉrê* is manifestly impossible: therefore when two *shᵉwas* occur together, as in יִקְטְלוּ (*they kill*), the first must be silent *shᵉwa* ending the syllable (*yiq*), and the second the vocalic *shᵉwa* beginning the new syllable *ṭᵉlû* (or perhaps even constituting by itself the second syllable *ṭᵉ*; cf. § 5. 2).

(4) *Position of the vowel sign.*—(a) The vowel sign stands under the consonant after which it is pronounced, as מַר *mar, bitter,* נָמֵר *nāmèr, a leopard*; with the exception of *ḥôlem*, which stands over the left corner of the consonant which it follows, as חֹק *ḥōq, statute,* קָטֹן *qāṭōn, little,* and *shûreq*, which has the compound sign, as סוּס *sûṣ, a horse.* Final *kaph* occurs only with *qāmeç* and *shᵉwa*, and these ᵗt takes in its bosom (not beneath it), as בְּךָ, בָּךְ, *bᵉkhā, bākh, in thee.*

(b) A *ḥôlem* preceding שׁ coincides with its point, as מֹשֶׁה *môshe, Moses*, not מֹשֶׁה. But there is no possible ambiguity; for as the consonant מ at the beginning *must* have a vowel to follow it, and as none is visible, not even a shᵉwa, the vowel must be concealed somewhere—it is really the vowel ·

absorbed in the point of the שׁ.   Similarly a *ḥôlem* following
שׂ coincides with its point, as שֹׂנֵא *sônē', hating*.   Here again
there can be no dubiety : the word could not be read as *s⁽ᵉ⁾nē'*,
which would be שְׂנֵא.   The figure שׁ will be *sho* at the beginning
of a syllable, and *os* elsewhere, as שֹׁמֵר *shô-mēr, keeper*.   This
could not be *osmēr*, for then we should have a word beginning with a vowel, which is impossible ; יִרְפֹּשׁ *yir-pōs, he
treads*.   There is no temptation to read the last syllable of
this word as *shō*, for the פ could not then be construed in
the word at all.   The first syllable is manifestly *yir* : the פ
must therefore begin a new syllable, and be accompanied, if
not by a full vowel, at least by a sounded *sh⁽ᵉ⁾wa*.   But there
is no *sh⁽ᵉ⁾wa*, therefore the dot on the right tip of the שׁ indicates the vowel *ō*, and the second syllable must be *pōs*.

(c) When *ḥôlem* precedes the letter א at the end of a
word or syllable, the point is placed on the right apex of the
letter, as בֹּא *bô' (enter)* ; when it follows, the point is on the
left apex, as אֹב *'ôbh (necromancer)*.   When the א begins a
syllable, the *ḥôlem* occupies its proper place, as בֹּאָם *bô'ām*
(*their entering*).

EXERCISE.   TRANSLITERATE THE FOLLOWING HEBREW
  WORDS INTO ENGLISH, AND ENGLISH INTO HEBREW
  WITH MASS. VOWELS.

יָד, גֵּר, חֵן, חֹק, גַּם, עַל, שׁוֹם, אִם, אַף, עָבֹד, בְּה, דֹּב, צַר,
צָרָה, עִיר, אֹכֶל, חֲזַק, אֲשֶׁר, רְפֹשׁ, שֹׁפֵט, קֶם, רָץ, רוּץ, הַגַּם,
וָו, דִּבֵּר, אֱמֶת :

gam, bôr, bôsh, shûbh, shîr, shôr, shām, ḥōq, 'im, ʻim, kōl,
qôl, ʻam, har, rōbh, rûç, hᵃrōgh, çēl, ḥêq, māshāl, m⁽ᵉ⁾shal,
qôṭēl, shālôm, yārûç, qômam, poʻᵒlô, ᵃçōph, heḥᵉzîq.

§ 4. COALITION OF THE MASSORETIC AND
TEXTUAL VOCALIZATION.

(a) The Massoretes are supposed to have abstained from
any alteration of the written consonantal text.   The rudi-
mentary vowel system expressed by the vowel letters remained

untouched.   At the same time their own system was not a mere supplement to this, but a thing complete in itself.   It thus happens that in all those cases where a textual vowel already existed, there is now a double vocalization, the textual and the Massoretic, the effect of which is to confuse the beginner.   Thus on the older system, *qôl* would be קול (*voice*), and *shîrâ* שׁירה (*song*); with the Massoretic vowels alone, these words would be respectively written קֹל and שִׁרָ. But in reality the vowels were added to the existing consonantal text, which motives of reverence left intact, and in which the naturally long vowels were, largely, already consonantally represented.   Therefore we have the forms קוֹל and שִׁירָה, in which the vowels are practically written twice.   Forms like these graphically represent to us two widely separated stages in the development of Hebrew vocalization.

(b) A vocalic consonant, used as a *consonant*, is not usually followed by that same consonant used as a vowel: in such a case only the vowel sign is written, *e.g.* מִצְוֹת *miçwôth* (*commandments*), in which the ו must be consonantal (*w*; cf. sing. מִצְוָה *miçwâ*), is better than מִצווֹת (in which the first ו would be consonantal and the second vocalic).   Again, in such a word as עָוֹן *ʿāwôn* (*iniquity*), the ו must be consonantal (*w*), as the first syllable is עָ, and a consonant is needed to start the new syllable.

(c)   There is a manifest disinclination to multiply these consonants, in their vocalic use, within the same word: consequently the same consonant is seldom twice thus used in consecutive syllables; *e.g.* שִׁרִים (*shîrîm* for שִׁירִים *songs*), קְטָלְהוּ (*qᵉṭālûhû* for קְטָלוּהוּ *they slew him*).

(d) When the consonantal letter is present (as in חֵיק *ḥêq*, *bosom*) the syllable is said to be written fully (*scriptio plena*); when it is absent (חֵק) the syllable is said to be written defectively (*scriptio defectiva*).   See also § 9.

(e) When vowels are written fully, *i.e.* with the vowel sign and the vocalic consonant, the Massoretic point stands in its proper place under the consonant which it follows, except *ḥôlem*, which is placed over the *waw*; *e.g.* חִיל (not חיִל) *ḥîl* (*to writhe*); חֵיל *ḥêl* (*rampart*), but הוֹל (not הֹול) *ḥôl* (*sand*).

Exercise.   *Write the words in Exercise § 2 with the Massoretic as well as Textual vowels.*

§ 5. PRINCIPLES OF THE SYLLABLE. READING.

1. (a) Hebrew is a strongly accented speech, and the Accent or Tone to a great extent rules the various vowel changes in the language. It is important to know where the accent falls, as the same word, differently accented, may have two widely different meanings; *e.g.* נָחָה *nā́ḥâ, she rested*, but נָחָה *nāḥá', he led*; so (בָּנוּ) *bānú', they built*, but *bā́nû, in us*. *Usually, however, the accent falls on the last syllable of the word, e.g.* יָשָׁר *yāshár, upright*, זָקֵן *zāqḗn, old*; in certain cases it may fall on the penult, *e.g.* קֶרֶן *qéren, horn*; אֹזֶן *'ózen, ear* (§ 29).

(b) If the accent be on the penult, either the accented penult or the unaccented final must be open; *e.g.* סֵפֶר *sḗpher, book*; קָטַלְתָּ *qāṭáltâ, thou hast killed*.

2. *Kinds of syllable.*——A syllable ending in a vowel is called *open*, as קָ *qā*; one ending in a consonant is called *shut*, as קַל *qal* (*light, swift*). Every syllable must contain a vowel, and the shᵉwas or indistinct sounds are not usually considered sufficiently vocalic to form syllables; *e.g.* זְקֵנִים (*elders*) would contain two syllables, *zᵉqḗ|nîm*. Some, however, regard shᵉwa, simple and composite, as (like the full vowel) constituting a syllable, and would consider this word trisyllabic *zᵉ|qē|nîm*. In prose, little depends upon the decision of this question.

3. (a) *Vowel of the syllable.*——The vowel of an open syllable is long, *e.g.* חָ in חָכָם *ḥākhām* (*wise*); it *may* be short if it has the accent, as מַ in שָׁמַיִם *shā-má-yim* (*heavens*). The vowel of a shut syllable is short; it *may* be long if it has the accent. In נִקְטָל *niqṭál* (*killed*, ptc.), *e.g.*, the *i* of the first syllable, which is shut, is short, while the *ā* of the last syllable, though it is also shut, is long, because that syllable, being the last, is accented. (The sign ָ could not therefore be *o*, which, being short, would imply that the syllable was unaccented.) So קָטֹנְתִּי *qāṭónti, I am little*.

(b) The vowels *î* and *û* cannot stand in a shut syllable before *two* consonants, even with the accent. We shall see the bearing of this in § 40. 6 a.

4. (a) Another kind of syllable, not uncommon, is the *half open*. It has a short unaccented vowel, but the consonant that would naturally close it is pronounced with a

slight vowel sound after it represented by *sh^ewa*, and thus hangs loosely between this syllable and the one following, *e.g.* בְּקְטֹל *biq̌ṭōl, in killing*; which is not *biq-ṭōl* nor *bi-q̌ṭōl*; יִשְׁרֵי *yišhrê*, which is not *yish-rê* nor *yi-sh^erê* (though, without dividing into syllables a fair transliteration would be *biq^eṭōl, yish^erê*). If the first syllable were absolutely closed, the *sh^ewa* would then necessarily be silent, whereas *sh^ewa* in words of this kind (as will be seen when the forms are mastered) always represents an ultimate full vowel; *e.g.* the original word from which יִשְׁרֵי comes is יְשָׁרִים *y^eshārîm* (sing. יָשָׁר *yāshār, upright*), and the second vowel, it is felt, ought not to be allowed to disappear absolutely. The vocalic sh^ewa therefore retains it, so far as it can be retained.

(b) Some scholars, however, emphatically deny the existence of the half-open syllable, treating the *sh^ewa* in such cases as silent and the first syllable as shut. Sievers,[1] *e.g.*, says: "A syllable is *either* open *or* closed: there is no such thing as an intermediate." The truth probably is that, for the reason given above, the *sh^ewa* was originally sounded, but that in course of time, through rapid or careless speech, it gradually disappeared (just as the *e* has been lost in *past(e)ry*, and as in careless speech the *i* tends to be lost in *family*, and the *o* in *history*). We shall throughout regard the *sh^ewa* in such cases as sounded, and the syllable as half open, as some phenomena we shall soon meet can perhaps be better accounted for on this assumption than on the other (§ 6. 2 d. i.).

5 *Beginning of the syllable.*—Every syllable must begin with a consonant: such a word as *ore* would therefore in Hebrew have to begin with an א; thus אֹר or אוֹר.

(The only exception is the conjunction וּ *w^e*, which in certain cases is written וּ *û*; cf. § 15. 1 c.)

No syllable can begin with more than two consonants (nor even with more than one, if the *sh^ewa* under the first consonant be held to constitute a syllable). When a syllable begins with two consonants, *i.e.* if the first consonant has no *full* vowel of its own, the two consonants must be separated by the slight vocalic sound indicated by sh^ewa, simple or composite, which is placed under the first, as קְטֹל *q^eṭōl*,

[1] *Metrische Studien*, i. p. 22.

kill, חֲלֹמִי *lĕ'lô-mî*, *my dream*; *i.e.* קְטֹל and חלמי are not possible. Hebrew would not say *dream* or *plan* or *umbrella*,
but *d'ream*, *p'lan*, *umb'rella*—forms which one may hear
from very slow speakers,[1] especially if uneducated. So in
modern Semitic speech, *Protestant* becomes *b'rootestanti*.
The Semites seem almost constitutionally incapable of
pronouncing two consonants together, and Greek, Latin, or
modern words involving this collocation are treated, in
transliteration, either as above, or by prefixing what is known
as the prosthetic aleph (א) to the initial consonant: thus
Scotland becomes *'iscotalandi*[2] (cf. אֶזְרֹעַ (rare) and זְרֹעַ *arm*;
so Fr. *esprit* from *spiritus*; Ital. *lo specchio* for *il specchio*).

Thus *the place of shĕwa vocal, simple or composite, is
under the first of two consonants that begin a syllable.*

6. *End of the syllable.*—(a) A syllable may end in a
vowel or consonant, that is, be either open or shut (§ 5. 2).
None but a final syllable can end in more than one consonant, and a final in not more than two (*e.g.* יַשְׁקְ *yashq, he
waters*), and the two cannot be a double letter. Therefore
such a form as קַלּ *qall* (letters are doubled by the insertion
of a point, cf. § 7. 3) is impossible. In its stead appears
simply קַל *qal* (*light*, adj.). A true double letter requires a
vowel after it; *e.g.* קַלָּה *qallâ* (fem. of קַל). The seemingly
exceptional אַתְּ (*'att*) *thou* (fem.), is explained by the fact
that the word was originally אַתִּי *'attî* (then probably *'attĕ*).

(b) *Simple shĕwa silent is placed under the consonant that
ends the syllable*, if the consonant be sounded and not the
last letter of a word, as נִקְטָל *niq-ṭāl* (*killed*). A consonant
not sounded (*i.e.* quiescent) does not take shĕwa; *e.g.* רֵאשִׁית
(*beginning*), not רֵאְשִׁית *rê-shîth*; בִּימֵי (*in the days of* . . .), not
בִּיְמֵי (because the א and ' are not sounded), nor does a single
final consonant (*e.g.* שָׁם *there*, not שָׁםְ), except *kaph*, which
takes shĕwa in its bosom, probably to distinguish *kaph* ך from
nun ן (thus לָךְ *to thee*, ׃ לָךְ *lākh*). But two sounded consonants at the end of a word both take shĕwa, as קֹשְׁטְ *qōshṭ*

---

[1] Cf. Mr. Chadband's eulogy of "Terewth" in *Bleak House* (ch. xxv.).
[2] Cf. Principal G. A. Smith, *The Early Poetry of Israel* (Schweich
Lectures for 1910), p. 4. Ch. i. has a brief but illuminating discussion
on the characteristics of the Hebrew alphabet.

(*truth*).   If, however, the first is silent and consequently drops the sh°wa, the second drops it too ; thus לִקְרַאת *liqrath,* because the א is silent.

Words ending in two consonants are rare.

(c) In a few words, *e.g.* חֵטְא *ḥēṭ, sin,* וַיַּרְא *way-yar, and he saw,* or *showed,* גַּיְא *gay, valley,* the presence of the א, though now otiose, is justified etymologically, like the *n* in *condemn.*

(d) Rule for placing *Sh°wa.*—The rules in 5 and 6 regarding sh°wa (simple and composite alike) may be put briefly thus: *Sh°wa* (simple or composite) *is to be placed under every consonant without a full vowel of its own,* if the consonant be sounded (not quiescent) and not the single final letter of a word.

Examples on the Syllable :

קָטַל *qā-ṭál,* קָטַלְתִּי *qā-ṭál-tî,* קְטַלְתֶּם *q'ṭal-tém,* כְּרֻבִים *k°rû-bhî'm,* יִשְׁקְלוּ *yish-q'lû',* הַבְדִּיל *habh-dî'l,* מַמְלֶכֶת *mam-lé-kheth,* עֲבָדִים *°bhā-dhî'm,* אֱלֹהֶיךָ *'lô-hé-khā,* יַלְדֵי *y'lî-dhé',* יַשְׁק *yashq,* יֹאמֵר *yē-'ā-mér,* חֲלָיֵנוּ *h°lā-yé'-nû.*

If, however, the vocal sh°was be counted as syllables (cf. § 5. 2), then we shall have *q°-ṭal-tem, h°-lā-yê-nû,* &c.

EXERCISE.   WRITE THE FOLLOWING WORDS IN ENGLISH, DIVIDING THEM INTO SYLLABLES.

אֱלֹהִים, חֲלִי, חֲמוֹר, אֲרִי, מֵרָחָק, הֲלָהֶן, נִשְׁקָלוּ, מְצֻפְצָפִים, קַמְנוּ, קְצִיר, לָאֲנָשִׁים, הַקְטְלָה, הַקְטִיל, יַפְתְּ :

Write these Hebrew words: qôṭēl, qâm, 'ekhtōbh, māqôm, wlô, mizmôr, qiṭlû, shāmáyim, qû'mû, lmînēhû, ûlyāmîm, yéreq, lilqōṭ, mamlākhâ, lshālôm, shmônîm, shnê, mqômî, yôr-shîm, nilḥam, yisrā'ēl, shmô, ná'ar, h°môrîm, ʲe'°ṣōph, 'amalnû.

Note.—In the above English words simple sh°wa, silent or vocal, is not expressed : the exercise is set partly for practice in placing it. The accent, unless marked, is on the last syllable, both in the Hebrew words and English transliterations.

§ 6. THE VOWEL SYSTEM AND THE TONE.

The principles of this paragraph are of fundamental importance : practically the whole vocalization of the language depends on them. They should therefore be very clearly grasped before passing on.

The following table is the same as that on p. 15, though the classes of vowels are placed in a different order, to show better some points of connection between them :

FIRST CLASS. A sound.	SECOND CLASS. I and E sounds.	THIRD CLASS. O and U sounds.
(a) naturally long vowels		
(b) pure short		
(c) tone-long		
(d) vanishing of tone-long		
(e) .... under gutturals		

As we have already seen, § 3. 2. 2 b, ֶ, though usually short, may be regarded as tone-long in the first syllable of words like מֶלֶךְ, and (written ֵ‎) as pure long in forms like תִּגְלֶינָה *tighlénâ* (*they reveal*, fem.), סוּסֶיהָ *sûséhâ* (*her horses*).

1. *Unchangeable vowels.*—The vowels in the first line being naturally long, whether pure or diphthongal, remain unaltered in all forms of the word. They are the vowels *â î û ê ô*. Thus the long vowel in the words קָם *qâm* (*he arose*), חֵיק or חֵק *héq* (*bosom*), שִׁיר *shîr* (*song*), קוֹל *qôl* (*voice*), סוּם *sûs* (*horse*)— being naturally long, and therefore (in the case of second and third class vowels) usually, though not necessarily or inevitably, having consonantal representation—remains unchanged through all possible transformations of the word. The pure short vowels also, standing generally in shut syllables (§ 5. 3 a), are from position unchangeable, because, if the syllable be truly shut, it cannot be entered, and the vowel within it is therefore invulnerable. They are *a i u e o*. Thus the first vowel in the words קַמְנוּ *qámnû* (*we arose*), מֶרְחָק *merḥâq* (*distance*), מִזְרָק *mizrâq* (*basin*), מָשְׁחָת *moshḥâth* (*ruined*, ptc.), מֻשְׁלָךְ *mushlâkh* (*thrown*, ptc.), is unchangeably short, because the syllable is shut.

2. *Changeable vowels.*—It will be well at this point to remind ourselves that, though Hebrew has strongly marked peculiarities of its own, the effect of the tone upon adjacent vowels is not without parallel even in our own language

The vowels in the first three syllables of the words *ánalogue*, *análogy*, *analógical*, for example, obviously are seriously modified by the shifting of the tone.

The most important vowels in reference to inflection are those in the third line called *Tone-long, ā ē ō*; that is, vowels not long by nature but from occupying a certain position in relation to the place of tone (§ 5. 1 a), and therefore changeable, when their relation to the tone alters, by change in the place of accent. *Tone-long vowels are therefore vowels long through their relation to the place of the tone.* We shall see in sub-paragraph (b) precisely what this means.

With the tone-long vowels must be taken the shᵉwas (whether simple ֳ or composite ֱ ֲ ֳ), § 2. 2. 3, which are full vowels reduced to the vanishing point by reason of their relation to the tone. This will become clear in sub-paragraph (c).

(a) There are only three tone-long vowels, ֡ ֡ ֡ *ā ē ō*, one for each class; a short *ḥireq* (ִ) when tone-lengthened becomes not long *ḥireq* but *çere* ֵ, and a *qibbuç* (ֻ) when tone-lengthened becomes not long *qibbuç* but *ḥôlem* (ֹ).

(b) Tone-long vowels are produced by proximity to the tone, and are found in the open syllable immediately *before* the tone (rarely after it), and in the shut syllable, chiefly the *final*, under the tone. In יָשָׁר *yāshár, upright, e.g.* the last syllable, though shut, has a *long* vowel, *because it is accented*—the last syllable is usually accented (§ 5. 1 a); therefore יָשַׁר would be wrong (but cf. f). Again, the first syllable, being immediately before the tone, *and open*, must also be long; therefore יְשָׁר would be wrong and impossible. Of course, if the syllable before the tone is shut, its vowel is short and must remain so; thus מַזְלֵג *mazlégh, fork* (not מָזְלֵג, which, if the form existed, would really be *mozlégh*—short o).

(c) i. The indistinct vowels or shᵉwas are produced by distance from the tone, their common position being what would be an open syllable two places from the tone, or any open syllable further removed. The end of the word being, as we have seen, so heavily weighted, the earlier part is made as light as possible, consistently with the laws of the language. Thus in יְשָׁרִים *yᵉshārîm* (plur. of יָשָׁר) the last syllable, as usual, has a long vowel; the pretonic is open (because the last syllable is רִים *rîm*) and therefore requires a long vowel, שָׁ; and the syllable before the pretonic being open (יָ *yā* in the original singular), must be accelerated by its vowel being reduced to the faintest vocalic sound, viz. sh°wa: יְ *y°*. Thus the word whose original is יָשָׁר becomes יְשָׁרִים and can become nothing else. No more serious violations of Hebrew vocalization could be conceived than such forms as יְשַׁרִים or יָשָׁרִים. Naturally, the vowel of the syllable before the pretone cannot vanish into a sh°wa if it be an unchangeably long vowel (*e.g.* כּוֹכָבִים *kôkhābhîm* (*stars*), manifestly could not become כְּכָבִים *k°khābhîm*, as the *ô* with its consonantal representation is unchangeable); nor can it so vanish if the syllable be shut (*e.g.* נִקְטָלִים *killed*, ptc. pl., could not become נְקְטָלִים. The syllable נִק *niq* is closed, and its vowel cannot be touched; besides, נְ would be an impossible form, as a syllable requires a full vowel).

In the illustration יָשָׁר the vowel of both tone and pretone happens to be *ā*; but 'any of the long vowels may appear in either place; *e.g.* זָקֵן *zāqēn* (*old*), קָטֹן *little*, לֵבָב *heart*.

ii. The rules may be summed up as follows: *the final accented shut syllable, and the pretonic syllable, if open, have tone-long vowels; the vowels before the pretonic are, where possible, reduced to sh°wa.*[1]

The vowel of the tone or pretone may, of course, happen to be long by nature: לָשׁוֹן *lāshôn* (*tongue*), נָשִׂיא *nāsî'* (*ruler*), קוֹטֵל *qôṭēl* (*killing*), כּוֹכָב *kôkhābh* (*star*).

iii. The indistinct vowel arising from the loss of a vowel of *any* class under ordinary consonants is *simple sh°wa vocal*; thus יְשָׁרִים from יָשָׁר, לְבָבִי (*my heart*) from לֵבָב, רְמָחִים (*spears*) from רֹמַח.[2] Under *Gutturals* (§ 8), it is one of the *ḥaṭephs*, generally ḥ. *pathaḥ* for vowels of first *and* second class (i.e. *not* ḥ. s°ghol for second class) and ḥ. *qāmeç* for vowels of third

---

[1] Only in very rare cases and with vowels long by nature in the tone, do indistinct vowels fall in the place immediately preceding the tone, as כְּתָב *k°thābh* (*a writing*), יְקוּם (*substance*).

[2] This word, accented on the penult in seeming contravention of the rule, will be explained in § 29, and need not now perplex or detain us.

class ; thus חֲכָמִים from חָכָם (*wise*), חֲלָבִים (not הֲלָבִים) from חֵלֶב [1]
(*fat*, noun), חֳדָשִׁים from חֹדֶשׁ [1] (*new moon, month*).

(d) i. Two sounded shᵉwas must never come together
(§ 3. 2. 3 d). When, therefore, through processes of inflection
(*e.g.* יְשָׁרִים *pl. absolute,* יִשְׁרֵי *pl. construct,* § 17) or composition
(as when, *e.g.*, the prepositions בְּ *in*, כְּ *as*, לְ *to*, precede a word
beginning with shᵉwa : *e.g.* לִמְשִׁיחוֹ *to his anointed*; cf. § 14. 1 b)
this would happen, *the first becomes a full short vowel, most
commonly* the vowel *ḥireq*. Thus the impossible יְשְׁרֵי becomes
יִשְׁרֵי *yishᵉrê*, and לְמְשִׁיחוֹ becomes לִמְשִׁיחוֹ *limᵉshîḥô*. In the
former word, as so frequently, an original *a* (seen in *sing.*
yashar, יָשָׁר) has been thinned to *i* (cf. *instant, covenant*
becoming in careless speech *instint, covenint*; cf. § 2. 2. 4).

ii. If the first of the shᵉwas be a composite (as will happen
when the first consonant is a guttural, cf. § 8. 2 a) the short
vowel arising is not *i*, but is generally the full vowel corresponding to the composite shᵉwa. Thus חַכְמֵי (from חָכָם
wise) becomes not חִכְמֵי but חַכְמֵי *ḥakhᵉmê*. That is, the flavour
of the original vowel is retained ; and this occasionally, but
rarely, happens with other than guttural consonants ; *e.g.*
כְּנְפֵי (from כָּנָף *a wing*) becomes not כִּנְפֵי but כַּנְפֵי *kanᵉphê*.

(e) The *new syllable* arising with this short vowel in such
cases is generally *half open* (§ 5. 4). That is, the יְשׁ in יִשְׁרֵי
and the חַכְ in חַכְמֵי are not completely closed, for the shᵉwa
is not silent but sounded ; nor yet are the י and the ח completely open, for that would make these vowels long, thus
giving them an importance which the history of the forms
shows that they do not deserve. A shᵉwa in such a place
(יְשְׁרֵי) would have no right to become a long vowel. The
syllable is therefore commonly regarded as half open, because it is neither quite open nor quite closed.

These loose or half-open syllables become perfectly easy
to understand when we remember that the shᵉwa represents
an original full vowel. Or conversely, if by processes of inflection or composition, an original full vowel is reduced to
a shᵉwa, the shᵉwa must be sounded, and the syllable to

---

[1] These words, accented on the penult in seeming contravention of
the rule, will be explained in § 29, and need not now perplex or detain us.

which it belongs is regarded as half open. If it were to be regarded as closed, then the sh^{e}wa would be silent, and the original full vowel would have disappeared without trace: whereas it is one of the fundamental principles of Hebrew to conserve, in whatever way possible, the ultimate elements of words. *E.g.* to consider the first syllable of יִשְׁרֵי as closed and the sh^{e}wa as silent would obliterate the fact that originally a full vowel (*a*) stood between *sh* and *r* (pl. יְשָׁרִים, sing. יָשָׁר). The only way of preserving this in the derivative form of the word is to treat the sh^{e}wa as sounded, not silent, and therefore to regard the syllable as half open: we therefore transliterate *yish^{e}rê* rather than *yishrê*. This principle covers most of the illustrations of the half-open syllable. *E.g.* Imperatives (2nd pl.) like קִטְלוּ (*kill*) are half open, because the sh^{e}wa corresponds to a full vowel in the singular קְטֹל *kill* (i.e. *qit^{e}lû* from *q^{e}tōl*: the original *ō* is now represented by ^{e}).

Similarly with nouns: בְּרָכָה *b^{e}rākhâ* (*blessing*) with a suffix becomes (first בְּרָכְתִי, then) בִּרְכָתִי, *i.e.* not *birkāthî*, but *bir^{e}khāthî* (*my blessing*).

(f) The principles stated in sub-paragraphs (b) and (c) are carried out both in nouns and verbs. There are, however, two remarkable exceptions.

First, the law in (b) regarding the tone-long vowel in the final accented shut has not been carried out fully in the case of the vowel *a*. (i.) *Verbs* always write *á* for *ā* (except in pause; cf. § 10. 4 a). Thus קָטַל *qātál, he killed*, not קָטָל— that is, the last syllable, though accented, has the *short* vowel, if it be *a*. This *á* in verbs is subjected to change precisely as if it were *ā*. (ii.) *Nouns* regularly write *a* for *ā* in the hurried form known as the construct state, to be described in § 17. 2 a. Thus the construct of יָשָׁר is יְשַׁר (not יְשָׁר).

Second, in opposition to the law in (c), in the case of *verbs*, the sh^{e}wa stands not in the second place from the tone but immediately before it. Thus, while the noun (or adjective) inflects יָשָׁר, יְשָׁרָה (fem.) *y^{e}shārâ* (*upright*), the verb inflects יָשַׁר, יָשְׁרָה *yāsh^{e}râ* (*he, she, was upright*), the sh^{e}wa being sounded to represent the original vowel *a*. So adj. חָכָם (*wise*), חֲכָמָה; vb. חָכַם (*he was wise*), חָכְמָה. (But see § 10. 2 b.)

EXERCISE.   CORRECT THE FOLLOWING WORDS.

לְבָבִי, מִדְבַּרִים, זַקֵנִים, חֳדָשִׁים, כּוֹכָבִים, קָטְלוֹ, קְטַלְתֶּם,
קָטַלְנוּ, קְטַּלְנוּ, סְפָרִים, עֲנָבִים, צִדְקַתֵּנוּ, דָּבָרֶיךָ, גְּדוֹלִים,
הָקִימוֹתֶם, שְׁמַיִם, חָכְמָה, אֲלָפִים, תָּשׁוּב, יָקִים׃

Note.—The accent falls on the last syllable, unless where otherwise indicated.

§ 7. DĀGHÉSH.   THE LETTERS
" BᴱGHADHKᴱPHATH."   (SPIRANTS.)

1. The word *Daghesh* is from a root which possibly expressed the idea of *hardness.*   The sign of Daghesh is a
point in the bosom of a letter, and this point was used
(i.) with the ב ג ד כ פ ת letters to indicate their harder pronunciation (בּ *b*, &c.); and (ii.) with consonants generally, to
denote duplication—or more strictly, a strengthening, which
can best be indicated by duplication.   The former is called
Daghesh lene, the latter *D. forte.*

2. *Daghesh lene.*—(a) Hebrew has not two sets of consonants for the sounds *b g d k p t* and their softer forms
bh gh dh kh ph th.   It distinguished the sounds by means
of the point Daghesh (§ 1. 3).   The harder sounds it expressed by inserting the point, as בּ *b*, פּ *p*, תּ *t*, &c., leaving
the unmodified consonant ב פ ת, &c., to express the weaker
bh ph th, &c.   The softer sounds were natural or easy only
after vowels; hence the rule:

The six letters בּ גּ דּ כּ פּ תּ (therefore known as *bᵉghadhkᵉphath*) *are hard and therefore have* Daghesh lene *whenever
they do not immediately follow a vowel sound: when they do
immediately follow a vowel sound they do not take the Daghesh
—thus זָכַר zā-khār (he remembered), יִזְכֹּר yiz-kōr (he remembers).*   The first כ follows a vowel (*ā*), and therefore has no
daghesh; the second כ does not follow a vowel (as the first
syllable is closed, *yiz*), and therefore has the daghesh.   Hence
these letters receive the point: *always* at the beginning of
a sentence or clause; *always* in the middle of a word after
a shut syllable; and *generally* at the beginning of words.

(b) For this purpose vocal sh°wa, simple or composite, has the same effect as the full vowels ; *e.g.* זְכֹר *z^ekhōr* (*remember*), חֲכַם *ḥ^akham* (*wise*; § 6. f, I. ii.). Such forms as זְכֹּר, חֲכַּם are impossible, as they would imply that no vowel preceded the כ, which would again imply that ְ and ֲ were silent—a manifest absurdity. In this way we can easily tell, in the case of the *b^eghadhk^ephath* letters, whether a syllable is half open or not ; *e.g.* בִּלְבָבוֹ (*in his heart*) must be *bil^ebhābhō* (pronounce *bil^evavo*). If pronounced *bilbavo*, it would require to be written בִּלְּבָבוֹ. This would be wrong, as the original word for *heart* is לְבָב ; *his heart*, by § 6. 2 b c, is לְבָבוֹ (§ 19) ; and this *vocal* sh°wa, representing an original full vowel *ē*, must not be allowed to disappear into a *silent* sh°wa. Being therefore sounded, it keeps the possible daghesh out of the following *beth*.

(c) The only other thing that need here be said is that Hebrew does not point mechanically, but considers words in their relations to each other. Therefore, if a word beginning with a *b^eghadhk^ephath* letter be very intimately connected with an immediately preceding word ending in a vowel, the two words are treated practically as one, and the daghesh is not inserted. Contrast, *e.g.*, וַיְהִי־כֵן *and it was so*, Gen. I. 7 (where the connection is very intimate, and further indicated in Hebrew by the hyphen ; cf. § 10. 3) with וַיְהִי כִּי *and it came to pass, when*, &c., Gen. 6. 1 (where the connection is broken, and a new start is made with כִּי).

3. *Daghesh forte.*—(a) Hebrew does not write a double consonant. To indicate that a consonant is doubled, or rather strengthened, it inserts in it a point, as קַלּוּ *qal-lû* (*they were swift*). When so used the point is called D. *forte*. The syllable before this daghesh is necessarily shut, for קַלּוּ = קַלְלוּ, and its vowel therefore short. Daghesh forte can be inserted in the letters י and ו when they are used consonantally ; thus צִיָּה *çiyyâ* (*dryness*), חִיָּה *ḥiyyâ* (*he preserved alive*), צִיּוֹן *çiyyôn* (*Zion*), צִוָּה *çiwwâ* (*he commanded*), צַוּוּ *çawwû* (*command*, imp.), קַוָּם *qawwām* (*their line ?*). There is no danger of this duplicated *waw* being confused with the vowel *shûreq*, because, in the nature of the case, a duplicated letter must be preceded by a vowel, and, conversely, if there be a vowel before the ו, then the ו must = *ww* and not *û*. If, *e.g.*, in קַוָּם

we gave ו the value of *û*, there would be no consonants with which to read the vowels ▁ and ▁ָ. The word is therefore = קַוְיִם, i.e. *qawwām*.

The duplicated consonant should be distinctly and firmly enunciated, as in Italian.

(b) When, by processes of inflection, a consonant is written twice, with a *silent* shᵉwa between, d. forte is used; thus נְתַנְנוּ *nāthannû* (*we gave*) becomes נַתַּנּוּ. But if the shᵉwa be *vocalic*, the daghesh f. must not be used; thus קִלְלַת *qilᵉlath* must not be written קִלַּת *qillath*, because the shᵉwa is sounded, representing as it does an original *ā* (קְלָלָה *qᵉlālâ*, *curse*, noun).

(c) It is important to note that the gutturals (*i.e.* א ה ח ע) cannot be duplicated, and therefore cannot take daghesh forte. Thus we cannot write בִּעֵר (*he burned, consumed*), or שִׁחֵת (*he destroyed*). See § 8. 4 c.

4. D. *lene* is peculiar to the six *Bᵉghadhkᵉphath*; but these letters, like all consonants except the gutturals, may be doubled and take daghesh forte; thus שִׁבֵּר *shibbēr* (*he broke in pieces*). In these cases it is the hard sound of the consonant that is doubled: *i.e.* we say *shibber*, not *shivver*; so סַפֵּר *sappēr* (*relate*, imp.), not *saffēr*.

Daghesh forte and daghesh lene can never be confused, because daghesh forte, as we have seen, is always preceded by a vowel; daghesh lene, never. Thus in מִדְבָּר *midhbār* (*wilderness*) the daghesh in the ב is necessarily d. lene: were it d. forte, it must have a full vowel before it to constitute the closed syllable ending in the first *beth*, whereas it has no vowel at all. Even if it were possible, as it is not, to regard the shᵉwa as vocalic, it could not form the vowel of the assumed closed syllable. Consequently this word could not conceivably be read as *midhᵉbbar*: the last syllable is בָּר, but the one before it could not possibly be דִב—between the ד and the ב there would need to be a full vowel, *e.g.* דַב. On the other hand, the daghesh in the *beth* of the word מְדַבֵּר *mᵉdhabbēr* (*speaking*, ptc.) is necessarily d. forte, because it is preceded by a vowel. Consequently there is never any real confusion.

5. *Omission of Daghesh forte.*—In the case of the consonants ק נ מ ל ו י, when written to a shᵉwa, the d. forte is very frequently omitted where

usage would lead us to expect it ; *e.g.* הַיְאֹר (not הַיְאֹר) *the Nile,* עִוְרִים (not עִוְרִים) *blind* ; הַלְלוּ (not הַלְלוּ) *praise ye,* הִנְנִי (not הִנְנִי) *behold me,* מְבַקְשִׁים (not מְבַקְשִׁים) *seeking,* יִקְחוּ (not יִקְחוּ) *they will take.* This also applies to sibilants, esp. when followed by a guttural ; *e.g.* כִּסְאוֹ (not כִּסְאוֹ) *his throne* ; so יִשְׂאוּ (not יִשְׂאוּ) *they will lift up.* It is most natural to regard the sh^ewa as vocalic (since it must have been sounded in the original form of the word) and the previous syllable consequently as half open.

6. *Insertion of Daghesh forte.*—D. forte is sometimes inserted in a consonant to secure the more audible enunciation of the sh^ewa under it ; *e.g.* עִנְּבֵי '*in-n^ebhê* for עִנְבֵי '*in^e-bhê* (*the grapes of . . .*). This is known as *D. forte dirimens.* In certain cases two words, of which the first ends in ֶ , הֶ or הֶ., may be closely connected by the insertion of a D. forte at the beginning of the second word ; *e.g.* עָשִׂיתָ זֹּאת *thou hast done this.* This always happens when זֶה (*this*) or מַה (*what*) is joined by maqqēph to the following word ; *e.g.* זֶה־שְּׁמוֹ *this is his name,* מַה־לְּךָ *what to thee ? what aileth thee ?* This is known as *D. forte conjunctivum.*

7. The short unaccented vowel of the *third* class in syllables ending with a double letter, *i.e.* Daghesh forte—so-called sharpened syllables—is *u.* *E.g.* הֻקְטַל, but הֻגַּד (not הֻגַּד) *it was declared.* (Rarely—and chiefly under gutturals—it may appear as *o* ; *e.g.* עֻזִּי, also עֹזִּי *my strength.*)

8. *Mappîq* (extender).—A point is also inserted in the letter *Hē,* when final, to indicate that it is to be pronounced, and is not a mere sign of a vowel. When so used the point is called *Mappîq,* as אַרְצָהּ *arçáh* (*h* sounded), *her land,* whereas אַרְצָה = *árçâ, towards* (*the*) *land* (cf. § 17. 3).

EXERCISE ON DAG. *LENE* AND *FORTE.*

Write these Hebrew Words.

1. gam, kōl, dām, bēn, 'ēt, môt, pat, kap, keleb, tiktöb, kātabtā, bkû, lbad, dābār, blektkā, mishpāṭ, midbār, btôk, malkî, yabdēl, kôkābîm, kbadtem, tikbdî, kaṣpkā, ḥelqkā, midbrêkem, lāredet, yirb, yibk, gdôlîm, wtāgēl.

2. mbaqqshîm, ḥallôn, hammáyim, wayyinnāgpû, limmadt, dibbēr, mdubbār, ṣappdû, miṣpēd, bkaṣpkem, shabbāt, mibbnê, çippôr, ykattēb, bqiçrkem, baddām, bôdēd, yittnû, lbaddô.

Note.—In this exercise the *B^eghadhk^ephath* are expressed by ordinary hard letters, and *sh^ewa* is not expressed, as the exercise is set for practice on the syllable.

3

§ 8. THE GUTTURALS.

The letters ע ח ה א are called *gutturals*. The ע is a firmer sound of the same kind as א, and ח a firmer sound of the same kind as ה. ח and ע are much stronger letters than ה and א. The gutturals have the following peculiarities:

1. They prefer about them, particularly *before* them, the *a* vowels, and a final guttural must be preceded by *pathah* or *qāmeç*.

(a) *Pathah furtive.*—Any short vowel before a final guttural becomes pathah; and between any long vowel (other than qāmeç) and the final guttural there steals in, in utterance, the sound of short *a*. In other words, a short vowel is dislodged in favour of *pathah*; a long vowel is retained, but a *pathah* is inserted. Thus we write מֶלֶךְ *melekh* (*king*), but מֶלַח *melah*, *salt* (not מֶלֶח *meleh*): so הִשְׁלִיךְ *hishlîkh* (*he threw*), but הִשְׁלִיחַ *hishlîah, he sent*—very rare (not הִשְׁלִיח *hishlîh*), גָּבוֹהַּ *gābhôah, high* (ה, as the mappîq shows, is consonantal, § 7. 8). A remote analogy may be found in the faint vowel that is sometimes allowed to creep in before the *r* in such words as *here, fire* (*he*ᵃ*r, fi*ᵃ*r*) This short *a* is therefore called path. *furtive.* This pathah, as the last illustration shows, is written *under* the final guttural, but pronounced *before* it. Thus רוּחַ *spirit*, is pronounced *rûah* (not *rûha*: no Hebrew word ends in a short *a*). The pathah furtive disappears when the guttural ceases to be final; thus רוּחִי *rû-hî, my spirit*; הִשְׁלִיחָה.

Pathah furtive is never written to final א, which is silent; thus נָבִיא *nābhî'* (*prophet*), not נָבִיַא. Further, if the final guttural is preceded by *qāmeç*, which is already a vowel of the *a* class, it does not require and cannot tolerate pathah furtive; thus נִשְׁלָח *nishlāh, sent* (not נִשְׁלָח *nishlāah*).

(b) The short *i*, falling before gutturals not final, is usually depressed to *e*; thus יִכְבַּד *he is heavy*, but יֶחְדַּל *he ceases* (not יִחְדַּל). This depression of *i* to *e* may also take place *after* a guttural; thus סִפְרִי *my book*, but עֶזְרִי (not עִזְרִי) *my help*. A similar depression of the vowel may be observed in careless Scotch pronunciation; thus *sick* becomes *seck ; give, gev ;*— though here it is not confined to gutturals; thus, *deliver* becomes *dellevver*.

(c) The letter ר, which, alike in sound and treatment, has many affinities with the gutturals, not always (cf. בֹּסֶר *unripe grapes*) but very frequently has the vowel *a* before it. Thus וַיָּסֹר *wayyásor* (*and he turned aside*) and וַיָּסֶר *wayyáser* (*and he caused to turn aside*) both become וַיָּסַר *wayyásar*.

2. (a) The gutturals cannot take simple sh⁽ᵉ⁾wa vocal, they require the composite sh⁽ᵉ⁾was; therefore a sh⁽ᵉ⁾wa under an initial guttural must be composite; *e.g.* קְבֹר *q⁽ᵉ⁾bhōr* (*bury*, imp.), but עֲבֹר *ᵃbhōr, cross*, imp. (not עְבֹר). In many cases they dislike simple sh⁽ᵉ⁾wa silent, preferring the composite; *e.g.* רַגְלִי *my foot*, but בַּעֲלִי *my lord* (not בַּעְלִי). The ḥaṭeph that takes the place of silent sh⁽ᵉ⁾wa always corresponds to the preceding short vowel; thus בַּעֲלִי becomes בַּעֲלִי, so פָּעֳלִי *po⁽ᵒ⁾lî* becomes פָּעֳלִי *po⁽ᵒ⁾lî* (*my work*). ח, which is very hard, has a distinct tendency to prefer the silent sh⁽ᵉ⁾wa; *e.g.* פַּחְדּוֹ *paḥdō, his fear* (not פַּחֲדוֹ *paḥᵃdhō*). But with other gutturals the composite is usual; thus נאְמַר becomes first, by paragraph 1 b, נֶאְמַר and then נֶאֱמַר *it was said*.

(b) By far the most common ḥaṭeph is ֲ. Initial ע ה ח prefer ֲ, initial א prefers ֱ; *e.g.* (קְטֹל) עֲמֹר *stand*, אֱמֹר *say*; but when further from the tone א also takes ֲ; *e.g.* אֲלֵי *to, towards* (very rare and poetic), but אֲלֵיכֶם *to you*.

3. (a) As two vocal sh⁽ᵉ⁾was cannot come together, a simple sh⁽ᵉ⁾wa before a ḥaṭeph becomes the full (short) vowel corresponding to the *ḥaṭeph*; thus לִקְטֹל becomes לִקְטֹל *to kill*; but לְעֲבֹר becomes לַעֲבֹר *to cross*. This used to be expressed by saying that the guttural pointed itself and the consonant preceding. We further saw, in paragraph 2 a, that, if the guttural was preceded by a short vowel, it took under it the sh⁽ᵉ⁾wa, if composite, which corresponded to the short vowel; *e.g.* בַּעֲלִי *my lord*. Therefore the resultant combination in either case is ֲ ַ or ֳ ָ or ֱ ֶ; *e.g.* הֶעֱמִיד *he caused to stand, stationed*, הָעֳמַד *he was stationed*. Either the short vowel before the guttural (as *a* in the original בַּעֲלִי) or the composite sh⁽ᵉ⁾wa under the guttural (as ᵃ in עֲבֹר) is sure to be determined, and then the above combination follows as a matter of course.

(b) If the guttural is preceded by a *long* vowel, it takes ֱ in place of ֲ; *e.g.* שָׁחֲטָה *she slaughtered*, מֵאֲנָה *she refused*, כֹּהֲנִים *priests*.

4. (a) The gutturals cannot be doubled.   In this peculiarity ר agrees with the gutturals.   Hence the short vowel that would precede the guttural were it doubled (§ 7. 3 c) falls into an open syllable before the undoubled letter and becomes the corresponding tone-long vowel (§ 5. 3 a ; § 6. 2 a) ; *e.g.* הַדֶּרֶךְ *haddérekh, the way*, but הָעֶבֶד *hā-'ébhedh, the servant* (for הֶעְעֶבֶד = הָעֶבֶד.   But as the ע cannot be doubled, the first must be dropped.   We therefore get הָעֶבֶד, because the vowel *a*, short in the shut syllable, becomes long, *ā*, now that the syllable is open).   So שִׁלֵּשׁ *he did a third time*, but שֵׁרֵשׁ *he uprooted*, because שֵׁרֵשׁ = שִׁרֵּשׁ (short *i*) = שֵׁרֵשׁ (tone-long *ē*).   So קִטֵּל, but בֹּרַךְ *he was blessed*, because בְּרֹרַךְ = בֹּרַּךְ (short *u*) = בֹּרַךְ (tone-long *ō*).

(b) It is important to note that, as the cause that produces the tone-long in this case is permanent, the vowel is unchangeable.   *E.g.* בֵּרַכְתֶּם (on the analogy of קְטַלְתֶּם) becomes (first בֵּרַרְכְתֶּם, then) בֵּרַכְתֶּם *you blessed*; but although the accent falls on the תֶּם, the בֵּ must not be reduced to בְּ (§ 6. 2 c), because it represents a syllable originally ideally closed (בֵּר), and thus could not be allowed to degenerate into a בְּ.   This would be unjust to its origin.   The word therefore remains בֵּרַכְתֶּם (not בְּרַכְתֶּם).   Similarly the plural of חָרָשׁ *artificer* is not חֲרָשִׁים but חָרָשִׁים, because חָרָשׁ is a word of the type of גַּנָּב *thief*, and therefore strictly חַרְרָשׁ, so that the first syllable, ideally closed, must, when it becomes open, have its vowel *unchangeably* long.

(c) This compensation, as it is called, represented by the lengthening of the short vowel, takes place practically always with א and ר, and usually with ע ; *e.g.* מֵאֵן becomes מֵאֵן *he refused*, הָרֵעָה becomes הָרָעָה *the evil*, הַעָם becomes הָעָם *the people*.   Usually with ה, and very frequently with ח, the preceding vowel remains short: the consonant is thus felt to be virtually doubled, or in other words the daghesh forte is implied, whence it is known as the *d. f. implicitum*.   *E.g.* מַהֵר (not מָהֵר from מִהֵר *hasten*), הַהוּא (not הָהוּא *that*), הַחֶרֶב (not הָחֶרֶב for הַחֶרֶב *the sword*), הַחֹדֶשׁ (not הָחֹדֶשׁ *the month*).

EXERCISE.   CORRECT THE FOLLOWING WORDS.

בְּאֱמֹר, אֲבַדְתֶּם, אָמֹר, יִשְׁחְטוּ, חְזַק, שָׁלוּחַ, הִשְׁלִיחַ, שָׁמֹע,

שְׁמַע, רֶגַע, וַיַּהְפֹּךְ, בְּרַךְ, שָׂרִים, הֶחֱזִיק, טָעֲמוּ, כֶּאֱמֶת, נֶאֱמַר,
לְחֶלִי, לְאָרִי, בַּחֲמֹר, מָעֳמָד, יַעֲמֹד, יַעֲמִדוּ:

§ 9. THE QUIESCENT LETTERS.

The letters א ה ו י show the same kind of feebleness that
the letters *h w y*, that correspond to three of them, have in
English: they frequently coalesce in various ways with the
vowel sounds about them.

1. They are real consonants at the beginning of a syllable,
but at the end of a syllable after a full vowel they generally
surrender their consonantal power and are silent; *e.g.* מִצְוָה
commandment (*miçwâ*, ו consonantal); so אָמַר *'ā-mar* (*he said*),
but יֹאמַר *yô-mar* (*he says*) (א quiescent); יְמֵי *y°mê* (*the days
of . . .*), but בִּימֵי *bî-mê, in the days of* (from בִּימֵי, § 6. 2 d)
not בִּימֵי *biy-mê*; so בִּיהוּדָה (from בִּיהוּדָה) *in Judah*. Pronounced rapidly, *biymê* is practically = *bîmê*, and is therefore
fairly represented by בִּימֵי. In other words, the י quiesces,
or is silent: and *under the silent consonant the sh°wa is not
placed*; thus בִּימֵי (not בִּימֵי); so יֹאמַר (not יֹאמַר), and רֵאשִׁית *beginning* (not רֵאשִׁית). Conversely, if it takes the sh°wa, it is
regarded as a consonant; *e.g.* נֶאְדָּר *ne'-dār* (*glorious*). Here
the ד has the daghesh lene, because the preceding syllable
is closed, ending, as it does, in a *consonant* (§ 7. 2 a). This,
however, is rare. At the end of a word א is always silent,
and usually at the end of a syllable; that is, as a consonant
it practically disappears. The effect of this is that the
syllable ends in a vowel, which is therefore usually lengthened
(§ 5. 3 a). Thus מָצָא (on the analogy of קָטַל) becomes מָצָא
he found, because, as the final א practically disappears, the
syllable is as good as open, and its vowel therefore long.
So for מָצָאתָ (cf. קָטַלְתָּ) we write מָצָאתָ *thou hast found*, because
א at the end of the syllable is silent, and the following ת
does *not* take the daghesh lene, because, now that the א has
vanished, it follows a *vowel* (§ 7. 2 a).

A certain analogy to the quiescents may be found in
the English *w* and *y*, which are consonants at the beginning
of a word and silent at the end; cf. *was, saw; yes, say*.

2. It is never difficult to decide whether final י and ו are

consonantal or quiescent.   If accompanied by a homogeneous vowel—*i.e.* י by *e* or *i*, and ו by *o* or *u* (§ 2. 3 *c*)—they are obviously quiescent, being simply the consonantal signs of these vowels ; *e.g.* לִי *lî* (*to me*), לוֹ *lô* (*to him*).   If accompanied by a heterogeneous vowel, they are necessarily consonantal ; *e.g.* חַי *ḥay* (*living*), הוֹי *hôy* (*ah !*), גָּלוּי *gālûy* (*uncovered*, ptc.) ; יַחְדָּו *yaḥdāw* (*together*), עַוְלָה *'awlâ* (*injustice*), זִו *ziw* (*April–May*), דָּוִד or דָּוִיד *Dāwîdh* (*David*).   The suffixal form (to be explained in § 19) יָו is sounded *âw*, as סוּסָיו *sû-sâw* (*his horses*).

קְרוּאָיו, אַל, לֹא, וּבֵיתוֹ, נוֹלְדוּ, יִיטַב, צְבָאוֹת, בָּאוּ, בָּרָא,
בְּרֵאשִׁית, אֶרְאֶה, לִקְרַאת, יִשְׁמָעֵאל, מָאתַיִם, שָׁאוּנִי, שְׁלֹמֹה,
בְּיָמָיו, תִּגְלֶינָה, יַקְנִיאֵהוּ, מְלֵאתָיו, כָּסוּי, שָׁלֵו, גּוֹי, קַו, אֲדֹנָי,
רָאשִׁים, בָּאְשׁוֹ, כְּלָיוֹת, לוּלֵי, קְנֵה׃

§ 10. THE ACCENTS.[1]   METHEGH, MAQQÊPH, PAUSE, QᵉRÊ, &c.

1. *Use of the Accents.*—The accents have three uses : (1) they mark the tone-syllable ; (2) they are signs of logical interpunction, like our comma, &c. ; and (3) they are musical expressions.   In the first case they are guides to the pronunciation of the individual words ; in the second they are guides to the sense, being a kind of commentary ; and in the third they are guides to the proper reading of the text as a whole, which is a kind of recitative or cantillation.   The last use, of course, embraces the other two.

2. *The secondary accent (Methegh) and the Tone.*—The main accent or Tone falls generally upon the last syllable of the word (§ 5. 1 a), *e.g.* דָּבָר *dābhár, word* ; in one class of nouns (the *Ṣegholates*, § 29), *e.g.* דֶּבֶר *dĕbher, pestilence*, and in some Verbal forms, *e.g.* קָטַלְתִּ *qāṭáltî, I killed*, it falls on the penult.

(a) According to the natural rhythm of the language the syllable immediately before the Tone has a fall, but the syllable *second* from the Tone a certain emphasis or ac-

---

[1] A brief account of the more common accents will be found on pp. 230 f.

centual rise. To prevent this emphasis or anti-tone being neglected the syllable was often marked by a sign called *Methegh*, מֶתֶג (*bridle*), a small perpendicular stroke to the left of the vowel.[1] An open syllable was most apt to be hurried over, and hence: *the second full syllable from the Tone, if open, is uniformly marked by Methegh*, whether the vowel is long (הָאָדָם *the man*) or short (הַהֵיכָל *the palace*); *e.g.* אָנֹכִי *I*, וְזָכַרְתָּ *and thou shalt remember*, הֶחָכָם *the wise*, הֶעָפָר *the dust*. That is, in the onward rush towards the tone-syllable, it safeguards the vowel which is otherwise likely to get less than justice. (The interests of the tone and the pretone syllables are already safeguarded by the principle laid down in § 6. 2 b.) The methegh is rarely used with the vowel of a shut syllable, because such a vowel is already safe and in little danger of being slurred (therefore not מְדַבְּרִים); or with a sh°wa, because so insignificant a vowel does not deserve special attention (therefore not דְּבָרִים).

(This is no violation of the principle laid down in § 6. 2 c; in all the above illustrations there are good reasons, which will afterwards be clear, why the vowel second from the tone should remain a full vowel and not be reduced to sh°wa.)

(b) When the open syllable is separated from the tone even by only vocal sh°wa, its vowel is marked by methegh;[2] *e.g.* אָכְלָה *'ā-khᵉlâ* (accent on last syllable), *she ate*, חָכְמָה *ḥā-khᵉmâ, she is wise.* (In these cases the sh°wa is vocal, representing as it does a full vowel in the original masc. form אָכַל, חָכַם.) In such positions methegh clearly indicates that the sh°wa is *vocal*, and thus serves to distinguish between *ā* and *o*, and between *î* and *i*; *e.g.* אָכְלָה *food* (— silent, because no methegh with the —: the word is therefore a pure dissyllable: last syllable, accented, *lâ*: the first, unaccented *and shut*, therefore with *short* vowel; therefore *'okh*: so *'okhlâ*); חָכְמָה *ḥokhmâ, wisdom*; יִרְאוּ *yi-rᵉʾû, they will fear* (open syllable, long *i*); יִרְאוּ *yir-ʾû, they will see* (shut syllable, short *i*).

(c) If the vocal sh°wa in this case be a *ḥaṭeph*, the preceding vowel, though *short*, has that distinctness that requires

---

[1] Under the consonant, if the vowel is *ḥôlem*; *e.g.* כּוֹכָבִים *stars*, כֹּהֲנִים *priests*, אֹיְבִים *enemies*.

[2] This fact tends to confirm the view that vocal sh°wa constitutes a syllable (§ 5. 2). Cf. Sievers, *Metrische Studien*, i. pp. 145 f.

to be preserved by methegh ; hence the combination referred to in § 8. 3 a always appears in the form ‑ַ ‑ִ ‑ְ ‑ֲ ‑ִ ‑ָ ‑ִ ; *e.g.* יַעֲמִיד *he stations*, הֶעֱמִיד *he stationed*, הָעֳמַד *he was stationed.*

3. *Maqqēph* (binder).—(a) Part of the accentual or rhythmical machinery is the *Maqqēph* or hyphen, which binds two or more words together. The sign indicates that all the words so joined are pronounced in the rhythmical reading as one word, *e.g.* אֶת־כָּל־אֲשֶׁר־לוֹ *all* (acc.) *that (was) to him, all that he had.* The occurrence of two accented syllables in immediate succession is contrary to the rhythm, and this conjunction is avoided by throwing several words into one. All the words joined by maqqēph lose their accent except the last, and in consequence of this their long vowels, if changeable, become short (§ 5. 3 a), כֹּל הָעָם but כָּל־הָעָם *all the people, i.e.* the ‑ֹ of כֹּל, which is now shut and *unaccented*, becomes the corresponding short (not *kōl*, but *kol-hā-'ām*). *Çere*, followed by maqqēph, is usually reduced to *s̆ghol*; thus הִשָּׁמֵר *hishshāmēr*, but הִשָּׁמֶר־נָא *beware*; so תּוֹדָה תֶּן־לוֹ so וְהַגֶּד־נָא *give praise to him and tell*, &c.

(b) The maqqēph is used almost invariably with אֶל *to*, כֹּל *all* (thus כָּל־), אֶת sign of accus. (thus אֶת־), and a few other common words (*e.g.* מִן־ *from*, פֶּן־ *lest*).

4. *Pause.*—The natural pause which occurs at the middle, and especially the end of a Hebrew verse, affects the vowels as follows :

(a) A short vowel in the tone becomes long, as מַיִם *water*, pause מָיִם ; שָׁמַר *he kept*, pause שָׁמָר ; שָׁמַרְתִּי *I kept*, pause שָׁמָרְתִּי : —the long vowel can stand in the shut syllable, now that it has the accent. If the short vowel has been modified from another, it is the long of the *primary* sound that appears, אֶרֶץ *earth*, p. אָרֶץ (from a primary אַרְץ *'arç*).

(b) Occasionally the tone is shifted from the last syllable to the penult, which is lengthened if it was short, עַתָּה *'attâ* (*now*), pause עָתָּה *'āttâ* (not, of course, *'ottâ*, as it would be if it were an ordinary non-pausal form).

(c) Perhaps the commonest pausal effect is what looks like a combination of (a) and (b). In verbal forms with vocal sh^ewa before the tone, this sh^ewa becomes the tone-long of the primary sound whose place it had taken, and the tone

is then shifted to it, as שָׁכְנָה *she dwelt*, pause שָׁכֵנָה from
שָׁכֵן; עִמְדוּ *stand ye*, pause עֲמֹדוּ from עֲמֹד *stand*.

Similarly the composite sh°wa under a guttural is raised,
in pause, to the corresponding long vowel; thus אֲנִי *I*, pause
אָנִי; חֳלִי *sickness*, pause חֳלִי.

i. Sh°wa before the suffix *kha* becomes in pause *é*, סוּסְךָ *thy
horse*, pause סוּסֶךָ.

ii. There is a fondness shown in many cases for the sharp *a* in
pausal syllables : *e.g.* יִגָּמֵל, pause וַיִּגָּמַל *and he was weaned*.

iii. If two accented syllables of different words occur in immediate succession, the tone is often shifted from the last syllable to
the penult of the first word, though only when this is open ; *e.g.*
קָרָא לַיְלָה *he called night* (not קָרָא, which would otherwise be correct),
תֹּאכַל לֶחֶם (not תֹּאכַל *thou shalt eat bread*).

5. *Q°ré* (קְרִי *read*, i.e. *to be read*) and *K°thîbh* (כְּתִיב *written*).

(a) The *K°thîbh* is the consonantal text as it lay before the
punctuators, being held inviolable. When however for any
reason, whether of grammar or propriety, the punctuators
preferred another reading, the *vowels* of this reading were
put under the *K°thîbh* in the text, while the consonants,
which could not find a place in the text, were set in the
margin. This recommended reading is the *Q°ré*. Attention
is called to the margin by a small circle placed over the
K°thîbh, thus : הַנַּעַר Gen. **24**. 14. The marginal or foot note
(unpointed) to which attention is thus called runs הנערה קרי [1],
i.e. הנערה is to be read : and the vowels to accompany this
recommended reading are the vowels of the other word
which stands in the text. The word to be read is therefore
in full הַנַּעֲרָה *the maiden*; the unpointed הנער, which would
normally represent הַנַּעַר *the youth* (masc.), would be am-
biguous. In other words, the consonants of the *margin*
are to be read with the vowels of the *text*.

(b) In the case of יהוה and a few other words of very
frequent occurrence, the *Q°ré* is not placed in the margin, but
its vowels are simply inserted in the text. *E.g.* יְהוָֹה (whence
our *Jehovah*, probably originally יַהְוֶה *Yahweh*) is always
written either thus—with the vowels of אֲדֹנָי *Lord* (which

---

[1] Or simply 'ק.

word, however, is not actually written in the margin)—or (when it follows אֲדֹנָי) to avoid repetition, יֱהוִֹה with the vowels of אֱלֹהִים (*God*). Thus the proper pronunciation of יהוה (doubtless *Yahweh*), for which the Hebrew equivalent for *Lord* (or *God*) was always substituted, came in course of time to be completely forgotten.

OF WORDS AND FORMS.

Roots may be considered to be of three classes : (1) the simplest and instinctive *interjection*, expressive of mere feeling, as *ah !* ; (2) the higher *demonstrative*, expressing locality, direction, and distinction between one object and another ; and (3) roots embodying thoughts, *nouns* and *verbs*. The first class, being uninflected and individual, do not need any separate treatment. And of the others it is better to begin with the second, which is next in simplicity.

§ 11. THE ARTICLE.

Hebrew has no *indefinite* Article ; *e.g.* יוֹם *yôm*, *a day*, אִישׁ *'ish*, *a man*.

The Definite Article, which before ordinary consonants is הַ (i.e. *ha*, with the following consonant duplicated), was originally a demonstrative pronoun. Something of this force still attaches to it in one or two phrases ; *e.g.* הַיּוֹם *hay-yôm*, *the* day, *i.e.* this day, to-day ; הַלַּיְלָה *the* night, *i.e.* to-night. The article is an inseparable particle prefixed to words, and, like *the* in English, suffers no change for Gender or Number.

The origin of the article is quite uncertain. Its primary form may have been *hā* (which, because of its very close connection with the following word—cf. *the*—may have emphasized or strengthened its opening consonant, which has therefore *Dag. forte*, § 7. 3 a); or it may even have been *han*.[1] All the phenomena can be satisfactorily explained on either assumption. Assuming, however, for simplicity's sake, a

---

[1] The former explanation is the more probable ; the latter, however, though it has met with little favour, is at least possible ; and I mention it here because, on this assumption, the pointing of the article becomes readily intelligible to the beginner.

primary *han*, the usage works out very naturally, especially when we remember how readily in other languages *n* assimilates with the consonant before it; e.g. *inmotus = immotus, inlotus = illotus, ἐνλείπω = ἐλλείπω*, &c.

(a) Before ordinary consonants the *n* is assimilated to the next consonant, which is thus doubled; *e.g.* קוֹל *voice* (הַנְקוֹל = הַקְקוֹל =) הַקּוֹל *haq-qôl, the voice*; so הַשֶּׁמֶשׁ *hashshémesh, the sun.*

(b) Before gutturals, the principles laid down in § 8. 4 apply. As they cannot be doubled, the *pathah* of the Art., falling in an open Syllable, expands to *qāmeç*; thus הַאִישׁ becomes הָאִישׁ *the man.* This expansion is universal before א and ר, *e.g.* הַרֹאשׁ *har-rôsh =* הָרֹאשׁ *hā-rôsh,*[1] *the head,* and general before ע, *e.g.* הָעִיר *the city.* Before the strong gutt. ה and ח, *pathah* usually remains; *i.e.* the daghesh is *implicit*, and the vowel before it, being in a practically shut syllable, remains short; *e.g.* הַהֵיכָל (from *hah-hêkhāl*) *the palace,* הַחָכְמָה (from *hah-hokhmā*) *wisdom.*[2]

(c) The rule in (b) applies to א and ר with any vowel. But when ה, ע, ח are pointed with *qāmeç*, the punctuation of the Art. varies—

Before הָ and עָ in the Tone, the Art., falling in the *pretone*, takes *ā* (§ 6. 2 b), as הָהָר *the mountain,* הָעָם *the people.*

Before הָ, עָ, not in the Tone, the Art., falling *before* the pretone, becomes *e* (*séghol*),[3] as הֶהָרִים *the mountains,* הֶעָמָל *the trouble.*[2] Before חָ (*hā*) in all positions, and also before חֶ, the Art. takes *séghol,* הֶחָכָם *the wise,* הֶחָג *the feast,* הֶחֳלִי *the sickness.*

The following will be a useful summary of the facts. It should not, however, be mechanically committed to memory,

---

[1] The א is silent, but it points to an earlier stage in the history of the word when it was consonantal; cf. § 5. 6 c (חֵטְא).

[2] These words would, in strict writing, all require methegh with the first vowel, as it is in the open syllable, and two places from the tone; *e.g.* הֶהָרִים, הַחָכְמָה, &c.

[3] This comes under the general rule that a *pathah* before an originally duplicated guttural *which has* —— *under it* becomes *séghol*; thus אֶחָי *my brothers*, pausal form of אַחַי (p. 153), originally *ah-hay* (§ 10. 4 a).

but read in the light of the principles that govern it, and
then it will be remembered with little difficulty.

Before ordinary conss.   הַקּוֹל, הַ——

Before gutturals $\begin{cases} א, ר, ע & הָ——, הָאִישׁ, הָרֹאשׁ, הָעִיר \\ ה, ח & הַ——, הַחֶרֶב, הַהֵיכָל \end{cases}$

Before gutturals with qāmeç $\begin{cases} עָ, הָ & הֶ——, הָעָם, הָהָר \\ עָ, הָ & הֶ——, הֶעָמָל, הֶהָרִים \\ (חֲ)חָ & הֶ——, הֶחָכְם, הֶחָלִי \end{cases}$

אִישׁ	man [1]	אִשָּׁה	*f.* woman	בֹּקֶר	morning
יוֹם	day	לַיְלָה	*m.* night	עֶרֶב	evening
חֹשֶׁךְ	darkness	רָקִיעַ	firmament	אוֹר	light
מַיִם	*pl.* water, waters	גָּדוֹל	great	עָפָר	dust
רָם	high	עַל-	upon	טוֹב	good
שָׁמַיִם	*pl.* heaven	כֶּסֶף	silver	וְ	and
		זָהָב	gold		

The conjunction *and* is a particle inseparably prefixed
to words, וְאִישׁ *and a man.*

Rule 1.——The adjective, when it qualifies, stands after the
noun ; e.g. *a good man*, אִישׁ טוֹב, not טוֹב אִישׁ. If the noun
be definite, the adj., as well as the noun, has the article ; e.g.
the good man, not הַטּוֹב אִישׁ, but הָאִישׁ הַטּוֹב *i.e.* the man, viz.
the good (one).

If two or more adjectives go with the same noun, each
of the adjectives has the article ; e.g. *the great and good man*,
הָאִישׁ הַגָּדוֹל וְהַטּוֹב.

Rule 2.——The adjective, when used *predicatively*, must
not take the article. It may come before or after the noun
——usually before ; e.g. *the man is good* = הָאִישׁ טוֹב or טוֹב הָאִישׁ
(lit. *good is the man*)——in neither case does the adj. take the
art. The copula *is*, *are*, &c., is not usually expressed.
This, however, occasions no ambiguity ; *e.g.* הָאִישׁ טוֹב could
not be mistaken for *the good man*, which would require הַטּוֹב.

---

[1] Throughout the vocabularies, *feminine* nouns are marked *f.*, those
unmarked are *masculine*.

EXERCISE.   TRANSLATE.

הַלַּיְלָה וְהַיּוֹם: 2 הָאִישׁ וְהָאִשָּׁה: 3 הַחֹשֶׁךְ הַגָּדוֹל: 4 רָם
הָרָקִיעַ: 5 טוֹב הַכֶּסֶף: 6 הָעֶרֶב וְהַבֹּקֶר: 7 גָּדוֹל הַחֹשֶׁךְ
עַל־הַמָּיִם: 8 טוֹב הָאִישׁ: 9 היום הגדול:

To-day. The morning. The night. The light (is)[1] good.
The good light. The lofty firmament. The man and the
woman. The darkness is great. The good man. A great
day. The gold (is)[1] good. The dust (is)[1] upon the waters.

§ 12. THE PERSONAL PRONOUNS.

	Sing.		Signif. part.	Plur.		Sig. part.
1 *pers. c.*	אָנֹכִי, אֲנִי	I	i, ni, ki	אֲנַחְנוּ	we	nu
2 *pers. m.*	אַתָּה	thou	ta	אַתֶּם	ye	tem
f.	אַתְּ	„	t	אַתֶּן, אַתֵּנָה[3]	„	ten
3 *pers. m.*	הוּא	he[2]	w, hu	הֵם, הֵמָּה[4]	they	m
f.	הִיא	she[2]	y (ha)	הֵנָּה	„	n

The above forms of the Pers. Pronouns are used only
to express the Nominative: they must not be put as *oblique
cases* after a verb or preposition: therefore *I-buried him* is
not קְבַרְתִּי הוּא (§ 31); *declare to* (לְ) *me* is not סַפְּרוּ לְאֲנִי (§ 14. 1 f).
When, as in these cases, the Pers. Pronouns do not express
the Subject, they become attracted in a fragmentary form to
be explained later (§§ 19. 31; 14. 1 f; 15. 2, &c.) to the
end of other words. These fragments (the *significant parts*
above) are named *Pronominal suffixes*.

עַיִן *f.* eye	יָד *f.* hand	הַר mountain	חֳלִי disease
אֶרֶץ *f.* earth	אֶבֶן *f.* stone	עֶבֶד servant	עַם people
חֶרֶב *f.* sword	אֱלֹהִים *pl.* God	הֵיכָל palace	חָכָם wise
עָצוּם powerful	רַע bad, sore	מְאֹד very	רַע מְאֹד very bad

A few words, *e.g.* הַר, עַם, חַג, when preceded by the

---

[1] Throughout the exercises, bracketed words are not to be translated.

[2] In הוּא *hû* and הִיא *hî*, the א, which is silent, represents doubtless
an earlier stage in the history of the word, when it was consonantal
(*hû'a? hî'a?*).

[3] Both forms extremely rare.

[4] Long vowel tolerated in shut syllable, because accented (§ 5. 3 a).

article, lengthen the pathaḥ to *qāmeç*; thus הֶחָג, הֶהָר. So also אֶרֶץ (original אִרְץ) becomes הָאָרֶץ.

In sentences of the type *the people is wise* (cf. § 11. Rule 2), the predicate is sometimes followed by the third personal pronoun (in the appropriate gender and number); thus הָעָם חָכָם הוּא. Sometimes (esp. when subj. and pred. are coextensive) this pronoun precedes the predicate; *e.g.* יהוה הוּא הָאֱלֹהִים *Yahweh*[1] *is the God*. But in such cases it is not strictly correct to say that the pronoun *is* the copula; it really resumes the subject,—in the former case, without emphasis, *as for the people, it* (הוּא) *is wise*; in the latter, with emphasis: *Yahweh, he* (and no other) *is the God*.

EXERCISE. TRANSLATE.

רָם הַהֵיכָל׃ 2 הָהָר הוּא רָם מְאֹד׃ 3 טוֹב הָעֶרֶב׃ 4 אַתָּה הוּא הָאֱלֹהִים׃ 5 אַתְּ הָאִשָּׁה׃ 6 הַחֶרֶב הִיא עַל־הֶעָפָר׃ 7 הָעֶבֶד הַטּוֹב׃ 8 עַם רָם וְגָדוֹל׃ 9 הָעָם הוּא עָצוּם מְאֹד׃ 10 הַיָּד וְהָעַיִן׃ 11 הַשָּׁמַיִם וְהָאָרֶץ׃ 12 הָעָם הֶעָצוּם וְהַגָּדוֹל׃ 13 אֲנִי הָאִישׁ הֶחָכָם׃ 14 חכם האיש׃ 15 החלי הרע׃

The eye. The hand. The mountain is very lofty. The dust is upon the waters. I (am) the man. We (are) the people. The sword. The good man is the wise man. The good and powerful people. The morning and the evening are the day. The darkness is the night. The great and lofty mountain. The darkness is very great upon the earth and upon the waters. Thou (art) the man. They (are) the heavens. The stone.

§ 13. DEMONSTRATIVE, INTERROGATIVE, AND OTHER PRONOUNS.

	Sing.	*Plur.*		*Sing.*	*Plur.*
mas.	זֶה this			הוּא that	הֵם, הֵמָּה those
f.	זֹאת „			הִיא „	הֵנָּה „
c.		אֵלֶּה these			

[1] יהוה should be pronounced and translated thus, not by *the Lord*. As the traditional vocalization of the word (יְהֹוָה) is erroneous, we shall throughout leave it unpointed.

1. The demonstratives may be used predicatively or adjectivally. Like adjectives when used predicatively they do not take the article, and the order is as in English : e.g. *this is the man,* זֶה הָאִישׁ ; *this is the good man,* זֶה הָאִישׁ הַטּוֹב. When used as adjectives their noun is definite, and they are written, with the definite article, after the noun—exactly like adjs. (§ 11. Rule 1) ; *e.g.* הָאִישׁ הַזֶּה *this man* (i.e. *the man—this one*), הַתּוֹרָה הַזֹּאת *this law,* הַיּוֹם הַהוּא *that day,* הַדְּבָרִים הָאֵלֶּה *these words.* With another adj., the demonstr. stands last : *this good man,* הָאִישׁ הַטּוֹב הַזֶּה.

Note that though, with the art., the sing. is הַהוּא, the plur. is הָהֵם.

2. *Relative pronoun.*—(a) אֲשֶׁר [1] used for *who, which,* invariable for all genders, numbers, and cases, is, strictly speaking, not a relative *pronoun,* but only a general word of relation ; and, as it is used to introduce clauses begin‑ ning not only with *who, whom, whose, which,* but also with *where, whence, whither,* it might be fairly said to correspond to the *wh* in these words, or to the *that* in such sentences as *the man* that *I spoke to, the house* that *I lived in.* The Hebrew way of turning such relative sentences is to throw the vague אֲשֶׁר (*wh, that*) at the beginning, and to clinch it at the end by the definite word which the sense requires ; *e.g.* the man *that* (אשר) I spoke *to him* (wh . . . to him = to whom) ; the house *that* (אשר) I lived *in it* (wh . . . in it = in which). The force of the אֲשֶׁר in such cases is practically = *as to whom* or *which* (e.g. the man *as to whom* I spoke to him, the house *as to which* I lived in it). So *whose* = אשר followed by *his* ; *e.g.* הָאָדָם אֲשֶׁר נְשָׁמָה בְּאַפּוֹ *man* in whose nostrils (אשר . . . באפו) *is* (*but*) *a breath* (*i.e.* man *as to whom* but a breath is in his nostrils). So *there* שָׁם, *where* שָׁם . . . אֲשֶׁר ; *thither* שָׁמָּה *shámmā, whither,* שָׁמָּה . . . אֲשֶׁר ; *thence* מִשָּׁם (מִן *from* ; *n* assimilated), *whence* מִשָּׁם . . . אֲשֶׁר.

(b) Almost always, however, when the English relative pronoun is in the nominative, and frequently also when it is in the accusative, אֲשֶׁר is used alone, *i.e.* without being

---

[1] The form שׁ prefixed inseparably to words, usually as שֶׁ or שַׁ followed by Dag. *forte, e.g.* שֶׁלִּי = אֲשֶׁר לִי (*which is to me,* i.e. *mine*), is mostly late.

clinched at the end by a definite pronoun ; *e.g.* the king *who pursued*, אֲשֶׁר רָדַף (the אשר is *not* followed up by a word for *he*) ; he put there the man *whom he had formed*, אֲשֶׁר יָצַר (here the אשר may or may not be followed by the word for *him*). It is doubtless this familiar usage that has led to the statement that אֲשֶׁר is a relative pronoun, and = *who, which.*

(c) אֲשֶׁר can also = *he who, him who, that which,* and may take a preposition before it ; e.g. *that which* (אֲשֶׁר) *he had done, displeased Yahweh* ; he said *to the man who* (לַאֲשֶׁר) *was over his house.*

3. *Interrogative pronoun.*—The interrogative is מִי *who?* for persons, and מָה *what?* for things, both words indeclinable.

The emphasis of the question not being on the interrogative particle it falls forward on the next word (§ 7. 6), and מה assumes a *pointing quite like the Article* (§ 11).

Before non-gutturals *path. and dag.* מַה־זֶּה what is this ?
before א and ר   *qāmeç*   מָה־אֵלֶּה what are these ?
before other gutturals *pathah*   מַה־הִיא what is it ?
before gutt. with qam. *s°ghol*   מֶה עָשָׂה what has he done ?

מִי is also used to express the indefinite *whoever, whosoever* ; and מָה *whatever, whatsoever* ; e.g. מִי לַיהוה אֵלָי *whoever (is) for Yahweh (let him come) unto me.* But while מִי can be thus used, אֲשֶׁר can never be used interrogatively. E.g. *Who will trust in Yahweh?* מִי יִבְטַח בַּיהוה (not possibly אֲשֶׁר) ; but *blessed is the man who trusts,* בָּרוּךְ הָאִישׁ אֲשֶׁר יִבְטָח.

מָה is also the exclamation *how !* מָה־אַדִּיר שִׁמְךָ *how glorious is thy name !*

4. *Other pronominal expressions.*—*Each* אִישׁ ; *e.g.* kings were sitting *each* (אִישׁ) upon his throne. So *any* ; *e.g.* if *any one* (אִישׁ) can number, &c.

Every, all, כֹּל (which is strictly a noun = *the whole*) ; e.g. *every day,* כֹּל יוֹם ; *all the day,* כָּל־הַיּוֹם (§ 10. 3).

No, none, אִישׁ . . . לֹא or אִישׁ לֹא (lit. *not a man*) : לֹא . . . כֹּל or כֹּל . . . לֹא (lit. *not every,* i.e. *not any*) ; e.g. *none living is just before thee,* לֹא . . . כָל־חַי ; *no work shall be done,* כָּל־מְלָאכָה לֹא־יֵעָשֶׂה.

The one, the other, זֶה . . . זֶה : *the one called to the other,* קָרָא זֶה אֶל־זֶה.

For other forms of reciprocal and for reflexive pronouns,
see pp. 90, 93, 150.

מֶלֶךְ king   רֹאשׁ head   יֶלֶד boy   יהוה Yahweh [1]
בָּרָא to create   קָרָא to call   יָלַד to bear   שָׁפַךְ to shed
לָקַח to take   שָׁמַע to hear   אָמַר to say   בָּא to come
יָשַׁב to sit   לֹא not   רָעָב famine   אֶל־ unto

5. The root of the verb is held to be, not the infinitive,
but the 3rd pers. sing. perf. act., which is the simplest form ;
e.g. בָּרָא is really not *to create*, but *he created*, לָקַח *he took*, &c.
It is as if in Latin we spoke of *amat* rather than *amare*.

6. Sentences are of two kinds: (i.) verbal—having a *finite*
verb for predicate, e.g. *the angel cried*; and (ii.) nominal—
having any other kind of predicate, such as noun, adj., partic.;
e.g. *Thou art God, God is good*, &c.   The order in a verbal
sentence (unless the subj. is emphatic) is verb, subject, *e.g.*
קָרָא הַמַּלְאָךְ *the angel cried*; in a nominal sentence, subject,
predicate, *e.g.* יהוה מַלְכֵּנוּ *Y. is our king.*   But in nom. sent.
the predicate, if emphatic, is placed first, *e.g.* עָפָר אַתָּה *dust
art thou*, and frequently also as we have seen (§ 11. Rule 2)
if it be an adj. צַדִּיק אַתָּה יהוה *righteous art thou*, Y.

The negative stands immediately before the verb or predicate : so that, in a verbal sentence, the order is (negative),
verb, subject, object ; e.g. *the boy did not hear the voice*,
לֹא שָׁמַע הַיֶּלֶד אֶת־הַקּוֹל.

7. (a) The *definite* accus. in nouns and pronouns, when
directly governed by an active verb, is, in prose, usually preceded by the particle אֵת, or rather אֶת־ (§ 10. 3), as in above
illustr.   But the accus. must be definite : "*a* voice" would have
been simply קוֹל, not אֶת־קוֹל.   The accusative is regarded as
definite (i.) if it be preceded by the def. art., (ii.) if it be par-
ticularized by a possessive pronoun (indicated in Hebrew
by a pronominal suffix, § 19), e.g. God heard *his voice*, אֶת־קוֹלוֹ,
(iii.) if it be a proper name, e.g. he smote *David*, אֶת־דָּוִד.

(b) אֶת־ is repeated with each of the accusatives, if there

---

[1] Usually pointed יְהֹוָה, occasionally יֱהֹוִה (cf. § 10. 5) : the true spelling (never found) is probably יַהְוֶה.   We leave it throughout unpointed.

4

be more than one ; *e.g.* Abraham took *Sarah and Lot,* אֶת־שָׂרָה וְאֶת־לֹוט.

(c) ־אֶת is used before מִי (= whom ?), but never before מָה. *Whom have I oppressed ?* אֶת־מִי עָשַׁקְתִּי, but *what have I taken ?* not אֶת־מָה.

EXERCISE. TRANSLATE.

מִי אַתֶּם׃ 2 רָם מְאֹד הָהָר הַזֶּה׃ 3 הַלַּיְלָה הַהוּא׃ 4 זֶה
הַיּוֹם אֲשֶׁר עָשָׂה אֱלֹהִים׃ 5 הָעָם הֶעָצוּם הַזֶּה׃ 6 זֶה הַיֶּלֶד
אֲשֶׁר שָׁמַע אֶת־הַקּוֹל׃ 7 מִי יָלַד אֶת־אֵלֶּה׃ 8 יָשַׁב הַמֶּלֶךְ
עַל־הֶעָפָר׃ 9 בָּא הָאִישׁ אֲשֶׁר שָׁפַךְ הַמַּיִם עַל־הָאָרֶץ׃ 10 מַה־
טוֹב הַיּוֹם הַזֶּה׃ 11 בָּרָא אֱלֹהִים אֵת הַשָּׁמַיִם וְאֵת הָאָרֶץ׃
12 וַקָּרָא זֶה אֶל־זֶה וְאָמַר קָדוֹשׁ יהוה׃ 13 לקח המלך את־
החרב׃ 14 זה המלך החכם׃

Who (are) these ? What (are) ye ? Who (is) this woman? I (am) the great king who (is) over (עַל) the land. That great day. This (is) a good head. This (is) the good head. This head (is) good. This good head. This (is) the bad boy who spilt the water upon the earth. What has the man done? What (are) these ? These (are) the heavens and the earth which God created this day. That great and sore disease. He sat by (עַל) those waters. How great (is) that palace !

§ 14. THE INSEPARABLE PREPOSITIONS.

1. Prepositions and similar words in Hebrew are usually nouns, sometimes entire, but oftener worn down and fragmentary. The following three fragments used as prepositions are, like the Art., inseparably prefixed to words :

בְּ *in, by, with* ; local and instrumental.

כְּ *as, like.*

לְ *to, at, for* ; sign of *dat.* and *infin.*

(a) The usual pointing of these light fragments is simple sh⁰wa ; *e.g.* בְּשָׁלֹום *in peace,* בְּיָד חֲזָקָה *with a strong hand,* כְּפַרְעֹה *like Pharaoh,* לְמֹשֶׁה *to Moses.*

(b) Before another sh⁰wa this becomes *ḥireq,* by § 6. 2 d. i., forming a half-open syllable בִּלְבַב, (= בְּלְבַב) בִּלְבַב *in the heart of*; the sh°wa is here sounded, because it was (necessarily) so in the original לְבַב (cf. § 5. 4 a); therefore not בִּלְבַב. If the consonant be י, it quiesces and the sh°wa is not written (§ 9. 1); *e.g.* יְמֵי, but בִּימֵי *in the days of*; לִיהוּדָה, יְהוּדָה *to Judah*.

(c) Before a ḥaṭeph the sh°wa becomes the corresponding short vowel, by § 8. 3, כְּאַרִי = כַּאֲרִי *like a lion*; לֶאֱכֹל, אֱכֹל *to eat*.

But with the very frequently recurring words אֱלֹהִים *God*, and אֱמֹר (in the phrase לֵאמֹר *saying*), the vowel under the guttural is swallowed up in a long vowel under the pre-position; thus, not בֶּאֱלֹהִים but בֵּאלֹהִים, לֵאלֹהִים *to God*, כֵּאלֹהִים *as God*, לֵאמֹר.

(d) Before the accent, the prep., falling in the *pretone*, often has tone-long *qāmeç* (§ 6. 2 b), as לְמַיִם *to water* (for לְמַיִם). This is found chiefly in one or two familiar expressions, לָעַד *for ever*, לָבֶטַח *securely*, and with a certain kind of infinitive; *e.g.* לָלֶכֶת *to go* (§ 33. 2 b, 3 d, § 39. 2 b, § 40, § 42. 2 a).

(e) In words with the Art. the weak *He* almost always surrenders its vowel to the prep. and disappears. An analogy for this disappearance of *h* may be seen in Cockney English, in many French words, e.g. *homme*, &c. *E.g.* הַשָּׁמַיִם (= בְּהַשָּׁמַיִם) בַּשָּׁמַיִם *in the heavens*, הָעָם, (= לְהָעָם) לָעָם *to the people*. לֶהָרִים (§ 11 c) *to the mountains*. To express it summarily, the Article disappears, but its vowel is written under the pre-position.

(f) Prepositions cannot be used immediately before pronouns; therefore *to me* is not לְאֲנִי, nor is *in you* בְּאַתֶּם. Instead, the significant parts of the pronouns (§ 12) are appended to the prepositions in more or less modified forms; thus—

Sing. לִי *to me*, לְךָ[1] (m.) לָךְ (f.) *to thee*, לוֹ *to him*, לָהּ *to her*.
Plur. לָנוּ *to us*, לָכֶם (m.) לָכֶן (f.) *to you*, לָהֶם (m.) לָהֶן (f.) *to them*.
בְּ is inflected like לְ, but it also takes בָּם in 3rd plur. masc.

2. The short word מִן, used as a prep. in the sense of *from, out of*, is also a worn down noun, and generally used as an inseparable particle.

(a) The weak liquid *n*, as in other languages, is assimilated to the next consonant, which is doubled, מִמַּיִם *from water*. מִמַּיִם = מִמְּמַיִם = מִן־מַיִם.

---

[1] Pause, לָךְ.

Dagh. f., with certain consonants, may be omitted (§ 7. 5); *e.g.*
מִקְצֵה (for מִקְצֵה) *at the end of.* When the consonant is י, it quiesces
(§ 9. 1); *e.g.* מִן־יְמִינִי *at my right hand* = מִיְמִינִי = מִיְמִינִי = מִימִינִי.

(b) Before gutturals, the short vowel expands in the open
syllable into the corresponding tone-long, מֵעֵץ *from a tree*
(מֵעֵץ = מֵעְ־עֵץ = מִן־עֵץ), by § 8. 4; and occasionally, with ח, hireq
remains, by § 8. 4; *e.g.* מִחוּץ (not מֵחוּץ), dagh. f. implicit., *outside.*

(c) Before the Art. either (b) is followed, or oftener the
prep. is prefixed entire to the word with help of Maqqeph,
מֵהָעֵץ or מִן־הָעֵץ *from the tree.* This fuller form is also common
in poetry. With these exceptions, the usual form is the
assimilated.

סֵפֶר	book	גַּן	garden	מָקוֹם	place
אֲדָמָה (*f.*)	ground	יַבָּשָׁה (*f.*)	dry land	בְּהֵמָה (*f.*)	beast, cattle
אֲרִי	lion	חֲמוֹר	ass	מְלָאכָה (*f.*)	work
שְׁבִיעִי	seventh	קָדוֹשׁ	holy	כָּתַב	to write
נָתַן	to give	אָכַל	to eat	שָׁבַת	to rest
מָשַׁל	{ to rule	מָחָה	{ to destroy	קָרָא	to cry, call
בְּ	over		to blot out	קָרָא לְ	to name
הָיָה	to be			עַד	unto, as far as

EXERCISE.   TRANSLATE.

קָרָא אֱלֹהִים לָאוֹר יוֹם וְלַחֹשֶׁךְ קָרָא לַיְלָה¹ 2 שָׁבַת אֱלֹהִים
בַּיּוֹם הַשְּׁבִיעִי מֵהַמְּלָאכָה אֲשֶׁר עָשָׂה: 3 שָׁמַע הָאָדָם אֶת־
הַקּוֹל ¹בַּגָּן: 4 מָשַׁל הַמֶּלֶךְ בָּעָם: 5 יָשַׁב הַיֶּלֶד בַּמָּקוֹם הַזֶּה:
6 מָחָה יהוה אֶת־כֹּל אֲשֶׁר עָשָׂה מֵאָדָם וְעַד בְּהֵמָה: 7 עָשָׂה
אֱלֹהִים אֶת־הָאָדָם עָפָר מִן־הָאֲדָמָה: 8 הָאֱלֹהִים הוּא
בַּהֵיכָל: 9 נתן את־החרב למלך: 10 כתב הילד בספר:

To a lion.   God gave the woman to the man for wife.
In the morning.   In these heavens.   In the earth.   In that day.
In the lofty palace.   The lion cried like an (the) ass.   God
called the firmament heaven, and the dry land called he
earth.   Man is dust out of the ground.   He ate of the tree.
The wise people rested on the seventh day.   To the dust.
In (לְ) pain.   On (בְּ) the high mountain.   One called to the
other and said, Yahweh is good.

¹ Pausal form (cf. § 10. 4 a).

§ 15. THE CONJUNCTION, &c.

1. The inseparable conjunction וְ *and*, is pointed very much like the inseparable prepositions in § 14.

(a) Its ordinary pointing is sh°wa, וְאַתָּה *and thou*, וְדָבָר *and a word*.

(b) Before the ḥaṭephs it takes the corresponding short vowel (§ 8. 3), וַאֲנִי *and I*, וֶאֱמַץ *and be strong.* חֶסֶד וֶאֱמֶת *kindness and faithfulness.*

וֶ (like בְּ כְ לְ, cf. § 14. 1 c) with אֱלֹהִים gives וֵאלֹהִים.

(c) Before simple sh°wa and the Labials (ב ו מ פ) its pointing is וּ, וּדְבָרִים *and words*, וּשְׁמַרְתֶּם *and ye shall keep*, וּבֵן *and a son*, וּפָרָה *and a cow.*

Rem.—Before *yodh* with sh°wa the pointing is *ḥireq*, after § 6. 2 d. i., and *yodh* is silent (§ 9. 1), וִימֵי *and the days of.*

(d) Before the accent, especially if disjunctive (see p. 230), it often takes *qāmeç* (§ 6. 2 b): טוֹב וָרָע *good and evil*, פָּרָה וָדֹב *a cow and a bear*, דֹּר וָדֹר *generation after generation*; especially with words that go in pairs: יוֹם וָלַיְלָה *day and night*, זָהָב וָכֶסֶף *gold and silver*, תֹּהוּ וָבֹהוּ *waste and void* (וָ in spite of Labial; cf. אֱלֹהִים וָמֶלֶךְ *God and king*).

(e) Naturally the conj. does not cohere so closely with the word as the prep. and does not displace the *He* of the Art., as וְהָעָם *and the people*, not וָעָם.

2. מִן appears with the pronominal suffixes as follows: Sing.: מִמֶּנִּי *from me*, מִמְּךָ (m.), מִמֵּךְ (f.) *from thee*, מִמֶּנּוּ *from him*, מִמֶּנָּה *from her.*

Plur.: מִמֶּנּוּ *from us*, מִכֶּם *from you*, מֵהֶם *from them.*

For the last two words, cf. § 14. 2 a b. The other words seem to postulate a reduplicated form *minmin.*

3. *The verb.*—Verbal inflection for persons is made by attaching to the root (*i.e.* 3 *sing. masc. perf. act.*) the significant elements of the personal pronoun (§ 12).

3 *sing. m. perf.* he ruled, has ruled, &c. מָשַׁל

2 „ „ „ thou hast ruled, &c. מָשַׁלְתָּ *ta* of אַתָּה

2 „ *f.* „ thou hast ruled, &c. מָשַׁלְתְּ *t* „ אַתְּ

1 „ *c.* „ I ruled, have ruled, &c. מָשַׁלְתִּי *ti = ki* of אָנֹכִי

3 *plur. m. perf.* they ruled, did rule, &c.   מָשְׁלוּ

2   „   „   „   ye ruled, &c.   מְשַׁלְתֶּם *tem* of   אַתֶּם

2   „   *f.* „   „   „   „   מְשַׁלְתֶּן *ten* „   אַתֶּן

1   „   *c.* „   we ruled, &c.   מָשַׁלְנוּ *nu* „   אֲנַחְנוּ

Thus these forms are not arbitrary : מָשַׁלְתָּ is really *having ruled* (art) *thou*, מָשַׁלְנוּ *having ruled* (are) *we*, &c.

דָּוִד David   יְהוֹנָתָן Jonathan   מֹשֶׁה Moses   מִרְיָם Miriam

יִשְׂרָאֵל Israel   יְהוּדָה Judah   אַבְרָם Abram   אַבְרָהָם Abraham

אֵלִיָּהוּ Elijah   אֱלִישָׁע Elisha   מִלְחָמָה *f.* battle, war,   זָעַק to cry

EXERCISE. TRANSLATE.

אָמַר יהוה לָאִשָּׁה : 2 מִן־הָעֵץ¹ אָכָלְתָּ : 3 בֵּאלֹהִים וּבְמֹשֶׁה :
4 לֵאלֹהִים זָעֲקוּ בַּמִּלְחָמָה : 5 דָּוִד וִיהוֹנָתָן : 6 אֲרִי וַחֲמוֹר :
7 יִשְׂרָאֵל וִיהוּדָה : 8 וּבַיּוֹם הַהוּא כָּתַבְתִּי בְּסֵפֶר : 9 משה
ומרים : 10 יום ולילה :

I said to the man. We rested on the seventh day. And of the tree we have eaten. God destroyed from the earth man and cattle. People and king. Elijah and Elisha. Who spilt the water upon the earth? I heard the voice in the garden. Thou hast said, Holy (is) Yahweh. And these, who (are) these? Dry land and water. Night and morning. Man is not wise as God. Thou (*f.*) hast ruled over this people.

§ 16. THE NOUN. INFLECTION.

1. Stems in Hebrew are considered to contain three consonantal letters, *e.g.* כבד, שׁמר. The noun may be regarded as expressing the stem idea in *rest*, and the verb the idea in *motion*. Hence the vowels of the verb are lighter than those of the noun. It is convenient to consider the verb as the root out of which other parts of speech grew, though there are many nouns not traceable to extant verbal stems. Nouns are thus primitive or derivative. We may on the other hand take a noun or particle and set it in motion

¹ Pausal form (cf. § 10. 4 a).

that is, verbalize it; such verbs are called *Denominatives*, &c., as *to dust*.

2. Inflection in Hebrew takes place after two modes, an outside and an inside mode. Both modes are to be observed in most languages, e.g. *boy, boys*, by the outside inflection; *man, men*, by the inside; so *fear, feared*, but *tread, trod; facio, feci; brechen, brach*. The Semitic languages have a preference for the inner inflection. This prevails greatly in the Heb. verb, though it has not gained great footing in the noun, the inflection of which is external. Great alterations do occur within the noun in Heb., but these are due to movements of the Tone, e.g. דָּבָר *word*, דְּבָרִים *words*, דִּבְרֵיכֶם *your words*, and differ altogether from such changes as appear in *foot, feet*. At the same time as the accentual changes take place to a certain extent on various principles, they afford means for classifying nouns into several *Declensions*. The external changes may be called *Inflection*.

3. *Inflection, external modifications in Nouns and Adjectives*.

(a) In Hebrew there are *two* genders: *mas.* and *fem.*

There are *three* numbers: *sing., dual*, and *plur*. The *dual* is not used to indicate *two* in general: *two captains* would not be שָׂרַיִם, nor *two fish* דָּגַיִם (see § 48. 1. 2).

(b) The *fem. sing.* is formed by adding הָ- (*á*) to the *mas.*, e.g. טוֹב, טוֹבָה.

(c) The *plur. mas.* is formed by adding ִים (*ím*) to the *sing.*, e.g. טוֹבִים; and the *plur. fem.* by changing הָ (*á*) into וֹת (*óth*), e.g. טוֹבָה, טוֹבוֹת, or by adding *óth* to the *sing.* if it has no *fem.* termination, e.g. רוּחַ *wind*, רוּחוֹת.

(d) The *dual* is formed by adding ַיִם (*áyim*: י consonantal) to the *mas. sing.* for the *mas.*, and to the original *fem. sing.* (which was תַ *ath*; § 16. 4. 8) for the *fem*. Thus: from סוּס, סוּסַיִם; from סוּסָה (orig. סוּסַת), סוּסָתַיִם (*a* under ס lengthened to *á*, because pretonic, § 6. 2 b).

	mas.	*fem.*	*mas.*	*fem.*
sing.	טוֹב *good*	טוֹבָה	סוּס *horse*	סוּסָה *mare*
plur.	טוֹבִים „	טוֹבוֹת	סוּסִים „	סוּסוֹת „
dual			סוּסַיִם „	סוּסָתַיִם „

4. *Classes of nouns feminine.*

(1) Words ending in ה ָ or ת; *e.g.* צְדָקָה *righteousness*, בְּרָכָה *blessing*, עַמּוֹנִית *an Ammonitess*, מִצְרִית *an Egyptian woman* (from מִצְרִי *an Egyptian*).

(2) Words of any termination that are names of creatures feminine, as אֵם *mother*.

(3) Names of cities, countries, &c., which may be considered *mothers* of their inhabitants; *e.g.* צִיּוֹן *Zion*, אַשּׁוּר *Assyria*.

(4) Names of organs of the body of men or animals, especially such organs as are double, as יָד *hand*, אֹזֶן *ear*, קֶרֶן *horn*; also of other utensils or instruments used by man, as חֶרֶב *sword*, כּוֹס *cup*, and even of *places* in which man is wont to move, as תֵּבֵל *world*.

(5) Names of things productive, the elements, unseen essences, &c., as שֶׁמֶשׁ *sun*, אֶרֶץ *earth*, אֵשׁ *fire*, נֶפֶשׁ *soul*.

In all these classes, however, there are numerous exceptions; and many words are of both genders, though in general where this is the case one gender is largely predominant in usage over the other; *e.g.* דֶּרֶךְ *way*, masc. (less often fem.).

(6) Words *fem.* usually assume the distinctive *fem.* termination in the *plural*; *e.g.* צְדָקָה, צְדָקוֹת. Many *fem.* nouns, however, have the *mas. plur.* ending, *e.g.* שָׁנָה *year*, regular pl. שָׁנִים (in poetry sometimes שָׁנוֹת), and on the contrary many *mas.* words have the *fem.* termination in the *plur.*, *e.g.* אָב *father*, pl. אָבוֹת, especially if they incline towards a *fem.* sense by (4) or (5); *e.g.* לֵבָב *heart*, pl. לְבָבוֹת, קוֹל *voice*, pl. קוֹלֹת or קֹלוֹת (§ 4), שׁוֹפָר *trumpet*, pl. שׁוֹפָרוֹת.

As a rule, the plur. takes the gender of the sing.; *e.g.* אָבוֹת טוֹבִים *good fathers*, שָׁנִים טֹבוֹת *good years*.

(7) The *fem.* often corresponds to the Greek or Latin neuter; *e.g.* טוֹבָה *welfare*, רָעָה *misery*, זֹאת *this* (τοῦτο).

(8) The original *fem.* ending was *ath* ת ַ. The ending occasionally appears, sometimes in this form, sometimes as simple ת (cf. מוֹאָבִית *Moabitess*, from מוֹאָבִי) under conditions to be afterwards explained (cf. § 17. 2 d).

Words ending in *î* (mainly ordinal numerals, § 48. 2, *e.g.* שְׁלִישִׁי *third*, and tribal names, *e.g.* עִבְרִי *Hebrew*) form the *fem.*

and *plur.* as follows :—*fem. sing.* שְׁלִישִׁית, עִבְרִיָּה (rarely שְׁלִישִׁיָּה), *masc. pl.* עִבְרִים and עִבְרִיִּים, *fem. pl.* עִבְרִיּוֹת.

5. *The Dual.*—(a) The *Dual* is confined to substantives (and the numeral שְׁנַיִם *two*); it is no more found in the adjective, pronoun, or verb. It is used for things that go *in pairs*, whether organs of the body or inanimate things ; e.g. *eyes* עֵינַיִם, *ears* אָזְנַיִם ('oznáyim), *hands* יָדַיִם, *feet* רַגְלַיִם, *lips* שְׂפָתַיִם (from שָׂפָה), *horns* קַרְנַיִם, *shoes* נַעֲלַיִם ; and with one or two other common words, e.g. יוֹמַיִם *two days*, שְׁנָתַיִם *two years.*

(b) Verbs and adjectives, having no dual, use the plural with a dual noun, עֵינַיִם רָמוֹת וְיָדַיִם שֹׁפְכוֹת דָּם *haughty* (high) *eyes and hands that shed blood.*

(c) When terms denoting members of the body are used to express inanimate objects, the *fem. plur.* is used ; e.g. קַרְנוֹת *horns* of the altar.

(d) The vowel before the dual termination, if open, is long, being pretonic (§ 6. 2 b), e.g. שְׂפָתַיִם *s^ephātháyim.*

(e) מַיִם *water*, and שָׁמַיִם *heaven*, are not duals, but plur. from unused sing. forms (מַי and שָׁמַי).

פַּר[1]	ox	פָּרָה	*f.* cow
סוּס	horse	סוּסָה	*f.* mare
דָּג	fish	דָּגָה	*f.* fish
שַׂר[1]	prince	שָׂרָה	*f.* princess
שִׁיר	song	שִׁירָה	*f.* song
צַר[1]	adversary	צָרָה	*f.* adversary

גִּבּוֹר	hero, mighty man	כּוֹכָב	star	בְּאֵר	*f.* well	זְאֵב	wolf
יַרְכָה	*f.* side	דָּם	blood	יְאֹר	river	חֲלוֹם / חֲלֹמוֹת	dream *pl.*
צַדִּיק	just	מַר[1]	bitter	נָתַן	to give, set	הָרַג	to slay
סָפַר	to count	רָאָה	to see			זָכַר	to remember
לֶחֶם	bread	חָדָשׁ	new	שָׁתָה	to drink		

EXERCISE. TRANSLATE.

לֹא שָׁתָה הַפַּר מִן־הַמַּיִם כִּי מָרִים הֵם : 2 אֵלֶּה הַפָּרוֹת הָרָעוֹת אֲשֶׁר רָאָה הַמֶּלֶךְ עַל־הַיְאֹר : 3 מָשַׁל הָאָדָם בַּבְּהֵמָה וּבַדָּגִים :

---

[1] The words פַּר, שַׂר, צַר, מַר, have, for etymological reasons (§ 43), *a* (path.) when uninflected or without the Article, cf. § 12 ; otherwise ā.

4 הֵמָּה הַשָּׂרִים וְהַגִּבּוֹרִים אֲשֶׁר נָתַן הַמֶּלֶךְ עַל־הָעָם : 5 אָמַרְתִּי
אֶל־הָעָם הַזֶּה צַדִּיקִים אַתֶּם : 6 הֶהָרִים הָאֵלֶּה רָמִים מְאֹד :
7 סָפַרְתָּ אֶת־הַכּוֹכָבִים : 8 מָה רָמִים הַהֵיכָלִים הָהֵם : הַיָּדַיִם :
יְַרְכָתַיִם : 9 ראה המלך בחלום את־הפרות הטבות על־
היאר : 10 זכר יהוה כי עפר אנחנו :

I remember (*perf.*) the songs which I heard in the temple.
These waters (are) bitter. Those heavens (are) very lofty.
These (are) the asses which we slew. Who (are) these princes
and heroes? Thou hast heard the cows. God remembers
the just (*pl.*). We sat on the hills two days. Bread he ate
and water he drank. The just are as the stars which (are)
in the firmament. The two-sides. He took oxen and cows
and horses and asses. We heard the wolves in the evening.
I counted the stars which God has set in the heavens.
Water from the wells. God gave me a new song. Thou (*f.*)
has spilt blood (*pl.*).

§ 17. CASES.   THE CONSTRUCT STATE.

1. *The construct state.*——There is some reason to believe
that Hebrew, like Arabic, once had three cases, the nominative, genitive, and accusative, ending respectively in *u*, *i*, and *a*.
The traces of case are clearest in the accusative. But
while there is now no external indication of the nomin. or
the accus., the genitive relation (e.g. *the palace of the king*)
is indicated by closely connecting the governing and governed
words in a way which demands special attention, as it has
no analogy in the corresponding Greek or Latin construction.
The first word (here *palace*), which is considered as dependent,
is said to be in the *construct state* or in construction ; the
second word (*king*), which is not dependent, is said to be in
the *absolute* state.

2. (a) The cstr. relation corresponds most nearly to the
relations expressed by *of* in English, in all its many senses :
e.g. *the palace of the king, the son of the father, a ring of
gold, the fear of God, a song of Zion.* This relation, though

usually, is not invariably expressed by *of*: when the first word is, as it may be and often is, an adjective or participle, it may be expressed by *in*, &c.; *e.g.* in " great in power, fair in appearance, broken in heart," *great, fair*, and *broken* would be in the construct, *power, appearance*, and *heart* in the absolute. The point is that the two words together make up one idea.

Now the first half of a relation like *son of*—, *great in*—, forming no complete idea of itself, the emphasis of the whole expression lies on the second half. The cstr. and the abs. are considered to form together an accentual unity, like words connected by maqqēph (§ 10. 3); the chief accent naturally falls on the second half or absolute, consequently the first half or construct is hurried. In this way *the cstr. is uttered as shortly as is possible in consistency with the laws of pronunciation* in the language; therefore any merely tone-long vowel within the word will be shortened or lost; *e.g.* abs. דָּבָר (ָ in both cases tone-long, § 6. 2 b), constr. דְּבַר. This is the shortest form such a word can assume.

(b) Further, the final *m* of the plur. *îm* and the dual *áyim* is elided, and these terminations become *ê*: thus, from plur. דְּבָרִים we get constr. דִּבְרֵי (since בָּ, when hurried, is reduced to בְּ, and דְּבְ must become דִּבְ, by § 6. 2 d. i.; and the shᵉwa is vocal, representing as it does an original ָ. Consequently, if the third radical is a *bᵉghadhkᵉphath*, it will not take daghesh lene: abs. pl. כְּבֵדִים [sing. כָּבֵד *heavy*], constr. כִּבְדֵי, not כִּבְדֵּי).

(c) The dual cstr. is similarly formed; *e.g.* abs. קַרְנַיִם *horns*, cstr. קַרְנֵי; abs. יָדַיִם *hands*, cstr. יְדֵי. So from שָׂפָה *lip*, dual abs. שְׂפָתַיִם (§ 16. 3 d, 5 d), cstr. שִׂפְתֵי.

(d) In *fem. sing.* the original ending ת— (§ 16. 4. 8) is resumed: abs. סוּסָה *mare*, cstr. סוּסַת; abs. צְדָקָה *righteousness*, cstr. צִדְקַת (because צְד = צִד: *çidlᵉqath*). אֲדָמָה *ground*, cstr. אַדְמַת (because אֲד = אַד, § 16. 2 d. ii.).

(e) *Fem. pl. cstr.* ends, like abs., in תֹ, but is shortened, like all constructs, as much as possible; pl. abs. צְדָקוֹת, cstr. צִדְקוֹת.

סוּס, with its unchangeable vowel, illustrates the endings in their simplest form: the other illustrations show how the changeable vowels are affected—יָשָׁר *upright*, יָד *hand*, שָׂפָה *lip*.

	Mas.		_Fem._	
	Abs.	_Cstr._	_Abs._	_Cstr._
sing.	סוּס horse	סוּס	סוּסָה mare	סוּסַת
plur.	סוּסִים „	סוּסֵי	סוּסוֹת „	סוּסוֹת
dual	סוּסַיִם „	סוּסֵי	סוּסָתַיִם „	סוּסְתֵּי

	Mas.	_Fem._		_Mas._[1]	_Fem._
abs. sing.	יָשָׁר	יְשָׁרָה	_abs. sing._	יָד	שָׂפָה
cstr. „	יְשַׁר	יִשְׁרַת	_cstr._ „	יַד	שְׂפַת
abs. plur.	יְשָׁרִים	יְשָׁרוֹת	_abs. dual_	יָדַיִם	שְׂפָתַיִם
cstr. „	יִשְׁרֵי	יִשְׁרוֹת	_cstr._ „	יְדֵי	שִׂפְתֵי

Rule 1.—_a._ The construct _never_ has the article: the absolute (if it be definite) has it—not of course with proper names. Thus _the king's horse_ (never in this order in Hebrew, but always _the horse of the king_), סוּס הַמֶּלֶךְ (not הַסּוּס הַמֶּלֶךְ) ; _the horses of the king,_ סוּסֵי הַמֶּלֶךְ (not הַסּוּסֵי הַמֶּלֶךְ) ; _the word of the prophet,_ דְּבַר הַנָּבִיא ; _the righteousness of the people,_ צִדְקַת הָעָם ; _the lips of the girl,_ שִׂפְתֵי הַנַּעֲרָה. So with adjs.: _a good-looking girl,_ נַעֲרָה טוֹבַת מַרְאֶה (lit. _good in appearance_), _a woman of good understanding_ (אִשָּׁה טוֹבַת שֵׂכֶל, lit. _good of understanding_); and with participles, _the broken-hearted,_ נִשְׁבְּרֵי־לֵב (lit. _those who are broken,_ pl. cstr. of נִשְׁבָּר _in heart_).

_b._ If the abs. is definite, the constr. is also definite ; _e.g._ אִישׁ הַמִּלְחָמָה _the_ man of war, _the_ warrior ; but אִישׁ מִלְחָמָה _a_ warrior ; מִזְמוֹר דָּוִד (_the_ psalm of David, bec. D. is definite). So הַר יהוה _the_ mountain of Yahweh. The indefinite in such cases is usually expressed by putting לְ (_to_) before the absolute: מִזְמוֹר לְדָוִד _a_ psalm of David.

Rule 2.—The construct must _immediately_ precede the noun with which it goes ; therefore two (co-ordinate) constructs cannot precede the same noun ; e.g. _the hands and lips of the man_ would _not_ be יְדֵי וְשִׂפְתֵי הָאִישׁ, because יְדֵי being construct must precede הָאִישׁ. Hebrew writes therefore _the hands of the man and his lips,_ יְדֵי הָאִישׁ וּשְׂפָתָיו ; _the prince's sons and daughters,_ not בְּנֵי וּבְנוֹת הַשָּׂר, but בְּנֵי הַשָּׂר וּבְנוֹתָיו. Similarly

[1] יָד is _fem._, but may be used here for illustration's sake, as it has not the fem. ending.

in phrases like *the God of heaven and earth*, the cstr. is, as a rule, repeated: thus אֱלֹהֵי הַשָּׁמַיִם וֵאלֹהֵי הָאָרֶץ rather than אלהי השמים והארץ (bec. then אֱלֹהֵי would be separated from הָאָרֶץ God *of the earth*).

Such a *succession* of constructs, however, as דֶּרֶךְ עֵץ הַחַיִּים *the way to the tree of life*; יְמֵי שְׁנֵי חַיֵּי אֲבוֹתַי *the days of the years of the life of my fathers*, constitutes a unity and is perfectly normal.[1]

Rule 3.—An adj. qualifying a noun in the cstr. state must stand *after the compound expression*, and, as the noun in the cstr. is definite, the adj. has the article; e.g. *the good horses of the king*, סוּסֵי הַמֶּלֶךְ הַטּוֹבִים (not סוסי הטובים המלך, because the cstr. must *immediately* precede its abs.) = *the horses of the king—viz. the good ones.* So *the king's good mare*, סוּסַת הַמֶּלֶךְ הַטּוֹבָה (הַטּוֹב would be *the good king's mare*).

If the gender and number of the cstr. and abs. happened to be identical, a certain ambiguity would arise: סוּסַת הַמַּלְכָּה הַטּוֹבָה *the queen's good mare, the good queen's mare*; but these cases would be obviously few, and the context would usually decide. Ambiguity may be definitely avoided by the use of a relative clause; e.g. *the queen's good mare*, הַסּוּסָה הַטּוֹבָה אֲשֶׁר לַמַּלְכָּה; i.e. *the good mare which (belongs) to the queen*.

The above illustrations show that, though an adj. agrees with its noun in gend. and numb. it does not agree in state. Even when a noun is in the cstr. its adj. is in the abs.

3. *Use of the accusative ending.*—The accus. ending *a* has been retained in one particular usage. ָה is added to words to express *direction* or motion towards. The ending in this use of it, which is probably a revival and extension of its former use, *has not the tone, e.g.* צָפֹ֫ונָה *northward* (not צָפוֹנָ֫ה, because the first syllable is pretonic), הָהָ֫רָה *towards the mountain* (not הָהָרָ֫ה, § 11 c). It may even admit a preposition before its word; e.g. לִשְׁאוֹלָה *to Sheol*. It may be appended to the plur.; e.g. הַשָּׁמַ֫יְמָה *heavenwards*, and even to the cstr. state, e.g. בֵּ֫יתָה יוֹסֵף *to the house of Joseph*.

This termination, called by some *He locale* because it

---

[1] Notice that the article (or its equivalent, *e.g.* pron. suff. *my, his,* etc., § 19) appears only at the *end*.

usually has reference to place, is sometimes extended to time ; *e.g.* מִיָּמִים יָמִ֫ימָה *from year* (lit. *days*) *to year*.

It cannot be used with persons : *to (towards) David* would not be דָּוִ֫דָה, but אֶל־דָּוִד.

צָפוֹן *f.*	north	מִצְרַ֫יִם	Egypt	מִטָּה *f.*	bed, אֶבְיוֹן poor
רוּחַ *f.*[1] {wind / spirit}		חַ֫יִל {valour / force, army}		יְשׁוּעָה *f.* {salvation / deliverance}	
מִצְוָה *f.*	command	עִיר *f.*	city	שֵׂ֫כֶל	understanding
תּוֹרָה *f.*	law	חוֹמָה *f.*	wall	בָּשָׂר	flesh
מַלְכָּה *f.*	queen	בַּת *f.*	daughter	אַרְבַּע	four
אֲבִגַ֫יִל	Abigail	שְׁאוֹל *f.*	Sheol, the underworld		
יָרַד	to go down	שָׁמַר	to keep	פָּקַד	to review
שָׁבַר	to break	נָתַץ	to break down	פָּרַץ	to break through (*e.g.* a wall)

EXERCISE. TRANSLATE.

לֹא שָׁתָה הָעָם מִמֵּי הַיְאֹר : 2 לָקַח דָּוִד אֲבִיגַ֫יִל לְאִשָּׁה וְהִיא אִשָּׁה טוֹבַת שֵׂ֫כֶל : 3 אֶבְיוֹנֵי הָעָם הֵם צַדִּיקִים : 4 לֹא שָׁמַ֫רְנוּ תּוֹרַת יהוה אֱלֹהֵי יִשְׂרָאֵל : 5 עָשָׂה הַשָּׂר כְּמִצְוַת הַמֶּ֫לֶךְ : 6 וּבְתוֹרַת יהוה לֹא [2]הָלָ֫כְתָּ : 7 אֵ֫לֶּה מִצְוֹת אֱלֹהֵי כָל־הָאָ֫רֶץ אֲשֶׁר כָּתַ֫בְתִּי הַיּוֹם הַזֶּה : 8 שָׁכַב הַיֶּ֫לֶד עַל־מִטַּת אִישׁ הָאֱלֹהִים : 9 בָּא חַ֫יִל גָּדוֹל [3]מִיַּרְכְּתֵי הָאָ֫רֶץ וּמֵאַרְבַּע רוּחוֹת [2]הַשָּׁמָ֫יִם : 10 אָכַ֫לְנוּ מִכָּל־עֵץ [2]הַגָּן : 11 וּמַלְכוּת הָאָ֫רֶץ בַּת אִישׁ גִּבּוֹר [2]חָ֫יִל : 12 הָיָה רָעָב בָּאָ֫רֶץ וְאַבְרָם יָרַד מִצְרַ֫יְמָה כִּי כָבֵד הָרָעָב בָּאָ֫רֶץ : 13 תּוֹרַת יהוה טוֹבָה : 14 בַּיּוֹם הַהוּא עָשָׂה יהוה יְשׁוּעָה בִּישְׂרָאֵל :

The great day of Yahweh. The day of Yahweh is great. The good queen of the land. All the people of the earth. All the king's good asses. The captain (prince) reviewed all the mighty-men of valour and all the people of war. In the two-sides of the temple. I have gone northward. We are gone down to Sheol. He went towards-the-mountain. We

---

[1] Less often *masc.*

[2] Observe the pausal vowels in 6, 9, 10, 11 (cf. § 10. 4 a).

[3] Dag. in *kaph* only in cstr.

slew the man's ass. The people did not drink from the waters of the river, for they (were) blood.[1] Ye have not kept the commandments of the God of all the earth. The spirit of God (was) upon the waters. God of the spirits (that belong) to all flesh. I have broken down all the walls of the city. Thou hast kept the poor of the land from all ill. Thou (*f.*) hast eaten of the tree of the garden.

§ 18. THE FIRST DECLENSION.

Nouns may be arranged in Declensions according to the internal vowel changes produced by alteration in the place of Tone occasioned by *Inflection* (§ 16. 2). Many forms of Nouns, however, contain unchangeable vowels, *i.e.* vowels pure long, or diphthongal (§ 2. 2. 1), or unchangeable by position, as גִּבּוֹר (*gibbôr*) *a hero*, אֶבְיוֹן (*'ebh-yôn*) *poor*, in both of which the first vowel is unchangeable by position (short, because in shut syllable, גִּבּ, אֶבְ), and the second pure long (as we might almost infer from its consonantal representation ו), and consequently unchangeable by nature (§ 6. 1). Such Nouns, as they suffer no internal change from inflection, do not seem to require classification; they are indeclinable. No additions at the end can in any way affect the vowels of either syllable; *e.g.* plur. אֶבְיוֹנִים, גִּבּוֹרִים.

The forms that suffer change are those having *tone-long* vowels, *e.g.* in each of the words דָּבָר, זָקֵן (not זָקִין), לֵבָב (not לֵיבָב) both vowels are tone-long, and are therefore both subject to change. These vowels, having been rarely expressed by the so-called *Vowel-letters* (§ 2. 3 *e*), may very generally be distinguished from pure long, and diphthongal, vowels, which were usually so expressed (§ 2. 3). In general only *qāmeç* and *çere* are tone-long in nouns, as in the above illustrations; *ḥôlem* being for the most part unchangeably long, and therefore usually represented by ו; *e.g.* גָּדוֹל (*gādhôl*), כּוֹכָב (*kôkhābh*). In these words the *ā* is subject to change, being only tone-long, but not the *ô*.

The forms with changeable vowels seem capable of being generalized under *three* classes or Declensions.

---

[1] In dependent clauses with כִּי *for, that,* &c., the pronoun is put last.

1. A large number of words are of the same form as the *perfect* of verbs, and are chiefly participles or adjectives, though many are substantives. With these may be classed some other forms of words that are subject to the same laws. Together they may be called

THE FIRST DECLENSION.

They are words having:

ā ָ in the pretone (גָּדוֹל, זָקֵן), or *ā* in the tone (כּוֹכָב, לֵבָב), or *ā* in both places (יָשָׁר, דָּבָר).

If the principles concerning the effect of the tone upon the vowels (§ 6) be clearly understood, and also the rules for the formation of the plur. (§ 16) and the construct (§ 17), no special rules for this declension are necessary. We have only to remember that when words are increased at the end (*e.g.* by ים ָ, ה ָ, &c.) the accent plants itself upon the significant inflectional addition; *e.g.* דָּבָר, but דְּבָרִים. The tone, falling on *bhār* in the sing., falls on *rîm* in the pl.: *bhā*, being pretonic, has the long *ā*, and the original *dā* of *dābhár*, being now *two* places from the tone (and open), becomes *dᵉ*. The construct, which, as we have seen, is always made as short as possible (§ 17. 2 a), becomes דְּבַר (sing.) and דִּבְרֵי (pl.): the shᵉwa in pl. is vocal, hence no daghesh in *bᵉghadhkᵉphath* letters; *e.g.* לִבְבוֹת, כּוֹכְבֵי.

Note that the form *ā–ē*, *e.g.* זָקֵן, has *a* in the constr. sing. זְקַן.

A few words have in the construct *sᵉghol* in both syllables: *e.g.* גָּדֵר *wall*, cstr. גֶּדֶר (pronominal suffix, § 19, regularly of the type גִּדְרוֹ *his wall*); כָּתֵף *shoulder*, c. כֶּתֶף; יָרֵךְ *thigh*, c. יֶרֶךְ; כָּבֵד *heavy*, c. both כְּבַד and כֶּבֶד.

	Sing.	*Plur.*	*Cstr. sing.*	*Cstr. plur.*
(1) upright	יָשָׁר	יְשָׁרִים	יְשַׁר	יִשְׁרֵי (= יִשְׁרֵי)
(2) old, old man, elder	זָקֵן	זְקֵנִים	זְקַן	זִקְנֵי (= זִקְנֵי)
(3) great	גָּדוֹל	גְּדוֹלִים	גְּדוֹל	גְּדוֹלֵי
(4) blessed	בָּרוּךְ	בְּרוּכִים	בְּרוּךְ	בְּרוּכֵי
(5) overseer	פָּקִיד	פְּקִידִים	פְּקִיד	פְּקִידֵי
(6) heart	לֵבָב	לְבָבוֹת	לְבַב	לִבְבוֹת (= לִבְבוֹת)
(7) star	כּוֹכָב	כּוֹכָבִים	כּוֹכַב	כּוֹכְבֵי
(8) desert	מִדְבָּר	מִדְבָּרִים	מִדְבַּר	מִדְבְּרֵי

Rem.—The forms 1, 2, 3 with vowels $\bar{a}$—$\bar{a}$, $\bar{a}$—$\bar{e}$, $\bar{a}$—$\bar{o}$, may be considered the typical forms of this declension, see § 22. 1. The forms 4, 5 are pass. participles, and 6 is a less common nominal formation.

2. *Feminine nouns* ending in ָה retain in the constr. sing. the original ת ַ of the feminine (cf. § 16. 4. 8). The construct, as usual, is pronounced as rapidly as is consistent with the laws of the language (§ 17. 2 a): abs. שָׂפָה *lip*, cstr. שְׂפַת.

Abs. sing. צְדָקָה *righteousness.*   cstr. (צִדְקַת =) צִדְקַת

„   plur. צְדָקוֹת *righteousnesses.*   „   (צִדְקוֹת =) צִדְקוֹת

„   sing. נְבֵלָה *corpse.*   „   (נִבְלַת =) נִבְלַת

The sh‘wa in the cstr. (sing. and pl.) is vocal. But in cstr. sing. of בְּרָכָה *blessing*, the first syllable is closed בִּרְכַּת.

Some fem. nouns retain the long $\bar{e}$ under inflection: *e.g.* גְּזֵלָה *plunder*, cstr. גְּזֵלַת ; גְּנֵבָה *thing stolen*, 3 sing. masc. suff. (§ 19) גְּנֵבָתוֹ.

3. A few monosyllables with changeable vowels ($\bar{a}$ $\bar{e}$) in the tone attach themselves to this declension. They are probably real dissyllables, which have undergone contraction. The chief are יָד *hand*, דָּם *blood*, דָּג *fish*, עֵץ *tree*. They are inflected exactly like the last syllable of דָּבָר (or זָקֵן); as this is in sing. abs. דָּבָר cstr. דְּבַר plur. abs. דְּבָרִים cstr. דִּבְרֵי

so we have   „   „   דָּג   „   דַּג   „   „   דָּגִים   „   דְּגֵי

עֵץ   „   עֵץ[1]   „   „   עֵצִים   „   עֲצֵי

So פָּנִים *face* (plur.), cstr. פְּנֵי.

WORDS FOR PRACTICE.

זָכָר	male	קָצֵר	short	תָּמִים	perfect
דָּבָר	word	מָאוֹר *m.*	luminary	שָׂפָה *f.*	lip
מָשָׁל	proverb	מְאוֹרֹת *pl.*		בְּרָכָה *f.*	blessing
כָּבֵד	heavy	נָבִיא	prophet	נְקָמָה *f.*	vengeance
נָמֵר	leopard	בְּרִיא	fat	נְבֵלָה *f.*	corpse
		קָדוֹשׁ	holy		

Exercise.—Write the *cstr. sing.* and the *abs.* and *cstr. pl.* of the above words. (The *abs.* and *cstr. dual* of שָׂפָה.)

שְׁנַיִם two   חוֹל sand   אָסַף to gather   נָשָׂא to lift up   יָם sea

---

[1] Same as abs.

5

יִצְחָק Isaac   יַעֲקֹב Jacob   עֵשָׂו Esau   עֶזְרָא Ezra

עֵצָה *f.* counsel   שָׁם there   לָמֶּה why ?   כַּרְמֶל[1] Carmel

EXERCISE.   PARSE AND TRANSLATE.

בְּרִיאוֹת, דְּגַת, נְבִיאֵי, יִשְׁרֵי, רָקִיעַ, לִבְבוֹת, מְאוֹר, מִשְׁלֵי, כְּבַד,
פְּקִידֵי, לְבַב, שִׂפְתֵי, נִקְמַת, בִּרְכוֹת, יָדַיִם : וְחֹשֶׁךְ עַל־פְּנֵי הַמָּיִם :
‏2 כָּתַב הַנָּבִיא אֶת־כָּל־הַדְּבָרִים בַּסֵּפֶר : 3 הָיָה דְבַר יהוה אֶל־
הַנְּבִיאִים : 4 תּוֹרַת יהוה בְּלֶבֶב הַצַּדִּיקִים : 5 כָּתַבְתִּי לָעָם הַזֶּה
אֶת־כָּל־דִּבְרֵי תוֹרַת יהוה : 6 לֹא הָיָה שָׁם אִישׁ מִזִּקְנֵי יִשְׂרָאֵל :
‏7 נָתַן אֱלֹהִים אֶת־שְׁנֵי הַמְּאוֹרוֹת הַגְּדֹלִים בִּרְקִיעַ הַשָּׁמָיִם :
‏8 אָסַף הַשַּׂר חַיִל כָּבֵד כְּכוֹכְבֵי הַשָּׁמַיִם וְכַחוֹל אֲשֶׁר עַל־שְׂפַת
הַיָּם : 9 אָמַר יִצְחָק הֲקוֹל קוֹל יַעֲקֹב וְהַיָּדַיִם יְדֵי עֵשָׂו : 10 נָשָׂא
הַנָּבִיא הַזָּקֵן אֶת־נִבְלַת אִישׁ הָאֱלֹהִים אֶל־הַחֲמוֹר : 11 כבד־
לשׁון אנכי : 12 ויקרא עזרא בספר תורת האלהים :

The law of Yahweh is perfect.   The king saw the fat kine
upon the bank (lip) of the river.   Ye have eaten the flesh
of fat oxen.   The words of the lips of Yahweh (are) upright.
I (am) not a man of words.   Good (are) the words of the law
of Yahweh.   The waters (are) upon the face of the ground.
We have heard the words of the prophets of the God
of all the earth.   Thou hast kept the heart of this people
from evil.   Very great (are) the righteousnesses of God.
Blessed (are) the upright of heart.   The vengeance of the
people (was) great.   The proverbs of the wise king (are)
perfect.   He destroyed all the fishes of the river.

§ 19. THE PRONOMINAL SUFFIXES.

The separate Personal Pronouns are used only to express
the Nominative or as Subject (§ 12).

I. Hebrew has not largely developed the adjective; instead of saying *holy hill, silver idols, eloquent man*, it says *hill
of holiness,* הַר קֹדֶשׁ ; *idols of silver,* אֱלִילֵי כֶסֶף ; *man of words,*
אִישׁ דְּבָרִים, and the like.   Similarly for *my horse* it says
horse-of-me; the possessive pronouns *my, thy, his, our,*

[1] Usually with def. art. = *the garden land.*

&c., are altogether wanting. In other words, what we have in such cases is—ideally—a noun in the construct, followed by a personal pronoun in the absolute, which, however, is not now written as a separate word, but attached to the noun as a suffix. There are a few words in which this process is still perfectly clear, and the pronoun is present in practically its original form ; e.g. אָבִיהוּ his father (father-of him, הוּא) ; but in all words the pronoun is really present, though not often so obvious ; e.g. סוּסוֹ his horse. Here the original sûs-hû (horse-of him) became first, by means of the helping vowel a (appropriate before the guttural h) sûsahû ; then h disappeared, as it so easily does (§ 14. 1 e), leaving sûsaû, which easily passes into sûsô (cf. § 2. 2. 1).

All the so-called pronominal suffixes correspond, with simple modifications similarly accounted for, to the (significant parts of the) personal pronouns § 12, except that in the second person k appears instead of t. The slight occasional differences between the forms of the suffixes, according as they are attached to singular or plural nouns, should be carefully noted. E.g. in סוּסֵיהֶם their horses, the ה of the original 3rd pers. pron. (הֶם) is preserved ; in סוּסָם their horse, it has disappeared (as in סוּסוֹ).

2. The suffixes are divided into *light* and *heavy* ; the heavy are those containing *two consonants*—כֶם, כֶן, הֶם, הֶן (not נוּ *nû*, for the ו is a vowel) ; all the others are light. Before the heavy suffixes, the noun, which is always an ideal construct, assumes the real construct form : e.g. דְּבַרְכֶם *the word of you, your word* ; דִּבְרֵיכֶם *the words of you, your words* ; דִּבְרֵיהֶם *the words of them, their words* (דְּבַר and דִּבְרֵי being respectively cstr. sing. and pl. of דָּבָר) ; so סוּסַתְכֶם *your mare,* צִדְקַתְכֶם *your righteousness,* שִׂפְתֵיכֶם *your lips.* Before the light suffixes, the regular rules of vocalization apply (§ 6), which are illustrated, e.g., in the formation of the plural—דְּבָרִים from דָּבָר. Thus, *my word* = דְּבָרִי : the accent falls at the end, on the suffix ; the pretonic, being open, is long ; the vowel before that, being in an open syllable, vanishes into sh°wa. (דְּבָרִי would exhibit the true construct form : but the short vowel in the open pretone would violate one of the fundamental principles of vocalization, and is manifestly impos-

sible.) So דְּבָרוֹ *his word,* דְּבָרֵנוּ *our word.* (The accent falls on the ֵ : hence דְּבָרֵנוּ would be again impossible.) So שְׂפָתִי *my lip,* not שִׂפְתִי. Similarly with a plural noun: *my words,* דְּבָרַי; *our words,* דְּבָרֵינוּ, not דְּבָרֵינוּ (because נוּ is not one of the heavy suffixes). The accent falls on the ֵ, and the vocalization follows as a matter of course. So שְׂפָתֶיךָ (*f.*) *thy lips,* שְׂפָתֵינוּ *our lips;* but שִׂפְתֵיהֶם *their lips.*

For purposes of vocalization, it is obviously important to know where the accent falls: in the paradigms it is specially marked, when it does not fall upon the last syllable. It may be put thus: the monosyllabic and all the heavy suffixes take the accent; *e.g.* דְּבָרִי *my word,* דִּבְרֵיכֶם *your words;* dissyllabic suffixes (except the heavy suffixes attached to plur. nouns) take the accent on the penult; *e.g.* סוּסֵנוּ *our horse,* דְּבָרֵנוּ *our word,* דְּבָרֶיהָ *her words,* but דִּבְרֵיהֶם *their words.*

NOUN WITH SUFFIXES.

	Mas.		*Fem.*		
Singular noun	סוּס	דָּבָר	סוּסָה	שָׂפָה	צְדָקָה
	(horse)	(word)	(mare)	(lip)	(righteousness)
sing. 1 *c.* my	סוּסִי	דְּבָרִי	סוּסָתִי	שְׂפָתִי	צִדְקָתִי
2 *m.* thy	סוּסְךָ	דְּבָרְךָ	סוּסָתְךָ	שְׂפָתְךָ	צִדְקָתְךָ
2 *f.* thy	סוּסֵךְ	דְּבָרֵךְ	סוּסָתֵךְ	שְׂפָתֵךְ	צִדְקָתֵךְ
3 *m.* his	סוּסוֹ	דְּבָרוֹ	סוּסָתוֹ	שְׂפָתוֹ	צִדְקָתוֹ
3 *f.* her	סוּסָהּ	דְּבָרָהּ	סוּסָתָהּ	שְׂפָתָהּ	צִדְקָתָהּ
plur. 1 *c.* our	סוּסֵנוּ	דְּבָרֵנוּ	סוּסָתֵנוּ	שְׂפָתֵנוּ	צִדְקָתֵנוּ
2 *m.* your	סוּסְכֶם	דְּבַרְכֶם	סוּסַתְכֶם	שְׂפַתְכֶם	צִדְקַתְכֶם
2 *f.* your	סוּסְכֶן	דְּבַרְכֶן	סוּסַתְכֶן	שְׂפַתְכֶן	צִדְקַתְכֶן
3 *m.* their	סוּסָם	דְּבָרָם	סוּסָתָם	שְׂפָתָם	צִדְקָתָם
3 *f.* their	סוּסָן	דְּבָרָן	סוּסָתָן	שְׂפָתָן	צִדְקָתָן
Plur. noun	סוּסִים	דְּבָרִים	סוּסוֹת	שְׂפָתַיִם	צְדָקוֹת
	(horses)	(words)	(mares)	(dual)	(righteousnesses)
sing. 1 *c.* my	סוּסַי	דְּבָרַי	סוּסוֹתַי	שְׂפָתַי	צִדְקוֹתַי
2 *m.* thy	סוּסֶיךָ	דְּבָרֶיךָ	סוּסוֹתֶיךָ	שְׂפָתֶיךָ	צִדְקוֹתֶיךָ
2 *f.* thy	סוּסַיִךְ	דְּבָרַיִךְ	סוּסוֹתַיִךְ	שְׂפָתַיִךְ	צִדְקוֹתַיִךְ
3 *m.* his	סוּסָיו	דְּבָרָיו	סוּסוֹתָיו	שְׂפָתָיו	צִדְקוֹתָיו
3 *f.* her	סוּסֶיהָ	דְּבָרֶיהָ	סוּסוֹתֶיהָ	שְׂפָתֶיהָ	צִדְקוֹתֶיהָ

plur. 1 *c.* our	צִדְקוֹתֵֽינוּ	סוּסֵֽינוּ	דְּבָרֵֽינוּ	סוּסוֹתֵֽינוּ	שְׂפָתֵֽינוּ
2 *m.* your	צִדְקוֹתֵיכֶם	סוּסֵיכֶם	דִּבְרֵיכֶם	סוּסוֹתֵיכֶם	שְׂפָתֵיכֶם
2 *f.* your	צִדְקוֹתֵיכֶן	סוּסֵיכֶן	דִּבְרֵיכֶן	סוּסוֹתֵיכֶן	שְׂפָתֵיכֶן
3 *m.* their	צִדְקוֹתֵיהֶם (תָם)	סוּסֵיהֶם	דִּבְרֵיהֶם	סוּסוֹתֵיהֶם	שְׂפָתֵיהֶם
3 *f.* their	צִדְקוֹתֵיהֶן	סוּסֵיהֶן	דִּבְרֵיהֶן	סוּסוֹתֵיהֶן	שְׂפָתֵיהֶן

Note (i.) that the shᵉwa before the 2nd pers. suff. sing.
and plur. attached to a sing. noun is vocal; hence the *kaph*
does not have the daghesh lene. דְּבָרְךָ *dᵉbhārᵉkhā* (in pause
דְּבָרֶךָ), דְּבַרְכֶם *dᵉbharᵉkhem*.

(ii.) The suffix יו֖ is pronounced *āw* (סוּסָיו = *sûsāw*).
The ' is ignored in pronunciation, but it represents an earlier
stage in the history of the word (cf. § 5. 6 c).

(iii.) Suffixes to fem. plur. nouns, curiously enough, are
preceded by ', which, appropriate with masc. plur. (because
it is really the cstr. plur. ending), is, with fem. nouns, strictly
speaking, neither necessary nor justified; with the result that
the plural is in such cases doubly indicated; *e.g.* סוּסוֹתֵֽינוּ.

(iv.) The helping vowel between stem and suffix is ultimately traceable
to *i* or *a* : *a* before gutturals, as we have seen, *sûs-a-*(*h*)*û* = סוּסוֹ, so סוּסָם
(*h* dropped); *i* in other cases סוּסֵֽנוּ (tone-long *ê*) is from an ultimate
sûs-i-nû.

(v.) The *dual* takes the same suffixes as the plural, *e.g.*
יָד *hand*, יָדַֽיִם *hands*, יָדֶֽיהָ *her hands*, יָדֵֽינוּ *our h.*, יְדֵיכֶם *your h.*

(vi.) The suffixes of *sing.* nouns are sometimes joined to
fem. pl., particularly 3 *pl.*; *e.g.* נַפְשׁוֹתָם *their souls* (instead
of נַפְשׁוֹתֵיהֶם), דּוֹרוֹתָם *their generations*.

---

face פָּנִים (*pl.*)	son, בֵּן, *pl.* בָּנִים	*daughter* בַּת, *pl.* בָּנוֹת
my face פָּנַי	*the man's face* פְּנֵי הָאִישׁ	
before me לְפָנַי	*before the man* לִפְנֵי הָאִישׁ	
before thee לְפָנֶיךָ	*before you* לִפְנֵיכֶם	
after אַחֲרֵי	*after me* אַחֲרַי	

Rule I.—The noun with suffix, being already definite,
does not take the def. art. (cf. § 1 3. 7 a), but naturally its
adj. does; e.g. *my good horse*, סוּסִי הַטּוֹב (*my horse, the good one*);
your evil words, דִּבְרֵיכֶם הָרָעִים; *thy strong hand*, יָדְךָ הַחֲזָקָה.

Rule II.—The suffix is repeated with each co-ordinate noun: e.g. *he took his sons and daughters,* לָקַח אֶת־בָּנָיו וְאֶת־בְּנוֹתָיו (cf. § 13. 7 b).

Particles, such as *Prepositions* and *Adverbs,* are generally *Nouns* in a fragmentary condition, and may take Suffixes which are attached to them precisely as to Nouns. For בְּ and לְ see § 14. 1 f; for מִן see § 15. 2. A number of words take the suffixes of *plur.* nouns. Some of the words are really *plur.*; *e.g.* אַחֲרֵי *after* (pl. cstr., *hinder parts*)—hence אַחֲרַי *after me,* אַחֲרֶיךָ *after you,* אַחֲרָיו *after him,* &c.; others, like עַל *upon,* אֶל *to,* resume before suffixes the *yodh* which originally formed part of the root (עֲלִי, אֱלִי), thus producing the impression of a plural.

עֲלֵיהֶם, עֲלֵיכֶם, עָלֵינוּ, עָלֶיהָ, עָלָיו, עָלַיִךְ, עָלֶיךָ, עָלַי

אֲלֵיהֶם, אֲלֵיכֶם, אֵלֵינוּ, אֵלֶיהָ, אֵלָיו, אֵלַיִךְ, אֵלֶיךָ, אֵלַי

Like עַל is עַד *unto, as far as.*

לוֹט Lot אֵהוּד Ehud שְׁמוּאֵל Samuel שְׁלֹמֹה Solomon אֶפְרַיִם Ephraim	

טוֹב good things, goodness   שִׂיחָה *f.* meditation   אֵת (אֶת־) with

נֶגֶד before, in presence of   פֶּתַח opening, door   דֶּלֶת *f.* door

סָגַר to shut, close   תָּקַע to thrust, strike, blow (a trumpet)

שׁוֹפָר
שׁוֹפָרוֹת *pl.* } horn (for blowing)   בְּרִית *f.* covenant   תְּפִלָּה *f.* prayer

חֶסֶד mercy, kindness   מִשְׁפָּט judgment, ordinance, justice

עוֹלָם long duration, age   מֵעוֹלָם from of old

עַד־עוֹלָם for ever   תָּמִיד continually

כָּרַת to cut off, cut down   כָּרַת בְּרִית to make a covenant

בָּטַח to trust   צָפַן to hide, lay up   אָהֵב to love   פָּעַל to do

EXERCISE. TRANSLATE.

תּוֹרָתוֹ, שְׂפָתָיו, בִּרְכָתָהּ, בָּנֶיהָ, מְשָׁלֵיכֶם, מְקוֹמָהּ, מִבְּשָׂרִי,

בְּשָׂרְכֶם, לְפָנַי, לְפָנֶיךָ, שְׂפָתֶיהָ, בָּנֵינוּ, לְבָבֵנוּ, בְּנֵיהֶם, יָדִי,

יָדוֹ, תּוֹרָתָם, יְדֵיהֶן:

יָצָא לוֹט אֶל־¹הָאֲנָשִׁים הַפֶּתְחָה וְהַדֶּלֶת סָגַר אַחֲרָיו: ² וְאֵהוּד

¹ *Pl. of* אִישׁ.

תָּקַע בַּשּׁוֹפָר בְּהַר [1]אֶפְרַיִם וּבְנֵי יִשְׂרָאֵל יָרְדוּ מִן־הָהָר וְהוּא
לִפְנֵיהֶם׃ 3 הוּא יהוה אֱלֹהֵינוּ בְּכָל־הָאָרֶץ מִשְׁפָּטָיו׃ 4 זָכַר
לְעוֹלָם בְּרִיתוֹ אֲשֶׁר כָּרַת אֶת־אַבְרָהָם׃ 5 חֶסֶד יהוה מֵעוֹלָם
וְעַד־עוֹלָם עַל־יְרֵאָיו וְצִדְקָתוֹ לִבְנֵי בָנִים׃ 6 וַאֲנִי עָלֶיךָ בָטַחְתִּי
יְהוָה אָמַרְתִּי אֱלֹהַי [2]אָתָּה׃ 7 מָה רַב טוּבְךָ אֲשֶׁר צָפַנְתָּ
לִירֵאֶיךָ [3]פָּעַלְתָּ לַבֹּטְחִים [2]בָּךְ נֶגֶד בְּנֵי אָדָם׃ 8 מָה אָהַבְתִּי
[4]תוֹרָתֶךָ כָּל־הַיּוֹם הִיא שִׂיחָתִי׃ 9 שָׁמַע יהוה אלהינו את־
תפלתנו׃ 10 ירד אל־בניו שאולה׃

Your blessings. Her corpse. My commandments. Her
lips. Thy words. His face; her face; my face. And his
words we heard out of the fire. Thy law (is) in my heart,
(O) my God. God has redeemed his holy (ones). Thou hast
heard my voice out of thy temple. We sat before her. The
words of thy (*f.*) lips (are) as the sand which (is) upon the
shore of the sea. He came and in his hand a sword. Very
good (are) the proverbs of his lips. We have sold our asses.
Ye (are) my sons and my daughters, saith (*perf.*) your God.
My heart (is) in his law continually. Thou hast kept their
heart. We have not kept the covenant of our God with all
our heart. The day of vengeance (is) in his heart. Ye have
kept my law and my commands. He lifted his corpse upon
the ass. Their hearts (are) fat. Thy perfect law. This
(is) flesh from my flesh. By (בְּ) all his great prophets.

§ 20. THE VERB.

1. *Root.*—The root of a verb is considered to be the *3rd
sing. masc. perf.* of the simple form (§ 13. 5), *e.g.* שָׁבַר *he
broke.* This form is called *Qal* (קַל) "light," in distinction
from all the other forms, which are heavy, being loaded by
additional inflectional letters, *e.g.* נִשְׁבַּר *he was broken*, or by
the duplication of a radical, *e.g.* שִׁבֵּר *be broke in pieces.*

[1] The sign ◌ known as *'Athnāḥ* indicates the chief pause within the
verse, as *Sillûq* ◌ indicates the last tone-syllable in the verse (cf. Gen. I. 1,
בְּרֵאשִׁית בָּרָא אֱלֹהִים אֵת הַשָּׁמַיִם וְאֵת הָאָרֶץ). The latter cannot be confused with *methegh*, which never stands on a tone-syllable (§ 10. 2).

[2] Pausal form. See § 10. 4 b.

[3] Relative unexpressed, as often in poetic style.   [4] See § 10. 4 c. i.

2. *Tenses.*—The verb has not *Tenses* strictly speaking.
It has two forms, which express not time but the quality
of an action as complete or incomplete; the one expresses
a finished action, and is called the *perfect*, the other an unfinished action, and is called the *imperfect*. It must be clearly
understood that these words are not used in the sense which
they bear, *e.g.* in English or in Latin grammar.

The perfect action includes all *past tenses* of other
languages, such as perfect, pluperfect, and future perf.
The imperfect includes all *imperfect tenses*, *e.g.* present
(especially of general truths), the classical imperfect, and
the future. The so-called *Tenses* will be dealt with more
fully in § 46. Suffice it here to say that Hebrew is not
so helpless in the expression of time as might be supposed.
As the perfect tense expresses completed action, it is the
natural tense to express the English past, *e.g.* רָדַף *he pursued*; and as the imperfect tense expresses incomplete action,
it is the natural tense to express the English future, *e.g.* יִרְדֹּף
he will pursue. It is wrong, however, to describe the tense
on this account as the *future*: this is at once to limit it
and to suggest a false point of view.

3. *Moods.*—The perfect and imperfect also do duty for
moods. Either may express the indicative: e.g. *he pursued*
= perf., *he will pursue* = impf. The subjunctive, optative,
&c., and, broadly, words implying potential or contingent
ideas, are generally expressed by the *imperfect* and its modifications (§ 23); *e.g.* of every tree *thou mayest eat*; hearken,
that *ye may live*; hasten, lest *thou be consumed; may he
judge! let us go!* This usage is thoroughly in accordance
with the fundamental idea of the impf.—incompletion—as
already explained. It might seem that this tense was
greatly overworked, and that its use would give rise to
endless obscurities and ambiguities: in point of fact, as
we shall see, this is rarely so.

Besides, there is an *imperative*, which is closely connected with the imperf.; two forms of *infinitive*, called
absolute and construct; and a *participle*.

4. *Degrees of the stem idea.*—The stem idea or meaning

of the verb is presented in *three* conditions or degrees ; the Simple (Qal), as *to eat* ; the Intensive, as *to eat much, often, greedily* ; and the extensive or Causative, extending the action over a second agent, as *to make to eat, to give one to eat.* These are formed by manipulating or adding to the radicals of the verb in a way which has no approximate analogy in English. It is as if the intensive idea of the verb "lament"—*to lament much, often, professionally*—were expressed by some such form as *limment*; and the causative idea, *to cause* some one *to lament*, were expressed by some such form as *hilmint.*

Each of these three conditions of the stem idea once appeared in three voices, Active, Passive, and middle or Reflexive, though some parts are now lost : only the intensive has all three. Thus :

Simple.	*Intensive.*	*Extensive* or *Causative.*
act.	act.	act.
—	pass.	pass.
reflexive	reflex.	—

5. *Conjugations.*—What are called in other languages conjugations, do not exist. The various classes of irregular or weak verbs most nearly correspond to conjugations ; but if the regular verbs be thoroughly learned, it will be found that the so-called irregular verbs follow naturally from them by the application of the fundamental rules of the language (§§ 3–10). The above seven parts are all growths of the original simple stem, which undergoes some modification, consonantal or vocalic or both (illustrated above by *lament*), to produce them.

6. *Inflection.*—Inflection to express person takes place by the connection of the significant parts of the personal pronoun with the stem (§ 12 and § 15. 3); and the third sing. as simplest is taken first, then the second, and finally the first. In an action which is finished, rather the action itself than the actor is prominent : hence in the perfect the stem is put before the personal designations. In the imperfect, or action going on, the actor is more prominent, and the personal modification is prefixed.

THE PERFECT.

	Sing.			*Plur.*	
3 *mas.*	קָטַל	he *killed*, &c.	3 *c.*	קָטְלוּ	they, &c.
3 *f.*	קָטְלָה	she „			
2 *m.*	קָטַלְתָּ	thou „	2 *m.*	קְטַלְתֶּם	ye
2 *f.*	קָטַלְתְּ	„	2 *f.*	קְטַלְתֶּן	„
1 *c.*	קָטַלְתִּי	I	1 *c.*	קָטַלְנוּ	we

7. Note carefully where the accent falls—usually on the טַל. The first syllable is pretonic and open, therefore has tone-long vowel, קָ (§ 6. 2 b), *e.g.* קָטַלְתִּי (not קְטַלְתִּי). The heavy terminations תֶּם, תֶּן, draw the accent upon them, so that the first vowel, being no longer pretonic and therefore tone-long, naturally vanishes into shᵉwa (§ 6. 2 c), *e.g.* קְטַלְתֶּם (not קָטַלְתֶּם).

8. It will be remembered that *nouns and adjs.* inflect thus: *m.* יָשָׁר, *f.* יְשָׁרה (§ 16. 3). *Verbs*, however, inflect thus: *m.* יָשַׁר, *f.* יָשְׁרה (cf. § 6. 2 f). In other words, in *verbal* inflection with vocalic additions—*e.g.* *â* of 3rd sing. fem. (הָ) or *û* of 3rd pl. (וּ)—the vowels *á ē ō*[1] in the tone-syllable become vocal shᵉwa, thus: *m.* קָטַל, *f.* קָטְלָה (not קָטָלָה), *m.* כָּבֵד, *f.* כָּבְדָה (not כָּבֵדה), *m.* יָכֹל, *f.* יָכְלָה. In the 3rd sing. fem. and the 3rd plur. the first vowel has methegh—קָטְלָה, קָטְלוּ, because the shᵉwa, representing as it does an original full vowel (*á*), is sounded (§ 6. 2 e, § 10. 2 b). This preserves the *a* sound: without methegh, the words would be *qotlâ, qotlû*. Naturally, if the third radical were a *bᵉghadhkᵉphath*, it would not take daghesh lene; *e.g.* כָּתְבָה *she wrote*, כָּתְבוּ *they wrote*.

9. *Uses of the perfect.*—The Perf. expresses:
    (a) The Aorist (Past), *he killed.*
    (b) The Perfect, *he has killed.*
    (c) The Pluperfect, *he had killed.*
    (d) The future Perfect, *he shall have killed.* (See § 46.)

10. אֵת or אֶת־, the sign of the accusative (§ 13. 7), when

---

[1] Most regular vbs. have their second vowel in *á*, many in *ē*, a few in *ō* (§ 22. 1).

used with the pronominal suffixes, appears as follows: אֹתִי
me, אֹתְךָ m. אֹתָךְ f. *thee*, אֹתוֹ *him*, אֹתָהּ *her*, אֹתָנוּ *us*, אֶתְכֶם m.
f. *you*, אֹתָם m. אֹתָן f. *them*.

The *scriptio plena* is also common: אוֹתִי, &c.

מְאוּמָה anything	אַחֲרִית *f.* latter end	שָׁכַח to forget
נָפַל to fall	עָף to fly	הֵן, הִנֵּה behold
פִּקּוּד statute	יוֹסֵף Joseph	מָכַר to sell
שָׂרַף to burn	שָׂרָף seraph	מֶלְקָחַיִם tongs
סָמַךְ to lean (*act.*)		כֹּפֶר ransom, bribe
עָשַׁק to oppress		שׁוֹר ox
זְקֵנָה *f.* } old age		זָבַח to sacrifice
זְקֵנִים *m. pl.* }		מִזְבֵּחַ altar
רִצְפָּה *f.* glowing stone, coal		כֹּהֵן priest

EXERCISE. TRANSLATE.

לֹא שָׁמַרְתָּ בְּרִיתִי: 2 לֹא שָׁמְרוּ תּוֹרָתֶךָ: 3 שָׁמַרְתִּי פִּקּוּדֶיךָ
בְּכָל־לִבִּי: 4 לֹא זָכְרָה אַחֲרִיתָהּ: 5 שָׁכְחוּ אֶת־אֱלֹהֵיהֶם:
6 אֶת־קוֹלְךָ שָׁמַעְנוּ מִן־הָאֵשׁ: 7 אֲנִי יוֹסֵף אֲשֶׁר־מְכַרְתֶּם אֹתִי
מִצְרָיְמָה: 8 לָמָּה נָפְלוּ פָנֶיךָ: 9 שָׁפְכוּ דָמִים כַּמָּיִם: 10 שְׂרַפְתֶּם
אֶת־הָעִיר בָּאֵשׁ: 11 רָאָה אֱלֹהִים אֶת־כָּל־אֲשֶׁר עָשָׂה וְהִנֵּה
טוֹב מְאֹד: 12 אָמַר שְׁמוּאֵל אֶל־הָעָם אֶת־שׁוֹר מִי לָקַחְתִּי
וַחֲמוֹר מִי לָקַחְתִּי וְאֶת־מִי עָשַׁקְתִּי וּמִיַּד מִי לָקַחְתִּי כֹפֶר:
וְכָל־הָעָם אָמַר לֹא עָשַׁקְתָּ אִישׁ וְלֹא לָקַחְתָּ מִיַּד אִישׁ מְאוּמָה:
13 עָף אֵלַי אֶחָד מִן ַהַשְּׂרָפִים וּבְיָדוֹ רִצְפָּה [1]בְּמֶלְקָחַיִם לָקַח
מֵעַל הַמִּזְבֵּחַ: 14 עמדה האשה לפני המלך: 15 שבת
אלהים ביום השביעי מהמלאכה אשר עשה:

Ye did not keep my words. The fire of God fell from
heaven. God set (gave) luminaries in the firmament of the
heavens. All the males fell before the sword. The heavens
of the heavens are God's (*dat.*), and the earth he has given
to the sons of man. Thou hast fallen, O (*art.*) city, in the
heart of the sea. I kept my tongue from evil words. These
(are) the proverbs of Solomon the wise king of Israel. We

----

[1] Relative unexpressed.

heard his voice from his temple. Their faces fell. We leant our hands upon her head. The blessing of Yahweh (be) upon thy children (sons). We sat by (עַל) the waters of the great rivers. Ye have burnt their city in the fire. She bare to her husband a son to his old age. They have forgotten my words and the proverbs of my lips.

§ 21. THE IMPERFECT, &c.

As in the perfect the pronouns were indicated at the end, so in the imperfect they are indicated, though not quite so obviously, at the beginning: *e.g.* א points to 1st pers. sing. (אֲנִי), נ to 1st plur., ת to 2nd sing., &c.

1. *Imperfect and Imperative.*

	Imperfect.		*Imperative.*
sing. 3 *m.*	יִקְטֹל	he *will, may*, &c., *kill, is, was, killing,* &c.	
3 *f.*	תִּקְטֹל	she ,, ,,	
2 *m.*	תִּקְטֹל	thou ,,	קְטֹל *kill* thou
2 *f.*	תִּקְטְלִי	thou ,,	קִטְלִי ,, ,,
1 *c.*	אֶקְטֹל	I ,,	
plur. 3 *m.*	יִקְטְלוּ	they ,,	
3 *f.*	תִּקְטֹלְנָה	they ,,	
2 *m.*	תִּקְטְלוּ	ye ,,	קִטְלוּ *kill* ye
2 *f.*	תִּקְטֹלְנָה	,, ,,	קְטֹלְנָה ,, ,,
1 *c.*	נִקְטֹל	we ,,	

Note carefully where the accent falls.

Note further that the first syllable is closed: in other words, the sh⁽e⁾wa is silent, consequently the second radical, if a *b⁽e⁾ghadhk⁽e⁾phath*, would take the dagh. lene; thus pf. כָּתַב *he wrote*, impf. יִכְתֹּב *yikhtōbh* (not יִכְתֹב).

(*a*) The original vowel in first syllable of impf. of active verbs appears to have been *a* (יַקְטֹל: cf. Arab. *yáqtulu*), which was later thinned to *i* (יִקְ: cf. דְּבָרִי for דְּבָרַי from *dabhâr*, § 2. 2. 4 and § 6. 2 d). This should be borne in mind, as the *a* reappears in certain forms of guttural and other verbs to be dealt with afterwards (§§ 34, 40, 42).

(b) The termination of the 2nd *plu.* and 3rd *plu.* sometimes appears as ן (יִקְטְלוּן), which always bears the tone.

(c) Note that the imperative is identical with the impf. except that it drops the pronominal prefixes: thus קְטֹל(תִּ). Obviously in the imperative the sh⁰wa is sounded; hence, in spite of יִכְתֹּב, the imper. is כְּתֹב (כְּתֹב is an impossible form, § 7. 4).

(d) The first syllable of imper. קִטְלִי *f. s.* קִטְלוּ *m. pl.* is half open; in other words the sh⁰wa is vocal, as it represents an original vowel (*ŏ*), § 6. 2 c; therefore כִּתְבוּ not כְּתְבוּ.

2. *The Infinitive.*—

Inf. cstr. קְטֹל *to kill* (admitting prepositions before it and pronominal suffixes).

Inf. abs. קָטוֹל (also קָטֹל) *to kill* (admitting neither prefix nor suffix).

(a) i. The inf. cstr. is the same as the 2nd sing. imperative. It corresponds roughly to English verbal nouns in -*ing*; e.g. עֵת סְפֹד a time *of* (i.e. *for*) *mourning*, a time *to mourn*.

ii. It is used very frequently with the preposition לְ (much like our *to* before inf.) : (i.) after such verbs as *begin, continue, cease*, &c.: e.g. חָדַל לִסְפֹּר he ceased *to count* (occasionally in such cases without לְ), and (ii.) to indicate purpose: e.g. I have come *to sacrifice* (לִזְבֹּחַ) to Yahweh. This לְ joins so closely with the inf. that the first syllable is closed; hence לִכְתֹּב *to write*, not לְכְתֹב. (Contrast § 14. 1 b.)

iii. It is used *very frequently* with pronom. suffixes; e.g. בְּכָתְבוֹ[1] (*b⁰khoth⁰bhô*) *in his writing*, i.e. when he wrote.

(b) To the absol. inf. nothing can be prefixed or added: it stands alone (לִקְטוֹל or קְטוֹלִי would be impossible), and it has the effect of throwing up prominently the bare idea of the verb. Usually it is accompanied by a finite verb. (i.) When placed before the verb, it strengthens it: שָׁמוֹר שָׁמַרְתִּי מִצְוֹתָיו (*keeping I kept*: i.e.) *I earnestly kept his commandments*. It is often rendered by an English adverb, such as "surely, utterly," e.g. he will *surely* visit, פָּקֹד יִפְקֹד ;

---

[1] The change which the cstr. inf. undergoes with pronom. suffixes will be explained in § 29. 2, § 31. 3 c

thou wilt *certainly* be king, מָלֹךְ תִּמְלֹךְ ; I will *utterly* (inf. abs.) destroy (impf.).   (ii.) When placed after the verb it usually suggests continuance ; *e.g.* שִׁמְעוּ שָׁמוֹעַ *hear ye continually*.

Etymologically the cstr. inf. is not related to the absol. as דְּבַר to דָּבָר ; the two forms are of independent origin.

3. *The Participle.*—

Act. Part. m. s.   קוֹטֵל or קֹטֵל *killing*, i.e. *one who kills*

    f. s. קֹטְלָה or (more often) קֹטֶלֶת[1]

    m. pl. קֹטְלִים   *f. pl.* קֹטְלוֹת

Pass. Part. m. s. קָטוּל *killed*, i.e. *one who is* or *has been killed*

    f. s. קְטוּלָה

    m. pl. קְטוּלִים   *f. pl.* קְטוּלוֹת

(a) The shᵉwa in fem. and pl. of act. ptc. is vocalic, *qô-ṭᵉ-lâ, -lîm*, as it represents an original full vowel.   The *ḥôlem* is unchangeable, whether written with or without *waw*.

The act. partic. denotes continuous action ; *e.g.* הוּא יֹשֵׁב *he is, was sitting* (not *he sat*).

(b) Of the *passive* voice there are few remaining traces besides the participle.[2]

Uses of the Imperfect.—The Impf. expresses :

(*a*) The Present, *he kills* (especially of general truths ; *e.g.* a bribe *blindeth* (impf.) the clear-sighted.   Ex. **23**. 8.

(*b*) The Imperfect, *he killed* (particularly of repeated past acts, i.e. *used to kill* : Latin or Greek impf.) ; *e.g.* a mist *used to go up*, Gen. **2**. 6.

(*c*) The Future, *he will kill.*

(*d*) The Potential, *he may* or *can kill, might, could, would,* &c., kill.   (See § 46.)

---

[1] When the *fem. ptc.* has the force of a substantive, it tends to retain the long *ē* of the masc. ; *e.g.* יֹלֵדָה *a woman in travail* (יָלַד *to bear*).

[2] For other traces see § 33. 3 c.

שָׁפַט to judge	גָּנַב to steal	כָּרַת to cut
שֹׁפֵט (*ptc.*) judge	שָׁמַר to watch	אִיזֶבֶל Jezebel
שָׁבַר to buy (grain)	שֹׁמֵר (*ptc.*) watchman	דְּבוֹרָה Deborah
מֵת dead	רָדַף to pursue	תֹּמֶר a palm tree
קָבַר to bury	אָכַל to eat	אֲבִימֶלֶךְ Abimelech
קֶבֶר grave	אֹכֶל food	עוֹד still, yet,
שָׁכַן to dwell	בַּעַל lord, husband, Baal	again
אֱמֶת *f.* faithfulness, truth	בָּעַל to marry, rule over	
אַרְבַּע four	מֵאָה *f.* hundred	שֻׁלְחָן table
דָּרַשׁ to seek	עֵת *f.* time	דָּבַר[1] to speak
קָבַץ to gather	עַל on account of	הָלַךְ to go

EXERCISE. TRANSLATE AND PARSE.

אֶשְׁמֹר, לִשְׁמֹר, שְׁמָרוּ, שְׁמֹר, תִּשְׁמֹר, יִשְׁמְרוּ, נִשְׁמֹר, גְּנוּבִים,
גָּנוּב, תִּפְקֹדוּ, תִּזְכְּרִי, זְכֹר, כְּרֵתִים, דֹּרְשֵׁי, רֹמֶשֶׂת, תִּשְׁמֹרְנָה:
לֹא תִגְנֹב: 2 לֹא תִשְׁמְרוּ אֶת־מִשְׁפָּטֵיהֶם: 3 אֲנַחְנוּ נִכְרֹת עֵצִים
מִן־הָהָר: 4 רָדְפוּ אַחֲרָיו: 5 אָמַרְתִּי לִשְׁמֹר דְּבָרֶיךָ: 6 מִשְׁלֵי
הָעָם הַזֶּה: 7 מִי יִשְׁכֹּן בְּהַר יהוה: הוֹלֵךְ תָּמִים וּפֹעֵל צֶדֶק
וְדֹבֵר אֱמֶת בִּלְבָבוֹ: 8 בָּא יוֹסֵף מֵאֶרֶץ מִצְרַיִם לִקְבֹּר אֶת־
יַעֲקֹב: 9 קָבְרוּ אֶת־נִבְלַת הַנָּבִיא הַזָּקֵן בַּקֶּבֶר אֲשֶׁר אִישׁ
הָאֱלֹהִים קָבוּר שָׁם: 10 יָרְדוּ בְּנֵי יַעֲקֹב מִצְרַיְמָה[2] לִשְׁבָּר־אֹכֶל:
11 וְעַתָּה קְבֹץ אֵלַי אֶת־כָּל־יִשְׂרָאֵל אֶל־הַר הַכַּרְמֶל וְאֶת־נְבִיאֵי
הַבַּעַל אַרְבַּע מֵאוֹת אֹכְלֵי שֻׁלְחָן אִיזָבֶל: 12 וּדְבוֹרָה אִשָּׁה
נְבִיאָה הִיא שֹׁפְטָה אֶת־יִשְׂרָאֵל בָּעֵת הַהִיא: וְהִיא יוֹשֶׁבֶת
תַּחַת־תֹּמֶר דְּבוֹרָה בְּהַר אֶפְרָיִם: 13 אָמַר אֱלֹהִים אֶל־אֲבִימֶלֶךְ
בַּחֲלוֹם הַלַּיְלָה הִנֵּה אַתָּה מֵת עַל־הָאִשָּׁה אֲשֶׁר לָקַחְתָּ וְהִיא
בְּעֻלַת בָּעַל: 14 אֹיְבֶיךָ לֹא יִרְדְּפוּ עוֹד אַחֲרֶיךָ: 15 בַּיּוֹם
הַהוּא אֶשְׁפֹּךְ אֶת־רוּחִי עַל־כָּל־בָּשָׂר:

I will pursue after her. I promised (said) to pursue after
them. Pursue after him. He set the stars in the firmament
of the heavens to rule over the night. Yahweh will judge
this people. A city shedding blood like water. Keep thy
tongue from evil. Ye shall keep the commandments of your
God with all your heart. They left off counting the proverbs

[1] In Qal used only in *act. ptc.*   [2] See § 10. 3 a.

of his lips, for they (were) as the sand which (is) upon the shore of the sea. His commandments and his words will we keep. His children (sons) will keep his covenant. Hands shedding blood. But I would seek unto God. He came to shed blood. We will burn your city with (in the) fire. Bury my corpse in the grave where the prophets (are) buried (*ptc.*).

§ 22. THE VERB ACTIVE AND STATIVE (TRANSITIVE AND INTRANSITIVE).

(See Paradigm of Regular Verb, p. 208.)

1. (a) The perf. Qal may end in any of the three vowels *á e ō*, *e.g.* קָטַל, כָּבֵד, קָטֹן, *á* taking the place of *ā* (§ 6. 2 f). Verbs are named according to these vowels *a, e* and *o* verbs. Verbs ending in *a* are transitive, verbs in *e* and *o* are intransitive, though these terms in Hebrew do not quite correspond to the same terms in the Western languages. The class of intransitive verbs is very wide, embracing words that describe the *condition* of the subject (as מָלֵא *to be full*, צָמֵא *to thirst*, יָרֵא *to fear*, אָהֵב *to love*), even though capable of taking an object after them. The term *Stative* verbs, *i.e.* verbs of *state*, is used by some grammarians. The state they describe may be either physical (גָּדַל *to be great*, זָקֵן *to be old*) or mental (שָׂמֵחַ *to rejoice*, שָׂנֵא *to hate*). But stative is not altogether synonymous with intransitive; not all intransitive verbs are stative; *e.g.* מָלַךְ *to reign*, nor are all stative verbs intransitive; *e.g.* לָבֵשׁ *to put on* (clothes), אָהֵב *to love*, חָצֵב *to hew, cleave*—actions in which the reflex influence of the action upon the subject is very prominent.

(b) In the perfect, vbs. in *ē* are inflected exactly like vbs. in *a*; *e.g.* קָטַלְתָּ, כָּבַדְתָּ. Vbs. in *ō*, which are very few, retain the *ō* in the accented shut syllable, *e.g.* קָטֹנְתָּ *qāṭóntā* (§ 5. 3 a), but naturally change it to *o* in the 2nd plur. where the second syllable is unaccented (§ 20. 7), *e.g.* קְטָנְתֶּם *q^etontém.*

2. *Formation of Impf.*—The Perf. in *á* (Active verb) gives the Impf. in *ō*, קָטַל, יִקְטֹל (originally יַקְטֹל, cf. § 21. 1 a); the Perf. in *ē* or *ō* (Stative verb) gives the Impf. in *á* כָּבֵד, יִכְבַּד (this too—*yi* in 1st syllable, not *ya*—is the *orig.* form in stat. vbs.), קָטֹן, יִקְטַן. Very rarely the impf. of a stat. vb. may be in *ō*; נָבֵל *to wither*, יִבֹּל; שָׁכַן (in pause שָׁכֵן) *to dwell*, יִשְׁכֹּן.

3. *Formation of Imper. and Inf. Cstr.*—As in Active vbs. the imperat. of Stative vbs. agrees with the impf., e.g. כְּבַד, כְּבַד יִכְבַּד; but the infin. cstr. of Stative vbs. is generally in ō (not a); e.g. קְרֹב, שְׂנֹא. Sometimes the inf. cstr. has a fem. ending of the type יִרְאָה from יָרֵא; e.g. לְיִרְאָה אֶת־יְהוה to fear Yahweh. Other rarer forms occur.

4. *Form of the Participle.*—The Active verb has the Ptc. of the form קֹטֵל; the Ptc. of the Stative verb is the same as the Perfect, קָרֵב *drawing near*, which is strictly a verbal adj. rather than a partic. The ô of act. ptc. is unchangeable, the ā of stat. is only tone-long, therefore changeable: כָּבֵד, f. כְּבֵדָה. These verbal adjectives frequently retain their ֵ in the cstr. plur.; e.g. שְׂמֵחֵי (as well as שִׂמְחֵי) from שָׂמֵחַ *rejoicing*. The cstr. pl. of יָרֵא *fearing*, is always יִרְאֵי; e.g. יִרְאֵי יהוה *those who fear Y.*

5. Of statives in ē, which are numerous, only a few have ē invariably, á frequently occurring instead; e.g. קָרֵב and קָרַב *to draw near.*

6. The perfect of Stative verbs usually corresponds to the English present; e.g. זָקַנְתִּי *I am old*, יָכֹלְתִּי *I am able*, יָדַעְתִּי *I know* (cf. Lat. *novi*). This use of the perf. is found with other verbs denoting affections or states of the mind: בָּטַחְתִּי *I trust* (have set my confidence), זָכַרְתִּי *I remember, memini*, μέμνημαι. The condition or state is regarded as the abiding result of a past experience.

גָּדַל	To be great / become great
יָכֹל	to be able
מָתֹק	to be sweet
עָמֹק	to be deep / „ deep

קָדֵשׁ	to be holy	יָרֵא	to fear	קָטֹן	to be little
קָדוֹשׁ	holy	„	fearing	„	little
זָקֵן	to be old	קָרֵב	to draw near	שָׁמַע	to hear
צָדֵק	to be just	לָמַד	to learn	רָעֵב	to be hungry
חָפֵץ	to delight in	שָׂבֵע (שָׂבַע)	to be sated (*acc.*)		
		מָלֵא	to be full (*acc.*)		

6

לֶחֶם bread   עוֹלָה *f.* burnt-offering

זֵכֶר remembrance, memorial   רָקֵב to rot

רִנָּה *f.* ringing cry   נְעוּרִים *pl.* (time of) youth

חַיִּים *pl.* life   מַחֲשָׁבָה *f.* (*cstr. pl.* מַחְ׳) thought

EXERCISE. PARSE AND TRANSLATE.

תִּשְׁפַּלְנָה, קָטֹנְתִּי, תִּקְטַן, יְכֻלֶּה, יְכָלְתֶם, אֶשְׂכַּל, לְבָשִׁי, נִכְבַּד, תִּכְבְּדִי, אֶגְדַּל, רָעֵבוּ:
קוֹל שׁוֹפָר לֹא נִשְׁמַע וְלַלֶּחֶם לֹא נִרְעָב: 2 לֹא יָכֹלְתָּ לִסְפֹּר הַכּוֹכָבִים: 3 יִגְדַּל שֵׁם יהוה עַד עוֹלָם: 4 קְרַב וּשְׁמַע אֶת־כָּל־הַדְּבָרִים אֲשֶׁר אָנֹכִי דֹבֵר אֵלֶיךָ: 5 עַתָּה יָדַעְתִּי כִּי יְרֵא אֱלֹהִים אָתָּה: 6 יהוה אֱלֹהַי גָּדַלְתָּ מְאֹד: 7 זֵכֶר צַדִּיק לִבְרָכָה וְשֵׁם רְשָׁעִים יִרְקָב: 8 קָרוֹב אַתָּה יהוה וְכָל־מִצְוֹתֶיךָ אֱמֶת תִּקְרַב רִנָּתִי לְפָנֶיךָ: 9 לְעֵת זִקְנַת שְׁלֹמֹה לֹא הָיָה לְבָבוֹ שָׁלֵם עִם־יהוה אֱלֹהָיו כְּלֵבַב דָּוִיד: 10 יִקְרָא הַמֶּלֶךְ בְּסֵפֶר הַתּוֹרָה כָּל־יְמֵי חַיָּיו לְמַעַן יִלְמַד לְיִרְאָה אֶת־יהוה אֱלֹהָיו: 11 לֹא יִצְדַּק לְפָנֶיךָ כָל־בָּשָׂר: 12 קדוש אתה יהוה מלאה כל־הארץ כבודך: 13 שבעתי עולות ודם פרים לא חפצתי:

I cannot draw near. I will be great. Draw near. The God who made the heavens and the earth I (am) fearing. Ye cannot keep my statutes with (בְּ) all your heart. Thou art little. Hear in order that thou mayest learn to fear Yahweh thy God. They are not able to pursue after me. I am bereaved. I know that thou shalt assuredly reign. Cease to draw near before me, for your hands are full of blood (*pl.*). How great art thou (O) my God, very deep are thy thoughts.

§ 23. JUSSIVE. COHORTATIVE. WAW CONSECUTIVE.

1. Besides the ordinary imperfect, which expresses the action simply, there are certain modifications of it which indicate the relation of the action to the speaker's will or feelings. The speaker may throw his own feeling into the word in two ways, either by a sharp, hasty utterance of it, thus expressing peremptory *wish*; or, on the contrary, by a

lengthening out of the word, giving expression to the *direction* of the mind or action. The short form that arises in the first way is called the *Jussive*, the other or lengthened form has been named the *Cohortative*.

(1) *The Jussive.*—The Jussive, which aimed at being as abrupt and brief as possible, arises through a contraction of the last syll. of the impf.; but the laws of the tone and of the formation of syllables usually make an actual shortening of the imperfect form impossible; *e.g.* יִקְטֹל *yiqṭōl*, could not, even in the interest of abruptness, become יִקְטָל *yiqṭol*, for that would violate the principle laid down in § 5. 1 b; it must therefore remain יִקְטֹל *yiqṭōl*. Consequently, in all parts of the regular verb except the *Hiph'il* (§ 27. 1 a: impf. יַקְטִיל, jussive יַקְטֵל—short *i* of an ultimate *yáqṭil*[1] lengthened to tone-long *ē*), *the Jussive coincides with the ordinary impf.*; and in all forms with inflectional terminations the juss. and ordinary impf. coincide. *The Jussive is found only in 2nd and 3rd persons.*

The Jussive (as the name implies) expresses *a command*, as יִקְטֹל *let him kill* (thus taking the place of the non-existent 3rd pers. imperative); or, less strongly, *an entreaty, request,* &c.—*may he kill*; or, with a negative, *a dissuasion*, as אַל־תִּקְטְלוּ *do not* (ye) *kill*.

Note (i.) that the imperative is used only for commands, *not for prohibitions*—these require the jussive (= impf.); e.g. *kill,* קְטֹל, but *do not kill,* אַל־תִּקְטְלוּ (not אַל־קְטֹלוּ).

(ii.) The regular negative with prohibitions is אַל; *e.g.* אַל־תִּקְטְלוּ, not לֹא תִקְטְלוּ. But לֹא can be used of a very emphatic, and especially of a divine, prohibition, exactly like our *thou shalt not*; *e.g.* לֹא תִגְנֹב *thou shalt not steal.*

(2) *The Cohortative.*—The Cohortative is formed by adding the syllable הָ *â* to the impf. As before ו of the plur., so before cohortative הָ, the vowel of the 2nd syllable becomes sh'wa; as יִקְטְלוּ, so אֶקְטְלָה (from אֶקְטֹל). *The Cohort. is found* (with rare exceptions) *in 1st pers. only*—sing. and plur.

The Cohort. expresses the direction of the will towards an action, consequently *desire, intention, self-encouragement,* or (in 1st plur.) *exhortation*: אֶשְׁמְרָה *let me keep, I would keep,*

---

[1] Cf. Arabic impf. *yúqtilu*, jussive *yúqtil.*

I will keep (but more emotional than the simple אֶשְׁמֹר),
נִשְׁמְרָה *let us keep*, &c.

2. *The Emphatic Imperative.*—The same termination
ה ָ *â* is added to the imper. 2 *m. s.* to give it emphasis, as
קָטְלָה *Oh kill!* qoṭ'lâ (half open, from q'ṭōl);[1] a form of the
type קִטְלָה qiṭ'lâ also occurs, but chiefly in verbs whose impf.
and consequently imperative end in *a*; *e.g.* impf. יִשְׁמַע, imper.
שְׁמַע *hear*, and שִׁמְעָה. This Emph. Imper. appears chiefly in
the irregular verb; *e.g.* קוּמָה *arise* (from קוּם)—frequently with
no appreciable emphasis.

3. *Waw Consecutive.*—The conjunction ו *and* is very frequently used not as a mere copulative to join or co-ordinate
clauses, but with a certain subordinating power, so as to
indicate that what is now added is the *result* or sequence
of the preceding: as, *he spake* and (and so, and thus, then)
it was done.

The usage is this:

After a simple *perfect* events conceived as following upon
this perf. are expressed by *waw* joined with the *imperfect*;
and conversely, after a simple *imperfect* the events conceived
as following on it are expressed by *waw* with the *perfect*.

But it must not be said or supposed—as was implied by
the old name *waw conversive*—that the *waw* really converts
the one tense into the other: that is impossible. Various
explanations of this curious phenomenon have been offered,
but none will be probable which contradicts the fundamental
character of the pf. and impf. as already explained (cf. § 46).

(1) (a) All the verbs following a perfect are put in the impf.
if they are immediately preceded by waw; but if any word,
however small (*e.g.* a pronoun, הוּא, or a negative, לֹא) intervene, then the construction reverts to the proper and natural
tense: *e.g.* In the beginning God *created* (pf., בָּרָא) the earth,
and the earth *was* (ו with *impf.*) without form, and God *said*
(ו with impf.), and so on with imperfects. But if the connection between waw and the verb is *in any way* broken, the
pf. is naturally and necessarily used. Hebrew says therefore
either *and-said* (*waw* impf.) *God*, or *and God said* (pf.).

(b) *Waw consecutive* with the imperf. is pointed *exactly*

[1] This form cannot be fully understood till §§ 29, 31 are reached.

like the Article (§ 11); *e.g.* וַיִּקְטֹל *and he killed,* וָאֶקְטֹל *and I killed,* וַנִּקְטֹל *and we killed.* Examples of usage:

He found the place and lay down   מָצָא אֶת־הַמָּקוֹם וַיִּשְׁכַּב

       „   *and did not lie down*   וְלֹא שָׁכַב   „

and the man lay down   וַיִּשְׁכַּב הָאִישׁ, וְהָאִישׁ שָׁכַב

(2) (a) Similarly all the verbs following an impf. are put in the pf. *if they are immediately preceded by waw,* cf. 1 Sam. 19. 3, אֵצֵא וְעָמַדְתִּי *I will go out and stand*; but if the connection is in any way broken, the imperfect reappears. *E.g.* In that day *I will raise up* (impf.) the tabernacle of David, and *close up* (וֹ with pf.) the breaches thereof, and-its-ruins *I will raise up* (impf.) and *I will build it* (וֹ with pf.) as in the days of old. (Am. 9. 11.) Cf. Ezek. 11. 20.

(b) *Waw consecutive* with the perf. is pointed exactly like *waw* copulative (§ 15); וְקָטַל *and he will kill,* וּקְטַלְתֶּם *and ye will kill,* וּמָרָה *and he will rebel.* Examples of usage:

he will find the place and lie down   יִמְצָא אֶת־הַמָּקוֹם וְשָׁכַב

       „   *and will not lie down*   וְלֹא יִשְׁכַּב   „

So completely does this construction with *waw consecutive* pervade the language that it may be employed even when no simple tense actually precedes: a book may even begin with it (cf. Ruth, Esther, Jonah).

(3) To summarize: *and* with English *past* tenses in continuous narrative is usually *waw* consec. *impf.* following an initial (expressed or implied) perfect: *and* with English *future* tenses is usually *waw* consec. *perf.* following an initial (expressed or implied) impf. *E.g.* (a) God was (הָיָה) with me and kept (וַיִּשְׁמֹר) me, and gave (וַיִּתֶּן) me bread. (b) God will be (יִהְיֶה) with me and keep (וְשָׁמַר) me and give (וְנָתַן) me bread. In translating into Hebrew, the choice of the first verb as pf. or impf. is scrupulously determined by the nature of the idea to be expressed (*e.g.* Eng. *past* usually by Hebr. pf., and Eng. *fut.* by Hebr. impf.), and all the subsequent verbs are expressed by waw consec. with the *other* tense.

(4) It is important to note that the Tone in the impf. with waw consec. is usually retracted from the last syll. to the *penult*, when this syll. is open (cf. § 5. 1 b), as וַיֵּשֶׁב *and he dwelt,* וַיֹּאמֶר *and he said*; while in the perfect the Tone is usually thrown forward—in the 1st and 2nd *sing.* regularly,

but not in 1st *pl.*—from the penult to the last syllable: וְקָטַלְתִּי *and I shall kill*, וְקָטַלְתָּ (note the *methegh* in what is now 2nd place from tone, § 10. 2 a), but וּקְטַלְנוּ.

The drawing backward of the Tone in *waw consec. impf.* very well suggests its connection with what precedes, and the throwing of it forward in *waw consec. perf.* suggests its connection with what follows.

(5) (a) Waw consec. with impf. may follow not only an actual perf. but an expression equivalent to a perf.: *e.g.* in the year of king Uzziah's death *I saw* וָאֶרְאֶה (= *and-I-saw*, impf. after an implied pf.—Uzziah *died*).

(b) Similarly waw consec. with pf. may follow not only an actual impf. but its equivalent, e.g. *a participle*, thus: Behold, I am about to raise up (*ptc.* מֵקִים) a nation, *and they shall oppress* you (וְלָחֲצוּ)—or an *imperative*, וְאָמַרְתָּ לֵךְ *go and say*.

(6) Final clauses, *i.e.* those indicating the purpose or design of a preceding act, may be expressed by *simple waw* (*not* waw consec.) and impf.—or to be more correct, jussive or cohortative, e.g. *Draw near that I may judge* קְרַב וְאִשְׁפְּטָה. *Serve him that he may deliver you* עָבְדֵהוּ וְיַצֵּל אֶתְכֶם (נצל Hiph.). That is, Hebrew simply places the facts side by side, *Draw nigh and I will judge.* It may, of course, also use (with the impf.) the final particle לְמַעַן *in order that*—which may or may not be followed by אֲשֶׁר; *e.g.* I will do marvellous things, *in order that thou mayst know* that there is none like me לְמַעַן (אֲשֶׁר) תֵּדַע.

(7) Two verbs of which the meaning is synonymous or the action contemporaneous are sometimes joined by *simple waw* rather than by waw consec. ; *e.g.* אֲנִי זָקַנְתִּי וְשַׂבְתִּי *As for me I am old and* (וְ pretonic, § 15. 1 d) *greyheaded*, כָּשְׁלוּ וְנָפָלוּ *they have stumbled and fallen.*

גָּדַל	*st.* to grow up	שָׂרַף	to burn	בְּכֹרָה	*f.* birthright
גָּוַע	*st.* to expire	פָּקַד	to visit	שָׂרָה	Sarah
קָצַף	to be angry	חֵת	Heth	עָמַד	to stand
לָכַד	to take (capture)	בְּנֵי־חֵת	the Hittites	מוֹאָב	Moab
מָכַר	to sell	הֲלֹם	hither	חָיָה	to live
רָמַשׂ	to creep	גָּבַר	to be strong, prevail	עֵגֶל	calf
שָׁלַח	to send, stretch out (the hand)			קֹדֶשׁ	holiness
עוֹף	(*coll.*) flying creatures, fowls, birds.			מְעָרָה	*f.* cave
בֵּין	between (*p.* 190)	פֶּן־	(§ 10. 3 b) lest	עֵד	witness

מַעֲלָל deed, practice (only in *plur.*, and usually in bad sense), כְּ ... כְּ (also כֵּן ... כְּ) *as ... so.*   Usually with כְּ ... כְּ the first term is the subject and the second the standard with which it is compared ; *e.g.* וְהָיָה כַצַּדִּיק כָּרָשָׁע and the righteous shall be as the wicked ; כַּגֵּר כָּאֶזְרָח the sojourner as the home-born ; כָּמוֹךָ כְּפַרְעֹה [1] thou art as Pharaoh.

EXERCISE.   TRANSLATE.

אֶשְׁמְרָה תוֹרָתְךָ תָמִיד: 2 נִכְרַתָה בְרִית אֲנִי וְאַתָּה וְהָיָה לְעֵד בֵּינִי וּבֵינֶךָ: 3 אָמַר אַבְרָהָם אֶל־בְּנֵי חֵת מִכְרוּ לִי קֶבֶר וְאֶקְבְּרָה מֵתִי מִלְפָנָי: 4 אַל־תִּתְקֹצַף יהוה עַד־מְאֹד: 5 אַל־תִּקְרַב הֲלֹם כִּי הַמָּקוֹם [2] אֲשֶׁר אַתָּה עוֹמֵד עָלָיו אַדְמַת קֹדֶשׁ הוּא: 6 אָמַר יַעֲקֹב אֶל־עֵשָׂו מִכְרָה [3] כַיּוֹם אֶת־בְּכֹרָתְךָ לִי וַיִּמְכֹּר לוֹ אֶת־בְּכֹרָתוֹ: 7 אָמַר יהוה הֵן הָאָדָם הָיָה כְּאַלֹהִים יֹדֵעַ טוֹב וָרָע וְעַתָּה פֶּן־ [4] יִשְׁלַח יָדוֹ וְלָקַח מֵעֵץ הַחַיִּים וְאָכַל וָחַי לְעוֹלָם: 8 וְהַמַּיִם גָּבְרוּ מְאֹד מְאֹד עַל־הָאָרֶץ וַיִּגְוַע כָּל־בָּשָׂר הָרֹמֵשׂ עַל־הָאָרֶץ בָּעוֹף וּבַבְּהֵמָה וְכֹל הָאָדָם: 9 וְהָיָה כָעָם כַּכֹּהֵן וּפָקַדְתִּי עָלָיו מֵעֲלָלָיו: וְאָכְלוּ וְלֹא יִשְׂבָּעוּ כִּי אֶת־יהוה עָזָבוּ: 10 נקרבה אל־יהוה וישפט ביני ובינך: 11 וישכחו בני־ישראל את־יהוה אלהיהם וימכר אותם ביד מלך מואב:

Thou shalt not lie down in that place.   Let me lie down. Do not (ye) draw near.   May Yahweh judge between me and (between) this people.   Hear my prayer (O) our God.

[1] The word כְּ *as, like,* uses the poetic form כְּמוֹ as the base for *light* suffixes, with which the accent is on the penult, with pretonic *ā* ; and the base כְּ for *heavy* suff., with which the accent is on the last syll., with pretonic *ā*.   Thus : כָּהֶם, כָּכֶם, כָּמֹנוּ, כָּמֹוֹהוּ, כָּמֹוֹהָ, כָּמוֹךָ, כָּמֹוֹךְ, כָּמֹוֹנִי.

[2] אֲשֶׁר ... עָלָיו =*on which* (cf. § 13. 2 a).

[3] = at (about) to-day, *i.e.* now, at once, first of all.

[4] Impf. of שׁלח.

[5] חַי pf. Qal of חָיַי, the ultimate form of חָיָה *to live* (cf. סב, סָבַב, § 42) ; and for change of ultimate ִי_ into ָה, see § 44.   The word cannot be completely understood till these later paragraphs are reached.   The *waw* has ָ, because it is in pretone, § 15. 1 d.

Sell to me this cave that I may bury my dead there. The man ate of the tree which (was) in the garden and God was very angry. And the calf I took and burnt it[1] with (in the) fire. Thus saith (*perf.*) Yahweh: Behold I will-give (*ptc.*) this city into the hand of the king of Bābel, and he will burn it[1] with fire. Sarah bare to her husband a son, and the boy grew up. And God called the light (*dat.*) day and the darkness he called night. And thou shalt keep his law continually. And I remembered his words. And it shall be, like prophet, like priest.

§ 24. SCHEME OF THE REGULAR VERB.

	simple.	*intens.*	*caus.*	*simp.*	*intens.*	*caus.*
act.	qal	pi'ēl	hiph'il	פָּעַל	פִּעֵל	הִפְעִיל
pass.	—	pu'al	hoph'al	—	פֻּעַל	הָפְעַל
refl.	niph'al	hithpa'ēl	—	נִפְעַל	הִתְפַּעֵל	—
				קָטַל	קִטֵּל	הִקְטִיל
				—	קֻטַּל	הָקְטַל
				נִקְטַל	הִתְקַטֵּל	—

1. The names *simple, intensive,* &c., have been explained § 20. 4.

2. The word פָּעַל *to do,* formed the paradigm of the original grammarians. Now the language, possessing no general terms like *reflexive, intensive act.,* and such like, made use of the parts of *this* verb that were *simple reflex., intens. act.* and the like, as names for the same parts in all verbs. Thus the *intens. act.* of פָּעַל *Pā'al* is פִּעֵל *Pi'ēl*; hence instead of speaking of the *intens. act.* of a verb we speak of its *Pi'ēl*: the *caus. act.* of פָּעַל is הִפְעִיל *Hiph'îl*; hence instead of speaking of the *caus. act.* of a vb. we speak of its *Hiph'îl*, &c.;— much as if, taking *amare* as the paradigm Latin verb, we should describe *monebo* as the *amabo* of *monere*, or *rexi* as the *amavi* of *regere*.

The *simple* form of the vb., however, is always called the *Qal*, not the *Pā'al*.

The use of פָּעַל as a Paradigm is unfortunate, because, its

<hr>

[1] אֵת with suffix, § 20. 10.

second radical being a guttural, the characteristics of several of the parts, such as the intensive, which duplicates the middle radical, are obscured; פִּעֵל necessarily fails to indicate this duplication, which is obvious, *e.g.*, in such a word as קִטֵּל. Hence the word קַטֵל (though poetical and defective) is generally used in modern grammars.[1]

3. "Intensive" means that which is increased *within*, and to express intensity the middle radical of the verb is doubled; *e.g.* קִטֵּל. "Extensive" or causative means what is increased *without*; and to express the causative a syllable is attached to the outside; *e.g.* הִקְטִיל.

4. Very few verbs are used in all these parts—only six, it is said, out of about fourteen hundred; but they must all be equally familiar to the student, because, with many verbs, the intensive or the causative forms are as frequent as, or more frequent than, the *Qal*, and are sometimes even the only form in use: *e.g.* נִסָּה, intensive, *to try, test*; הִשְׁלִיךְ, causative, *to cast*. But these forms are modelled exactly on the *Qal*; so that when the *Qal*, in its pf., impf., imper., inf., and ptc., is thoroughly understood, the other forms put no additional strain on the memory. Hence the importance of knowing the *Qal*.

WORDS FOR PRACTICE ON THE ABOVE SCHEME.

כתב to write	גדל to be great	כבד to be heavy	גנב to steal
מׁשׁל to rule	רדף to pursue	מלך to govern	פקד to visit
מכר to sell	לכד to capture	דבר to speak	קדׁש be holy

§ 25. THE SIMPLE REFLEXIVE OR *NIPH‘AL.*
(See Paradigm, p. 208.)

1. The characteristic letter of the Niph‘al is *n*. In the perf. *ni* (probably orig. *na*) is prefixed to the stem—thus נִקְטַל; and the first syllable is closed (נִׁשְׁבַּר); in the impf. the prefix is *yin*, the *n* of which naturally assimilates with

---

[1] The learner must not use קַטֵל in Prose composition for "kill." The word is rare in Heb., and in use only in Poetry. Its prose equivalent is הָרַג (*slay*) or *Hiph‘il* of מוּת *to die*—הֵמִית (*cause to die*); cf. § 40. 3.

the following consonant—thus (יִנְקָטֵל =) יִקָּטֵל. The imperative, as we have seen (§ 21. 1 c), is usually formed from the
impf. by dropping the pronominal prefix ; but, as such a form
as קָטֵל *qqāṭēl* is impossible, a secondary ה was prefixed (perhaps on the analogy of the Hiph‘il, § 27), yielding the form
הִקָּטֵל, which is also, as we should expect (§ 21. 2 a. i.), infinitive construct. With the perf. (נִקְטַל) the inf. abs. is נִקְטֹל ;
with the impf. it is הִקָּטֵל (also הִקָּטֹל). The participle is
like the pf., only with long *ā*: נִקְטָל *m.*, נִקְטָלָה *f.*

2. Niph. is inflected exactly like Qal : נִקְטַל, נִקְטְלָה, נִקְטַלְתָּ,
&c. ; impf. יִקָּטֵל (in pause often יִקָּטֵל, § 10. 4 c. ii.), תִּקָּטֵל, &c.
אֶקָּטֵל (or אִקָּטֵל), but cohortative always אִקָּטְלָה. With *waw
consec.*, as the penult is open, the tone is usually retracted
to it (§ 23. 3. 4) and the last syllable shortened : thus, יִקָּטֵל,
but וַיִּקָּטֵל.

3. In meaning the Niph‘al is (i.) properly the reflexive of
the simple form or Qal, as שָׁמַר *to keep,* נִשְׁמַר *to keep oneself, to
beware,* נִסְתַּר *to hide oneself.* (ii.) It is also used of reciprocal
action : נִלְחַם *to fight (i.e.* with *one another* ; cf. Greek middles
and Latin deponents, μάχεσθαι, *luctari*) ; נִדְבְּרוּ they spoke to
one another. But (iii.) the common use of Niph. is as *passive*
of Qal, as שָׁבַר *to break,* נִשְׁבַּר *to be broken,* נִקְבַּר *to be buried.*

4. The Niph. part. has sometimes the force of the Latin
gerundive ; *e.g.* נֶחְמָד *to be desired, desirable.* (ֶ for ִ before
guttural, § 8. 1 b.)

5. The agent after the Niph. is usually expressed by לְ ;
e.g. *And death shall be chosen by all the remnant,* וְנִבְחַר מָוֶת לְכֹל
הַשְּׁאֵרִית ; *And Yahweh let himself be entreated by him,* וַיֵּעָתֶר
לוֹ יהוה.

מָלֵא to be full	גָּמַל to wean	סָתַר *N.* { to hide oneself
Niph. to be filled	*N.* to be weaned	{ to be hidden
גָּרַשׁ to drive out	לָחַם *N.* to fight	מָלַט *N.* to escape
נָחַם *N.* to repent	שָׁחַת *N.* to be corrup-	מַבּוּל flood (of Noah)
דָּרַשׁ to seek	שָׁעַן *N.* to lean [ted	זְרוֹעַ *f.* arm
רָשָׁע wicked	חָמָם violence	מָצָא to find
שָׁקַל to weigh	בָּבֶל Babylon	פַּח bird-trap, snare
	בִּינָה *f.* understanding (*noun*).	

EXERCISE. TRANSLATE.

נִשְׁמָר, הִשָּׁפֵט, נִפְקַדְתֶּם, אֶשָּׁבֵר, נִכְתְּבוּ, נִשָּׁפְטָה, לְהִמָּלֵט,
יִשָּׁקֵל, תִּלָּחֵם, נִלְחַמְתִּי, תִּזָּכַרְנָה:
הָרְשָׁעִים לֹא יִכָּתְבוּ בְּסֵפֶר חַיִּים: 2 הַפַּח נִשְׁבַּר וַאֲנַחְנוּ
נִמְלָטְנוּ: 3 וַתִּשָּׁחֵת הָאָרֶץ לִפְנֵי אֱלֹהִים וַתִּמָּלֵא הָאָרֶץ חָמָס:
4 שֹׁפֵךְ דַּם הָאָדָם בָּאָדָם דָּמוֹ יִשָּׁפֵךְ: 5 וַיִּגְדַּל הַיֶּלֶד וַיִּגָּמַל:
6 נִגְרַשְׁתִּי הַיּוֹם מֵעַל פְּנֵי הָאֲדָמָה וּמִפָּנֶיךָ אֶסָּתֵר: 7 וַיִּנָּחֶם
יהוה כִּי עָשָׂה אֶת־הָאָדָם בָּאָרֶץ: 8 לֹא יִכָּרֵת עוֹד כָּל־בָּשָׂר
[1]מִמֵּי הַמַּבּוּל: 9 בָּא הָאוֹיֵב אֶל־הָעִיר וְלֹא יָכֹל לְהִלָּחֵם עָלֶיהָ:
10 ותשרף העיר באש : 11 השמר לך פן־תכרת ברית ליושב
הארץ ולקחת מבנותיו לבניך:

Yahweh is near to the broken of heart. I am hidden
from the face of my God. Hide thyself from his face. Ye
shall hide yourselves on that day. And the earth was
corrupted, and all flesh was cut off by the waters of the flood.
The arms of the wicked shall be broken. Let me escape
in the day of fighting (*inf. cons.*). And the earth was filled
with blood (*acc.*). His dead was buried out of his sight.[2]
Thus saith (*perf.*) Yahweh the God of Israel: Behold I
give (*ptc.*) this city into the hand of the king of Babylon
and he shall burn it with fire, and thou shalt not escape
from his hand, but thou shalt be captured and given into
his hand. Trust in Yahweh with all thy heart, and lean
not unto (אֶל־) thine own understanding.

§ 26. THE INTENSIVE ACT., PASS., AND REFLEX.,
PI'ĒL, &C.
(See Paradigm, p. 209.)

The characteristic of the Intensive, both in verbs (קִטֵּל)
and nouns (גַּנָּב *a thief*), is the duplication of the middle stem-
letter. Nouns of this class frequently indicate one who

---

[1] מֵי and מֵימֵי, *cstr. pl.* of מַיִם : always the longer form before suffixes.
[2] *From before him.*

practises a trade or profession—one who performs a certain
act *often, habitually*; *e.g.* גַּנָּב *a thief*, טַבָּח *a cook*, חָרָשׁ *an
artificer* (primarily חָרָּשׁ; therefore the cstr. is not חַָרַשׁ but
חָרַשׁ, § 8. 4 b).

I. *The Pi‘ēl.*—(*a*) i. The perf. of the Pi‘ēl, or intensive,
has the vowel *i* in the first syllable; in the second usually *ē*
(קִטֵּל: hence the word Pi‘ēl), frequently *a* (אִבַּד *to destroy*,
לִמַּד *to teach*), and three times *e* (דִּבֶּר *to speak*, כִּבֶּס *to wash*,
כִּפֶּר *to atone*). The impf. is of the type יְקַטֵּל (י without
dagh. f. in waw consec. וַיְקַטֵּל, not וַיּ, § 7. 5); hence the
imper. and the inf. cstr. (usually also inf. abs., which rarely
has קַטֹּל) are of the type קַטֵּל (§ 21. 1 and 2 a).

ii. Pi‘ēl is inflected exactly like Qal: קִטֵּל, קִטְּלָה, &c., except
that in pf. (after 3rd person) the second syllable, when closed,
has the vowel *a* (doubtless the orig. vowel of the Pi.); *e.g.*
קִטַּלְתָּ. The impf. is also regular, תִּקַּטֵּל יְקַטֵּל (the *ē* is retained
in the 2nd and 3rd pl. fem. תְּקַטֵּלְנָה). See Paradigm, p. 209.

iii. The dagh. f. is omitted from certain letters when they are followed by vocal sh⁰wa (cf. § 7. 5); *e.g.* בִּקְשׁוּ (not בקשׁו) *they sought*,
הַלְלוּ (§ 7. 5, § 3. 2 3 b) *praise ye* (not הללו).

(*b*) Pi‘ēl is (i.) properly intensive of Qal; that is, it adds
such ideas as *often, much, for a long time*, &c., to the simple
idea of the verb, as שָׁבַר *to break*, שִׁבֵּר *to break in pieces*, שָׁאַל
to ask, Pi. שִׁאֵל *to beg* (cf. סָפַר *to count*, סִפֵּר *to recount, relate*);
or it implies less often, that the action of the verb is done
by many or *to many*. Cf. קָבַר *to bury*, קִבֵּר *to bury many*.
(ii.) Since eagerness may show itself in urging others to
similar action, the Pi‘ēl frequently has a *causative force*:
לָמַד *to learn*, לִמַּד *to cause to learn*, i.e. *to teach*. So חָיָה *to
live*, חִיָּה (§ 44. 1 a) *to let live, to spare*. For similarly
strengthened consonant producing intensive force, cf. Germ.
wachen, wecken (*watch, wake*).

2. *Pu‘al.*—Pu‘al is the proper *passive* of Pi‘ēl in its
various senses; *e.g.* בִּקֵּשׁ *to seek*. Pu. בֻּקַּשׁ *to be sought*.

It is inflected exactly like Qal: pf. קֻטַּל, קֻטְּלָה, קֻטַּלְתָּ, &c.;
impf. יְקֻטַּל, תְּקֻטַּל, תְּקֻטְּלִי, &c.

Characteristic of impf. Pi. and Pu. is the ֽ at the beginning; the 1st pers., of course, begins with אֲ. (§ 8. 2 a.)

3. *Hithpa'ēl.*—(*a*) i. The Hithpa'ēl is formed by prefixing the syllable *hith*, having reflexive force, to the root-form
of the Pi'ēl, as קַטֵּל, הִתְקַטֵּל.

ii. When the syllable *hith* precedes the sibilants ס, שׂ, שׁ,
the ת changes places with the sibilant, as הִשְׁתַּמֵּר for הִתְשַׁמֵּר *to
take heed to oneself*; with צ the ת further becomes ט, as
הִצְטַדֵּק *to justify oneself*, from צָדֵק.

iii. With unsibilant dentals (ד, ט, ת) the ת is assimilated,
as הִטַּהֵר for הִתְטַ׳ *to purify oneself*, from טָהֵר *to be clean, pure*;
מִדַּבֵּר (ptc.) *conversing*.

(*b*) In meaning Hith. is (i.) properly reflexive of Pi'ēl, as
קִדֵּשׁ *to sanctify*, הִתְקַדֵּשׁ *to sanctify oneself*. (ii.) But it very
often implies that one *shows himself as*, or *gives himself out as*,
performing the action of the simple verb; *e.g.* הִתְנַקֵּם *to show
oneself revengeful*, הִתְעַשֵּׁר *to give oneself out to be rich*, הִתְנַבֵּא
to act like an ecstatic prophet, rave. (iii.) It may express
reciprocal action תִּתְרָאוּ (fr. רָאָה *to see*, cf. § 36. 1. 3, § 44) *ye
look upon one another*. (iv.) It may express action *upon* or
for oneself; cf. הִתְהַלֵּךְ (fr. הָלַךְ *to go*) *to go to and fro for
oneself*, i.e. *to walk about*.

(*c*) As in Pi. pf. the final vowel is frequently (the original) *a*; cf.
הִתְאַנַּף *he was angry* (so also in impf. and imper.) and always in
pause (as *ā*); *e.g.* הִתְאַזָּר *he has girded himself*.

4. The participles of Pi., Pu., and Hithp. follow the imperfect, and all begin with *m*: מְקַטֵּל, מְקֻטָּל, מִתְקַטֵּל. The מ of
Pi. and Pu. is written without a dagh. f. after the article
(cf. § 7. 5), but methegh is used to indicate that the first
syllable is not closed: הַמְהַלֵּךְ *he who walks in majesty* (not
הִמּ׳), לַמְנַצֵּחַ *for the musical director* (not לִמּ׳).

5. Some rarer intensives are formed by doubling the last
radical, *e.g.* שַׁאֲנָן *to be quiet*; or the last two, *e.g.* סְחַרְחַר *to
palpitate*; or the first and last (omitting the weak middle
letter), *e.g.* כִּלְכֵּל *to sustain*, pass. כָּלְכַּל (*kolkāl*) from כּוּל (cf.
§ 40. 5). These last forms are known as *pilpēl*.

שָׁבַר to break	שִׁבֵּר to break in pieces	דִּבֵּר to speak
סָפַר to count	סִפֵּר to recount, tell	בִּקֵּשׁ to seek
קָדַשׁ to be holy	*Pi.* to sanctify	*Hithp.* to sanctify oneself
כָּבֵד to be heavy	*Pi.* to honour, harden	*Hithp.* to get honour
גָּדַל to be great, grow	*Pi.* to bring up, magnify	*Hithp.* to magnify oneself
הָלַךְ to go	*Hithp.* to walk	חבא \ סתר / *Hithp.* to hide oneself
אַיִן no, none	כִּי אִם except	פָּשַׁע to rebel
פַּרְעֹה Pharaoh	(לְ, כָּה) לָמָּה for what reason? why?	

EXERCISE. TRANSLATE.

שִׁמְעוּ שָׁמַיִם כִּי יהוה דִּבֵּר בָּנִים גִּדַּלְתִּי וְהֵם פָּשְׁעוּ בִי:
2 וְלָמָּה תְכַבְּדוּ אֶת־לְבַבְכֶם כַּאֲשֶׁר כִּבְּדוּ מִצְרַיִם וּפַרְעֹה אֶת־
לְבָבָם: 3 הַשָּׁמַיִם מְסַפְּרִים כְּבוֹד אֱלֹהִים: 4 זִכְרוּ אֶת־יוֹם
הַשַּׁבָּת לְקַדֵּשׁ אֹתוֹ: 5 אֶת־הָאֱלֹהִים [1]הִתְהַלֶּךְ־נֹחַ: 6 וַיִּשְׁמְעוּ
אֶת־קוֹל יהוה מִתְהַלֵּךְ בַּגָּן לְרוּחַ הַיּוֹם וַיִּתְחַבֵּא הָאָדָם
[2]וְאִשְׁתּוֹ מִפְּנֵי יהוה: 7 וְלָאָרֶץ לֹא יְכֻפַּר לַדָּם אֲשֶׁר שֻׁפַּךְ בָּהּ
כִּי אִם בְּדַם שֹׁפְכוֹ: 8 מַה־נְּדַבֵּר וּמַה־נִּצְטַדָּק: 9 הָאֶבְיוֹנִים
מְבַקְשִׁים מַיִם וָאָיִן: 10 אֶת־פָּנֶיךָ יהוה אֲבַקֵּשׁ: 11 נִמְצְאוּ
הַחֲמוֹרִים אֲשֶׁר הָלַכְתָּ לְבַקֵּשׁ: 12 וַיִּקְרָא פַרְעֹה אֶת־כָּל־חַכְמֵי
מִצְרַיִם וַיְסַפֵּר לָהֶם אֶת־חֲלֹמוֹ:

These are the words which I have spoken. Harden not your heart, lest Yahweh your God be angry. Seek ye his face. Walk before me and sanctify yourselves. I cannot speak to this people, for they have hardened their heart. We heard the voice of Yahweh walking in the garden and we hid ourselves from his face. He said unto the woman, Speak, and the woman spoke. I will honour them that honour me. And now, behold, the king walketh (*ptc.*) before you, and I am old, and I have walked before you from my youth until this day.

[1] See § 10. 3 a.
[2] 3 s. m. suff. from אִשָּׁה, *cstr.* אֵשֶׁת (cf. pp. 153, 101, 2nd col.).

§ 27. THE CAUSATIVE, *HIPH'ÎL, HOPH'AL.*
(See Paradigm, p. 209.)

1. *Hiph'îl.*—(*a*) i. The perfect of the Hiph. or causative is formed by prefixing the letter *h* with *i* (properly a thinned *a*) to the stem, and expanding the final vowel to *î*, הִקְטִיל. In the impf. the final syllable is the same (טִיל), and the first syllable has the vowel *a*: thus יַקְטִיל (יְהַקְטִיל with ה dropped, § 14. 1 e). The jussive (which in the regular vb. differs from the impf. *only in the Hiph.*) is יַקְטֵל (cf. § 23. 1. 1); so *waw consec.* וַיַּקְטֵל. Hence the imper. is of the type הַקְטֵל (§ 21. 1). So also inf. abs.; inf. cstr. is הַקְטִיל.

ii. The Hiph. is inflected regularly. We have only to remember that the final *î*, being long, is maintained, as is natural, in open syllables, *i.e.* with vocalic affixes (*a i u*) and has the accent; *e.g.* הִקְטִילָה f., הִקְטִילוּ pl., הַקְטִילִי imper. s. f., הַקְטִילָה emph. imper. (§ 23. 2); in shut syll. it becomes *a* (probably the original vowel) in perf. (*e.g.* הִקְטַלְתָּ), and generally *ē* after the perf. (*e.g.* תַּקְטֵלְנָה). In both these respects it resembles the Pi'ēl.

iii. Pf. הִקְטִיל, הִקְטִילָה, הִקְטַלְתָּ, &c.; impf. יַקְטִיל, תַּקְטִיל, &c. See Paradigm.

(*b*) In meaning Hiph. is (i.) causative of Qal, as פָּקַד *to oversee*, הִפְקִיד *to make one oversee, to entrust to*; קָדֵשׁ *to be holy*, הִקְדִּישׁ *to sanctify*. A rough analogy to the formation of the Hiph. may be found in Lat. cado, *caedo*; Ger. fallen *fällen*; Eng. fall, *fell*; rise, *raise*: a still closer analogy in the causative suffix *ig* in Esperanto; e.g. *veni*, to come, *venigi*, to cause to come, send for; *sani*, to be healthy, *sanigi*, to make healthy. (ii.) The Hiph. may be declaratory; *e.g.* הִצְדִּיק *to declare one to be* צַדִּיק *in the right*, i.e. *to acquit*; הִרְשִׁיעַ *to declare to be* רָשָׁע *in the wrong*, i.e. *to condemn*. (iii.) The Hiph. is very frequently used of actions or states which we express by a neuter or intransitive vb.; cf. הֶאֱמִין *to trust*, הֶחֱזִיק *to be strong*. But we must not say that the Hiph. is intrans. or that it stands for the Qal: the transitive idea is genuinely present to Semitic feeling; *e.g.* הֶחֱזִיק *to develop strength*, הֶחֱרִישׁ *to keep silence (to be silent)*, &c.

(*c*) Since the Pi'ēl, as we have seen (§ 26. 1 *b*) frequently

has this meaning, it happens that in some vbs. *both* forms
are used causatively; *e.g.* אִבַּד (Pi.) and הֶאֱבִיד (Hiph.) *to
destroy*; but generally if both forms are in use, they
differ in meaning; *e.g.* כָּבֵד *to be heavy*, Pi. כִּבֵּד *to honour*,
Hiph. הִכְבִּיד *to make heavy* (also *to bring to honour*).

(*d*) If the Qal is transitive, the Hiph. takes two accu-
satives: לָבֵשׁ *to put on* (clothes, acc.); וַיַּלְבֵּשׁ אֹתוֹ בִּגְדֵי־שֵׁשׁ *and
he clothed him with garments of fine linen.*

2. *Hoph'al.*—The Hoph. is *passive* of the Hiph. in its
various senses; *e.g.* הִשְׁלִיךְ *to cast*, הָשְׁלַךְ (*hoshlakh*) *to be cast.*
It is inflected exactly like Qal in pf.: impf. יְקְטַל (fr. יְהָקְטַל,
h dropped). See Paradigm, p. 209. In the first syllable,
especially in the participle under the influence of the מ, the
vowel is sometimes *u*; cf. מֻשְׁלָךְ.

3. The first syllable of Hiph. and Hoph. in all parts is
closed: hence הִצְדִּיק (not ר). The participles begin with מ
and follow the impf. (only Hoph. like Niph. has ָ in 2nd
syllable) מָקְטָל, מַקְטִיל.

מָלַךְ to be king, rule	*Hiph.* to make king	שָׁלַךְ *Hiph.* to cast
צָדַק to be just	*Hiph.* to justify	שָׁמַד *Hiph.* to destroy
שָׁכַן to dwell	*Hiph.* to place	בָּדַל *Hiph.* to divide
זָכַר to remember	*Hiph.* to commemor- ate	שָׁחַת *Hiph.* to corrupt, deal corruptly
פָּשַׁט to strip off (a garment)	*Hiph.* to strip (one of a garment) —*two accus.*	

מטר *Hiph.* to send rain, rain   יֵשׁ (יְשׁ־) there is

בְּעַד away from, behind; through (a window), over (a wall)

רֵק (רִיק) empty   כָּרַע to bow down

עֵדֶן Eden (delight) רְאוּבֵן Reuben יָרָבְעָם Jeroboam

כְּרוּב cherub   בּוֹר pit, well

יַסְתִּיר פָּנָיו *he will hide his face*

יַסְתֵּר „ *may he hide his face*

וַיַּסְתֵּר „ *and he hid his face*

הַסְתֵּר, הַסְתִּירָה פָּנֶיךָ *hide thy face*

אַל־תַּסְתֵּר „ *hide not thy face*

אַסְתִּירָה פָנַי *let me hide my face*

הַסְתֵּר יַסְתִּיר פָּנָיו *he will assuredly hide his face*

EXERCISE. TRANSLATE.

אַתָּה הִמְלַכְתָּ אֹתִי תַּחַת דָּוִד אָבִי: 2 הִנֵּה פָנַי בָּעָם הַזֶּה
וְהִשְׁמַדְתִּי אֹתָם מֵעַל־פְּנֵי הָאֲדָמָה: 3 וַיַּשְׁכֵּן אֱלֹהִים לִפְנֵי גַן
עֵדֶן אֶת־הַכְּרֻבִים לִשְׁמֹר דֶּרֶךְ עֵץ הַחַיִּים: 4 נָתַן אֱלֹהִים
מְאֹרֹת בִּרְקִיעַ הַשָּׁמַיִם לְהַבְדִּיל בֵּין הַיּוֹם וּבֵין הַלָּיְלָה:
5 וְאָנֹכִי הַסְתֵּר אַסְתִּיר פָּנַי בַּיּוֹם הַהוּא 6 הִנֵּה רֹאשׁוֹ מֻשְׁלָךְ
אֵלֶיךָ בְּעַד הַחוֹמָה: 7 וַיִּשְׁלָחֻהוּ וַיִּקְרְאוּ אֶת־יָרָבְעָם וַיַּמְלִיכוּ
אֹתוֹ עַל־יִשְׂרָאֵל: 8 וְהָרָקִיעַ הָיָה מַבְדִּיל בֵּין מַיִם לָמָיִם:
9 אַל־תַּסְתֵּר אֶת־פָּנֶיךָ מֵהָעָם הַזֶּה: 10 וַיַּמְטֵר יהוה עַל־
הָעִיר אֵשׁ מִן־הַשָּׁמַיִם וַיַּשְׁמֵד אוֹתָהּ מֵעַל־פְּנֵי הָאֲדָמָה:

There is a time to keep and a time to cast away. Justify
not the wicked. Let me hide my face from this evil people,
for they have done-corruptly (*Hiph.*) before me upon the
earth. The king said, Cast his head unto us over the wall;
and they cast his head unto them. For he will surely (*inf.
abs.*) rain fire from heaven upon that evil city and will destroy
it, and it shall not be remembered any more for ever. The
prophet found the child laid (*Hoph. ptc.* of שָׁכַב) upon his
bed. We went down unto the city to fight against it, but
we could not destroy it. Reuben said, Spill not blood,
cast him into this pit which (is) in the wilderness; and they
stripped Joseph and cast him (into) the pit (*acc.*, § 17. 3),
and the pit (was) empty.

§ 28. SKELETON PARADIGM OF THE REGULAR VERB.

	simple		intensive			causative	
	qal	niph.	pi‘ēl	pu‘al	hithp.	hiph.	hoph.
	act.	*reflex.*	*act.*	*pass.*	*reflex.*	*act.*	*pass.*
perf.	קָטַל	נִקְטַל	קִטֵּל	קֻטַּל	הִתְקַטֵּל	הִקְטִיל	הָקְטַל
imperf.	יִקְטֹל	יִקָּטֵל	יְקַטֵּל	יְקֻטַּל	יִתְקַטֵּל	יַקְטִיל	יָקְטַל
imper.	קְטֹל	הִקָּטֵל	קַטֵּל		הִתְקַטֵּל	הַקְטֵל	
inf. cstr.	קְטֹל	הִקָּטֵל	קַטֵּל	קֻטַּל	הִתְקַטֵּל	הַקְטִיל	הָקְטַל
inf. abs.	קָטוֹל	הִקָּטֹל	קַטֵּל	קֻטֹּל		הַקְטֵל	הָקְטֵל
ptc. act.	קֹטֵל		מְקַטֵּל		מִתְקַטֵּל	מַקְטִיל	
ptc. pass.	קָטוּל	נִקְטָל		מְקֻטָּל			מֻקְטָל

1. The names N*i*ph'al, Pi'ēl, &c., indicate what *vowels* verbs have in the *perfects* of these parts.

The *i* in first syll. of Pi'ēl and Hiph'îl is a thinned *a*, which shows itself in all parts after the perf.; cf. יַקְטֵל, יַקְטִיל; and even the *ē* and *i* of second syll. seem to have arisen out of *a*.

2. The imperfect may be considered the part regulative of the imperat. and infin. cstr. (§ 21. 1 c, 2 a. i.), and these three parts end alike, cf. Qal יִקְטֹל, קְטֹל, Pi. יְקַטֵּל, קַטֵּל; and after the Niph. the participle also agrees, cf. Hiph. יַקְטִיל, מַקְטִיל.

The imperf. *ends like the perf.* after Niph., cf. Pi. pf. קִטֵּל, impf. יְקַטֵּל; and in Niph. it ends in *ē*, cf. יִקָּטֵל.

> To this rule that the imperf. imper. and inf. cstr. end alike there is, first, the known exception of the Qal of intrans. verbs, in which infin. cstr. usually adopts *ō*, though the other two are in *a* (§ 22. 3); and second, the Hiph. imper. agrees, of course, not with the ordinary, but with the *jussive* imperf., and ends in *ē*; *e.g.* impf. יַקְטִיל, juss. יַקְטֵל, Hiph. הַקְטֵל (but pl. הַקְטִילוּ).

3. The infin. abs. has *o* in the last syll., except in Hiph. and Hoph., where it has *e*; though see § 26. 1 *a* on infin. abs. Pi'ēl.

4. The passives usually have no imperative.

5. After Niph. the preformative letter of the participle is מ, pointed as the preform. of imperf.; cf. Pi. יְקַטֵּל, מְקַטֵּל, Hoph. יָקְטַל, מָקְטָל. This מ is possibly the pron. מִי *who? whoever* (§ 13. 3).

6. Finally, it is of much consequence that the learner, before leaving the regular verb, should carefully note the following points, which must not, however, be committed to memory, but will be seen to be simply summary expressions of facts which ought by this time to be familiar; where the first radical has sh°wa vocal under it (2 pl. perf., inf. cstr., imper. Qal קְטֹל, קְטַלְתֶּם); where the 2nd rad. has sh°wa vocal (all parts—except Hiph.—with vocalic affixes *a i u*, Qal קָטְלָה, יִקְטְלוּ, Niph. נִקְטְלָה, יִקָּטְלוּ, Pi. קִטְּלוּ, יְקַטְּלוּ, Hoph. הָקְטְלָה, יָקְטְלוּ, but Hiph. הִקְטִילָה, יַקְטִילוּ); where the 1st rad. has sh°wa silent (at the end of a syll., imperf. Qal, perf., part. Niph., all Hiph. Hoph. יִקְטֹל—*e.g.* יִכְתֹּב—נִקְטַל, נִקְטָל, הִקְטִיל &c.); where the 1st rad. is doubled (imperf. Niph. and cognate parts יִקָּטֵל), where 2nd rad. is doubled (Pi. Pu. Hithp. קִטֵּל, &c.). These and such points are of importance in the irregular verbs.

EXERCISE. PARSE.

כָּתַבְתִּי, כְּתֻבִים, כְּתוּבִים, תִּכְתֹּב, יִכָּתֵב, שְׁמֹר, נִשְׁמָר, נִשְׁמֹר, הִשָּׁמֵר, מְשַׁמֵּר, יְרַדֵּף, אֶשְׁבֹּר, אֲשַׁבֵּר, מַזְכִּיר, הַמְשֵׁל, וְדַף, הָשְׁבַּר, זָכוֹר, תַּמְשִׁילוּ, תִּשְׁקְלִי, שְׁקֹל, שָׁכַב, מֹלֶכֶת, יַמְטִיר, יַפְקֵד, מִסְתַּתֵּר, יְקַדֵּשׁ, הִלָּבֵשְׁנָה, תִּזְכְּרֶנָּה׃

§ 29. SECOND DECLENSION.

1. The words embraced under the first declension were chiefly concrete words, having a resemblance in form to the *perfect* of verbs. A very large class of nouns have an affinity in form with the *imperfect*, that is, with the abstract noun at the base of that form. They are thus themselves largely abstract nouns. They are properly monosyllables, but are pronounced and spelled as dissyllables through the slipping in of a furtive vowel between the last two radicals.

(a) *a.* The process will be best illustrated by examples. From מַלְכִּי *my king* (first syllable closed), we may infer that the word for *king* must, strictly speaking, have been מַלְךְ *malk*: so סִפְרִי *my book*, comes from an ultimate סִפְר *siphr*; and קָדְשִׁי (*qodhshî*) *my holiness*, from קָדְשׁ *qodhsh* (ultimately *qudhsh*). But Hebrew dislikes the collocation of two consonants at the end, as at the beginning (§ 5. 5) of a word, doubtless from constitutional inability to pronounce them easily together; consequently it separated them, as other languages have done,[1] by a furtive vowel—here ş°ghol. Thus we have סֵפֶר, &c. But the *ḥireq*, originally short in the doubly shut syllable *siphr*, is now the vowel of an open syllable (סִ|פֶר) and must therefore become tone-long, hence סֵפֶר—with the accent, of course, on the penult, as the ֵ represents the original, and strictly the only, vowel of the word. All nouns of this kind —so-called *şegholates*,[2] because of the furtive ş°ghol—are

---

[1] Cf. alarm and alarum ; Gaelic tarbh = tárabh, Dutch Delft = Déleft ; so *Peter* from *Petr-us* ; *schism* (almost = siz°m), but *schismatic*.

[2] The name is not an altogether happy one, because (i.) it calls attention to a feature that is of secondary rather than of primary importance, and (ii.) ş°ghol is sometimes replaced by other vowels, *e.g.* by pathaḥ, if the 2nd or the 3rd radical be a guttural, *e.g.* רֹחַב *breadth*, זֶרַע *seed*

accented on the penult, whose vowel, being in an open syllable, is most naturally, as we have seen (סֵפֶר), tone-long; cf. קֹדֶשׁ. On this analogy we should expect nouns of the *a* class, like מַלְךְ, to pass first into מַלֶךְ and then into מָלֶךְ *mālekh*. In point of fact this form is found only *in pause* (*e.g.* כָּסֶף for כֶּסֶף *silver*) — and not always even then (*e.g.* מֶלֶךְ *king*, and צֶדֶק *righteousness*, are always written thus—never מָלֶךְ צָדֶק). In place of מָלֶךְ with the long *ā*, which we expect, the regular and normal form is מֶלֶךְ *mélekh*. The first „, which is manifestly accented, may fairly be regarded as a (tone) long sᵉghol (§ 3. 2. 2 b, § 6); and the original *a* has assumed this form probably by attraction—the more so as the two vowels have a certain affinity.

Forms without a helping vowel, *i.e.* monosyllabic forms, are rare ; *e.g.* גַּיְא *valley*, נֵרְדְּ *nard*, חֵטְא *ḥēṭ, sin*, קֹשְׁטְ *qōshṭ, truth*.

A class   I class   U class
(1) קַטְל *qaṭl* קִטְל *qiṭl* קֹטְל *qoṭl* (קֻטְל *quṭl*) primary form
(2) קַטֶל *qaṭel* קִטֶל *qiṭel* קֹטֶל *qoṭel* (קֻטֶל *quṭel*) with furtive sᵉghol
(3) קֶטֶל *qéṭel* קֶטֶל *qéṭel* קֹטֶל *qóṭel* regular form

β. *Rules for declension.*—(1) The cstr. state of the sing. is, of course, like the absolute : מֶלֶךְ, abs. and cstr.

Rarely it assumes (esp. before *gutt.* or *r*) the form זֶרַע (as well as זֶרַע) from abs. זֶרַע *seed*.

(2) With inflectional additions in the sing. and dual, the word appears *in its primary monosyllabic form*, *qaṭl*, *qiṭl*, *qoṭl*: *my king*, not מֶלְכִּי (an impossible form) but מַלְכִּי *mal-kî*, because the primary form is *malk* ; סִפְרוֹ *his book* (from סֵפֶר, orig. *siphr*) ; אָזְנָיו *'oznāw, his ears* (from אֹזֶן, orig. *'ozn, 'uzn*).

(3) The plural,*both mas. and fem.*,assumes the form *qᵉṭālîm*, *qᵉṭālôth*, with pretonic *ā*. The presence of this *ā* (cf. מְלָכִים) is difficult to explain in a word whose ultimate form has no vowel between the 2nd and 3rd radicals, *malk* ; it has possibly followed the analogy of nouns of the first declension, cf. דְּבָרִים.

(§§ 36, 37) ; while if the 2nd radical be ', it either becomes ḥireq, cf. זַיִת *an olive-tree*, or contracts (*ay = ê*, § 2. 2. 1) into monosyllabic form, cf. חֵיק *bosom* (§ 41).

γ. Note that while the feminine of an original *malk* is naturally *malkâ*, כַּלְכָּה (cstr. מַלְכַּת, with suff. מַלְכָּתִי, &c., regular), the plur. is not מַלְכּוֹת, but, on the analogy of the masculine, מְלָכוֹת.

δ. When in the plur. the pretonic *ā* becomes lost, the *primary* vowel is resumed; *e.g.* cstr. of מְלָכִים is not מִלְכֵי (like דִּבְרֵי), but, as was natural, the original vowel (a, *malk*) reasserted itself, hence מַלְכֵי ; so בָּקְרֵי, סִפְרֵי *boq'rê* (from בֹּקֶר, orig. *boqr*).

Masc.

sing. abs.	מֶלֶךְ	סֵפֶר	בֹּקֶר
cstr.	„	„	„
1 *sing.*	מַלְכִּי	סִפְ[1]	בָּק[1]
2 *m.*	מַלְכְּךָ	„	„
2 *f.*	מַלְכֵּךְ	„	„
3 *m.*	מַלְכּוֹ	„	„
3 *f.*	מַלְכָּהּ	„	„
1 *pl.*	מַלְכֵּנוּ	„	„
2 *pl.*	מַלְכְּכֶם	„	„
3 *pl.*	מַלְכָּם	„	„
pl. abs.	מְלָכִים	סְפָ	בְּקָ
cstr.	מַלְכֵי	סִפְ	בָּק
1 *sing.*	מְלָכַי	סְפָ	בְּקָ
2 *m.*	מְלָכֶיךָ	„	„
2 *f.*	מְלָכַיִךְ	„	„
3 *m.*	מְלָכָיו	„	„
3 *f.*	מְלָכֶיהָ	„	„
1 *pl.*	מְלָכֵינוּ	„	„
2 *pl.*	מַלְכֵיכֶם	סְפָ	בְּקָ
3 *pl.*	מַלְכֵיהֶם	„	„

Fem.

sing. abs.	מַלְכָּה	סִפְ	בָּק
cstr.	מַלְכַּת	„	„
1 *sing.*	מַלְכָּתִי	„	„
2 *pl.*	מַלְכַּתְכֶם	„	„
pl. abs.	מַלְכוֹת	סְפָ	בְּקָ
cstr.	מַלְכוֹת	סְפָ	בְּקָ
1 *sing.*	מַלְכֹתַי	„	„

Dual.

abs.	רַגְלַיִם[2]	בִּרְכַּיִם[3]	אָזְנַיִם[4]
cstr.	רַגְלֵי	בִּרְכֵּי	אָזְנֵי
1 *sing.*	רַגְלַי	בִּרְכַּי	אָזְנַי
2 *sing.*	רַגְלֶיךָ	בִּרְכֶּיךָ	אָזְנֶיךָ
2 *pl.*	רַגְלֵיכֶם	בִּרְכֵּיכֶם	אָזְנֵיכֶם

(b) In many nouns of the *a* class the *a* has been thinned before suffixes to *i* (cf. § 2. 2. 4, § 6. 2 d. i.); *e.g.* שֶׁמֶשׁ *sun*,

[1] In the 2nd and 3rd columns only the first syllable is given : the rest follows the exact analogy of the first column ; בָּקְרִי, סִפְרְךָ, סִפְרִי, &c.

[2] *Feet* (רֶגֶל). The dual termination ‏ם ַ‎ִ is usually attached to the ground form ; consequently the first syllable is closed. This differentiates the cstr. dual from the cstr. plur.

[3] *Knees* (בֶּרֶךְ).

[4] *Ears* (אֹזֶן).

שִׁמְשֵׁךְ (not שִׁמְשֵׁךְ) *thy* (f.) *sun*; צֶדֶק *righteousness*, צִדְקֵנוּ *our righteousness*. Conversely a noun of the *i* class (בִּרְכַּיִם) may have an absolute form of the *a* type בֶּרֶךְ (not בֶּרֶךְ). Only a knowledge of the cognate languages can tell us whether a word whose vowels are *e . . . e* in the abs. and *i* before suffixes, really belongs to the *a* or the *i* class. Some nouns have both forms in the absolute; *e.g.* נִדְרִי *my vow*; abs. נֵדֶר or נֶדֶר *vow*.

2. In some nouns belonging to this general type the original *a, i* (lengthened to *ē*), *o* (or *u*; lengthened to *ō*) appears between the 2nd and 3rd radicals instead of between the 1st and 2nd: under the first radical, of course, must stand sh⁰wa (§ 5. 5); *e.g.* דְּבַשׁ *honey*, בְּאֵר *well*, בְּאֹשׁ *stench* (3 s. m. suf. בָּאְשׁוֹ). The last class is important, as to it belong the frequently recurring construct infinitives of the type קְטֹל (with suffixes 1 *s.* קָטְלִי, 3 *s.* קָטְלוֹ, &c.:—exactly like בָּקְרִי, בָּקְרוֹ, &c., except that in קָטְלִי the sh⁰wa is vocalic, because it replaces an original full vowel; hence כָּתְבוֹ, not כָּתְבוֹ, cstr. inf. of כָּתַב *to write*, whereas the noun אֹרֶךְ *length*, would yield אָרְכּוֹ).

3. *Feminines with ṣegholate ending.*—

mas.	(מַמְלָךְ)	קֹטֶל	מֵינִיק	²גְּבִיר	נָחוּשׁ	(קָטוֹר)
fem.	¹מַמְלָכָה	קְטָלָה	(מֵינִיקָה)	³גְּבִירָה	נְחוּשָׁה	קְטוֹרָה
or	(מַמְלַכְתְּ)	(קֹטַלְתְּ)	(מֵינִקְתְּ)	(גְּבִרְתְּ)	(נְחֹשְׁתְּ)	(קְטָרְתְּ)
abs., cstr.	מַמְלֶכֶת	קֹטֶלֶת	⁴מֵינֶקֶת	גְּבֶרֶת	⁵נְחֹשֶׁת	⁶קְטֹרֶת
suff.	מַמְלַכְתִּי	קֹטַלְתִּי	מֵינִקְתִּי	גְּבִרְתִּי	נְחֹשְׁתִּי	קְטָרְתִּי
plur.	מַמְלָכוֹת	קְטָלוֹת	מֵינִיקוֹת	גְּבִירוֹת	נְחוּשׁוֹת	קְטוֹרוֹת
cstr.	מַמְלְכוֹת	„	„	„	„	„

(a) Feminines ending in *t* (§ 16. 4. 8) belong to the segholate class.⁷ *E.g.* מַמְלַכְתּוֹ *his kingdom*, points back to מַמְלַכְתְּ *kingdom*, which becomes מַמְלֶכֶת exactly as מֶלֶךְ becomes מֶלֶךְ. In point of fact, however, while the segholate form (*e.g.* מַמְלֶכֶת) is invariably used for the construct, and sometimes

---

¹ *Kingdom.*   ² *Lord, master.*   ³ *Lady, mistress.*

⁴ *One who gives suck, a nurse*, Hiph. ptc. of יָנַק *to suck* (§ 39. 1. 2).

⁵ *Copper, bronze* (נְחוּשָׁה is only poetical).

⁶ *Smoke of sacrifice, incense.*

⁷ Not, of course, if preceded by an unchangeably long vowel (*e.g.* עִבְרִית). § 16. 4. 8 b.

for the absolute (*e.g.* מִשְׁמֶרֶת *guard, charge*), the absolute frequently assumes the form in ָה ; *e.g.* the abs. of *kingdom* is always מַמְלָכָה. Some nouns have both forms in the absolute ; *e.g.* עֲצֶרֶת and עֲצָרָה *an assembly*. Similarly ptc. *m.* קֹטֵל, *f.* קֹטְלָה or קֹטֶלֶת cstr. קֹטֶלֶת, suff. קֹטַלְתִּי, &c.

(b) So with nouns in *o* or *u*. *E.g.* נְחֻשְׁתִּי comes from נְחֹשֶׁת (bronze) which becomes (first נְחֹשֶׁת and then) נְחֹשֶׁת (cf. בֹּקֶר), which is abs. as well as cstr. Similarly from גְּבִיר *master*, גְּבִירָה *mistress*, גְּבִרְתּוֹ *his mistress*, we should expect the cstr. to be גְּבֶרֶת (cf. סֵפֶר, סִפְרוֹ). In point of fact, however, it is גְּבֶרֶת, and so almost always with fem. nouns whose origin would lead us to expect ֶ ֶ ; *e.g.* מֵינִקְתּוֹ *his nurse*, מֵינֶקֶת *nurse* (not נֶ).

(c) In general the plurals are formed regularly from the *ordinary* fem., or from what would be the ordinary fem. if it were found. Consequently the original *mas.* must be carefully attended to, e.g. *m.* גְּבִיר, *f.* גְּבִירָה, *pl.* גְּבִירוֹת (*i.e.* the plur. is *not* formed from ṣegholate form גְּבֶרֶת).

WORDS FOR PRACTICE.

דֶּרֶךְ	way [1]	קֶרֶן *f.*	horn	שִׁפְחָה *f.*	maid
יֶלֶד	boy	רֶגֶל *f.*	foot	בֶּרֶךְ[2] *f.*	knee *i*
יַלְדָּה *f.*	girl	חֶדֶר	chamber	צֶדֶק[2]	righteousness *i*
נֶפֶשׁ *f.*	soul	אֹזֶן *f.*	ear	קֶרֶב[2]	midst *i*
אָכְלָה *f.*	food	גֹּדֶל	greatness	מֵינֶקֶת[2] *f.*	nurse *i*
צֶלֶם	image	נֶדֶר	vow	יְרוּשָׁלַםִ	Jerusalem [3]
גֹּרֶן	threshing floor	חָכְמָה *f.*	wisdom	צִיּוֹן	Zion
כֶּרֶם	vineyard	שֵׁבֶט	tribe	נֵר	lamp
זֵכֶר	memory	אַדֶּרֶת *f.*	mantle	נְתִיבָה *f.*	path [4]

בִּקְעָה *f.* valley   שָׁמֵן to grow fat ; *Hiph.*, to make fat, dull
רְחוֹב *f.* broad open place, *pl.* רְחֹבוֹת.   קֶשֶׁת *f.* bow

(d) A suffix defining a compound expression in the construct relationship is appended to the last word of the

---

[1] Usually *masc.*, sometimes *fem.*

[2] These four words take *i* instead of *a* with suffixes, &c. ; *e.g.* בִּרְכַּיִם, צִדְקֵנוּ, &c.

[3] The older pronunciation was undoubtedly יְרוּשָׁלֵם. The later form, however, יְרוּשָׁלַיִם (jᵉrûshāláyim) is (like יְהֹוָה, § 10. 5 b) a so-called *Qᵉrê perpetuum*.   [4] Poetical ; also נָתִיב *m.*

expression, as the connection between construct and absolute must not be interrupted (§ 17. 2, Rule 2); *e.g.*

הַר קֹדֶשׁ (*a hill of holiness =*) *a holy hill*

הַר קָדְשִׁי *my holy hill* (*the hill of my holiness*; or more strictly, *my* הַר קֹדֶשׁ *my hill-of-holiness*)

אֱלִיל כֶּסֶף *an idol of silver*   אֱלִיל כַּסְפִּי *my idol of silver*

בְּלֵי מִלְחַמְתּוֹ *his weapons* [1] *of warfare* (the weapons of his w.)

EXERCISE.   TRANSLATE.

וַיִּבְרָא אֱלֹהִים אֶת־הָאָדָם בְּצַלְמוֹ׃ 2 לֹא דָרְכֵי דַּרְכֵיכֶם׃

3 וְעַתָּה יוֹשֵׁב יְרוּשָׁלַם וְאִישׁ יְהוּדָה שִׁפְטוּ־נָא בֵּינִי וּבֵין כַּרְמִי׃

4 וַיִּסָּתְרוּ אֶת־הַיֶּלֶד וְאֶת־מֵינִקְתּוֹ מִפְּנֵי הַמַּלְכָּה׃ 5 נֵר לְרַגְלִי

דְבָרֶךָ וְאוֹר לִנְתִיבָתִי׃ 6 הַשְּׁמֶן לֵב־הָעָם הַזֶּה וְאָזְנָיו הַכְבֵּד׃

7 וּרְחֹבוֹת הָעִיר יִמָּלְאוּ יְלָדִים וִילָדוֹת׃ 8 פְּנֵי יהוה בְּרְשָׁעִים

לְהַכְרִית מֵהָאָרֶץ זִכְרָם׃ 9 כַּסְפְּךָ וּזְהָבְךָ לֹא חָפַצְתִּי׃

My king. Our kings. His books. Her righteousness. Our knees (*du.*). Thy feet (*du.*). Our horn. Their silver. My way is hid (*perf. fem.*) from my God. For all flesh had corrupted his way upon the earth. Their ways are not our ways. And all the people bowed-down upon their knees before their king. Let thine hand-maid speak in the ears of the king. My God and my king reigns upon Zion his holy hill. My mantle. Her mistress. His kingdom is an everlasting kingdom (k. of eternity). I will cut off their bow and all their weapons of warfare.

§ 30. THIRD DECLENSION.

1. Besides the words resembling the perfect which form the chief elements of the first declension and the nouns having affinity with the imperfect and infinitive forming the second, there is another formation which along with the words that follow it may be called a *third declension*. This is the *act. participle* Qal, קוֹטֵל or קֹטֵל, probably a later development and not found in all verbs.

Third declension.—The type of this declension is the *act. part.* Qal; and the declension comprises all words, whether

---

[1] Weapon (article, instrument, vessel) כְּלִי, pl. כֵּלִים.

participles or nouns, ending in *ē* (çere) with a vowel unchangeable (by nature, *e.g.* קוֹטֵל, or position, *c.g.* מִסְפֵּד) in the place of the pretone. It therefore does not include nouns like זָקֵן whose pretonic vowel is changeable (§ 18).

Rules for inflection.—(1) In words of this class the *verbal* law of inflection is followed (§ 6. 2 f); that is, with vocalic additions, *e.g.* ָי, ִי, נוּ, ◌ָם, &c., the vowel in the tone, the *ē*, becomes vocal shᵉwa; *e.g.* קְטֹל, קְטָלִי, קְטָלֵנוּ, שְׁמוֹ *his name* (from שֵׁם).

(2) *a.* With consonantal additions, *e.g.* ך, כֶם, the *ē* being thrown into an unaccented shut (half-open) syllable, becomes the short vowel, i.e. *e* or *i*; *i* particularly with *labials*, *e.g.* קְטֶלְךָ, but שִׁמְךָ (not שֶׁמְךָ) *thy name.*

b. As קוֹטֵל and similar forms come from an ultimate qâṭil, § 2. 2. 1 (the short *i* in the last syllable becoming in Hebrew, where it is accented, the tone-long *ē*, § 6. 2 a), the real vowel is strictly *i*, but this has been modified in the majority of words into *e* before the consonantal addition.

(3) Words of the participial form (קֹטֵל, מְקֻטֵּל) retain *ē* in cstr. and generally other words, though some take *a*; *e.g.* מִסְפֵּד *mourning*, cstr. מִסְפַּד.

abs.	קֹטֵל	מְקֻטֵּל	מַקֵּל	מִסְפֵּד	שֵׁם
cons.	קֹטֶל	מְקֻטַּל	מַקֵּל	מִסְפַּד	שֵׁם
vocalic suff.	קְטְלִי	מְקֻטְּלִי	מַקְלִי	מִסְפְּדִי	שְׁמִי
conson. suff.	קְטֶלְךָ	מְקֻטֶּלְךָ	מַקֶּלְכֶם		שִׁמְךָ

2. *a.* A few monosyllabic words in *ē* attach themselves to this declension, the chief being בֵּן *son*, and שֵׁם *name*, which are irregular in the plural—בָּנִים, שֵׁמוֹת.

b. Many nouns are formed by prefixing מ (probably connected with מָה, cf. § 28. 5) to the stem. Such words express *place* (מַרְבֵּץ *stall*, from רָבֵץ *to lie*) or *instrument* (מַפְתֵּחַ *key*, from פָּתַח *to open*) or some more general idea (מַלְקוֹחַ *plunder*, from לָקַח *to take*).

אֹיֵב	enemy	אִלֵּם	dumb	מַקֵּל	staff
מִסְפֵּד	mourning	מִזְבֵּחַ	altar	נַעַל	*f.* sandal, shoe,
עוֹלֵל עוֹלָל	}child	עִוֵּר	blind		*dual* נַעֲלַיִם
		שָׁלַח	to send, *Pi.* send	שָׁרַץ	to swarm
כֹּהֵן	priest		away, let go	שָׁבַע	*Niph.* to swear

מִשְׁפָּט judgment	קָלַל to be light or slight,	חָגַר to gird
צְפַרְדֵּעַ f. frog (pl. *îm*)	*Pi.* to curse: ptc.	פֶּסַח passover
יֶרַח moon	מְקַלֵּל one who curses	עִם with
מֻרְבֵּין stall	נָבַח to bark	כִּסֵּא throne
מַפְתֵּחַ key	מָתְנַיִם loins	חֻקָּה f. statute

עָשָׂה חֶסֶד עִם to do or show kindness to (*i.e.* in dealing *with*), deal kindly with   צָרַף to smelt, test, prove

Exercise.—Write the above nouns in cstr. sing. and with a vocalic and consonantal suff., observing which of them are of first declens. ; and translate:

אָכְלוּ בְּנֵי־יִשְׂרָאֵל אֶת־הַפֶּסַח מַתְּנֵיהֶם חֲגוּרִים נַעֲלֵיהֶם בְּרַגְלֵיהֶם ¹וּמַקְלָם בְּיָדָם : 2 עָשָׂה מַלְכְּכֶם חֶסֶד עִם־מַלְכֵּנוּ וְעִם כֹּהֲנֵינוּ וְעִם־נְבִיאֵינוּ : 3 שָׁלַחְתִּי אֶת־אֹיְבִי וַיִּמָּלֵט : 4 מֵת אֹיְבָהּ הַמְבַקֵּשׁ אֶת־נַפְשֶׁהּ : 5 וְהָלְכוּ יוֹשְׁבֵי הָאָרֶץ כְּעִוְרִים וְשָׁפַךְ דָּמָם כֶּעָפָר : 6 בני אתה : 7 אתם בני : 8 לא־אדבר עוד בשמו : 9 ולקחתם את־מקלכם ²בידכם :

This (is) my son and these (are) my son's sons. He sent the frogs upon all the land. All his prophets are dumb dogs, they cannot bark. In Jerusalem is my holy throne. We took our staves in our hand. Our enemies dealt kindly with our children. These are the statutes and the judgments which ye shall keep in the land whither ye (are) crossing, thou and thy son and thy son's son. Their land swarmed-with frogs (*acc.*) in the chambers of their kings.

§ 31. VERBAL SUFFIXES.

(See Paradigm, p. 210.)

1. (a) The pronominal object after a verb may be expressed by the appropriate form of the particle את (*me*, אֹתִי, &c.; cf. § 20. 10). In point of fact, however, this construction, though relatively common in the later style, is, in the earlier style, usually reserved for cases of emphasis: אֹתְךָ

---

¹ ק without dagh. forte ; cf. § 7. 5.
² יֶדְכֶם (not יְדְכֶם), cf. Scotch *gless, Glesca,* for *glass, Glasgow.*

אֹתוֹ אָהֵב אֲבִיהֶם מִכָּל־אֶחָיו thee *have I seen righteous,* *their father loved* him *more than* (§ 47. 1) *all his brethren,* אֹתְךָ הָרַגְתִּי וְאֹתָהּ הֶחֱיֵיתִי thee *had I slain, but* her *had I kept alive.* Note that in such cases the obj. precedes the verb.

(b) Ordinarily the pronom. obj. is expressed by a pronom. suffix to the verb, after the fashion of the suffixes appended to nouns ; *e.g.* הִכְעִיסוֹ *he provoked him* (הִכְעִים, Hiph. of כָּעַס). יִשְׁמָרְךָ *he will keep thee,* וַיִּמְכְּרֵם *and he sold them.*

2. The following table on p. 108 illustrates the use of the verbal suffixes, the study of which will be greatly facilitated by careful attention to the following points :

(a) The 3 *s. m. Hiph.* is chosen for the paradigm rather than the Qal because, both its vowels being unchangeable (the first short in the shut syllable, the second naturally long) the suffixes are unable to affect in any way the earlier part of the word, and thus their real nature and form can be most simply seen. Thus הִקְטִיל with 3 *s. m.* suffix gives הִקְטִילוֹ, but קָטַל would not give קָטַלוֹ (but קְטָלוֹ), because, the first two syllables being now both open, the law of the tone (§ 6. 2 b, c) instantly begins to affect their vowels and some-what complicates the issue for the beginner. Hence the special suitability of the Hiph.

(b) The suffixes to the vb., alike in pf. and impf. (which differ slightly) very closely resemble those to the noun (§ 19). The chief differences are in the 1st pers. sing. suffix, which is not *î*, but *nî*, and in the 3 *s. m.* and *f.* suff. to the impf. which are *êhu* and *êha* : the latter forms, however, are regularly found with nouns ending in הָ (§ 45. 3. 3); cf. מִקְנֵהוּ, מִקְנֶהָ *his, her cattle* (from מִקְנֶה); cf. § 19. 1.

(c) i. The so-called connecting vowel between the vb. and the suffix is *a* in the pf. (cf. הִקְטִילָם) and *e* in the impf. (cf. יַקְטִילֵם), and of course imperative (cf. הַקְטִילֵם).

ii. This vowel, however, is not really an arbitrary *connecting* vowel, but the *a* is, strictly speaking, the final vowel in the ultimate form of the *verb*, seen, *e.g.*, in the Arabic *qatala* = Hebr. קָטַל. The origin of the *e* is not so obvious ; probably it is due tc the analogy of Lamedh He vbs., § 44, where the *ē* is really part of the verb (*ay* = *ai* = *ê* = *ē*, cf. § 2. 2. 1).

VERBAL SUFFIXES TO HIPHʻÎL.

PERF.	הִקְטִיל	INFIN. CSTR.		הִקְטַלְתָּ
1 *s. c.*	הִקְטִילַנִי	הַקְטִילִי (subj.) הַקְטִילַנִי (obj.)		הִקְטַלְתַּנִי
2 *s. m.*	הִקְטִילְךָ	הַקְטִילְךָ (subj. and obj.)		—
„ *f.*	הִקְטִילֵךְ	„		—
3 *s. m.*	הִקְטִילוֹ	„	PARTIC.	הִקְטַלְתּוֹ
„ *f.*	הִקְטִילָהּ	„	מַקְטִיל	הִקְטַלְתָּהּ
1 *pl. c.*	הִקְטִילָנוּ	הַקְטִילֵנוּ	מַקְטִילִי	הִקְטַלְתָּנוּ
2 *pl. m.*	הִקְטִילְכֶם	&c.	&c., mostly as	—
„ *f.*	הִקְטִילְכֶן	as noun	the noun	—
3 *pl. m.*	הִקְטִילָם			הִקְטַלְתָּם
„ *f.*	הִקְטִילָן			הִקְטַלְתָּן
IMPERF.	יַקְטִיל	IMPER. AS IMPF.		יַקְטִילוּ
1 *s. c.*	יַקְטִילֵנִי	הַקְטִילֵנִי		יַקְטִילוּנִי
2 *s. m.*	יַקְטִילְךָ	—		יַקְטִילוּךָ
„ *f.*	יַקְטִילֵךְ	—		יַקְטִילוּךְ
3 *s. m.*	יַקְטִילֵהוּ	הַקְטִילֵהוּ		יַקְטִילוּהוּ
„ *f.*	יַקְטִילֶהָ	הַקְטִילֶהָ		יַקְטִילוּהָ
1 *pl. c.*	יַקְטִילֵנוּ	הַקְטִילֵנוּ		
2 *pl. m.*	יַקְטִילְכֶם	—		
„ *f.*	יַקְטִילְכֶן	—		
3 *pl. m.*	יַקְטִילֵם	הַקְטִילֵם		יַקְטִילוּם
„ *f.*	יַקְטִילֵן	הַקְטִילֵן		יַקְטִילוּן

3. (a) i. The case seems more complicated when one
or both of the syllables before the suffix is open: in reality
it is perfectly simple, as the tone laws strictly apply (§ 6).
Thus קָטַל with 3rd sing. masc. suff. becomes קְטָלוֹ; the accent
falls on the *ô*, in the open pretonic syllable the original ־ַ
naturally becomes the tone (long) ־ָ, and the original ־ָ being
now two places from the tone vanishes into shᵉwa. It follows exactly the analogy of דְּבָרוֹ. Thus קָטַל with the verbal
suffixes becomes קְטָלָם קְטָלְכֶם קְטָלָנוּ קְטָלָה קְטָלוֹ קְטָלָךְ קְטָלֵךְ קְטָלַנִי.
This *first declension* analogy (§ 18) is followed by the pf.
Qal in *all* its forms (*e.g.* שְׂנֵאָהּ *he hated her*) and by the

impf. and imper. Qal in *a* (*e.g.* וַיִּשְׁכָּחֵהוּ not "יִּשַׁ *and he forgot him*, from יִשְׁכַּח ; שְׁלָחֵנִי *send me*, from יִשְׁלַח).

  ii. Note that the vb., with 1st sing. suff. ends in נִי (*ánî*) ; with 1st pl. suff., in נוּ (*ánú*).

(b) Imperfects in *ō* (Qal) or *ē* (Pi'ēl, &c.) may be said to follow the analogy of the *third declension* (§ 30). *E.g.* Pi'ēl יְקַבֵּץ *he will gather*, יְקַבֶּצְךָ *he will gather thee*, אֲקַבְּצֵם *I will gather them*. Similarly יִשְׁמֹר *he will keep*, יִשְׁמְרֵנִי *he will keep me*, יִשְׁמְרֵהוּ *he will keep him*, but (before a consonantal suffix) יִשְׁמָרְךָ *he will keep thee* (*yishmor^ekhâ*).

(c) The imperat. Qal in *ō* and the infin. cstr. follow the analogy of the *second declension*, the form קְטֹל being a ṣeġholate of the *third* class (cf. § 21. 2 a.iii., § 29. 2). Thus שְׁמֹר *keep*, שָׁמְרֵנִי *shom^erēnî*, *keep me*, שָׁמְרֵם *keep them*, בְּשָׁמְרִי *when I kept* (lit. *in my keeping*). As the sh^ewa is vocal (cf. § 6. 2 e) the third radical does not take daghesh lene ; *e.g.* כָּתְבֵם *kothbhēm*, *write them*, בְּכָתְבוֹ *when he wrote*. This sh^ewa, however, is necessarily silent when the suffix is ךָ or כֶם, as two vocal sh^ewas cannot come together ; *e.g.* בְּעָבְרְכֶם *when you cross* (*'obh*, closed syllable), בְּעָבְדְךָ *when thou servest*. (With these two suffixes, the *o* sometimes appears between the second and third radical instead of between the first and second ; thus קְטֹל would give קְטָלְךָ (*q^etol^ekhâ*) as well as קָטְלְךָ *qotl^ekhâ* (cf. impf. יִשְׁמָרְךָ יִשְׁכֹּר). Hence בְּיוֹם אֲכָלְךָ *in the day of thine eating*, אֲכָלְכֶם *your eating*.)

4. (a) When the vb. already ends in a vowel, no " connecting " vowel is necessary—or possible ; the suffix is directly appended, *e.g.* קְטָלַתְנִי, קְטָלַתּוּ (note that the accent moves a place forward—hence ַ), קְטַלְתִּים ; in the 3rd pers. it appears as הוּ or ו (masc.), and הָ (fem.), *e.g.* קְטַלְתִּיהוּ, קְטַלְתִּיו (*-tiw*), קְטַלְתִּיהָ ; so יִקְטְלוּךְ (3 pl. impf.) יִקְטְלוּם, &c. With suffixes ending in וּ the *û* of the vb. is usually written ֵ , *e.g.* יִקְטְלֵנוּ, יִקְטְלֵהוּ, cf. § 4 c (*they will kill him, us*).

(b) Similarly in the 2nd pers. (קְטַלְתְּ) the vowel ַ is maintained with all the suffixes except the *first sing.*, *which always ends in* נִי ְ (except in pause נִי ָ), *e.g.* קְטַלְתַּנִי ; with the 3 s. m. suffix, *ā-hû* by dropping the *h* (§ 14. 1 e) contracts (through *au*) to *ô*, קְטַלְתּוֹ (§ 19. 1).

(c) The gaps which appear in the paradigms are explained

by the fact that the reflexive idea which would be expressed
by the absent forms is in Hebrew expressed in other ways,
e.g. Niph. Hithp. &c. (§§ 25, 26). E.g. *I hid myself*, not
סְתַרְתִּ֫ינִי but נִסְתַּ֫רְתִּי.

5. Before the suffixes, original verbal forms are restored.

(a) The 3rd sing. fem. pf. ־ָה becomes ־ַת or ־ָֽת, *e.g.*
הִקְטִילָ֫תַם, הִקְטִילַ֫תְנִי.

(b) The 2nd sing. fem. pf. ־ְתּ becomes ־ְתִּי (or ־ְתּ); *e.g.*
הִקְטַלְתִּ֫ינִי (Hiph.), קְטַלְתִּ֫יהוּ (Qal). Only the context enables
us to distinguish this from the suff. to the 1st pers.

(c) The 2nd pl. masc. pf. ־ְתֶּם becomes—but very rarely
—תּוּ; *e.g.* הֶעֱלִיתֻ֫נוּ *you have brought us up* (Hiph. of עלה,
§§ 34, 44).

6. In the 3 s. f. pf. קָֽטְלָה and the 3 pl. קָֽטְלוּ, it has to be
remembered that the sh°wa represents an original full vowel
in the second syllable (קָטֹל). When suffixes therefore are
added, not only does the initial ־ָ become ־ְ under the influence of the tone, as we have seen in the masc. (קְטָלַ֫נִי,
קְטָל֫וֹ, &c.), but the original pathaḥ which had become sh°wa
reasserts itself, and, standing in the open pretonic, becomes
־ָ; hence we get קְטָלַ֫תְנִי, קְטָלָ֫תַם, &c., קְטָל֫וּנִי, קְטָל֫וּךָ, קְטָל֫וּהוּ, &c.

7. Singular suffixes to the impf. and imper. are occasionally strengthened by the addition of *nûn* (known as the *nûn
energicum*) which is usually assimilated to the following consonant, or if that be נ, the נ is usually dropped and the
nûn doubled. The following forms result : יִקְטְלֶ֫נּוּ יִקְטְלֶ֫ךָ יִקְטְלֵ֫נִי
יִקְטְלֶ֫נָּה. They occur chiefly in pause.

8. *Participle.*—The suffixes to the participle are practically always those of the *noun*, not of the verb ; *e.g.* מַצְדִּיקִי
(not מַצְדִּיקֵ֫נִי) *he who justifies me* (Hiph. ptc. of צדק), מְבַקְשָׁיו
(not מְבַקְשֵׁ֫יהוּ) *those who seek him* (Pi. of בקש ; cf. § 7. 5),
רֹדְפַי *those who pursue me, my persecutors*.

9. (a) *Inf. construct.*—The suffixes to the inf. constr. are
also those of the *noun*, except that the *first* pers. sing. suff. is
both nominal (־ִי) and verbal (־ֵ֫נִי), the nominal being used
to denote the *subject*, and the verbal the *object*; *e.g.* יוֹם
פָּקְדִי *the day of my visiting*, i.e. *when I visit* (*poq°dhî*) ; but
לְפָקְדֵ֫נִי *to visit me*. In the other persons the suffix may express either subject or object; *e.g.* עַל־שָׂרְפוֹ (*sor°phô*) *because
he burned* (lit. *on account of his burning*), לְשָׂרְפוֹ *to burn it.*

(b) The *infin. cstr.*, partaking as it does of the character of both verb and noun, has (like a verb) the power of governing an object, besides (like a noun) being able to take suffixes and prefixes.   The usual order is infin., subject, object.

when he kept בְּשָׁמְרוֹ   *when the man kept* בְּשְׁמֹר הָאִישׁ
before he kept me   לִפְנֵי שָׁמְרוֹ אֹתִי
before the man kept me   לִפְנֵי שְׁמֹר הָאִישׁ אֹתִי
on the day when I visit them   בְּיוֹם פָּקְדִי אֹתָם

(c) Instead of the infin. cstr. with preposition the finite form may be used with a conjunctional expression formed of the prep. and relative.

when I kept the man   כַּאֲשֶׁר שָׁמַרְתִּי אֶת־הָאִישׁ or בְּשָׁמְרִי אֶת־הָאִישׁ
until I keep the man   עַד אֲשֶׁר אֶשְׁמֹר or „ עַד שָׁמְרִי
after they had made a covenant   אַחֲרֵי אֲשֶׁר or אַחֲרֵי כָּרְתָם בְּרִית כָּרְתָם בְּרִית

נָּמַל to deal fully with, recompense, requite   טָמַן to hide
דָּרַךְ to tread   קִבֵּץ (*Qal*) *Pi'êl*, to gather   מִצְרִי Egyptian
קְבוּרָה *f.* burying-place   לוּחַ } tablet   בֵּיתְאֵל Bethel
                לוּחֹת } *pl.*

EXERCISE.   TRANSLATE.

שְׁמָרְתַּנִי, שְׁמַרְתִּיהָ, וּשְׁמָרוֹ, לְשָׁמְרָהּ, וּלְשָׁמְרָה, שָׁמְרֵנִי, וַיִּשְׁמְרֵנִי,
וַיִּלְבָּשֵׁנִי, תִּשְׁמְרֵם, וְאֶשְׁמְרֶנָּה, יִשְׁמְרֵהוּ, תִּשְׁמְרֶךָ; שְׁפָטוּנִי,
שְׁפָטוּם, בְּשָׁפְטֶךָ, שְׁפָטֵנִי; זְבַרְתָּם, אֶזְכְּרֶנָּה, וַיִּזְכְּרֶהָ, יִזְכְּרוּנִי,
כְּהַזְכִּירוֹ, הַזְכִּירֵנִי, גְּנַבְתַּם, גְּנָבוּהָ; וְקִבְּצָהּ, קִבְּצָם, וְקִבַּצְתִּים,
וּמְקַבְּצָיו, בְּקַבְּצִי, אֲקַבְּצֵךָ, יְקַבְּצָהּ:
אַתָּה גְמַלְתַּנִי הַטּוֹבָה וַאֲנִי גְמַלְתִּיךָ הָרָעָה: 2 כִּבְּדוּנִי
בְשִׂפְתֵיהֶם: 3 שְׁמֹר אֶת־דְּבָרֵי יהוה כָּתְבֵם עַל־לוּחַ לִבְּךָ:
4 בַּקֵּשׁ שָׁלוֹם וְרָדְפֵהוּ: 5 הַדְרִיכֵנִי בִּנְתִיב מִצְוֹתֶיךָ כִּי בוֹ
חָפָצְתִּי: 6 דְּרָשׁוּ יהוה בְּהִמָּצְאוֹ: 7 הָרַג משֶׁה אֶת־הַמִּצְרִי
וַיִּטְמְנֵהוּ בַחוֹל: 8 יהוה יִשְׁמָרְךָ מִכָּל־רָע יִשְׁמֹר אֶת־נַפְשֶׁךָ:

I have gathered thee.   I will gather her from the sides of the earth.   And thou shalt keep me in thy way.   Keep thou him.   Before she kept the man.   In the day when I visit (of my visiting) Israel, I will destroy the altars of

Bethel.   Judge me according-to my righteousness.   Bury me not in Egypt, but I will lie with my fathers and thou shalt bury me in their burying-place.   What is man that thou rememberest him, or (and) the son of man that thou visitest him?   Thy word[1] is proved and thy servant loveth it. Before he cut off all flesh by the waters of the flood.   He promised (said) to mention him before the priests of the temple.

§ 32. IRREGULAR OR WEAK VERBS.

1. The word פָּעַל *to do* was used as a paradigm by the older Grammarians.   Now the first letter of this verb being *Pe,* the first letter of any verb was called its *Pe*; and in like manner the second letter was called its *'Ayin,* and the third its *Lamedh.*   This mode of designation is employed in *weak verbs.*

2. A weak verb is a verb which has one or more of its three stem letters a weak letter.   The weak letters are the *Gutturals,* the *Quiescents,* and *Nun, i.e.* the letters ח ה א י ו ר ע נ.   Thus such a verb as נפל is called a *Pe Nun* verb, because its *Pe, i.e.* its first letter, is *nun*; יָלַד, a *Pe Yodh* verb; קוּם, a *'Ayin Waw* verb, because its second letter is *waw*; שָׁמַע, a *Lamedh Guttural* verb, because its third letter is a guttural: and so on.   The letters *'Aleph* and *He* being gutturals at the beginning of a word and quiescents at the end have a double nomenclature, thus גָּלָה is a *Lamedh He,* but הָלַךְ a *Pe Gutt.,* מָצָא a *Lam. 'Aleph,* but אָסַף a *Pe Gutt.* In a few verbs *'Aleph,* when first radical, quiesces in the impf., as in אָמַר; these are called *Pe 'Aleph* verbs (§ 35).   If a verb have more than one weak letter it is called after all the classes whose peculiarities it shares; *e.g.* ירה is a *Pe Yodh* and *Lam. He* verb.   A verb like גָּלַל whose second and third letters are the same is called a *Double 'Ayin* verb.

3. The phrase "irregular verbs" is really a misnomer. The verbs so called are neither arbitrary nor anomalous; most of them are absolutely regular, only the paradigm form of the regular verb is modified—in strictly natural and reasonable ways—by the presence of one of the weak letters.

---

[1] אִמְרָה.

E.g. the Pi'ēl which doubles the middle radical (קִטֵּל) will necessarily assume a special form when the middle radical is a guttural, as gutturals cannot be doubled; but that special form is determined by the laws affecting gutturals with which we are already familiar (§ 8) and is not some arbitrary thing to be laboriously committed to memory (*e.g.* מֵאֵן for מִאֵן *to refuse,* בֵּרֵךְ for בִּרֵךְ *to bless*). So it is with other types of "irregular" verb, which are thoroughly regular to one who clearly understands the fundamental principles of the language described in §§ 2–10.

DESIGNATE THE CLASSES OF THESE VERBS.

קְרָא, אָבַל, שָׁלַח, שָׁחַט, שָׁאַף, בִּין, יָלַד, יָשַׁע, בָּקַשׁ, רוּם,
בֵּרֵךְ, עָבַר, שָׁקַל, נָחָה, נָחַם, נָגַף, רָעַע, קָלַל, בּוֹא, סָבַב,
קָרַע, רָדַף, יָרֵא, ירה:

§ 33. PE NUN VERBS.
(See Paradigm, p. 212.)

The letter *n* in Hebrew shows the same kind of feebleness that it has in other languages; when it is not sustained by being followed by a full vowel, its sound is apt to be lost in that of the consonant after it, *in-licio = illicio*; ἐν-γράφω = ἐγγράφω; יִנְגֹּשׁ = יִגֹּשׁ (*yin-gash = yiggash*).

1. (*a*) When *n* stands at the end of a syllable (imperf. Qal, perf. and ptc. Niph., Hiph., Hoph.) it is in most cases assimilated to the next consonant, which is doubled, יִנְפֹּל = יִפֹּל, הִנְפִּיל = הִפִּיל (*yin-pōl = yippōl, hinpīl = hippīl*). נִנְגַּף = נִגַּף, Niph. of נָגַף *to smite.*

(*b*) In certain cases (*e.g.* verbs ending in ה) the Niph. and Pi'ēl would be indistinguishable, except for the context; cf. נָקָה, Niph. *to be clean, innocent*; Pi. *to declare innocent, acquit.*

(c) In the Hoph. *u* naturally appears instead of *o* before the duplicated consonant (§ 7. 7); *e.g.* נָגַד, הֻגַּד (pf.) יֻגַּד (impf.).

(d) The *n* is not usually assimilated in verbs whose middle radical is a guttural; *e.g.* נָחַל *to inherit,* impf. Qal יִנְחַל, Hiph. יַנְחִיל. But the Niph. of נָחַם is נִחַם *to repent* (cf. § 36. 1. 3).

2. Verbs whose impfs. are in *ō* and *a* should be carefully distinguished.

8

(a) In vbs. with impf. in *a* (*e.g.* נָגַשׁ, יִגַּשׁ) the נ is almost always dropped in the imperat. Qal; *e.g.* גַּשׁ (for נְגַשׁ), *f.* גְּשִׁי, *pl.* גְּשׁוּ.

(b) It is also usually dropped in the inf. cstr., which, however, by a sort of compensation, adds the fem. termination ת, and then assumes the form of a segholate noun גֶּשֶׁת; the steps are גֵּשׁ, גֵּשְׁתְּ, גֶּשֶׁת (exactly like מֶלֶךְ, מַלְךְ, § 29). Note, however, that the vowel is regularly *i* (not *a*) when inflected (cf. צֶדֶק, § 29. 1 b); *e.g.* גִּשְׁתּוֹ *his approaching*.

(c) ל before such (segholate) inf. constructs is pointed לְ; *e.g.* לְגֶשֶׁת (§ 14. 1 d).

(d) In vbs. with impf. in *ō*, the נ is not dropped in imper. or inf. cstr.; *e.g.* נָפַל, impf. יִפֹּל; imper. and inf. cstr. נְפֹל.

3. (a) The verb נָתַן *to give* assimilates its *final* n also in perf. נָתַתִּי, &c. (for נָתַנְתִּי), and infin. cstr. which is תֵּת (for תֵּנְת), and with suff. תִּתִּי (for תִּנְתִּי). It has *ē* in imperf. יִתֵּן and imper. תֵּן, emph. תֵּנָה (§ 23. 2), *f.* תְּנִי, *pl.* תְּנוּ.

(b) In the verb לָקַח *to take* the ל is treated like the *nun* of *Pe Nun* vbs.; *e.g.* impf. Qal יִקַּח (for יִלְקַח), *pl.* יִקְחוּ (§ 7. 5); imper. קַח, קְחוּ, inf. cstr. קַחַת, קַחְתִּי, &c. (§ 8. 1, *a* under influence of the guttural).

(c) The form יֻקַּח is probably not impf. Hoph. but impf. of the old passive Qal, of which now few traces exist except the participle. לֻקַּח, which also exists, is to be regarded as the (old) pf. pass. Qal rather than as pf. Puʻal. So יֻתַּן pass. Qal rather than Hoph. of נתן. The Hoph. is unlikely, as no causative idea is present in these words, and the Hiph. of these verbs is not found.

(d) ל before these (monosyllabic or segholate) inf. constructs is pointed לָ; *e.g.* לָקַחַת לָתֵת, (§ 14. 1 d).

4. *Nouns from Verbs* פ״ן.—Nouns with *m* preformative are of the form מַתָּן *gifts* (coll. from נָתַן), as מַפָּל *offal* (from נָפַל *to fall*), מַכָּה *stroke* (from נָכָה, Hiph. *to strike*).

נצל *Hi.* to deliver	נגע to touch (*Hi.* to reach)	נשק to kiss
נגש to approach	נשׁא *Hi.* to deceive	נפל to fall
נגף to smite	נדר to vow	נבט *Hi.* to look
נגד *Hi.* to tell	נצב *Hi.* to set	נחל to inherit
נָשַׁל to drop off *intr.*, draw off *tr.*	תַּרְדֵּמָה *f.* a deep sleep	
בָּנָה to build	אֹרֶךְ length	רֹחַב breadth
צֵלָע *f.* rib, side : *cstr.* צֶלַע ; *pl.* צְלָעוֹת, *cstr.* צַלְעוֹת		
אֶחָד *m.* אַחַת *f.* one	סֻלָּם ladder	אַיִל ram גַּת Gath

EXERCISE. TRANSLATE.

תֵּן, קְחוּ, נָפֹל, הִנָּגֵף, אַפִּיל, הִצַּלְתָּ, מַצִּיל, וַיִּנָּצְלוּ, תְּנָה,
תַּצִּילֵם, תִּגְּעוּ, נִגָּף, הֻגַּד, הַגִּידוּ, תַּבֵּט, לִנְפֹּל, לָגֶשֶׁת:
הַצִּילֵנִי מִדָּמִים אֱלֹהֵי תְּשׁוּעָתִי וּלְשׁוֹנִי תַּגִּיד צִדְקָתֶךָ: 2 כִּי
תִדּוֹר נֶדֶר [1] לַיהוה אַל־תְּשַׁבַּח לְשַׁלְּמוֹ: 3 יָרְאוּ אֹיְבָיו מִגֶּשֶׁת
אֵלָיו: 4 הַבֶּט־נָא הַשָּׁמַיְמָה וּסְפֹר הַכּוֹכָבִים: 5 וַיַּפֵּל יהוה
תַּרְדֵּמָה עַל־הָאָדָם וַיִּקַּח אַחַת מִצַּלְעוֹתָיו וְהַצֵּלָע אֲשֶׁר לָקַח
בָּנָה לְאִשָּׁה: 6 אָמַר הָאָדָם הָאִשָּׁה אֲשֶׁר נָתַתָּ [2] עִמָּדִי הִיא
נָתְנָה־לִּי [3] מִן־הָעֵץ: 7 אָמַר יהוה אֶל־אַבְרָם הִתְהַלֵּךְ בָּאָרֶץ
לְאָרְכָּהּ וּלְרָחְבָּהּ כִּי לְךָ אֶתְּנֶנָּה וַיִּפֹּל אַבְרָם עַל פָּנָיו:
8 חָלַם יַעֲקֹב וְהִנֵּה סֻלָּם מֻצָּב אַרְצָה וְרֹאשׁוֹ מַגִּיעַ הַשָּׁמָיְמָה:
9 נִתְּנוּ בְּיַד מַלְכֵי הָאֲרָצוֹת: 10 שַׁל נְעָלֶיךָ מֵעַל רַגְלֶיךָ כִּי
הַמָּקוֹם אֲשֶׁר אַתָּה עוֹמֵד עָלָיו אַדְמַת־קֹדֶשׁ הוּא: 11 וַיֹּאמֶר
לוֹ הַמֶּלֶךְ תְּנָה־לִּי אֶת־כַּרְמְךָ בְּכֶסֶף וַיֹּאמֶר לֹא־אֶתֵּן לְךָ
אֶת־כַּרְמִי:

Give ye. I will not give my silver and my gold. Tell
it not in Gath. Look not (*f.*) after thee, lest God smite
thee. Deliver me, for thou art my salvation. Let them
give glory to Yahweh because of his loving-kindness. When
I gave the woman to the man for wife. I will deliver thee,
and thy tongue shall tell-of righteousness. The serpent
deceived her and she took of the tree and gave to her
husband. They feared to draw near, lest they should be
smitten before their enemies. Thou hast caused a deep-sleep
to fall upon me. And he brought near the man and he took
him in his arms and kissed him (*dat.*).

§ 34. PE GUTTURAL VERBS.
(See Paradigm, p. 214.)

See the rules for Gutturals, § 8.

1. By § 8. 2 a, a gutt. requires a *ḥateph* for simple sh°wa
vocal (2 pl. perf., imper., infin. cstr., Qal: thus קְטֹל, קְטַלְתֶּם,
but עֲמֹד, עֲמַדְתֶּם; אָכֹל but אֲכַלְתֶּם, § 8. 2 b).

---

[1] לְ is pointed as if read to אֲדֹנָי which was substituted for יהוה, § 10. 5 b.

[2] Alternative form to עִמִּי = *with me*, 1 s. suff. to עִם *with* (cf. p. 142,
note 1).   [3] See § 7. 6.

2. (a) By § 8. 1 b, *i* before gutt. becomes *e*, and by § 8. 2 a the short vowel usually repeats itself under the gutt. in a *ḥaṭeph* corresponding to itself. Thus:

Niph. pf.	נִקְטַל	in gutt.	נֶעֱמַד	and then	נֶעֱמַד
Hiph. pf.	הִקְטִיל	„	הֶעֱמִיד	„	הֶעֱמִיד
Hiph. inf.	הַקְטִיל	„			הֶעֱמִיד
Hoph. pf.	הָקְטַל	„			הָעֳמַד
Qal impf.	(יִקְטֹל) primary form	יַקְטֹל in gutt.			יַעֲמֹד
Qal impf. of stat. vb.	יִכְבַּד in gutt.		יֶאֱהַב and then		יֶאֱהַב

(b) Note that in stative vbs. (impf. in *a*) the guttural has *e* in impf. Qal; in active vbs. (impf. in *ō*) it has *a*, which is really the original vowel of the impf. (§ 21. 1 a). Thus the combinations are ˈ _ֱ_ and _ֲ_; except that before א even imperfects in *ō* have *e*, e.g. יֶאֱסֹף *he will gather*.

(c) The gutturals usually, though not always, take a *composite* sh⁰wa at the end of a syllable, cf. יַעֲמֹד, נֶעֱזַב (Niph.) *he was forsaken,* הֶאֱמִין (Hiph.) *he trusted*; in most cases, however, though not in all (e.g. יַחֲלֹם *he will dream,* יַחֲרִישׁ *he will be silent*) ח takes *silent* sh⁰wa; e.g. יֶחְכַּם *he will be wise,* יֶחְדַּל *he will cease,* יֶחְסַר *he will lack,* יַחְמֹד *he will desire* (cf. § 8. 2). A few use both forms, חָשַׁב *to devise,* יַחְשֹׁב and יַחֲשֹׁב.

(d) Note that in forms ending ה‍ָ, ‍ִי, ‍וּ, the composite sh⁰wa of the guttural is necessarily changed into the corresponding short vowel, and the syllable is half open; e.g. sing. יַעֲמֹד, pl. (cf. יִקְטְלוּ) יַעַמְדוּ which, as two vocal sh⁰was cannot come together, becomes יַעַמְדוּ *yaʿamᵉdhû* (§ 6. 2 d. ii.); 3 s. m. Niph. נֶאֱסַף, f. (cf. נִקְטְלָה) נֶאֱסָפָה which becomes נֶאֶסְפָה *she has been gathered* or *taken away.*

3. (a) By § 8. 4 the gutt. cannot be doubled, but remaining single, causes the preceding short vowel to become its tone-long. Only the impf. (imper. and inf.) Niphal are affected; e.g. יִקָּטֵל, but יֵעָמֵד (for יֵעָמֵד). So with ר; יֵרָפֵא *he shall be healed.*

(b) In the Hiph. pf. with *waw cons.* and the consequent throwing forward of the accent (§ 23. 3. 4), the ‍ֱ becomes ‍ֲ: thus הֶעֱמַדְתָּ *thou hast stationed,* but וְהַעֲמַדְתָּ *and thou wilt station.* This change

occurs elsewhere at a distance from the tone ; *e.g.* אֵלַי (poetic form
of אֶל־), but אֲלֵיכֶם, cf. § 8. 2 b.

חלם	to dream	עמד	to stand	יְהוֹשֻׁעַ	Joshua
עבר	to pass, cross	חבק	*Pi.* to embrace	הרג	to slay
רחק	to be distant,	חטא	to sin	חשׁב	to count
	[withdraw, refrain	אחז	to take hold of	חזק }	to be strong
עזב	to leave, forsake	חבשׁ } to bind		אמץ }	
עבד	to serve, till	אסר }		אמן	*Hi.* to believe
חכם	to be wise	אָרַךְ	to be long :	אֵיךְ	how ?
נָהָר	river		*Hiph.* to prolong	עָשַׁן	to smoke

נְהָרִים, oftener נְהָרוֹת, *pl.*

4. *Nouns from Pe Gutt. verbs.*——

	First declension.			Second declension.		
sing. abs.	חָכָם	אֲדָמָה	מַאֲכָל	עֶבֶד	עֵגֶל	חֹדֶשׁ
cstr.	חֲכַם	אַדְמַת	מַאֲכַל	„	„	„
plur. abs.	חֲכָמִים	אֲדָמוֹת		עֲבָדִים	עֲגָלִים	חֳדָשִׁים
cstr.	חַכְמֵי	אַדְמוֹת		עַבְדֵי	עֶגְלֵי	חָדְשֵׁי
	(wise)	(ground)	(food)	(servant)	(calf)	(month)

(a) In *first declens.*——Rule 2 of Gutturals (§ 8. 2) applies.
Note cstr. pl. חַכְמֵי (not of course חִכְמֵי like דִּבְרֵי, cf. § 6. 2 d. ii.).

(b) In *second declens.*——2nd class, the gutt. often depresses
i to *e* (§ 8. 1 b) ; hence עֶגְלֵי not עִגְלֵי. With nouns of the 1st
and 2nd class the composite sh°wa, where necessary, is
ḥateph pathaḥ (עֲבָדִים, עֲגָלִים, cf. § 6. 2 c. iii.) ; with nouns of
the 3rd class it is naturally *ḥateph qāmeç* (חֳדָשִׁים, § 29).

(c). In *third declens.*——No effects follow, because the vowel
accompanying the guttural is unchangeable ; *e.g.* חֹמֵד, חֹמְדִים,
desiring, מְאַסֵּף, מְאַסְּפִים (Pi. ptc. *gathering* ; for ס, cf. § 7. 5).

EXERCISE. TRANSLATE.

וַיַּעֲזֹב כָּל־אֲשֶׁר לוֹ בְּיַד יוֹסֵף : 2 הִנֵּה שְׁנֵי הַמְּלָכִים לֹא
עָמְדוּ לְפָנָיו וְאֵיךְ נַעֲמֹד אֲנַחְנוּ : 3 וַיִּזְכֹּר אֱלֹהִים אֶת־נֹחַ
וַיַּעֲבֵר רוּחַ גְּדוֹלָה עַל־הָאָרֶץ : 4 [1] וַנַּחַלְמָה חֲלוֹם בַּלַּיְלָה אֶחָד

[1] The form with final הָ is often used in the 1st pers. both sing. and
pl. (esp. in the later books) ; *e.g.* וָאֶשְׁלְחָה *and I sent*, Gen. 32. 6.

אֲנִי וָהוּא : 5 חֲזַק וֶאֱמָץ כִּי אַתָּה תַּנְחִיל אֶת־הָעָם הַזֶּה
אֶת־הָאָרֶץ אֲשֶׁר נִשְׁבַּעְתִּי לַאֲבוֹתָם לָתֵת לָהֶם : 6 וְאַבְרָם
הֶאֱמִין בַּיהוה וַיַּחְשְׁבֶהָ לּוֹ צְדָקָה : 7 תְּנָה־לָּנוּ אֶת־הָאָרֶץ
הַזֹּאת וְאַל־תַּעֲבִרֵנוּ אֶת־הַנָּהָר : 8 שְׁלָחַנִי יהוה לַחֲבֹשׁ לְנִשְׁבְּרֵי
לֵב : 9 אִם־רָעֵב הַאֲכִילֵהוּ לָהֶם : 10 גַּע בֶּהָרִים
וְיֶעֱשָׁנוּ : 11 אַל־תַעֲזֹב חכמה אֶהֱבֶהָ ותשמרך : 12 ואתם
אל־תעמדו רדפו אחרי אויביכם כי נתנם יהוה אלהיכם
בידכם :

Abraham saw a ram taken by (בְּ) his horns. Pass not
the river, lest ye be smitten before your enemies. Our land
shall not be tilled, for our enemies shall stand in the midst-
of-her. Let me cross the river, that I may make this people
inherit the land which Yahweh sware unto their fathers to
give them. Love wisdom, forsake her not. They said unto
him, To bind thee have we come down, to give thee into
the hand of thine enemies. And the people served (*pl.*) their
God all the days of Joshua, and all the days of the elders
who prolonged days after Joshua. And he made to pass
his children in the fire.

§ 35. PE 'ALEPH VERB.
(See Paradigm, p. 215.)

1. (a) *Pe 'Aleph* verbs are a sub-class of *Pe Gutt.* verbs.
They have one peculiarity,—in impf. Qal *'Aleph* quiesces in
the vowel *ô*; in all other respects they are *Pe Gutt.* This
ô is for *â*: thus אֱמֹר = יָאֱמֹר = יָאמֹר (cf. Arab. *salâmu*, שָׁלוֹם,
§ 2. 2. 1) = יֹאמַר, by a curious process known as *dissimilation*,
intended to prevent two similar vowels (here *ō*) from following
one another in the same word (cf. רִאשׁוֹן *first*, from ראֹשׁ *head*).

The verbs belonging to this class are *five*: אָבַד *to perish*,
אָכַל *to eat*, אָמַר *to say*, אָבָה *to be willing*, אָפָה *to bake*.

(b) A few verbs have both this quiescent form and the regular *Pe Gutt.* form; *e.g.* אָחַז *grasp, seize,* impf. יֹאחֵז and (rarely)
יֶאֱחֹז; אָסַף *to gather,* impf. יֶאֱסֹף and (rarely) יֹסֵף (for יֹאסֵף).

(c) Note that in the last vb. the quiescent א is dropped,
as sometimes elsewhere; *e.g.* תֹּמְרוּ = תֹּאמְרוּ *ye shall say,* and

regularly in the 1st pers. sing. of these verbs; *e.g.* אֹמַר (for
אאֹמַר) *I will say.*

2. (a) The impf. is in *a* (יֹאכַל), but often (cf. יֹסֵף, יֹאחֵז),
especially in pause, in *ē* (יֹאכֵל).

(b) This does not apply to אָבָה and אָפָה, whose impf., like that
of all *Lamedh He* verbs (§ 32. 2), ends in ה ָ (§ 44. 1 b); *e.g.* יֹאבֶה.

3. (a) אָמַר in impf. with waw consec. and retracted accent
(§ 23. 3. 4) has the form וַיֹּאמֶר *and he said.*

(b) In inf. cstr. (אֱמֹר) with לְ, it becomes (לֶאֱמֹר =) לֵאמֹר
dicendo, *saying* (§ 14. 1 c). But not so with other verbs;
e.g. לֶאֱכֹל (not לֵאכֹל) *to eat.*

שָׁכַם *Hiph.* to rise early   פְּלִשְׁתִּים Philistines   שִׁמְשׁוֹן Samson
נְחֹשֶׁת *m.* copper, bronze: *dual* נְחֻשְׁתַּיִם fetters of copper or bronze
נָקִי (twice written נָקִיא) clean, innocent   מָחָר to-morrow
בִּשֵּׁל *Pi.* to boil, seethe   אַחֵר another (next)   חבא *Hiph.* hide

EXERCISE. TRANSLATE.

וַיֹּאמֶר יְהוָֹה אֶל־הָאָדָם מִכָּל־עֵץ הַגָּן אָכֹל תֹּאכֵל : 2 אִם־
¹תֹּאבוּ וּשְׁמַעְתֶּם טוּב הָאָרֶץ תֹּאכֵלוּ : 3 וְהַאֲכַלְתִּים אֶת־בְּשַׂר
בְּנֵיהֶם וְאֶת־בְּשַׂר בְּנוֹתֵיהֶם : 4 קַחֲ־לָהּ מִכָּל־מַאֲכָל אֲשֶׁר
יֵאָכֵל וְהָיָה לָהּ וְלָהֶם לְאָכְלָה : 5 יְהוָה אַל־נָא נֹאבְדָה בְּנֶפֶשׁ
הָאִישׁ הַזֶּה וְאַל־תִּתֵּן עָלֵינוּ דָּם נָקִיא : 6 וַיֹּאמֶר הַמֶּלֶךְ אֶל־
הָאִשָּׁה מַה־לָּךְ וַתֹּאמֶר הָאִשָּׁה הַזֹּאת אָמְרָה אֵלַי תְּנִי אֶת־
בְּנֵךְ וְנֹאכְלֶנּוּ הַיּוֹם וְאֶת־בְּנִי נֹאכַל מָחָר : וַנְּבַשֵּׁל אֶת־בְּנִי
וַנֹּאכְלֵהוּ וָאֹמַר אֵלֶיהָ בַּיּוֹם הָאַחֵר תְּנִי אֶת־בְּנֵךְ וְנֹאכְלֶנּוּ
וַתַּחְבֵּא אֶת־בְּנָהּ : 7 וַתִּקַּח הָאִשָּׁה מִפְּרִי הָעֵץ וַתֹּאבַל וַתִּתֵּן
גַּם לְאִישָׁהּ וַיֹּאכַל : 8 הַאֲכַלְתֶּם לָהֶם בַּמִּדְבָּר :

Ye shall eat of the fruit of your ways. Let us not perish
for his soul. And he called the people to eat and they ate.
And the children of Israel said, Who will let-us-eat (*Hiph.*)
flesh? Ye shall not eat any carcase; to the stranger ye
shall give it and he shall eat it. And the woman said, The
serpent beguiled me and I ate. Give me flesh that I may
eat.² It shall not be eaten, it shall be burned in the fire.
And the dogs ate the flesh of my calf. And the man rose-

¹ 2nd plur. impf., § 44. 2. 1.   ² *Waw* with *Cohort.*, § 23. 1. 2.

early in the morning and he told all these words in the ears of his servants. The Philistines gathered together (אָסַף, *Niph.*) and seized Samson and bound him with fetters of bronze.

§ 36. ʿAYIN GUTTURAL VERBS.
(See Paradigm, p. 216.)

1. (1) *a.* By § 8. 1 a the gutt. prefers the *a* sound, hence impf. and imper. Qal end in *a*; *e.g.* שָׁחַט, יִשְׁחַט, not יִשְׁחֹט, שְׁחֹט. (But inf. cstr. has *ō*; *e.g.* שְׁחֹט, § 22. 3.)

b. Impf. with suff. יִשְׁחֲטֵנִי not "יִשְׁחָ, cf. § 31. 3 a.

c. Often, too, the pf. Piʿēl has *a*; *e.g.* נִחַם (not נִחֵם) *to comfort*; but שִׁחֵת *to destroy*.

(2) By § 8. 2 a the gutt. must have a *ḥateph* as indistinct vowel, hence with the terminations הָ ֽ, י ֽ, וּ, the middle gutt. is pointed with *ḥ. pathaḥ*, as שָׁחֲטָה, שָׁחֲטוּ, not שָׁחְטוּ (cf. קְטָלָה), &c.; cf. 8. 3 b. The first vowel of the imper. *s. f.* and *pl. m.* is naturally *a*; *e.g.* שַׁחֲטִי, שַׁחֲטוּ.

(3) *a.* By § 8. 4 the gutt. cannot be doubled, hence Piʿēl, Puʿal, Hithp. must omit *dag. f.* from the middle radical. The preceding vowel becomes tone-long *always* before ר, as pf. Pi. בֵּרֵךְ for בִּרֵּךְ: 2 pl. בֵּרַכְתֶּם (not בְּ ; the ֵ remains unchangeable, as the first syllable is virtually closed, § 8. 4 b), Pi. יְבָרֵךְ for יְבַרֵּךְ (impf.), בָּרֵךְ (imper.), יְבֹרַךְ for יְבֻרַּךְ (impf. Puʿal).—The preceding vowel becomes tone-long *generally* before א, as מֵאֵן, impf. יְמָאֵן *to refuse*; before ה, ח, and ע the short vowel usually remains and the guttural is regarded as virtually doubled; *e.g.* נִחַם (not נִחֵם), impf. יְנַחֵם (not 'יְנָ), Pu. נֻחַם (not נֻחָם). So בִּעֵר *to burn, consume, remove.*

b. In ברך when the vowel of the כ is accented, the ר takes composite instead of simple shᵉwa; *e.g.* בֵּרֲכוּ *they blessed*, בָּרֲכֵנִי *bless me.*

2. *Nouns from ʿAyin Gutt. verbs.*

	First declension.		Second declension.		Third declension.	
sing. abs.	נָהָר	נַעַר	פַּחַד	פֹּעַל	רֹחַב	כֹּהֵן
cstr.	נְהַר	,,	,,	,,	,,	,,
voc. suff.	נְהָרִי	נַעֲרִי	פַּחְדִּי	פָּעֳלִי	רָחְבִּי	כֹּהֲנִי
cons. suff.	נְהָרְךָ	נַעַרְךָ	פַּחְדְּךָ	פָּעָלְךָ	רָחְבְּךָ	(כֹּהֶנְךָ)
plur. abs.	נְהָרִים	נְעָרִים	פְּחָדִים	פְּעָלִים	(רְחָבִים)	כֹּהֲנִים
cstr.	נְהֲרֵי	נַעֲרֵי	פַּחֲדֵי	פָּעֳלֵי	(רַחֲבֵי)	כֹּהֲנֵי
	(river)	(lad)	(fear)	(work)	(breadth)	(priest)

Like פַּחַד is the preposition תַּחַת *under, instead of*, which,
like אֶל, עַל, takes *plur.* suffixes, תַּחְתָּיו, תַּחְתֶּיךָ, תַּחְתַּי, &c.

(1) In *second declens.* words primarily of the form נַעַר,
פֹּעַל, &c. (§ 29), naturally take, under the influence of the
guttural, as their helping vowel ־ַ, not ־ֶ (as in בֹּקֶר, מֶלֶךְ),
and words of the 1st class or *a*-type (מֶלֶךְ) preserve the
original pathaḥ (cf. נַעַר), thus yielding the form נַעַר; words
of the 2nd class, with the vowels ־ ־ (cf. סֵפֶר), do not exist;
words of the 3rd class are formed as we should expect
(cf. בֹּקֶר), *e.g.* פֹּעַל.

(2) Suffixes are added in strict accordance with the rules;
e.g. נַעַר (cf. מַלְכִּי) becomes נַעֲרִי because gutturals except
ח (§ 8. 2 a) (cf. פַּחְדִּי) prefer the composite. נַעַרְךָ (cf. מַלְכְּךָ)
becomes first נַעֲרְךָ and then נַעַרְךָ because two vocal shᵉwas
cannot come together (§ 6. 2 d. ii.). Similarly פֹּעַל with suffix
becomes first פָּעֳלִי (cf. בָּקְרִי) then פָּעֳלִי: so פָּעֳלְךָ *poʿŏlkhâ* becomes first פָּעֳלְךָ and then פָּעֳלְךָ *poʿŏlkhâ*. But ח takes the
simple shᵉwa and closes the syllable, cf. רָחְבִּי.

(3) Sᵉghol appears instead of pathaḥ in the words לֶחֶם
bread, רֶחֶם *womb*, אֹהֶל *tent*, בֹּהֶן *thumb*.

טהר	to be clean	שׁרת	*Pi.* to serve	נרשׁ	*Pi.* to drive
שׁחט	to slay	לחם	*Ni.* to fight	סעד	{ to sustain / refresh
צעק / זעק	to cry	ברך	*Pi.* to bless	מִנְחָה	*f.* offering
אבל	to mourn	שׁען	*Ni.* to lean	נֶסֶךְ	drink-offering
טעם	to taste	בחר	to choose	עֵדֶן	Eden [1]
מִשְׁפָּחָה	*f.* clan	רחץ	to wash	כּוּשׁ	Cush (Ethiopia)
		שַׁעַר	gate		

EXERCISE. TRANSLATE.

טַהֲרֵנִי, טַעֲמוּ, בָּרְכוּ, יְשָׁרֵת, נַעֲקִי, וַיִּלָּחֲמוּ, יִטְהַר, אֶרְחַץ,
רְחַצְתָּ, אֶרְחָצֵךְ, נִבְחֲרָה, מִצַּעַק, בַּעֲלִי, שְׁעָרֶיךָ:
[2]יֻקַּח־נָא מְעַט מַיִם וְרַחֲצוּ רַגְלֵיכֶם וְהִשָּׁעֲנוּ תַּחַת הָעֵץ:
וְאֶקְחָה פַת־לֶחֶם וְסַעֲדוּ לִבְּכֶם אַחַר תַּעֲבֹרוּ: 2 וַיְגָרֶשׁ יהוה

---

[1] Perhaps connected in the Hebrew mind with עֵדֶן *delight.*
[2] See § 33. 3 c.

אֶת־הָאָדָם וַיְשַׁלְּחֵהוּ מִגַּן־עֵדֶן לַעֲבֹד אֶת־הָאֲדָמָה אֲשֶׁר לֻקַּח[1]

מִשָּׁם[2] ‏3 הָכְרַת מִנְחָה וָנֶסֶךְ אָבְלוּ הַכֹּהֲנִים מְשָׁרְתֵי יהוה:

‏4 וַיְבָרֲכוּ הַכֹּהֲנִים אֶת־בְּנֵי יִשְׂרָאֵל לֵאמֹר יְבָרֶכְךָ יהוה וְיִשְׁמְרֶךָ

יִשָּׂא יהוה פָּנָיו אֵלֶיךָ: ‏5 וַיִּזְעֲקוּ בְּנֵי יִשְׂרָאֵל אֶל־יְהוה לֵאמֹר

עֲזַבְנוּ אֶת־אֱלֹהֵינוּ וַנַּעֲבֹד אֶת־הַבְּעָלִים: ‏6 וַנְּבָרֶכְךָ וַאֲגַדְּלָה

שְׁמֶךָ וַאֲבָרֲכָה מְבָרֲכֶיךָ וְנִבְרְכוּ בְךָ כֹּל מִשְׁפְּחֹת הָאֲדָמָה:

‏7 ברכי נפשי את־יהוה ואל־תשכחי כל־חסדיו: ‏8 ביום

ההוא תאמרי לי אישי ולא תקראי לי עוד בעלי:

Beyond the rivers of Ethiopia.   Our feet shall stand in thy
(*f.*) gates (O) Jerusalem.   Thou shalt love Yahweh thy God
and him thou shalt serve.   And your fathers cried unto me
and said, We shall perish from the violence of our enemies.
And she said unto her husband, Drive out this maid-servant
and her son.   And they forgot Yahweh, and he sold them into
the hand of their enemies and they fought against[3] them.
And they took wives[4] from all whom they chose.

§ 37. LAMEDH GUTTURAL VERBS.
(See Paradigm, p. 218.)

1. The peculiarities of *Lam. Gutt.* arise chiefly from the
first law of gutturals—that all final gutturals must have an *a*
sound before them.   The real question is: in what cases does
the *pathaḥ* dislodge a long vowel (cf. יִשְׁלַח with יִקְטֹל), and in
what is it written additional to it, and furtive (cf. שָׁלוּחַ)?

(1) *Unchangeably* long vowels naturally are retained, taking *path. furtive* between them and the gutt.; *e.g.* שָׁלוּחַ (inf.
abs. Qal), שָׁלוּחַ (pass. ptc.), הִשְׁלִיחַ (Hiph. pf.), יַשְׁלִיחַ (impf.).

(2) a. The *tone*-long vowels *ē* and *ō* are displaced by
pathaḥ; *e.g.* impf. and imper. Qal יִשְׁלַח (cf. יִקְטֹל), שְׁלַח (with suff.
שְׁלָחֵנִי, יִשְׁלָחֵנִי, § 31. 3 a. i.); impf. Niph. יִשָּׁלַח (cf. יִקָּטֵל), impf. Pi.
יְשַׁלַּח, also pf. Pi. שִׁלַּח; Hiph. juss. יַשְׁלַח (waw consec. וַיִּשְׁלַח),
imper. הַשְׁלַח, &c.   (But inf. cstr. Qal retains *ō*, שְׁלֹחַ.)

---

[1] See § 33. 3 c.   [2] See § 13. 2 a.

[3] בְּ.   [4] נָשִׁים, *pl.* of אִשָּׁה (p. 153).

b. Exceptions : *ē* remains—(*a*) in pause, *e.g.* יִשָּׁלֵחַ (Niph.),
יְשַׁלֵּחַ (Pi.) ; (*b*) in participles abs., *e.g.* שֹׁלֵחַ (*f.* שֹׁלַחַת), מְשַׁלֵּחַ ;
(*c*) in infin. abs., *e.g.* שַׁלֵּחַ, Pi. (but constr. שַׁלַּח).

    c. Final ר usually has *ō* in impf. (*e.g.* יִסְפֹּר *to count*, יַעֲבֹר *to cross*)
except in stative verbs חָסֵר *to lack*, יֶחְסַר.

(3) Under the Tone the gutt. retains sh°wa silent, as שָׁלַחְתִּי ;
except before another vowel-less consonant in 2 *fem. sing.*
where a furt. path. slips in between the consonants without
removing *dag.* from the 2nd, שָׁלַחַתְּ *shaláḥat* (probably an
attempt to combine two traditions, שָׁלַחְתְּ and שָׁלַחַת).

    2. *Nouns from verbs Lam. Guttural.*—

	First declension.		Second declension.		Third declension.	
sing. abs.	רָשָׁע	שָׂמֵחַ	זֶרַע	שֵׁמַע	רֹמַח	מִזְבֵּחַ
cstr.	רְשַׁע	שְׂמַח	,,	,,	,,	מִזְבַּח
cons. suff.	רִשְׁעֶךָ	שִׂמְחֲךָ	זַרְעֲךָ	שִׁמְעֲךָ	רָמְחֲךָ	מִזְבַּחֲךָ
plur. abs.	רְשָׁעִים	שְׂמֵחִים	זְרָעִים	(שְׁמָעִים) רְמָחִים		מִזְבְּחוֹת
cstr.	רִשְׁעֵי	שִׂמְחֵי	זַרְעֵי	(שִׁמְעֵי) רָמְחֵי		,,

and שִׂמֵחִי, § 22. 4.

    (wicked) (rejoicing) (seed) (report) (lance) (altar)

In *second declension* the final short vowel is naturally *a*
before the guttural (§ 8. 1), and in all the declensions the
quasi-vocal sh°wa before the consonantal suffixes *ka,* &c.,
becomes a *ḥateph* (therefore not simply רִשְׁעֶךָ, זַרְעֶךָ, &c.).

שׁלח to send	נטע to plant	שׁכח to forget
זרע to sow	שׂבע to be satisfied	צלע to halt
זרח to rise (shine)	לקח to take צמח to sprout	משׁח to anoint
שׁמע to hear	דּשׁא *Hiph.* to make grow	שַׁחַר dawn
יַבֹּק Jabbok	פְּנוּאֵל Penuel	אבק *Niph.* to wrestle
נַחַל torrent, torrent valley, wady		יֶשַׁע deliverance, salvation
שׁבע *Niph.* to swear, *Hiph.* cause to swear		כְּנַעֲנִי Canaanite
נתץ pull down, break down	מֶלַח salt	מַעֲבָר ford

EXERCISE.   TRANSLATE.

אֶשְׁמַע, אֶשְׁמְעָה, בְּהִשָּׁמַע, תִּשָּׁמַע, שֻׁלְּחָה, שָׁלַח, שְׁלַח,
שִׁלֵּחַ, אֲשַׁלְּחֶךָ, יְשַׁכְּחֵהוּ, שָׁכַחַתְּ, נִשְׁכַּחַת :
הִנֵּה אָנֹכִי שֹׁלֵחַ מַלְאָךְ לְפָנֶיךָ לִשְׁמָרְךָ בַּדֶּרֶךְ הַשָּׁמֶר מִפָּנָיו

וּשְׁמַע בְּקוֹלוֹ ׃ 2 אֶבְיוֹנֶי צִיּוֹן אַשְׂבִּיעַ ¹לֶחֶם וְכֹהֲנֶיהָ אַלְבִּישׁ

יֶשַׁע ׃ 3 וַיִּטַּע יְהוָֹה גַּן בְּעֵדֶן וַיַּצְמַח מִן־הָאֲדָמָה כָּל־עֵץ נֶחְמָד

לְמַרְאֶה וְטוֹב לְמַאֲכָל ׃ 4 וַיִּקַּח יַעֲקֹב אֶת־נָשָׁיו וְאֶת־יְלָדָיו

וַיַּעֲבֹר אֶת־מַעֲבַר יַבֹּק ׃ וַיִּקָּחֵם וַיַּעֲבִרֵם אֶת־הַנָּחַל וַיַּעֲבֵר

אֶת־אֲשֶׁר לוֹ ׃ וַיֵּאָבֵק אִישׁ עִם יַעֲקֹב וַיֹּאמֶר הָאִישׁ שַׁלְּחֵנִי כִּי

עָלָה הַשָּׁחַר וַיֹּאמֶר לֹא אֲשַׁלֵּחֲךָ כִּי אִם בֵּרַכְתָּנִי ׃ וַיֹּאמֶר לוֹ

הַמַּלְאָךְ לֹא יֵאָמֵר עוֹד יַעֲקֹב שְׁמֶךָ כִּי אִם יִשְׂרָאֵל וַיְבָרֶךְ אֹתוֹ

שָׁם ׃ וַיִּזְרַח לוֹ הַשֶּׁמֶשׁ כַּאֲשֶׁר עָבַר אֶת־פְּנוּאֵל וְהוּא צֹלֵעַ

עַל־יְרֵכוֹ ׃ 5 וישביעני לאמר לא־תקח אשה לבני מבנות

הכנעני אשר אנכי ישב בארצו ׃ 6 השמיעני בבקר חסדך

כי־בך בטחתי ׃

This song shall never be forgotten. In the day of his being anointed (*Niph.*). And now lest he put forth (send) his hand and take of the tree of life and eat and live [2] for ever. Yahweh will give you in the evening flesh to eat, and bread in the morning to be satisfied (*inf. Qal*). He caused thee to hear his words out of the fire. Let those-loving (*ptc. cstr.*) thy salvation say: Let God be great! Ye shall surely hearken to the voice of my messenger, when I send him to you. And Samuel said, Speak, Yahweh, for thy servant is listening (*ptc.*). And he fought against the city all that day, and he took the city, and the people that (was) in it he slew, and he pulled down the city and sowed it with salt (*acc.*).

§ 38. LAMEDH 'ALEPH VERBS.
(See Paradigm, p. 220.)

The irregularities of the remaining classes of verbs (except verbs *Double ʿAyin, e.g.* סָבַב) arise from the presence of some of the quiescents א ו י in the stem. Verbs פ״א, in which א quiesces in the imperfect only, have been already treated, § 35.

1. *Verbs Lamedh 'Aleph.*—When א is third stem-letter, it causes the following peculiarities:

(1) At the end of a syllable א is silent after the pre-

----

¹ On double *accus.* see § 27. 1 *d*; cf. § 38. 3.   ² Cf. p. 87, note 5.

ceding vowel, which is lengthened, as the syllable is now virtually open, § 9. 1.   Thus *a* in pf. and impf. Qal (cf. § 37), pf. Niph., &c., becomes *ā*.   Thus מְצָא (קְטַל) practically = מְצָ which must become מָצָ (§ 5. 3 a), that is, מָצָא.   So יִמְצָא (יִכְבַּד); with suff. יִמְצָאֵנִי, § 31. 3 a. i.), נִמְצָא (נִקְטַל), &c.

(2) In perf. Qal of *active* verbs (those in *ā*) the vowel *ā* remains throughout, as (מְצָאתָ =) מָצָאתָ.

(3) a. In perf. Qal of *stative* verbs (cf. מָלֵא *to be full*) and in *all* the other perfects the vowel is *ē*; e.g. Qal מָלֵאתִי, Niph. נִמְצֵאתִי, Pi. מִצֵּאתִי, &c.

b. This *ē*, natural in the Pi., is difficult to account for in the Niph., where we should have expected נִמְצָאתִי (cf. נִקְטַלְתִּי).   It probably follows the analogy of *Lamedh He* vbs. (§ 44).

c. All imperfects and imperatives take ֶ (*e*) before נָה, again probably on the analogy of *Lamedh He* vbs.; e.g. מְצֶאנָה, תִּמְצֶאנָה.

(4) The letter א, being silent, sometimes falls out in writing; e.g. מָצָתִי for מָצָאתִי.

(5) This class of verbs has a considerable tendency to adopt the vocalization and even the consonantal spelling of *Lamedh He* verbs (§ 44); e.g. רְפֵה *heal* (imperative) for רְפָא.   There is frequent confusion between the roots קָרָא *to call*, and קָרָה *to meet*.

(6) In pf. with *waw consec.* the accent is not usually thrown forward; e.g. וְקָרָאתָ, not וְקָרָאתָ *and thou shalt call.*

2. *Nouns from verbs ל״א.*—

	First declension.		Second declension.		Third declension.	
abs.	צָבָא	מִקְרָא	כֶּלֶא	חֵטְא	יֹצֵא	
cstr.	צְבָא	מִקְרָא	„	„	יֹצֵאת *fem.*	
suff.	צְבָאֲךָ	מִקְרָאֲכֶם	כִּלְאוֹ	חֶטְאוֹ		
pl.	צְבָאוֹת	מִקְרָאִים	כְּלָאִים	חֲטָאִים	יֹצְאִים	
cstr.	צִבְאוֹת	מִקְרָאֵי	(כִּלְאֵי)	חֲטָאֵי	יֹצְאוֹת *fem.*	
	(host)	(assembly)	(prison)	(sin)	(going out, *ptc.*)	

a. The quiescent retains the long vowel *ā* before it even in the *cstr. sing.*, though the heavy suffix כֶם admits the short vowel.

b. The long vowel often remains before the quiescent even in the *cstr. plur.*; e.g. חֲטָאֵי.   For the ֲ in חֲטָאוֹ, cf. § 8. 1 b.

c. In the *fem.* the א is apt to surrender its vowel to the preceding cons., יְצָאת for יָצְאָת, § 21. 3.

מצא to find	שָׂנֵא to hate	גְּבוּרָה *f.* ⎫ strength,
קרא to call, read	מוֹצָא *pl. im* ⎫	כֹּחַ ⎭ might, power
קָרָה ⎫	and *ôth* ⎬ outgoing	שׁתק to be quiet
קרא ⎭ to befall, meet	נשׂא to lift up	(*late word*)
חטא to sin	נבא *Ni.,* ⎫	חרשׁ to plough
מָלֵא to be full	*Hith.* ⎬ to prophesy	לוּלֵא ⎫
פֶּלֶא *i* a wonder	רפא to heal	לוּלֵי ⎭ if not, unless
נָסַע to journey,	חִידָה *f.* riddle	אַחֲרִית *f.* after-part,
decamp	עֶגְלָה *f.* heifer	issue, end
ברא to create	רעשׁ to quake	יַשְׁלֵךְ *Hiph.* to throw, cast

3. a. Stative verbs (*i.e.* those describing a condition of the subject) subordinate to themselves in the *accus.* the noun that supplements the description. When they become active (in Pi. or Hiph., §§ 26, 27) they take *two* accusatives.

b. Such verbs are those expressing the idea of *fulness* (מָלֵא *to be full,* שָׂבַע *to be satisfied,* שָׁרַץ *to swarm,* לָבֵשׁ or לָבַשׁ *to be clothed with,* &c.) and *want* (חָסֵר *to lack,* שָׁכֹל *to be bereaved,* &c.).

מָלֵא הַבַּיִת עָשָׁן   *The house was full of smoke*

    נִמְלָא   „   „   *The house was filled with smoke*

מִלֵּא הַבַּיִת עָשָׁן   *He filled the house with smoke*

EXERCISE.   TRANSLATE.

נִבְרָא, תֶּחֱטִיא, וַחֲטָאתֶם, תֶּחֶטָאוּ, מִלֵּאתִיהָ, קְרָאן, וַיִּמְצָאֻהוּ, יַמְצִאֶנּוּ, יָרְאַנוּ, אֲמַלְאָה, יִשָּׁאֵנִי:

וַיֹּאמֶר יַעֲקֹב אֶל־בָּנָיו הֵאָסְפוּ וְאַגִּידָה לָכֶם אֵת־אֲשֶׁר יִקְרָא אֶתְכֶם בְּאַחֲרִית הַיָּמִים: 2 וַיֹּאמֶר מֶלֶךְ יִשְׂרָאֵל שְׂנֵאתִיו כִּי לֹא יִתְנַבֵּא עָלַי טוֹב כִּי אִם רָע: 3 וַיֹּאמֶר אֲלֵיהֶם שָׂאוּנִי וַהֲשְׁלִיכֻנִי אֶל־הַיָּם וְיִשְׁתֹּק הַיָּם מֵעֲלֵיכֶם: 4 וּבְנֵי יִשְׂרָאֵל שָׁרְצוּ וַיַּעַצְמוּ וַתִּמָּלֵא הָאָרֶץ אֹתָם: 5 כֹּה אָמַר יהוה אֲנִי מַרְעִישׁ אֶת־כָּל־הַגּוֹיִם וּמִלֵּאתִי אֶת־הַבַּיִת הַזֶּה כָּבוֹד:

6 נִמְצֵאתִי לַאֲשֶׁר לֹא בִקְשֻׁנִי אָמַרְתִּי הִנֵּנִי הִנֵּנִי אֶל־גּוֹי ¹לֹא
קֹרָא בִשְׁמִי : 7 אמר הכהן הגדול ספר התורה מצאתי ויתן
את־הספר אל־הסֹפֵר ויקראהו : 8 וימצאהו איש וישאלהו
לאמר מה־תבקש :

Yahweh will hear when thou criest to him.   I am full
(*perf.*) of the spirit of judgment and of power, to tell to
Jacob his transgression and to Israel his sin.   And the earth
was filled with violence.   Hast thou found-me, mine enemy?
and he said, I have found-thee.   Thou hast filled this house
with thy glory.   Thou hatest (*perf.*) all workers of iniquity.
And the spirit of Yahweh lifted-him up and cast him to-
(the)-earth.   Thou shalt love thine enemy, thou shalt not
hate him in thy heart.   Unless ye had ploughed (*perf.*) with
my heifer, ye would not have found (*perf.*) my riddle.

§ 39. PE YODH AND PE WAW VERBS.
(See Paradigm, p. 222.)

As Hebrew words hardly ever begin with ו (*w*), and a
primary *w* at the beginning of a word (cf. Arab. *walada*)
becomes in Hebrew י (*y*), *e.g.* יָלַד (*yalad*), it is impossible
to distinguish in the Qal between *Pe Yodh* and *Pe Waw*
verbs—vbs. whose first radical is ultimately י (*e.g.* יָנַק *to suck*)
and ו (*e.g.* יָלַד *to bear*)—as both necessarily begin with י.
Nevertheless they must be carefully distinguished, and in
Hebrew the distinction is most obvious in the Hiph. (and
Niph.); *e.g.* הֵינִיק (from ינק), but הוֹלִיד (Niph. נוֹלַד : from an
ultimate ולד).   Let us take the *Pe Yodh* vbs. first—*i.e.* those
whose י in the Qal is a real ultimate י.

I. *Pe Yodh vbs.*—(1) The impf. Qal (יִינַק) is formed quite
regularly: the final vowel is *a*.   Thus יִינַק (cf. יִכְבַּד) becomes
יִינַק, as the second י quiesces (§ 9. 1).

(2) The impf. Hiph. (יַיְנִיק) is also regular.   Thus יַיְנִיק (cf.
יַקְטִיל) becomes יֵינִיק (*ay = ai =* diphth. *ê,* cf. § 2. 2. 1).

(3) The pf. Hiph., which we should expect to be הֵינִיק
(from הֵינִיק, הִקְטִיל; cf. impf. Qal), is הֵינִיק, probably on the
analogy of the impf.

¹ Relative unexpressed, as often in poetic style.

(4) The verbs of this class, which are very few, are chiefly יָנַק *to suck* (Hiph. *to suckle*), יָטַב *to be good* (Hiph. *to do good*), יָלַל in Hiph. הֵילִיל *to howl*.

2. *Pe Waw vbs.*—(1) *a.* In the Hiph., as we have seen (pf. הוֹשִׁיב, impf. יוֹשִׁיב), the original *waw* (seen in Arab.) reappears. Impf. יַוְשִׁיב (cf. יַקְטִיל) becomes יוֹשִׁיב (*aw = au =* diphth. *ô,* cf. § 2. 2. 1). The pf. is הוֹשִׁיב, formed probably on the analogy of the impf. (Impf. with *waw cons.* וַיּוֹשֶׁב, § 23. 3. 4.) In the Niph. נוֹשַׁב the *waw* also reappears.

b. The (prob. orig.) Niph. prefix *na* (which ordinarily appears as *ni,* cf. נִקְטַל) combined with *w* (נַוְשַׁב) yields *nô* (נוֹשַׁב).

c. In the impf. Niph. (and derived parts) the *waw* is retained and quite properly treated as a consonant; *e.g.* יִוָּלֵד (cf. יִקָּטֵל).

d. The 1st pers. impf. has always the form אִוָּלֵד not אֶוָּלֵד (§ 25. 2).

e. Waw is sometimes found in the Hithp.; *e.g.* הִתְוַדַּע *to make oneself known.*

f. The Hoph. is הוּשַׁב (*hûshabh,* from הֻוְשַׁב *huwshabh*), cf. הָשְׁלַךְ (altern. form to הֻשְׁלַךְ).

(2) Of the impf. Qal (and related parts: inf. and imper.) there are two types:

(*a*) In some vbs. it is formed exactly as in impf. Qal of *Pe Yodh* vbs.; *e.g.* יָרַשׁ, יִירַשׁ *to possess,* יָרֵא, יִירָא *to fear,* יָבֵשׁ *to be dry,* יָעַץ *to counsel,* יָעֵף *to be weary,* &c.

(*b*) In others the initial י falls out. In this case the vowel of the preformative is *ē* (pretonic, long), and the final vowel is also *ē* (*e.g.* יֵשֵׁב, יֵלֵד: with *waw cons.* וַתֵּלֶד, וַיֵּשֶׁב, § 23. 3. 4) or *a* before gutturals (*e.g.* יֵדַע).

(*c*) The chief verbs which inflect thus are six in number, and as they are of very common occurrence, they should be carefully noted: יָדַע *to know,* יָלַד *to bear,* יָצָא (impf. יֵצֵא) *to go out,* יָרַד *to go down,* יָשַׁב *to sit, dwell,* and הָלַךְ *to go* (impf. יֵלֵךְ as if from יָלַךְ, *i.e.* ולך; cf. Hiph. הוֹלִיךְ).

(*d*) i. The imper. (שֵׁב, צֵא, דַּע, &c.) and inf. cstr. (שֶׁבֶת, רֶדֶת, דַּעַת, צֵאת, &c.) follow, as always, the impf. (§ 21. 1 c, 2 a. i.). The inf. cstr., by the addition of ת, assumes ṣegholate form, exactly as in *Pe Nun* vbs., § 33. 2 b: with suff., דַּעְתִּי, רִדְתִּי, שִׁבְתִּי, צֵאתִי, but לְכִתִּי (*sᵉghol,* under influence of following palatal).

ii. ל before such (ṣegholate or monosyllabic) inf. constructs is pointed לָ; *e.g.* לָשֶׁבֶת, לָצֵאת (§ 14. 1 d, cf. § 33. 2 c).

3. *Verbs assimilating the first radical.*—The initial *w y* are subject to still another mode of treatment; instead of coalescing with a preceding vowel as (*iy̆* = *î*, *uw* = *û*, *ay* = *ê*, *aw* = *ô*), they may be assimilated, like *n*, to the following consonant, which is then doubled, as יָצַק *to pour*, impf. יִצֹּק; יצג in Hiph. הִצִּיג *to set, place*, יָצַת *to burn* (Niph. נִצַּת, Hiph. הִצִּית).

4.   *to be able* יָכֹל, perf. Qal; impf. יוּכַל

   to add   יָסַף, perf. Qal; impf. Hiph. יוֹסִיף

English adverbs, e.g. *again, well*, are rendered idiomatically by Hebrew verbs: thus

and she bore again	וַתּוֹסֶף לֶרֶדת
(lit. "*added to bear*," or	לָלֶדת ,,
"*added and bore*")	וַתֵּלֶד ,,
he played the instrument well	הֵיטִיב נַגֵּן
(lit. *he did well as regards playing*)	לְנַגֵּן ,,
thou hast found it quickly	מִהַרְתָּ לִמְצֹא
(lit. *thou hast hastened*—מהר,	מְצֹא ,,
Pi. — *as regards finding*)	

נֶגַע	stroke, plague	אַרְבָּעִים forty	יָגוֹן	sorrow
אוּר	Ur	שֵׂיבָה *f.* grey hair	בַּעֲבוּר	for the sake of
כַּשְׂדִּים	Chaldeans	תֵּבָה *f.* ark [1]	יקץ	to awake: only in
יעץ	to advise counsel, *Niph.* to take or			impf. Qal יִיקַץ
	exchange counsel with	שֶׁבֶר grain, corn		
אָח	brother	אָחוֹת sister	אִשָּׁה *cstr.* אֵשֶׁת wife
אָב	father	מוֹלֶדֶת *f.* kindred	אָסוֹן mischief, harm (*very rare*)
הַ ,הֲ	particle of interrogation (§ 49. 2. 2)	יִשָּׁאר, *Niph.* remain,
פֶּה	mouth, *cstr.* פִּי		be left

עַל פִּי according to the measure of, in accordance with

יקד to be kindled, burn   יצע, *Hiph.* הִצִּיעַ to lay spread

בַּמֶּה (בַּמָּה in pause and before א) by what?   חַי alive

EXERCISE.   PARSE AND TRANSLATE.

רְדָה, לָרֶדֶת, דַּע, דַּעַת, נֵלְכָה, אִינַק, תִּירָא, הַנּוֹרָא, אִירַשׁ,

---

[1] Never the ark of the covenant (which is always אָרוֹן, הָאָרוֹן) but Noah's ark in Gen. **6**–**9** (and in Ex. **2**. 3, 5 the papyrus vessel in which the infant Moses was laid).

9

וַיֹּרֶשׁ, וָאִישָׁנָה, תּוּקַד, בְּהוֹרִידִי, תֵּרַדְנָה, וַיִּרְדֻּהוּ, הֻצַּע,
מַצִּיג, וַגְּדָעֵם, יִירָשׁוּם :

וַיֵּרֶד אַבְרָם מִצְרַיְמָה וַיֹּאמֶר אֶל־אִשְׁתּוֹ אֹמְרִי־נָא אֲחֹתִי אָתְּ
לְמַעַן יִיטַב־לִי בַעֲבוּרֵךְ : וַיִּקַּח אֹתָהּ הַמֶּלֶךְ וּלְאַבְרָם הֵיטִיב
בַּעֲבוּרָהּ : וַיְנַגַּע יהוה אֹתוֹ ¹נְגָעִים גְּדֹלִים וַיֵּדַע כִּי אִשְׁתּוֹ
הִיא : 2 אָמַר יהוה אֶל־אַבְרָם אֲנִי יהוה אֲשֶׁר הוֹצֵאתִיךָ
מֵאוּר כַּשְׂדִּים לָתֶת לְךָ אֶת־הָאָרֶץ הַזֹּאת לְרִשְׁתָּהּ : וַיֹּאמֶר
אֲדֹנָי יהוה בַּמָּה אֵדַע כִּי אִירָשֶׁנָּה : 3 וַיֹּאמְרוּ בְּנֵי יַעֲקֹב
אֵלָיו ²שָׁאוֹל שָׁאַל הָאִישׁ לָנוּ וּלְמוֹלַדְתֵּנוּ לֵאמֹר הַעוֹד אֲבִיכֶם
חַי ³הֲיֵשׁ לָכֶם אָח וַנַּגֶּד־לוֹ עַל־פִּי הַדְּבָרִים הָאֵלֶּה הֲיָדוֹעַ
נֵדַע כִּי יֹאמַר הוֹרִדוּ אֶת־אֲחִיכֶם : 4 וַיַּעֲזֹב אֶת־עֲצַת־הַזְּקֵנִים
אֲשֶׁר יְעָצֻהוּ וַיִּוָּעַץ אֶת־הַיְלָדִים : 5 הַבֹּטְחִים בַּיהוה יֵלְכוּ וְלֹא
יִיעָפוּ : 6 וזכרת את־כל־הדרך אשר הוליכך יהוה אלהיך
זה ארבעים שנה במדבר לדעת את־אשר בלבבך הֲתִשְׁמֹר
מצותיו אם־לא :

And the ark went upon the face of the waters.   Make
me to know thy ways.   And they said unto her, Wilt thou go
with this man ? and she said, I will go.   And he said, Cause
every man to go out of the house ; and there stood no man
with him, when he made himself known to his brethren.
And the man opened the doors of the house and went out
to go on (*dat.*) his way.   And the daughter of Pharaoh said
to her, Take this child and nurse (suckle) it for me, and
she took the child and nursed it.   Behold I have heard that
there is corn in Egypt, go down thither and buy us a little
food.   And Yahweh said unto him, Go not down to Egypt,
dwell in the land which I shall say unto thee.   And he
was afraid and said, How terrible (ירא, *Niph. ptc.*) is this
place !   And he said, My son shall not go down, for his

¹ Cognate acc.
² Infin. abs.＝we did not tell him of our own accord, he *asked* us
(§ 21. 2 b).
³ יֵשׁ *there is, there are* (opposite of אַיִן, p. 136 *note*), a particle,—with
suffixes, יֶשְׁךָ *thou art*, יֶשְׁכֶם *you are* (הֲ is interrogative particle).

brother [1] is dead and he alone is left, and should mischief befall [2] him in the way in which ye shall go, then [2] shall ye bring down my grey-hairs in sorrow to Sheol.

§ 40. 'AYIN WAW AND YODH VERBS.
(See Paradigm, p. 224.)

This class includes the verbs whose middle letter, ו or י, is a *vowel* letter (*e.g.* קוּם *to arise*, רִיב *to contend*), but not the vbs. in which that letter is a real consonant (*e.g.* גָּוַע *to expire*, חָיָה *to live*). Whether these vbs. were always mono-syllabic, or whether they are contracted forms of verbs of the ordinary type, the middle letter being originally con-sonantal (*e.g.* pf. קָם from קָוַם? מֵת from מָוֵת *to die*? cf. the noun מָוֶת *māweth, death*), is a question difficult to decide, and need not be here discussed. In these verbs the inf. cstr. (קוּם, רִיב, &c.), not the pf. Qal, is treated as the ground-form, as the pf. Qal (קָם, רָב, &c.) does not exhibit the characteristic ו or י. The following vbs. illustrate the various types.

Inf. cstr. קוּם *to arise*, מוּת *to die*, בּוֹשׁ *to be ashamed*, בּוֹא *to come*; בִּין *to discern*.

ל before such (monosyllabic) inf. constructs is pointed לְ; *e.g.* לָקוּם (§ 14. 1 d); cf. § 39. 2. 2 d. ii.

1. *Qal pf.*—As in the regular verbs (קָטַל, כָּבֵד, קָטֹן) the vowel may be *a e* or *o*; *e.g.* קָם, מֵת, בּוֹשׁ, בָּא, בֹּן.

 fem. קָמָה, מֵתָה, &c.; 1 *s. m.* בָּאתִי, בֹּשְׁתִּי, מַתִּי, קַמְתִּי, בַּנְתִּי, &c.

2. *Qal impf.*—a. The vowel of the ground-form (inf. cstr.) is preserved, and the preformative is not the ordinary *yi* (יִקְטֹל) but the old *ya* (§ 21. 1 a) necessarily lengthened in the open pretone to *yā* (§ 6. 2 b): hence יָקוּם, יָמוּת, יָבוֹא, יָבִין; *pl.* יָקוּמוּ, &c. In יֵבוֹשׁ preformative is the regular *yi* (proper and original to *stative* vbs.; § 22. 2) lengthened to *yē* (§ 6. 2 b).

b. Jussive יָקֹם; impf. with *waw cons.* וַיָּקָם (*way-yā́-qom*); with final guttural or *r* וַיָּסַר *and he turned aside* (§ 8. 1 c), from סוּר.

c. Participle קָם, מֵת, &c.: *fem.* קָמָה, *pl.* קָמִים, *cstr.* קָמֵי (*â* un-changeable, § 41. 1 a).

d. Only in impf. Qal do ו״ע and י״ע vbs. differ (יָקוּם, יָבִין): there the characteristic ו or י appears. But in Hiph., *e.g.*, they are alike: הֵקִים, הֵבִין.

 [1] אָחִיו (see p. 153).   [2] *Waw consec.* with *perf.*

3. *Hiph.*—a. The Hiph. is of the regular form (יַקְטִיל, הִקְטִיל);
only the vowel of the preformative (*hi, ya*), being now in the
open syllable, becomes the corresponding tone-long vowel
(*hē, yā*): הֵקִים (*f.* הֵקִימָה), impf. יָקִים; ptc. מֵקִים (formed fr. pf.).
Hoph. הוּקַם.

b. Jussive יָקֵם: impf. with *waw consec.* וַיָּקֶם; with final
guttural or *r* וַיָּסַר (same as Qal) *and he removed* (§ 8. 1 c).

4. *Niph.* נָקוֹם (נִקְטַל).—a. The preformative of the pf. is
the (orig.) *na* lengthened to *nā* in the open syllable, and
qâm has passed into *qôm* (§ 2. 2. 1); hence נָקוֹם (*f.* נָקוֹמָה).
Impf. יִקּוֹם (from יִנְקוֹם).

b. Notice that the closing syllables of *Niph.* and *Hoph.* are not,
as in the regular verb, alike.

5. *Piʿēl,* &c.—The regular intensive forms, duplicating the
middle radical (*e.g.* עַוֵּד *to surround*, from עוּד), are very rare and
late. The intensive is usually formed by doubling the last
radical—*Pôlēl* (*e.g.* קוֹמֵם, *pass.* קוֹמַם *to raise up*, רוֹמֵם *to exalt*), or
the first and last—*Pilpēl* (*e.g.* כִּלְכֵּל *to sustain*). Cf. § 26. 5.

6. (a) The vowels *î û* being so characteristic of these
verbs, a great effort is made to give them expression; but as
they cannot stand in a shut syllable with two consonants
following them, § 5. 3 b (*e.g.* תְּקוּמֶינָה, 3 *f. pl. impf. Qal,* הֲקִימְתָּ,
2 *s. m. pf. Hiph.,* are impossible), a vowel is often inserted
between the stem and the consonantal afformatives, and *î û*
thus remain in the open syllable. The inserted vowel is *ô* in
perf., and *ê* in impf.; *e.g.* תְּקוּמֶׂינָה, impf. Qal, הֲקִימׂוֹתִ, pf. Hiph.,
נְקוּמׂוֹתִי, pf. Niph. (by dissimilation, § 35. 1 a) for נְקוּמׂתִי.

(b) Sometimes the regular vb. is followed, and no vowel
is inserted. In that case *î û* become *ē* (*a* in pf. Hiph.) *ō* in
the shut syllable; *e.g.* תָּשֹׁבְנָה (*they shall return,* fem. impf. Qal
from שׁוּב; but also תְּשׁוּבֶינָה), תָּשֵׁבְנָה (impf. Hiph.), הֵנַפְתָּ (pf. Hiph.
of נוּף *to wave, swing*; but also הֲנִיפׂוֹתָ). Sometimes, as we
have just seen, both forms are found.

7. Some vbs. are both וʹʹע and יʹʹע, though one form
usually predominates; *e.g.* שׂוּם or שִׂים *to place* (impf. יָשִׂים,
very rarely יְשׂוּם), שׂוּשׂ or שִׂישׂ *to rejoice.*

8. A few יʹʹע verbs have forms which look like, and probably are,
Hiphʿils with the preformative dropped; *e.g.* בִּינׂתִי (as well as בַּנׂתִי; at
least בַּנׂתָ is attested) רִיבׂוֹתָ as well as רַבְתָּ *thou strivest.* These
abbreviated forms appear to be late.

קוּם } to arise *Hiph.* } to establish	שִׂים שׂוּם to set שׁוּב } to return *Hiph.* } to restore	שִׁית to set יוֹנָה *f.* } dove יוֹנִים } *pl.*
נוּחַ to rest		
Hiph. { הֵנִיחַ to cause to rest, give rest to הִנִּיחַ to place, set down	רוּם to be high בּוֹשׁ to be ashamed בּוֹא to come כּוּן to be firm (?) (not found in *Qal*)	לִין, לָן to pass the night נוּס to flee צוּד to hunt מוּג to melt
מוּת to die	כּוֹנֵן, הֵכִין *Hiph. Pô'lēl* to establish	אוֹר to shine רִיב to contend
רוּץ to run		
זֵעָה[1] *f.* sweat	סוּר } to turn aside *Hiph.* } to remove	עוּד *Hiph.* to testify מָנוֹחַ resting-place

אַף nostril, anger ; *dual* אַפַּיִם face (§ 43. 4)

כַּף *f.* palm (of hand), sole (of foot)   נֹחַ Noah

EXERCISE. PARSE AND TRANSLATE.

נָס, סָרָה, שָׁבָה, וּבָאָה, וְסָרוּ, אָרוּם, תָּשׁוּבִי, תְּשׁוּבֶינָה, יָרֹם,

אָמוּתָה, וַיָּקָם, לָצוּד, תָּכוּן, הָרִימוֹת, וַהֲשִׁבֹתִי, יָאִיר, וְיָרֶם,

אַל־תֵּשֵׁב, הֲבִיאָה, נָשִׂימָה, יְכוּנֶּהָ, מוּבָא, תְּמִיתֵת׃

בְּזֵעַת אַפֶּיךָ תֹּאכַל לֶחֶם עַד שׁוּבְךָ אֶל־הָאֲדָמָה כִּי עָפָר אַתָּה

וְאֶל־עָפָר תָּשׁוּב׃ 2 וַאֲנִי הִנְנִי מֵבִיא אֶת־הַמַּבּוּל[2] מַיִם עַל־

הָאָרֶץ לְשַׁחֵת כָּל־בָּשָׂר מִתַּחַת הַשָּׁמָיִם׃ 3 יָדֹעַ תֵּדְעוּ כִּי אִם

מְמִיתִים אַתֶּם אֹתִי כִּי־דָם נָקִי אַתֶּם נֹתְנִים עֲלֵיכֶם׃ 4 וְלֹא

מָצְאָה הַיּוֹנָה מָנוֹחַ לְכַף רַגְלָהּ וַתָּשָׁב אֶל־נֹחַ אֶל־הַתֵּבָה

וַיִּשְׁלַח יָדוֹ וַיִּקָּחֶהָ וַיָּבֵא אֹתָהּ אֵלָיו אֶל־הַתֵּבָה׃ 5 יהוה

אֱלֹהַי תְּשִׁיבֵנָא נֶפֶשׁ הַיֶּלֶד הַזֶּה׃ 6 הנה אנכי מת והיה

אלהים[3] עִמָּכֶם והשיב אתכם אל־ארץ אבותיכם׃ 7 אם־

שכח תשכח את־יהוה אלהיך והלכת אחרי אלהים אחרים

ועבדתם[4] העדתי בך היום כי אבד תאבד׃

[1] *ê* unchangeable ; because strictly זֵעָה from יֶזַע.

[2] מַיִם is either a gloss on, or in apposition to, הַמַּבּוּל.

[3] *With you*, from עַם (see p. 142, *note* 1).

[4] הַעִדֹתִי.   The pf. Hiph. of עוּד has ˍ instead of ˍ: .   The pf. (*I testify*) is used "to express actions which, although really only in process of accomplishment, are nevertheless meant to be represented as already accomplished in the conception of the speaker," Gesenius-Kautzsch, § 106. i.

And they fled the way of the wilderness. Depart not from-after Yahweh, but (and) ye shall serve him with all your heart. Arise, shine, for thy (*f.*) light is come. And he took not from his hand (that) which he had brought. I will surely-return (*inf. abs.*) unto thee (*f.*). And he arose in the morning and saddled his ass and went with the princes of Moab. And he called the man (*dat.*) and said unto him, Thou hast brought upon me and upon my kingdom a great sin. And his wife said to him, If Yahweh had wished (*pf.*) to kill us, he would not have taken (*pf.*) from our hand a burnt-offering. And the woman went out to meet the captain of the king's host and she said, Turn aside, my lord, turn aside unto me, fear not; and he turned aside unto her to the tent.

§ 41. NOUNS FROM ʿAYIN WAW AND YODH.

1. First declension. See § 18.

קָם (*rising*)	*plur.* קָמִים	*cstr.* קָמֵי	; *fem.* קָמָה
מֵת (*dead*)	„ מֵתִים	„ מֵתֵי	„ מֵתָה
טוֹב (*good*)	„ טוֹבִים	„ טוֹבֵי	„ טוֹבָה
מָקוֹם (*place*)	„ מְקוֹמוֹת &c.		
(מָגוֹר) (*sojourning-place*)	„ מְגוּרִים	(גּוּר *to sojourn*)	
מָנוֹחַ (*resting-place*)	*fem.* מְנוּחָה	(נוּחַ *to rest*)	
	„ מְדִינָה *a province* (דִּין *to judge*)		

(a) Whether or not the first three words are to be regarded as contracted from קוֹם, כְּוֵת, טוֹב (§ 22. 1), and therefore ideally falling within the first declension (§ 18), it is important to note that words of this type, derived from roots whose middle letter is ‎י‎ or ‎ו‎, have *unchangeable* vowels; e.g. *pl. cstr.* קָמֵי, not קְמֵי (unlike דָּם *blood*, which, not being from a root דּוֹם, has pl. cstr. דְּמֵי), מֵתֵי, not מְתֵי.

(b) Note, too, that ע״וּ nouns with מ preformative have often, with inflectional additions (e.g. *pl.* or *fem.*), ‎וּ‎ instead of ‎וֹ‎; cf. pf. Niph. נָקוֹם, נְקוּמֹת (§ 40. 6 a; so מָתוֹק *sweet*, מְתוּקָה, &c.).

2. Second declension. See § 29.

ע"ו Nouns.

	A class.			I class.	U class.	
abs.	אוֹר	שׁוֹר	מָוֶת	none	סוּס	שׁוּק (שׁוֹק)
cstr.	,,	,,	מוֹת		,,	,,
suff.	אוֹרִי	שׁוֹרִי	סוֹתִי		סוּסִי	שׁוּקִי
plur.	אוֹרִים	שְׁוָרִים	מוֹתִים		סוּסִים	שְׁוָקִים
cstr.	אוֹרֵי	שׁוֹרֵי	מוֹתִי		סוּסֵי	שׁוּקֵי
	(light)	(ox)	(death)		(horse)	(street)

ע"י Nouns.

	A class.			I class.	U class.
abs.	הֵיק	זַ֫יִת	חַיִל	שִׁיר	none
cstr.	,,	זֵית	חֵיל	,,	
suff.	חֵיקִי	זֵיתִי	חֵילִי	שִׁירִי	
plur.	(הֵיקִים)	זֵיתִים	חֲיָלִים	שִׁירִים	
cstr.	(חֵיקֵי)	זֵיתֵי	חֵילֵי	שִׁירֵי	
	(bosom)	(olive)	(force)	(song)	

(a) Some of these words, in the absolute form, are manifestly ṣegholates ; *e.g.* מָ֫וֶת, זַ֫יִת (p. 100, *footnote*) ; others, the majority, are not, *e.g.* אוֹר, הֵיק—they are now simply monosyllables, with long unchangeable vowels.

Originally, however, words of the latter type will have been 'awr (or 'aur) and ḥayq (or ḥaiq)—contracting respectively into 'ôr (אוֹר) and ḥêq (הֵיק), but corresponding in their uncontracted form to *malk*, and therefore not unfairly regarded, in their ultimate form, as ṣegholates.

(b) There is a distinct preference for the shorter form. Note that the shorter form appears in *all* the constructs (*i.e.* even where the abs. is dissyllabic, *e.g.* מָוֶת *c.* מוֹת, זַיִת *c.* זֵית, חַיִל *c.* חֵיל), and of course with suffixes (מוֹתִי, זֵיתִי, &c.) ; also, in most cases, even with the abs. plur. ; *e.g.* מוֹתִים, זֵתִים.

(c) In a few cases, however, the plur. has the longer form as in ordinary ṣegholates (*e.g.* חֲיָלִים from חַיִל, cf. מְלָכִים) even (though rarely) when the sing. is monosyllabic (cf. שְׁוָרִים from שׁוֹר, שְׁוָקִים from שׁוּק).

(d) With the rare exception just mentioned, the inflection

of monosyllabic nouns of this type proceeds with absolute regularity, because of the unchangeableness of the vowel (cf. סוּס, § 19).

3. (a) In ʿ*Ayin Waw* nouns of the *a* class the primary vowel *a* is not assimilated to *e* (as, *e.g.*, in *malk, mélekh,* מֶלֶךְ) but lengthened, probably under the influence of the *waw*, to *ā* (the form reserved in ordinary ṣegholates for pause ; *e.g.* דֶּרֶךְ, p. דֶּרֶךְ, § 29. 1 a): thus מָוֶת (not מֶוֶת), תָּוֶךְ. (With suffix, בְּתוֹכָם *in their midst.*)

(b) In ʿ*Ayin Yodh* nouns of the *a* class the primary *a* was not lengthened to *ā*, probably because the word was pronounced practically as a monosyllable, and the helping vowel is not *s̆ghol* but *ḥireq*, which is homogeneous with the י ; *e.g.* not זֶיֵת but זַיִת.

4. There are no ו״ע nouns of the *i* class, nor י״ע nouns of the *u* class, because these consonants have no affinity for these vowels (§ 2. 3 *c*, § 9. 2).

-----

death	מָוֶת	and so :	midst תָּוֶךְ, evil אָוֶן.
light	אוֹר	„	thorn קוֹץ, voice קוֹל, *pl. ôth*, pit בּוֹר *ôth*, generation דּוֹר *îm* and *ôth*, fowl עוֹף. Like שׁוֹר,—thorn חוֹחַ.
horse	סוּס	„	whelp גּוּר, spirit רוּחַ *ôth*, street חוּץ *ôth*. Like שׁוּק,—pot דּוּד.
olive	זַיִת	„	ram אַיִל, wine יַיִן, no אַיִן.[1]
force	חַיִל	„	eye עַיִן *ôth* (wells), colt עַיִר, buck תַּיִשׁ.
bosom	חֵיק	„	egg בֵּיץ only in *pl.*, calamity אֵיד, smell רֵיחַ.
song	שִׁיר	„	vanity רִיק, judgment דִּין, joy גִּיל.

5. Many words have some irregularity :
house בַּיִת, *pl.* בָּתִּים, probably *bāttîm* or *bâtim* (see p. 153).

[1] אַיִן, which often appears with a sort of verbal function, and is = *there is not* (cf. יֵשׁ *there is*, p. 130), not unnaturally takes verbal suffixes, occasionally strengthened by the *nun energicum* (§ 31. 7) ; they are אֵינָם, אֵינְכֶם, אֵינֶנּוּ, אֵינֶנָּה, אֵינֶנּוּ, אֵינֶךָ, אֵינְךָ, אֵינֶנִּי. *E.g.* Enoch walked with God וְאֵינֶנּוּ *and he was not.* A verb accompanying אַיִן must be in the participle ; e.g. *ye do not keep* my ways, אֵינְכֶם שֹׁמְרִים.

Somewhat similarly עוֹד *yet, still* : עוֹדֶנִּי (עוֹדִי), עוֹדְךָ, עוֹדָךְ, עוֹדֶנּוּ, 3 *pl.* עוֹדָם.

eye   עַיִן, *du.* עֵינַיִם eyes, *pl.* עֲיָנוֹת *wells.*

night   לֵיל, more usually לַיְלָה, where הָ is acc. termination ; *cstr.* לֵיל, *pl.* לֵילוֹת.

day   יוֹם, *pl.* (יוֹמִים =) יָמִים, § 9.   This word is very irregular in treating its *â* as merely tone-long : hence *pl. cstr.* יְמֵי.

head רֹאשׁ, probably = רָאשׁ (§ 2. 2. 1), i.e. *raʾsh* (like *malk*), *plur.* רָאשִׁים contracted from רְאָשִׁים, cf. מְלָכִים. The א, now silent and superfluous, preserves the memory of the time when the letter was a really integral part of the word—in its old form *raʾshu.*

פָּקַח to open (eyes)   אַרְבֶּה locusts (*coll.*)   עָוֺן iniquity, guilt

EXERCISE.   TRANSLATE.

עֵינַי עַל־כָּל־דַּרְכֵיהֶם לֹא נִסְתְּרוּ מִלְּפָנַי וְלֹא־נִצְפַּן עֲוֺנָם מִנֶּגֶד עֵינָי : 2 לֹא תָמוּתוּ כִּי יֹדֵעַ אֱלֹהִים כִּי בְּיוֹם אֲכָלְכֶם מִן־הָעֵץ [1]וְנִפְקְחוּ עֵינֵיכֶם : 3 כַּרְמֵיכֶם וְזֵיתֵיכֶם יֹאכַל הָאַרְבֶּה : 4 חֵיל גּוֹיִם יָבֹאוּ לָךְ : 5 הִצַּלְתֶּם אֶת־נַפְשֹׁתֵינוּ מִמָּוֶת : 6 לֹא אֶחְפֹּץ בְּמוֹת הַמֵּת : 7 וַיִּשְׁמְעוּ אֶת־קוֹל יהוה מִתְהַלֵּךְ בְּתוֹךְ עֵץ הַגָּן לְרוּחַ הַיּוֹם וַיִּתְחַבֵּא הָאָדָם וְאִשְׁתּוֹ מִפָּנָיו : 8 וְלִמַּדְתֶּם אֶת־דְּבָרַי אֶת־בְּנֵיכֶם לְדַבֵּר בָּם בְּשִׁבְתְּךָ בְּבֵיתֶךָ וּבְלֶכְתְּךָ בַדֶּרֶךְ וּבְשָׁכְבְּךָ וּבְקוּמֶךָ :

Behold I am old, I know not the day of my death.   In those days there-was-not a king in Israel, (every) man did [2] the (thing) upright in his (own) eyes.   And Noah awoke from his wine and knew what his younger (little) son had done to him.   And the prophet said unto her, And thou (*fem.*) arise, go to thy house ; when thy feet come to-the-city, then (*waw cons.*) the boy shall die.   And he offered the ram of the burnt-offering.   And the men feared to return to their houses.

§ 42. DOUBLE ʿAYIN VERBS.

(See Paradigm, p. 226.)

Verbs *Double ʿAyin* (*e.g.* סָבַב) so entirely resemble in their inflection verbs *ʿAyin Waw*, that it is best to treat them immediately after this class.   It is an open question whether

---

[1] Waw consec. pf. : *then … shall be opened.*   [2] יַעֲשֶׂה *impf.*, § 46. II. 2.

the root is to be regarded as monosyllabic and biliteral (סַב),
expanded in certain parts to סָבַב, or dissyllabic and triliteral
(סְבַב), contracted in certain parts to סַב. The duplication
which is so common a feature of these verbs (*e.g.* סַבּוֹתִי,
I *s. pf. Qal*; קַלּוּ, 3 *pl. pf.* &c.) might seem to point conclusively
to the presence of a repeated letter in the stem (קָלַל, סָבַב);
it may equally well be due, however, simply to the desire
to strengthen the second consonant of the short biliteral
stem (סַב, קַל), § 7. 3 a. But whatever the explanation may
be, the facts are simple enough; they are these—

(1) The longer form (סבב) is necessary when an unchangeably long vowel or double letter requires the presence
of a third stem-letter; *e.g.* pres. and pass. ptc. Qal סוֹבֵב,
סָבוּב; inf. abs. Qal סָבוֹב; Pi. סִבֵּב.

It is also usual in the 3rd pers. pf. : סָבַב, סָבְבָה, סָבְבוּ.

(2) a. In other cases the shorter form is used and the
vowel is that which is found in the *second* syllable of the
regular verb; *e.g.* inf. cstr. סֹב (cf. קְטֹל), impf. Qal יָסֹב (יִקְטֹל),
pf. Niph. נָסַב (נִקְטַל).

   a. לְ before such (monosyllabic) inf. constructs is pointed לְ; *e.g.*
לָבֹז *to plunder,* לָרֹב *to become many* (§ 14. 1 d); cf. § 39. 2. 2 d. ii.

   β. With suffixes to the inf. cstr., *u* naturally appears in the
sharpened syllable (§ 7. 7); *e.g.* בְּחֻקּוֹ *when he inscribed* (from חָקַק).
Cf. § 43. 1 a.

   b. Exceptions.—(i.) In the Hiph. the vowel has not risen
to *î*, but remains *ē* (sometimes *a*, esp. with gutt. and ר; *e.g.* הֵמַר
he has made bitter); *e.g.* הֵסֵב, הֵחֵל *to begin* (impf. יָסֵב, יָחֵל).
(ii.) The Niph. impf. follows the pf. : יִסַּב (cf. נָקוֹם, יִקּוֹם, § 40. 4 a).
(iii.) Stative vbs. always end in *a*, not *ē*; *e.g.* קַל, מַר, רַךְ.

(3) a. As in *ʿAyin Waw* vbs. (§ 40. 2) the vowels of the
preformative, standing in the open pretone, are tone-long;
e.g. impf. Qal יָסֹב—the original *ya* (§ 21. 1 a) lengthened
to *yā*—with *waw cons.* וַיָּסׇב (way-yā-ṣobh); pf. Niph. נָסַב—the
primary *na* lengthened to *nā* (cf. נָקוֹם, § 40. 4); pf. Hiph.
הֵסֵב—*hi* lengthened to *hē* (§ 6. 2 b), ptc. follows the pf. מֵסֵב
(cf. מֵקִים, § 40. 3 a), impf. יָסֵב, with *waw cons.* וַיָּסֶב, Hoph. הוּסַב,
יוּסַב.

   b. In stat. vbs.—impf. in *a*—the *yi* of the preformative
(§ 22. 2) is naturally lengthened to *yē*; cf. יֵמַר, יֵרַךְ.

(4) The double letter shows itself with all inflectional

afformatives; and the tone (except in participles) is, as a rule, on the penult; as Niph. pf. נָסַב, *f.* נְסַבָּה (נ pretonic; therefore not נ), 2 *m.* נְסַבֹּות, but ptc. נָסָב, *f.* נְסַבָּה, *pl.* נְסַבִּים.

(5) Before the afformatives beginning with a consonant a vowel is inserted, viz. in the perfects *ô*, and in the impff. and related parts, *ê*; as pf. Qal סַבֹּותִ, impf. Niph. תִּסַּבֶּינָה; cf. § 40. 6 a.

(6) The tone-long *ē ō*, which under the tone maintained themselves before the double letter, cf. § 5. 3 (2 f. s. impf. Qal תָּסֹבִּי, impf. Hiph. תָּסֵבִּי), when they lose the tone become the sharp *i u* (§ 7. 7); as 2 pl. fem. imper. Qal סֻבֶּינָה, impf. תְּסֻבֶּינָה; impf. Hiph. תְּסִבֶּינָה.

(7) a. The regular Intensive is quite common; *e.g.* הִלֵּל *to praise.* Another form of Intensive, also much in use, is the so-called *Pôʿēl*; *e.g.* סֹובֵב (cf. קֹומֵם, § 40. 5) *to encompass,* עֹולֵל *to act severely,* pass. עֹולַל, reflexive הִתְעֹולֵל. More rare is the *Pilpēl*; *e.g.* גִּלְגֵּל *to roll* (§ 26. 5).

    b. In the regular verb the *Pôʿēl* is found, though rarely, in the sense of aim or endeavour; *e.g.* שֹׁרֵשׁ *to take root.*

(8) In the impf. some vbs. duplicate the *first* radical, as in Aramaic; *e.g.* קָבַב, impf. יִקֹּב *to curse,* יִקֹּד קָדַד *to bow down,* יִדֹּם דָּמַם *to be silent,* יִתֹּם תָּמַם *to be finished.* Some vbs. have both forms; *e.g.* סָבַב, Qal יָסֹב and יִסֹּב, Hiph. יָסֵב and יַסֵּב; שָׁמֵם *to be desolate* or *astonished,* יָשֹׁם and יִשֹּׁם.

בז to plunder	מד to measure	שָׁלֹשׁ three
חם *st.*[1] to be hot	מר *st.* to be bitter	כָּרַע to bow down
חן to be gracious	הל *Hiph.* to begin	נָעֳמִי Naomi
רע *st.* to be evil	צל *st.* to tingle	(Noʿmi)
גל to roll	רב to be *or* become	רחם *Pi.* to have
אר to curse	many, multiply	compassion
חג to hold a feast	גּור to sojourn	עָנָה to answer
רך *st.* to be soft	הִתְגֹּורֵר to seek hospi-	עָנָה בּ to testify
מק *Niph.* to waste away	tality (with)	against
מש to feel (grope)	גִּדְעֹון Gideon	בַּד separation
לק to lick, lap	שַׁדַּי Almighty (?)	(always pre-
לק *st.* to be light (*Pi.*	יֶתֶר remainder, rest	ceded by לְ)
to curse)		לְבַד apart

[1] i.e. *stative.*

EXERCISE.   PARSE THESE WORDS.

בַּזֹּונוּ, קַלּוּ, וְחַגֹּתֶם, אָאֹר, וַיָּחָן, גֹּל, תֵּרַע, בֹּזוּ, לָקֹב, וְנָקַל,
וּנְמַקֹּתֶם, יְמַד, הַשְׁמֹּות, הֵתַמּוּ, תֻּדֹּם, אֵקֹב, וַיִּתַּמּוּ, תַּתֶּם:
אֲנִי אַעֲבִיר כָּל־טוּבִי עַל־פָּנֶיךָ וְחַנֹּתִי אֶת־אֲשֶׁר אָחֹן וְרִחַמְתִּי
אֶת־אֲשֶׁר אֲרַחֵם: 2 הֵחֵל הָאָדָם לָרֹב בָּאָרֶץ וּבָנֹות יֻלְּדוּ
לָהֶם: 3 וַיִּגַּשׁ יַעֲקֹב אֶל־יִצְחָק אָבִיו וַיְמֻשֵּׁהוּ: 4 עַל־הָאִשָּׁה
אֲשֶׁר אֲנִי מִתְגּוֹרֵר עִמָּהּ הֲרֵעוֹתָ לְהָמִית אֶת־בְּנָהּ: 5 וַתֹּאמֶר
אֲלֵיהֶן אַל־תִּקְרֶאנָה לִי נָעֳמִי ¹קְרֶאןָ לִי מָרָא כִּי הֵמַר שַׁדַּי
לִי מְאֹד: אֲנִי מְלֵאָה הָלַכְתִּי וְרֵיקָם הֱשִׁיבַנִי יְהוָה לָמָּה
תִּקְרֶאנָה לִי נָעֳמִי ²וַיהוה עָנָה בִי וְשַׁדַּי הֵרַע לִי: 6 וַיּוֹרֶד
את־העם אל־המים ויאמר יהוה אל־גדעון כל אשר ילק
בלשונו מן־המים כאשר־ילק הכלב תציג אתו לבד:

I will curse (אר) them that curse (קל) thee.   May Yahweh
cause his face to shine upon thee and be gracious to thee.
In the place where the dogs licked his blood shall they lick
thy blood, even thine.[3]   Roll thy way upon Yahweh thy God
and trust in him.   The number of those who lapped (*Pi. ptc.*)
was three hundred, and all the rest of the people bowed
down upon their knees.

§ 43. NOUNS FROM DOUBLE 'AYIN VERBS.

There are biliteral nouns and adjectives, as there are
verbs, which duplicate the second radical before afformatives ;
e.g. קַל *fem.* קַלָּה *light* ; עַם *people, suff.* עַמִּי *my people, pl.* עַמִּים.

	A class.		I class.	U class.
abs.	עַם	הַר	חֵץ	חֹק
cstr.	עַם	הַר	חֵץ	חָק־
suff.	עַמִּי	הָרִי	חִצִּי	חֻקִּי
plur.	עַמִּים	הָרִים	חִצִּים	חֻקִּים
	(people)	(mountain)	(arrow)	(statute)

¹ Defective spelling, § 4 d.
² *Circumstantial clause,*—in which the order is : *waw*, then *subject*,
and last *predicate*.   *Waw* would be translated here " when."
³ See § 43. 6.

1. (a) In their monosyllabic form the primary vowels *i* and *u* (evident in the forms with suffixes, plurs., &c. ; *e.g.* חִצִּים *arrows*, חֻקִּים *statutes* ; cf. 42. 2 a. β : notice *u*, not *o*, before double letter, § 7. 7) become tone-long *ē* and *ō*, *e.g.* חֵץ, חֹק. The vowel *a*, however (cf. עַמִּי), usually remains, *e.g.* עַם (not עָם), except, in certain nouns, in combination with the article, when it becomes *ā* ; *e.g.* הָעָם, הָהָר, § 12. Sometimes the *a* is thinned to *i* before suffixes and plur. ; *e.g.* פַּת *morsel*, פִּתִּים (§ 2. 2. 4, § 6. 2 d. i.).

(b) The vowel under מ preformative is sometimes lost (*e.g.* מְסַב *circle*, מְסִבִּים) and sometimes preserved (*e.g.* מָסָךְ *curtain*, cstr. מְסַךְ ; מָגֵן *shield*, מָגִנִּי *my shield*.

(c) Rarely a triliteral form, of the segholate type, has been developed in the plur. ; *e.g.* עֲמָמִים *peoples*, צְלָלִים from צֵל *shadow* (צִלִּי *my shadow*), הֲרָרֵי, cstr. pl. of הַר.

2. As gutturals and ר cannot be doubled, the preceding vowel is usually lengthened ; thus קַל, *f.* קַלָּה, *m. pl.* קַלִּים, *f.* קַלּוֹת ; but רַע *evil*, רָעָה, רָעִים, רָעוֹת. So הַר, 1 *s.* הָרִי, *pl.* הָרִים. Before a virtually doubled ח the short vowel remains. פַּח *snare*, פַּחִים. In either case, of course, the vowel is unchangeable, hence pl. cstr. רָעֵי (not רֵ֥ר), הָרֵי, &c. § 8. 4 b.

3. This class of words can best be distinguished from other classes by a knowledge of derivation ; but it may be observed that—(i.) Words of this class ending in *a* sound have usually short *a*, while the words of other classes which they resemble, as דָּם *blood*, § 18, קָם *standing*, § 41, have *ā* (notice the very different cstr. plurals קְמֵי, דְּמֵי, עַמֵּי). (ii.) Words of this class ending in *e* sound are distinguished from segholates of 'Ayin Yodh like חֵיק, § 41, by wanting *yodh*. They quite agree in form with words like מֵת, § 41, and שֵׁם, § 30, which, however, are not a numerous class (notice the difference before suffixes, שְׁמִי, מֵתִי, חִצִּי). (iii.) Words of this class ending in *o* sound are distinguished from adj. and segholates of 'Ayin Waw like טוֹב and קוֹל, § 41, by wanting *waw*.

4. To this class may also be relegated (i.) a few words of the first declension type ; *e.g.* גָּמָל *camel*, pl. גְּמַלִּים ; עֶצֶב *idol*, pl. עֲצַבִּים ; אוֹפָן *wheel*, קָטָן *little*, קְטַנִּים ; עָמֹק *deep*, fem. עֲמֻקָּה, &c. ; (ii.) two or three monosyllables from roots with medial *n* (always assimilated) ; *e.g.* אַף, *nostril, anger* (=anp, from root אנף), suff. אַפִּי, du. אַפַּיִם ; עֵז (root עַנַז) *she-goat*, pl. עִזִּים ; (iii.) words that double the last consonant ; *e.g.* שַׁאֲנָן *at ease*, שַׁאֲנַנִּים.

light קַל and so: weak דַּל, fine דַּק, bitter מַר, living חַי,
cold קַר, hot חַם.

people עַם „ hill הַר, garden גַּן, prince שַׂר, ox פַּר, palm
(hand) כַּף *f.*

shadow צֵל „ heart לֵב, mother אֵם, end קֵץ, arrow חֵץ,
with (prep.) אֵת, עִם.¹

statute חֹק „ bear דֹּב, tambourine תֹּף, all כֹּל, yoke עֹל,
strength עֹז, heat חֹם, cold קֹר, statute
חֻקָּה.

5. The indeterminate subject (Engl. *they*) may be expressed—(*a*) by the 3rd pers. plur.; or (*b*) by the 3rd sing.; or (*c*) by the passive voice, *i.e.* Niph. (Hoph. Pu.)—in the last case the Pass., used impersonally, still remains the government of the Act.; *e.g.*

they called his name Sheth { קָרְאוּ אֶת־שְׁמוֹ שֵׁת
„ קָרָא
„ נִקְרָא }

6. When the Personal Pronoun is repeated for the sake of emphasis, it is repeated in the separate or simple form; *e.g.*

bless me, even me בָּרְכֵנִי גַם אָנִי
thy blood, even thine דָּמְךָ גַם־אָתָּה
to Sheth, even him לְשֵׁת גַם־הוּא

יֶתֶר cord, string נָשִׂיא ruler, prince
עַלְמָה *f.* young woman מָאַס to reject
זָעֵף ² displeased.

EXERCISE.   TRANSLATE.

וַיָּבֹא דָוִד אֶל־בֵּיתוֹ וְהִנֵּה הַנְּעָרָה יֹצֵאת לִקְרָאתוֹ בְּתֻפִּים: 2 וּבְצִלּוֹ יֵשְׁבוּ גוֹיִם רַבִּים: 3 כּוֹנְנוּ חִצָּם עַל־יֶתֶר: 4 וְאַתְּנֵם לַכֹּהֵן וּלְבָנָיו לְחָק־עוֹלָם: 5 וַתָּבֹא הָאִשָּׁה אֵלָיו וַתֹּאמֶר הִנֵּה שָׁמְעָה שִׁפְחָתְךָ בְּקוֹלֶךָ וָאָשִׂים נַפְשִׁי בְכַפִּי: 6 קָרַב קִצֵּנוּ מָלְאוּ

¹ With suff. אֹתָם, אֶתְכֶם, אֹתָנוּ, אֹתָהּ, אֹתוֹ, אֹתָהּ, אֹתָךְ, אֹתְךָ, אֹתִי. So עִמִּי, &c., except 2 *pl.* which is עִמָּכֶם. (Another form of 1 sing. is עִמָּדִי.) Like אֵת too is הִנֵּה *behold*, except in 1 pers. sing. and plur. It is as follows: הִנְנִי (or הִנֶּנִּי, *pause* הִנֵּנִי), הִנְּךָ, הִנֶּךָ, הִנּוֹ, הִנָּהּ, הִנֶּנּוּ (or הִנֵּנוּ), הִנָּם, הִנְּכֶם (*pause* הִנֵּנוּ).

² Very rare.

יְמֵינוּ: 7 הִנֵּה הָעַלְמָה יֹלֶדֶת בֵּן וְקָרָאת[1] שְׁמוֹ עִמָּנוּ אֵל׃
8 וַיָּבֹא אֶל־בֵּיתוֹ זָעֵף וַיִּשְׁכַּב עַל־מִטָּתוֹ וַיַּסֵּב אֶת־פָּנָיו וְלֹא
אָכַל לָחֶם׃ 9 אֱלֹהִים לֹא תְקַלֵּל וְנָשִׂיא בְעַמְּךָ לֹא תָאֹר׃
10 אלה החקים והמשפטים אשר תשמרו בארץ אשר
נתתי לכם לרשתה כל הימים אשר־אתם חיים על־האדמה
כי עמי אתם׃

Comfort ye my people, speak to (עַל־) their heart, and
cry unto them that their warfare is fulfilled (full).   Plead
with your mother, plead, for she is not my wife, and I am
not her husband.   Thou shalt fall upon the mountains of
Israel, thou and all the peoples that are with thee.   And the
captain of the host sent messengers to the king, saying:
Make thy covenant with me, and behold, my hand (shall
be) with thee, to turn-round [2] unto thee all Israel.

§ 44. LAMEDH HE (LAMEDH WAW AND YODH) VERBS.

(See Paradigm, p. 228.)

The ה in this class of verbs (e.g. גָּלָה *to uncover, reveal*)
is not a genuine letter of the root, but a mere vowel sign,
indicating *ā*.   (When the ה is truly consonantal, it takes
mappiq, § 7. 8, *e.g.* גָּבַהּ *to be high*, and the vb. is treated
like a *Lamedh guttural*, § 37.)

The last letter of the stem is properly either י (גלי *gālay*)
or ו (*e.g.* שלו *shālaw*), though forms with *yodh* have acquired
such a preponderance that only a few traces of stems with
waw now appear.   *Lamedh Yodh* (or *Lamedh Waw*) would
therefore be a more appropriate term, as ה is not integral
to the root.

The original י of גלי (now גָּלָה) is still seen in the pass. ptc.
Qal, גָּלוּי (*gāluy*, cf. קָטוּל), and in some pausal forms ; *e.g.* חָסָיוּ *they
seek refuge* (cf. קָטְלוּ).   The original ו of שלו (שָׁלָה) is seen in the
words שָׁלֵו (*shālēw*) *at ease*, שַׁלְוָה (*shalwâ*) *ease* (שָׁלַוְתִּי *I was at
ease*, 1 s. pf. Qal, in Job 3. 26).

---

[1] Probably to be regarded as a rare form of the 3rd sing. fem. pf.
[2] Hiph. סבב.

1. The letter ה, appropriate (as = $\bar{a}$) in the 3rd s. m. pf. Qal, came to be regarded as part of the root, and consequently (just like the ל of קָטַל) appears in *all* (3rd s. m.) perfects, imperfects, participles (except pass. Qal, *e.g.* גָּלוּי), and absolute infinitives.

The vowel preceding ה frequently differs, in a way difficult to account for, from that of the corresponding part of the regular verb: the respective endings are as follows:

(a) הָ in *all* perfects, *e.g.* הִגְלָה, נִגְלָה, גִּלָּה, גָּלָה, &c.

(b) הֶ in *all* imperfects, *e.g.* יִגְלֶה, יְגַלֶּה, יַגְלֶה, &c.

(c) הֶ in *all* participles (exc. pass. Qal) absolute; *e.g.* מַגְלֶה, מְגַלֶּה, נִגְלֶה (*f.* גֹּלָה), גֹּלֶה, &c.

   Ptc. cstr. is in הֵ; *e.g.* גֹּלֵה, &c.

(d) הֵ in *all* imperatives; *e.g.* הַגְלֵה, גַּלֵּה, גְּלֵה, &c.

(e) Inf. abs. has the ordinary vowel of the regular vb.; Qal גָּלֹה, Hiph. הַגְלֵה.

(f) Inf. cstr. adds the fem. ending ת (cf. § 33. 2 b), making the termination וֹת; *e.g.* Qal גְּלוֹת, Pi. גַּלּוֹת, Hiph. הַגְלוֹת.

   The ordinary form of the 3rd s. fem. גָּלְתָה, נִגְלְתָה, &c., has in reality a double fem. termination.

2. When the third radical (*i.e.* the ultimate י) is not final but stands under inflection:

(1) Before vocalic afformatives, וּ, ִי, or הָ, the *yodh*, coming between two vowels (*e.g.* קְטָלוּ, גָּלְיוּ *gāl'yû*) disappears and is dropped; thus גָּלוּ.

It is also dropped before suffixes; *e.g.* (from עָנָה) עָנָנִי *he answered me*, עָנָהוּ . . . *him* (always the form הוּ with pf.), עָנָם . . . *them*, יַעֲנֵם *he will answer them*, וַיִּרְאֵהוּ *and he saw him* (רָאָה).

(2) At the end of a syllable (*i.e.* before a consonantal afformative; *e.g.* Niph. נִגְלֵיתִי, נִקְטַלְתִּי) the *yodh*, preceded as it always is by *a*, creates primarily, as we have seen, by strict analogy, the combination *ay*.

(a) This *ay* most naturally becomes the diphthongal $\hat{e}$, § 2. 2. 1. Thus נִגְלֵיתִי becomes נִגְלֵיתִי. This $\hat{e}$ prevails exclusively in perff. pass., *i.e.* Niph. Pu. (גֻּלֵּיתִי) and Hoph.;

(b) but in the other parts it also appears as $\hat{\imath}$, which in perf. Qal is found exclusively, and in other perff. alternatively with *ê*, as *Qal* גָּלִיתָ; Pi. גִּלִּיתָ and גִּלֵּיתָ;

(c) before נָה of imperf. and imper. it becomes *ê* (sᵉghol fairly regarded as pure long; cf. § 3. 2. 2 b), as תִּגְלֶינָה, גְּלֶינָה.

3. Of the few vbs. ending in *waw*, שָׁחָה (שׁחו) is found very frequently, usually in the Hithpaʿlēl (הִתְקַטְלֵל) *to bow down, prostrate oneself*. The pf. would be strictly הִתְשַׁחֲוַ (*waw*), then (as all pfs. end in הָ,) הִשְׁתַּחֲוָה (§ 26. 3 *a.* ii.), impf. יִשְׁתַּחֲוֶה, *pl.* יִשְׁתַּחֲווּ (*wū*). Apoc. impf. sing. (§ 45. 1) strictly יִשְׁתַּחְו. But, as it is characteristic of final (consonantal) *w* to pass into the unaccented homogeneous (vocalic) *û*, this becomes יִשְׁתַּחוּ (not תְּ, perhaps because the ח was felt to be virtually doubled).

4. In pf. with *waw consec.* the accent is not usually thrown forward: *e.g.* וְעָשִׂיתָ, not וְעָשִׂיתָ *and thou shalt make*; cf. § 38. 1. 6.

הִיה to be	שׁתה to drink	רדה to rule
עשׂה to do	שׁקה[1] *Hiph.* to give drink, water	נכה *Hiph.* to smite
קנה to acquire		פִּנָּה *f.* corner
מנה to count	הרה to conceive	אָרוֹן (with article
בכה to weep	עלה to go up	הָאָרוֹן)chest, ark
מחה to blot out	גלה to reveal, open	הַיַּרְדֵּן the Jordan
בנה to build	ראה to see	עָנָן cloud
כסה *Pi.* to cover	פרה to be fruitful	עָנַן *Pi.* to bring
רבה to increase	צוה *Pi.* to command	clouds

Not before the inf. is rendered by לְבִלְתִּי with inf. cstr.; *e.g.*

He commanded the man to eat צִוָּה אֶת־הָאִישׁ לֶאֱכֹל

„ „ „ *not to eat* לְבִלְתִּי אֲכֹל „ „

EXERCISE. TRANSLATE.

כֹּה אָמַר יְהוָה לָעֲצָמוֹת הָאֵלֶּה הִנֵּה אֲנִי מֵבִיא בָכֶם רוּחַ וִחְיִיתֶם: 2 צַוֵּה אֶת־הַכֹּהֲנִים נֹשְׂאֵי אֲרוֹן יְהוָה וְיַעֲלוּ מִן־הַיַּרְדֵּן: 3 לֹא אֹסִף עוֹד לְהַכּוֹת אֶת־כָּל־חַי כַּאֲשֶׁר עָשִׂיתִי: 4 אֶבֶן[2] מָאֲסוּ הַבּוֹנִים הָיְתָה לְרֹאשׁ פִּנָּה: 5 וְהָיָה[3] בְּעַנְנִי עָנָן עַל־הָאָרֶץ וְנִרְאֲתָה הַקֶּשֶׁת בֶּעָנָן: וְהָיְתָה הַקֶּשֶׁת בֶּעָנָן וּרְאִיתִיהָ לִזְכֹּר בְּרִיתִי: 6 שָׂא נָא עֵינֶיךָ וּרְאֵה כִּי אֶת־כָּל־

---

[1] Used instead of Hiph. of שׁתה. [2] Relative unexpressed.

[3] § 3. 2. 3 b, § 7. 5.

10

הָאָרֶץ אֲשֶׁר אַתָּה רֹאֶה לְךָ אֶתְּנֶנָּה ׃ וְשַׂמְתִּי אֶת־זַרְעֲךָ כַּעֲפַר
הָאָרֶץ אֲשֶׁר אִם־יוּכַל אִישׁ לִמְנוֹת עֲפַר הָאָרֶץ גַּם־זַרְעֲךָ
יִמָּנֶה ׃ 7 וַיֹּאמֶר פַּרְעֹה לְךָ מֵעָלַי הִשָּׁמֶר לְךָ אַל־תֹּסֶף רְאוֹת
פָּנַי כִּי בְּיוֹם רְאוֹתְךָ פָּנַי תָּמוּת ׃ 8 מִי יַשְׁקֵנִי מַיִם ׃ 9 וַאֲנִי
הנני ממטיר על־הארץ ארבעים יום וארבעים לילה ומחיתי
את־כל אשר עשיתי מעל פני האדמה ׃ 10 נער הייתי
גם־זקנתי ולא ראיתי צדיק נעזב וזרעו מבקש־לחם ׃

Behold, thy maid is in thy (*f.*) hand, do to her the (thing)
good in thine eyes. And they left off building the city. I
am not able to do (any)thing until thou come thither. And
the waters increased very (much), and the heads of the mountains were covered. I have commanded thee not to eat of
the tree which is in the midst of the garden, lest thou die.
For thou, Yahweh of hosts, God of Israel, hast opened the ear
of thy servant saying, A house will I build for thee. And
he said unto the children of Israel, (At)-evening [1] (*acc.*) then
(*waw. cons. pf.*[2]) shall ye know that Yahweh hath brought
you out from the land of Egypt, and (in-the)-morning (*acc.*)
then shall ye see his glory.

§ 45. APOCOPATED FORMS AND NOUNS OF VERBS LAM. HE.

1. (1) The *Jussive* or shortened impf. and the imper.[3] in
verbs *Lam. He* is formed by loss of the final vocalic syllable
(*He* and vowel sign), and hence is often called the *Apocopated*
impf. &c. The contraction occasions some alterations within
the word. Thus: *impf. Qal* יִגְלֶה, apoc. (by loss of הֶ) יִגֶל.
(*a*) This form is found in some vbs. ; *e.g.* וַיִּשְׁבְּ *and he took cap-*
tive (from שָׁבָה). (*b*) But, just as סִפֵּר becomes סֵפֶר (§ 29. 1 a. *a*),
so, in certain vbs., the form יִגֶל has become יֵגֶל; *e.g.* וַתֵּפֶן
and she turned (פָּנָה), (gutt. וַתֵּתַע *and she wandered* תָּעָה).

---

[1] The *modal* accus. embracing all definitions of *time, place, measure,*
and in general all expressions defining the *mode* of the verbal action.

[2] Following עֶרֶב, which is *equivalent to* a clause in the impf. (§ 23. 5 b).

[3] The Qal—גְּלֵה—of course cannot contract. In the other parts both
longer and shorter forms are found ; *e.g.* צַוֵּה and צַו, *command*, Pi. imper.
of צִוָּה.

(c) Other vbs. have the long vowel, but no helping s͑ghol, e.g. וַיֵּבְךְ *and he wept.*   (d) Others, again, have the helping vowel, but only the short vowel in the open syllable; e.g. וַיִּבֶן *and he built* (gutt. וַיִּשַׁע *and he gazed* יָשְׁעָה).   Thus there are four types, יֵגֶל, יֵגֶל, יֵגֶל, יֵגֶל.

(2) Similarly with *impf. Hiph.* יַגְלֶה, *apoc.* יֶגֶל.   (a) This form is found in some vbs., e.g. וַיַּשְׁקְ *and he watered.*   (b) But just as מֶלֶךְ becomes מֶלֶךְ (§ 29), so in certain vbs. the form יֶגֶל has become יֶגֶל; e.g. וַיֶּפֶר *and he made fruitful* (פָּרָה).

So *imper. Hiph.* (הַגְלֵה = הַגֶל =) הֶגֶל; e.g. הֶרֶב *make abundant* (apoc. Hiph. imp. of רָבָה; through הַרְבֵּה, הַרְבֶּה).

(3) Gutturals in the *Pe guttural* vbs. naturally take *pathah*: apoc. impf. Qal, Hiph. of עָלָה *to go up* (יַעֲלֶה) = יַעַל, cf. נַעַר, § 36. 2. 1; *apoc. imper.* (הַעֲלֵה =) הַעַל.   In such vbs. the impf. Qal and Hiph. are identical.

(4) These contracted forms of impf. are used with *waw consec.*, e.g. וַיַּעַל *and he went up* (Qal), or *brought up* (Hiph.), though full forms with *waw* are not uncommon.   The following list summarizes the chief facts:

impf. Qal	יִגְלֶה	*apoc.*	יֵגֶל or יֶגֶל = יֵגֶל or יֵגֶל.
impf. Hiph.	יַגְלֶה	„	יֶגֶל = יֶגֶל.
imper. Hiph.	הַגְלֵה	„	הֶגֶל = הֶגֶל.
impf. Niph.	יִגָּלֶה	„	יִגָּל.
impf. Pi.	יְגַלֶּה	„	יְגַל.
imper. Pi.	גַּלֵּה	„	גַּל.
impf. Qal, Hiph.	יַעֲלֶה	„	יַעַל.
impf. Qal	יִרְאֶה	„	יֵרְא, &c. With waw cons. 3 *s. m.* alone וַיַּרְא (*and he saw*; also Hiph. *and he showed*), 3 *s. f.* וַתֵּרֶא, 1 *s.* וָאֵרֶא. *impf. Niph.* יֵרָאֶה, *apoc.* יֵרָא.

2. The common verb הָיָה *to be* has some irregularities, which may be summarized thus:

(1) The gutt., when initial, takes hat. s͑ghol. as imper. הֱיֵה.

(2) With *any* prefixed letter the gutt., when without a vowel, takes simple sh͑wa, and the prefix *hireq*, as impf. יִהְיֶה.

(3) Apocopated impf. is primarily יִהְי *yihy.*   But, as it is characteristic of final (consonantal) *y* to pass into the accented homogeneous (vocalic) *î*, this becomes יְהִי *y͑hî*, with simple

waw וְיִהִי, with *waw consec.* וַיְהִי *and it came to pass.* See nouns of 2nd declension in this § (45. 3 b. 1).

The verb חָיָה *to live* has mostly the same peculiarities.

a. Waw before the imp. sing. takes —– as וְהָיָה (not וּ) and of course א in 1st sing. impf. אֶהְיֶה. The preform. letter always takes *Methegh* ; *e.g.* יִהְיֶה, etc.

b. As the ultimate form of the vb. for *to live* is חָיַי, which appears in the form of חַי (§ 43) as well as of חָיָה (§ 44, also p. 87, note 5), the plur. of חַי *living* is חַיִּים (which also means *life*).

3. *Nouns from Verbs* ל"ה.

First and third declensions.

						fem.
abs.	מִקְנֶה	קֹנֶה	עָלֶה	שָׂדֶה	יָפֶה	יָפָה
cstr.	מִקְנֵה	קֹנֵה	עֲלֵה	שְׂדֵה	יְפֵה	יְפַת
suff. 1	מִקְנִי	קֹנִי	עָלִי	שָׂדִי		
3 *m.*	מִקְנֵהוּ	קֹנֵהוּ	עָלֵהוּ	שָׂדֵהוּ		
3 *f.*	מִקְנָהּ	קֹנָהּ	עָלָהּ	שָׂדָהּ		
pl.	מִקְנִים	קֹנִים	עָלִים	שָׂדוֹת	יָפִים	יָפוֹת
cstr.	מִקְנֵי	קֹנֵי	עֲלֵי	שְׂדוֹת	יְפֵי	יְפוֹת
	(possession)	(possessor)	(leaf)	(field)	(fair)	(fair)

Second declension.

A class. · I class. U class.

						I class	U class	
abs. sing. אֲרִי	(קֹצוּ)	גְּדִי	פְּרִי	פְּתִי	חֲצִי	חֳלִי	תֹּהוּ	
pause „		גֶּדִי	פֶּרִי	פֶּתִי	חֵצִי	חֹלִי		
suff. 3 *m.*	(גְּדִיוֹ)	פִּרְיוֹ		חֶצְיוֹ	חָלְיוֹ		
plur. אֲרָיִים		גְּדָיִים		פְּתָאִים		חֳלָיִים		

and

cstr.	גְּדָיֵי קַצְוֵי		פְּתָיִים		חֲלָיֵנוּ 1 *pl.*	
	(lion)	(end)	(kid)	(fruit)	(simple)	(half) (sickness) (waste)

a. First and third declensions.—(1) The vocalic sound at the end of these words is, in the absolute (cf. מִקְנֶה), the broad *sĕghol*, which becomes the closer *çere* in the construct (מִקְנֵה). Comp. the relation of the impf. יִגְלֶה and imper. גְּלֵה in the verb.

(2) The vocalic termination is absorbed in the vowel of the afformative, *e.g.* מִקְנִי—the ה ָ of מִקְנֶה has disappeared. So רֹעֶה *shepherd,* רֹעִי *my shepherd* ; יָפֶה, יָפִים, &c.

(3) *a.* The final *e* sound naturally admits the suffixes *hu,*

ha, &c., of 3 pers.—the original form of this suffix (§ 19. 1);
cf. suffix to impf. of vbs. (§ 31. 2 b).   In 3 m. s. הוּ֖— is found
exclusively (*e.g.* מִקְנֵהוּ, not מִקְנוֹ); in 3 f. usually הָ, (cf. suffix
to impf. of vbs.), *e.g.* עָלֶהָ; rarely ה ָ (*e.g.* שָׂדֶה).

> β. Forms like מִקְנֶיךָ *thy cattle*, שָׂדֵינוּ *our field*, are probably not
> plur. but sing. written with the original י of the root, seen, *e.g.*, in
> שָׂדַי, the poetic form of שָׂדֶה.

b. *Second declension.*—(1) a. Nouns of the regular forma-
tion, *e.g.* בְּכֶה *weeping*, הֶגֶה *murmuring* (like מֶלֶךְ), are rare.   As
a rule the fundamental י or ו appears.   It is characteristic, as
we have seen (§ 45. 2. 3), of final (consonantal) *y* to pass into
accented (vocalic) *î*, which has the effect of reducing the
preceding vowel to sh^ewa; and of final (consonantal) *w* to
pass into unaccented (vocalic) *û* (§ 44. 3).   Thus an original
פֶּרְי *pary* (from פָּרָה = פרה *to be fruitful*) becomes פְּרִי *p'rî* (in
pause פֶּרִי with the accent on the orig. syllable); an orig. חֶצְי
hicy (from חָצָה = חצה *to divide*) becomes חֵצִי (*p.* חֵצִי, the
orig. *i* becomes tone-long *ē*); an orig. חֶלְי *holy* or חָלְי (from
חָלָה = חלי *to be sick*) becomes חֳלִי *h'lî* (*p.* חֹלִי).

> β. Nouns ending in ו are few.   An original קַצְו would
> become קָצוּ (1st syll. open and accented, therefore *ā*; not
> found, but cf. שָׂחוּ *swimming*), cstr. pl. קַצְוֵי (like מַלְכֵי) in which
> the *waw* resumes its primary consonantal power.   So an
> orig. *tohw* or *tuhw* becomes *tôhû*, תֹּהוּ.

(2) When any afformative or suffix is appended, the
vowel as in other segholates removes to the first syllable;
e.g. the *a* in אַרְיֵה (an alternative word for אֲרִי) *lion*; חָלְיוֹ *his
sickness* (cf. קׇדְשׁוֹ), *holyô*.   In many nouns of the A class the
a has been thinned to *i* (cf. פֶּרְיוֹ, גְּדִיוֹ) so that with suffixes
they have all the appearance of I class nouns (cf. שִׁמְשׁ, שִׁמְשֶׁךָ,
§ 29. 1 b).

(3) In the plur. *yodh* is sometimes softened into *'aleph*
before another *yodh*; *e.g.* פְּתָאִים oftener than פְּתָיִים; and in
the *cstr.* the pretonic *ā* many times remains; *e.g.* גְּדָיֵי.

> c. The short words יָד *hand*, דָּם *blood*, &c., which follow in their
> inflection the *first* declension, and the words בֵּן *son*, שֵׁם *name*, &c.,
> which follow the *third*, appear to be contractions of forms derived
> from stems ל״ה.   The words אָב *father*, אָח *brother, fem.* אָחוֹת

sister, חָם *father-in-law*, &c., are also shortened forms belonging to this class of stems ; in which, however, the rejected letter generally appears under inflection, *e.g.* sing. cstr. אֲבִי, 2 m. אָבִיךָ, 3 m. אָבִיהוּ or אָבִיו, 3 f. אָבִיהָ, &c. See Table of Irreg. Nouns, p. 153.

4. Our reciprocal pronouns are expressed in Hebrew more concretely by nouns, *man, woman, brother, sister, friend*, &c. ; *e.g.*

and they spake to one another	וַיְדַבְּרוּ אִישׁ אֶל־רֵעֵהוּ
	,, ,, אֶל־אָחִיו
and they smote one another	וַיַּכּוּ אִישׁ אֶת־אָחִיו
and they (f.) *clave to one another*	וַתִּדְבַּקְנָה אִשָּׁה בַּאֲחוֹתָהּ
	,, ,, בִּרְעוּתָהּ

5. Our reflexive pronouns are rendered chiefly in two ways : (i.) by the Niph. or Hithp. of the verb. ; *e.g. they hid themselves* נִסְתְּרוּ, *they girded themselves* הִתְאַזְּרוּ ; (ii.) by nouns, such as לֵב heart, קֶרֶב inward part, נֶפֶשׁ soul ; *e.g. And he said to himself* וַיֹּאמֶר אֶל־לִבּוֹ, *And she laughed within herself* וַתִּצְחַק בְּקִרְבָּהּ, *He has sworn by himself* נִשְׁבַּע בְּנַפְשׁוֹ.

מַעֲשֶׂה work	עֳנִי affliction	רִיב (מְרִיבָה *f.*) strife
יְפִי beauty	מִכְסֶה covering	חִתִּים Hittites
רֵעֶה friend	רֹעֶה shepherd	לוּז Luz בְּאֵר *f.* well
מַרְאֶה appearance	חָלָה to be sick	חֵמֶת (rare) water-
שְׁבִי *i* captivity	קָוָה (rare) *Niph.* to	skin, bottle
מַשְׁקֶה } butler	be gathered	מָבוֹא entrance
(butlership)	together	מַכָּה *f.* blow, plague
מִקְנֶה cattle	לְחִי cheek, *dual* לְחָיַיִם	שָׁכַר to be drunken

EXERCISE.   TRANSLATE.

וַתַּהַר וַתֵּרֶא כִּי הָרָתָה וַתֵּקַל גְּבִרְתָּהּ בְּעֵינֶיהָ: 2 הִתְהַלֵּךְ לְפָנַי וֶהְיֵה תָמִים וַהֲקִמֹתִי אֶת־בְּרִיתִי לִהְיוֹת לְךָ לֵאלֹהִים: 3 וַיָּסַר נֹחַ אֶת־מִכְסֵה הַתֵּבָה וַיַּרְא וְהִנֵּה חָרְבוּ פְּנֵי הָאֲדָמָה: 4 וַיִּטַּע נֹחַ כֶּרֶם וַיֵּשְׁתְּ מִן־הַיַּיִן וַיִּשְׁכָּר וַיִּתְגַּל בְּתוֹךְ אָהֳלֹה[1]:

[1] This form of the 3 *s. m.* suff. infrequently met with, points back to the older ending הוּ (cf. § 19. 1) ; the ה, which was there consonantal (*hû*), is here retained as a vowel letter.

5 וַיַּחַל הַמֶּלֶךְ בְּרַגְלָיו וְגַם־בְּחָלְיוֹ לֹא דָרַשׁ אֶת־יהוה : 6 נָטָה
יָדְךָ וְהַעַל אֶת־הַצְפַרְדְּעִים : 7 וַיְהִי רִיב בֵּין רֹעֵי מִקְנֵה אַבְרָם
וּבֵין רֹעֵי מִקְנֵה לוֹט וַיֹּאמְרוּ אִישׁ אֶל־רֵעֵהוּ אַל־נָא תְהִי
מְרִיבָה בֵּינִי וּבֵינֶךָ : 8 וַיֵּרָא יהוה אֶל־אַבְרָם וַיִּבֶן שָׁם אַבְרָם
מִזְבֵּחַ לַיהוה הַנִּרְאֶה אֵלָיו : 9 וִיְהִי שֵׁם יהוה מְבֹרָךְ : 10 ויראו
השמרים איש יוצא מן־העיר ויאמרו לו הראנו נא את־מבוא
העיר ועשינו עמך חסד : ויראם את־מבוא העיר ויכו את־
העיר לפי־חרב ואת־האיש שלחו : וילך האיש ארץ החתים
ויבן עיר ויקרא שמה לוז הוא שמה עד היום הזה :

And Noah did according to all that Yahweh commanded
him.   And he commanded the priests, saying, Come up out
of the Jordan ; and they went up.   And the man of God
stretched out his hand and brought up the frogs, and Pharaoh
saw the plagues, and he feared (with) a great fear.   And it
came to pass, when they were in the field, that the man rose
up against (אל) his friend and slew him.   Let the waters be
gathered together unto one place, and let the dry land
appear ; and it was so.   And God opened her eyes and she
saw a well of water, and she went and filled the bottle with-
water,[1] and made the boy drink   And the captain of the
host said, Who (ever) shall smite Qiryath Sepher and take it,
then (*waw cons.*) I will give him my daughter to wife.   Bow
(נטה, *Hiph.*) thy heavens and come down.

Note on doubly weak and defective verbs.

1. Many verbs have more than one weak letter.   They are mostly
ל״א or ל״ה with some other peculiarity.   Some common verbs are these :
(1) ל״א and פ״ן.—נָשָׂא *to lift*, impf. יִשָּׂא, pl. יִשְׂאוּ (§ 7. 5) ; imp. שָׂא,
suff. שָׂאֵהוּ, שָׂאוּנִי ; inf. c. שְׂאֵת (rarely נְשֹׂא), בִּשְׂאֵת, &c., but לָשֵׂאת.

(2) ל״א and פ״ו.—יָצָא *go out*, impf. יֵצֵא, imp. צֵא, inf. c. צֵאת,
לָצֵאת.   Hiph. הוֹצִיא, הוֹצֵאתָ, &c.

(3) ל״א and ע״ו.—בּוֹא *to come*, perf. בָּא, בָּאתָ, &c., impf. יָבוֹא, inf.,
imp. בּוֹא, part. בָּא.   Hiph. הֵבִיא, הֵבֵאתָ, &c., but usually הֲבִיאֹתָ,
&c., before suff.

(4) ל״ה and פ״ן.—נָטָה *to stretch*, impf. יִטֶּה, apoc. יֵט, וַיֵּט.   Hiph.

---

[1] Acc. (cf. § 38. 3).

נכה *to smite*, הִכָּה, impf. יַכֶּה, apoc. יַ֫ךְ, וַיַּ֫ךְ, imp. הַךְ, inf. הַכּוֹת, part. מַכֶּה.

(5) ל״ה and א״ל.—אָבָה *be willing*, impf. יֹאבֶה, apoc. אַל־תֹּבֵא, Pr. **1.** 10. אָלָה *to swear*, apoc. וַיֹּאֶל; 1 S. **14.** 24 (יֹאלֶה=יֹאלֶה=יֹאלֶה, § 2. 2. 1, § 35. 1 a). Poet. אָתָה *to come*, impf. יֹאתֶה יֶאֱתֶה, apoc. וַיֵּאת, Is. **41.** 25, cf. Deut. **33.** 21.

(6) ל״ה and פ״י.—יָרָה *to cast, shoot*, imp. יְרֵה, inf. יְרוֹת. Hiph. הוֹרָה *to direct, teach, instruct* (cf. תּוֹרָה *direction, instruction, law*), impf. יוֹרֶה, apoc. וַיּוֹר, 2 K. **13.** 17. יָפָה *be beautiful*, impf. יִיפֶה, apoc. וַיִּיף, Ez. **31.** 7, cf. **16.** 13.

2. Stems composed of two strong radicals and any of the three weak letters י, ו, נ, are often allied in meaning. Thus: עָיִן יָעַץ *to advise*, יָגֹר, נֻּר *to fear*, נָצַב יָצַב *to place*, פּוּחַ נָפַח *to blow*, עָטָה יָעַט *to cover*. Hence one root supplements itself often from another. In many verbs also the forms in Qal have fallen into disuse, and the Qal supplements itself out of the other conjugations.

(1) בּוֹשׁ *be ashamed*, see Parad. § 40. Hiph. הֵבִישׁ reg., and also הוֹבִישׁ from יבשׁ.

(2) טוֹב *be good*, perf., part., inf. טוֹב; but impf. יִיטַב and Hiph. הֵיטִיב from יטב.

(3) הָלַךְ *to go*, perf., inf. abs. הָלוֹךְ, part. הֹלֵךְ; impf. יֵלֵךְ, inf. c. לֶכֶת, suff. לֶכְתִּי, imp. לֵךְ, Hiph. הוֹלִיךְ from ילך (ולך). Later style forms impf. and inf. cons. from הָלַךְ (הֲלַךְ, יַהֲלֹךְ).

(4) יָגֹר *to fear*, perf., part. יָגֹר; impf. יָגוּר, imp. גּוּר, Job **19.** 29, from נּוּר.

(5) יָכֹל *be able*, inf. abs. יָכוֹל, inf. cons. יְכֹלֶת, impf. יוּכַל (regarded by some, less probably, as impf. Hoph.).

(6) יָסַף *to add*, perf., part., in Qal; Hiph. הוֹסִיף in perf., impf. (יוֹסִף, וַיּוֹסֶף), and inf. cstr. הוֹרִיף. An imp. סְפוּ, Is. **29.** 1, Jer. **7.** 21.

(7) יָקַץ *to awake*, only impf. יִיקַץ in Qal; Hiph. הֵקִין, perf., impf., imp., infin., from קוּץ.

(8) כָּשַׁל *to fall*, perf., inf. abs., part., in Qal; impf., inf. cons. from Niph.

(9) נָגַשׁ *to draw near*, impf., imp., inf. cons. in Qal, but perf. and part. borrowed from Niph., which has only these two parts.

(10) נָחָה *to lead*, perf., imper. in Qal; impf. and inf. cons. in Hiph., which has also perf. twice.

(11) נָקַע *be alienated*, perf., 3 *f.* נָקְעָה, Ez. **23.** 18, impf. 3 *f.* תֵּקַע, Jer. **6.** 8, from יקע.

(12) נתך *to pour* (intr.), only impf. יִתַּךְ in Qal, in Niph. נִתַּךְ, perf. and part.

(13) שָׁתָה *to drink*, in Qal, but Hiph. הִשְׁקָה *to give to drink*, from שָׁקָה (the Qal of which is not used in Hebrew).

TABLE OF SOME COMMON IRREG. NOUNS.[1]

אָב *father*, cstr. אֲבִי, *my f.* אָבִי, *thy f.* אָבִיךָ, *his f.* אָבִיהוּ or
אָבִיו, *her f.* אָבִיהָ, *your f.* אֲבִיכֶם, *their f.* אֲבִיהֶם, &c.;
plur. אָבוֹת, *their f.* אֲבוֹתָם (rarer and late אֲבוֹתֵיהֶם).

אָח *brother*; in the sing. like אָב—cstr. אֲחִי, *my b.* אָחִי,
our b. אָחִינוּ, *your b.* אֲחִיכֶם, &c. *Plur.* אַחִים (with *dagh.*
f. implicitum)—but cstr. אֲחֵי, *my b.* אַחַי (pause אֶחָי,
p. 43, note 3), *his b.* אֶחָיו, *our b.* אַחֵינוּ, *your b.* אֲחֵיכֶם, &c.

חָם *husband's father*, like אָח.

אָחוֹת *sister*, cstr. אֲחוֹת, *suff.* אֲחוֹתִי, &c.; *pl.* (abs. אֲחָיוֹת not
found), with *suff.* אַחְיוֹתָיו, אַחְיוֹתֵיהֶם, but also אַחְווֹתֶיךָ,
אַחְווֹתֵיכֶם.

חֲמוֹת *husband's mother* (not found in pl.), like אָחוֹת.

אִישׁ *man*, *pl.* אֲנָשִׁים, cstr. אַנְשֵׁי.

אִשָּׁה *woman*, *wife* (probably for אִנְשָׁה). The primary אִנְשַׁת
(fem. *t*) would give first אִשְׁתְּ, then אִשְׁתְּ, which
naturally becomes אֵשֶׁת (cf. כֵּפֶר, § 29. 1 a. *a*). This
is, in point of fact, the *cstr.* form, hence *my w.* אִשְׁתִּי,
&c.; *pl.* נָשִׁים 1, cstr. נְשֵׁי.

אָמָה 1 *maid*, *pl.* אֲמָהוֹת 1, *suff.* אַמְהֹתַי.

בַּיִת 2 *house*, cstr. בֵּית, *pl.* בָּתִּים (not *bottîm*, but probably
bāttîm, or *bâtîm*; in latter case *dagh.* would be *lene*
—irregularly: on any view the ָ is unchangeable,
and is usually marked by methegh, probably to
keep it from being mistaken for *o*), cstr. בָּתֵּי.

בֵּן 3 *son*, cstr. בֶּן, rarely בִּן; *suff.* בְּנִי, בִּנְךָ, &c.; *pl.* בָּנִים 1,
cstr. בְּנֵי, *suff.* בָּנַי, &c.

בַּת 2 *daughter*, *my d.* בִּתִּי (for בִּנְתִּי, &c.); *pl.* בָּנוֹת 1.

יוֹם 2 *day* (contracted from *yawm* or *yaum*), *pl.* יָמִים (for
"יָמְ"); cstr. יְמֵי, cf. § 41. 5. (The plur. of יָם *sea* is יַמִּים.)

כְּלִי *vessel*, *suff.* כֶּלְיְךָ; *pl.* כֵּלִים, cstr. כְּלֵי, *suff.* כֵּלַי.

מַיִם *pl. water*, cstr. מֵי, מֵימֵי, *suff.* מֵימַי, מֵימֶיךָ, &c. (redupl.
form always before suff.).

עִיר *f. 2 city*, *pl.* עָרִים, cstr. עָרֵי.

פֶּה *mouth*, cstr. פִּי, *my m.* פִּי, פִּיךָ, פִּיו and פִּיהוּ, פִּיהָ, פִּיךָ, פִּיהֶם, &c.,
like אָב; *pl.* פִּיּוֹת.

רֹאשׁ 2 *head*, *pl.* רָאשִׁים, cstr. רָאשֵׁי. (§ 41. 5.)

---

[1] The numbers indicate the declensions.

שֵׁם *name, suff.* שְׁמִי, שִׁמְךָ, &c.   *Pl.* שֵׁמוֹת, *cstr.* שְׁמוֹת.
בְּהֵמָה *f. cattle*, though hardly irregular, should be carefully
    noted : *cstr.* בֶּהֱמַת ; *thy c.* בְּהֶמְתְּךָ, *his c.* בְּהֶמְתּוֹ (*pl.* בְּהֵמוֹת,
    cstr. בַּהֲמוֹת : rare and poetic).

שבה to take captive   אֲהָהּ alas !   בֶּגֶד garment
אַשְׁרֵי only used in cstr. plu. (from אֶשֶׁר or אָשָׁר ?), the happi-
    nesses of; used practically as a kind of interjection :
    happy (*is, are,* &c.) !   עכר to trouble
פצה to open (mouth)   פתח to open   תִּפְאָרָה *f.* glory
עֲטָרָה *f.* (*cstr.* (עֲטֶרֶת) crown   כלה to be complete, ended ; *Pi.*
ישע *Hiph.* to deliver   מַדּוּעַ wherefore ?   to finish
אוּרִיָּה Uriah   בזה to despise   קרע to tear, rend

EXERCISE.   TRANSLATE.

וַיָּבֹא דָוִד וַאֲנָשָׁיו אֶל־הָעִיר וְהִנֵּה שְׂרוּפָה בָּאֵשׁ וּנְשֵׁיהֶם
וּבְנֵיהֶם וּבְנֹתֵיהֶם נִשְׁבּוּ : 2 וַיְהִי כִּרְאוֹתוֹ אוֹתָהּ וַיִּקְרַע אֶת־
בְּגָדָיו וַיֹּאמֶר אֲהָהּ בִּתִּי הַכְרֵעַ הִכְרַעְתָּנִי וְאַתְּ הָיִית בְּעֹכְרָי
וְאָנֹכִי פָּצִיתִי פִי אֶל־יְהוָה וְלֹא אוּכַל לָשׁוּב : 3 עֲטֶרֶת זְקֵנִים
בְּנֵי בָנִים וְתִפְאֶרֶת בָּנִים אֲבוֹתָם : 4 אַשְׁרֵי יוֹשְׁבֵי בֵיתֶךָ :
5 וַיִּקַּח אֶת־בַּת־פַּרְעֹה וַיְבִיאֶהָ אֶל־עִיר דָּוִד עַד כַּלֹּתוֹ לִבְנוֹת
אֶת־בֵּיתוֹ : 6 וַיִּשְׁכַּב עִם־אֲבֹתָיו וַיִּקָּבֵר בְּעִיר אָבִיו : 7 וַיָּקָם
מֹשֶׁה וַיּוֹשִׁעָן[1] וַיַּשְׁקְ אֶת־צֹאנָם[2] וַתָּבֹאנָה אֶל־אֲבִיהֶן וַיֹּאמֶר
מַדּוּעַ[3] מִהַרְתֶּן בֹּא הַיּוֹם : 8 בְּתַתְּנִי וַתִּקַּח אֶת־אֵשֶׁת אוּרִיָּה
לִהְיוֹת לְךָ לְאִשָּׁה : 9 וְעַתָּה לֵךְ וְאָנֹכִי אֶהְיֶה עִם־פִּיךָ
וְהוֹרֵיתִיךָ אֲשֶׁר תְּדַבֵּר : 10 וַהֲקִימֹתִי אֶת־בְּרִיתִי אִתָּךְ וּבָאתָ
אֶל־הַתֵּבָה אַתָּה וּבָנֶיךָ וְאִשְׁתְּךָ וּנְשֵׁי־בָנֶיךָ אִתָּךְ :

Honour thy father and thy mother, as thy God commanded thee.   And his daughters spoke to one another,

---

[1] We should expect וַיֹּשַׁע, but the " connecting " vowel *a*, regular with
the pf., § 31. 2 c, is occasionally found with the impf.
[2] Masc. suffixes are occasionally used to refer to fem. nouns.
[3] Cf. § 39. 4.

saying : Let us make our father drink wine ; and he drank and was drunken.   And again his wife bore a son ; and, when he grew up, he loved his parents with all his heart, and did great good to his brothers and sisters.   They took captive their enemies' wives, and plundered their houses, and then went on their way ; but they did not slay (מוּת, *Hiph.*) any one.   His daughter abode in her father's house two years.   For two days his father did not open his mouth. My father and my mother have forsaken me.   His name shall continually be in my mouth.   I have found in thy house vessels of silver and gold.   Happy are thy men !

§ 46. PERFECT, IMPERFECT, AND PARTICIPLE.

In § 20 only so much was said regarding the Tenses of the Verb as seemed absolutely necessary for understanding the Exercises.   A full discussion of the subject belongs to the syntax ; but the sections on the Verb can hardly be closed without some additional notes on the simple verbal forms.

I. *The Perfect.*—The perfect expresses a completed action.   1. a. Now in reference to *time* such an action may be : (1) one just completed from the point of view of the present ; as, Against thee only *have I sinned* חָטָאתִי ; or (2) one completed in the indefinite past ; as, In the beginning God *created* בָּרָא ; or (3) one already completed from the point of view of another past act (pluperfect) ; as, And God saw every thing that *he had made* עָשָׂה ; or finally, on the opposite side, (4) one completed from the point of view of another action yet future (the future perfect) ; as, I will draw for thy camels also until *they have done* drinking כִּלּוּ לִשְׁתּוֹת (Pi. of כָּלָה).

b. It will make no difference in the usage of the perf. if the completed actions, instead of being expressed absolutely, as in the above sentences, should be conceived and expressed conditionally, or if they should have no existence except in conception : as, (1) O my God, *if I have done this* אִם עָשִׂיתִי זֹאת ; (3) *If ye had not ploughed* with my heifer לוּלֵא חֲרַשְׁתֶּם ("ל if not, unless); *Would that we had died* לוּ מַתְנוּ ;

(4) *If I bring him not* (i.e. *shall not have brought him*) *to thee* אִם־לֹא [1] הֲבִיאֹתִיו אֵלֶיךָ.

2. The perf. never expresses any action but one completed, or conceived as completed; but a difference in the manner of conceiving actions makes the perf. used in several cases where the present is rather employed in English: (1) In the case of general truths or actions of frequent occurrence—truths or actions which *have been* often experienced or observed (perf. of experience, the Greek *gnomic aorist*); as, The grass *withereth* יָבֵשׁ חָצִיר; the sparrow *findeth* a house מָצְאָה. This usage is particularly common when general truths are expressed *negatively*; e.g. *He does no evil to his neighbour* לֹא־עָשָׂה לְרֵעֵהוּ רָעָה (*i.e.* never did). (2) In the case of the actions or conditions expressed by *stative* verbs, § 22. What the language seizes upon in this case is not the fact that the condition expressed by the verb is one that *continues*, but rather the fact that it is a condition that has come into *complete existence* and realization, and hence the perf. is made use of to express it; but as, in point of fact, the condition continues, it is usually best rendered by the English present (§ 22. 6); as, *I know* יָדַעְתִּי that thou wilt be king; *I hate* שָׂנֵאתִי all workers of iniquity; so, *I remember*, זָכַרְתִּי; חָסִיתִי *I take refuge*, שָׂמַחְתִּי *I rejoice*, &c. To this class belongs the verb *to be* when it is, as it is not usually, expressed; *e.g.* Thy servants *are no spies* לֹא־הָיוּ מְרַגְּלִים. (3) A lively imagination is very apt to conceive things which are really future, especially if their occurrence be certain, as already done, and to describe them in the perf. This happens often in making promises or threats, and in the language of contracts; as, The field *give I* thee נָתַתִּי; And if not, I *will take it* לָקַחְתִּי. This usage is very common in the elevated language of the Prophets, whose faith and imagination so vividly project before them the event or scene which they predict that it appears already realized. It is part of the purpose of God, and therefore,

---

[1] Gen. **43.** 9. In a very similar sentence (Gen. **42.** 37) the impf. אֲבִיאֶנּוּ is used. The sense is practically the same, but the point of view is different: the *perfect* contemplates the case assumed *after* its occurrence.

to the clear eyes of the prophet, already as good as accomplished (*prophetic perfect*); *e.g.* גָּלָה עַמִּי my people *is gone into captivity* (i.e. *shall assuredly go*).

II. *The Imperfect.*—The impf. expresses an action conceived as *entering upon*, or *going on towards*, accomplishment.

1. (1) If the imperfect is used to describe a single (as opposed to a *repeated*) action in the past, it differs from the perfect in being more vivid and pictorial. The pf. expresses the *fact*, the impf. adds colour and movement by suggesting the *process* preliminary to its completion, and is thus often best rendered by our graphic historical present ; *e.g.* Jael יָדָהּ תִּשְׁלַח *puts forth her hand* to the pin—you see her in the act ; שָׁלְחָה would simply have stated the fact. (Contrast this with נָפַל שָׁכָב Sisera *fell, he lay.*) In prose this use of the impf. is only common after אָז then, טֶרֶם *not yet*, בְּטֶרֶם *before*; *e.g.* אָז יָשִׁיר *then he sang* (*i.e.* proceeded to sing). (2) A single action in the present time may similarly be expressed by the impf.; *e.g.* the man asked him, *What seekest thou ?* מַה־תְּבַקֵּשׁ.

2. The kind of progression or imperfection and unfinished condition of the action may consist in its frequent *repetition*: (1) Either in the present; as, It *is said* to this day, יֵאָמֵר (Niph.), Take of all food which *is* (regularly, customarily) *eaten*, יֵאָכֵל. This usage is very common in comparisons and in the statement of general truths founded in the nature of things; as, A wise son *maketh a glad* father יְשַׂמַּח ; As a (Heb. *the*) dog (habitually) *laps* כַּאֲשֶׁר יָלֹק הַכֶּלֶב (יָלֹק, impf. of לָקַק, § 42). Or (2) In the past; as, And so *he did* regularly, year by year וְכֵן יַעֲשֶׂה שָׁנָה בְשָׁנָה. This usage is of very frequent occurrence, A mist *used to go up* אֵד יַעֲלֶה ; We remember (note the *pf.*) the fish (collective, *fem.*) which *we used to eat* זָכַרְנוּ אֶת־הַדָּגָה אֲשֶׁר־נֹאכַל ; The manna *came down* regularly יֵרֵד הַמָּן ; *Moses spoke* repeatedly (kept speaking) *and God* repeatedly *answered* him מֹשֶׁה יְדַבֵּר וְהָאֱלֹהִים יַעֲנֶנּוּ (the tenses imply a colloquy). This is known as the frequentative imperfect.

3. The imperf. is used for the expression of the *future*— that which is conceived as entering upon accomplishment :

(1) This may be a future from the point of view of the real present; as, Now *shalt thou see what I will do* עַתָּה תִרְאֶה אֲשֶׁר אֶעֱשֶׂה; *We will burn* thy house בֵּיתְךָ נִשְׂרֹף.   Or (2) It may be a future from any other point of view assumed; as, He took his son that *was to reign* יִמְלֹךְ in his stead.

4. The usage in 3. (2) may be taken as the transition to a common use of the impf. in which it serves for the expression of that class of dependent actions and those shades of relation among acts and thoughts, for which we rather use the conditional moods (esp. the potential).   Such actions are strictly *future* in reference to the assumed point of relation, and the simple impf. sufficiently expresses them. For ex., Of every tree of the garden thou *mayest eat* תֹּאכֵל; *Could we* (were we to) *know* הֲנֵדַע, that he *would say* יֹאמַר; How *shall* (how *can*) we *sing Yahweh's* song in a foreign land? אֵיךְ נָשִׁיר.

5. (a) On the same ground the impf. follows particles expressing *transition, purpose, result*, and the like, as, לְמַעַן *in order that* פֶּן *lest*, &c.; *e.g.* Say thou art my sister, *that it may be well with me* לְמַעַן יִיטַב לִי; Let us deal wisely with the nation, *lest it multiplies* פֶּן־יִרְבֶּה.   The actions introduced by such particles are strictly consequent and future to something just stated.

(b) When, however, there is a strong feeling of *purpose*, or when it is meant to be strongly marked, then, of course, the moods are employed, § 23. 6; *e.g.* Raise me up *that I may require them* הֲקִימֵנִי וַאֲשַׁלְּמָה לָהֶם (cohort.); Who will entice Ahab *that he may go up?* מִי יְפַתֶּה אֶת־אַחְאָב וְיַעַל (juss.); What shall we do *that the sea may be calm?* מַה־נַּעֲשֶׂה וְיִשְׁתֹּק הַיָּם.   The moods are also employed to express that class of future actions which we express in the *Optative*, &c.: *May I die* אָמוּתָה (coh.); *May* Yahweh *establish* his word יָקֶם יהוה אֶת־דְּבָרוֹ (juss.); *May* the soul of this child *return* תָּשָׁב־נָא נֶפֶשׁ הַיֶּלֶד הַזֶּה (*tāshobh*, shortened before נָא, § 10. 3, from תָּשׁוּב, juss.).

(c) It must be remembered that the perf. and impf. are entirely distinct in meaning, and that the one is never used *for* the other or to express the same conception of an act with the other.   But it may readily happen that two distinct conceptions may be entertained of an action, which may thus be expressed either in the perf. or impf.   Any *general truth*, *e.g.*, may be conceived on the one side as a thing completed, having been many times realized, and this conception of it would be expressed in the *perf.* (I. 2. 1) ; or it may be conceived on the other side as a thing unfinished, ever repeating itself ; and to express this view of it, the *impf.* would be used (II. 2. 1).   *E.g.* the grass *withereth* might be either יָבֵשׁ or יִיבַשׁ, the former calling attention rather to the fact, the latter to the frequency.

III.   The *consecutive forms* have the same variety of use as the simple forms, the consec. impf. corresponding to the simple perf., and the consec. perf. to the simple impf.   *E.g.*, the perf. of general truths, like the ordinary historical pf., is followed by *waw consec. impf.*; *e.g.* כָּלָה עָנָן וַיֵּלַךְ *the cloud is consumed and departs* (pausal impf. of הלך).   Similarly the impf., in its frequentative as in its future sense, is followed by *waw consec. pf.*; *e.g.* אֵד יַעֲלֶה וְהִשְׁקָה a mist used to go up *and water* (the ground).

IV.   *The Participle.*—1.   The participle represents an action or condition in its unbroken continuity, and corresponds to the English auxiliary *to be* with the pres. ptc.—*I am, was, shall be doing*; *e.g.* הוּא יֹשֵׁב *he was sitting* (not simply *he sat*).   It may be used of present, past, or future time : (i.) *pres.*, מָה אַתֶּם עֹשִׂים *what are you doing ?* (ii.) *past*, *e.g.*, מֵת הַיֶּלֶד *the child is dead*; (iii.) *fut.*, מַשְׁחִתִים אֲנַחְנוּ אֶת־הַמָּקוֹם הַזֶּה we *are destroying*, i.e. *are about to destroy*, this place (Hiph. יֹשׁחת).   The ptc. in this (fut.) sense is frequently introduced by הִנֵּה *behold*; *e.g.*, הִנְנִי מֵקִים גּוֹי *Behold, I am about to raise up* a nation.

2.   The ptc. differs thus from the impf.: ptc. suggests continuity, impf. succession.   " The impf. multiplies an action, the participle prolongs it " (Driver).   The ptc. is a line, the impf. a succession of points.   *E.g.* הַשָּׁמַיִם מְסַפְּרִים כְּבוֹד־אֵל the heavens *are* unceasingly *declaring* the glory of God (ptc.); but יוֹם לְיוֹם יַבִּיעַ אֹמֶר (one) day *pours forth* (Hiph. נבע) speech to (another) day.

3. It must be carefully noted that the Hebrew participle cannot be used as the equivalent of the English past ptc. or the Greek aor. (or pf.) ptc.   For ἀφέντες πάντα ἠκολούθησαν αὐτῷ, *having left all they followed him*, Hebrew says, (*and*) *they left all and went after him*, וַיַּעַזְבוּ אֶת־הַכֹּל וַיֵּלְכוּ אַחֲרָיו.

רעה to pasture, shepherd		פַּת *f.* morsel (1 suff. פִּתִּי)	
שֶׂה a sheep (a goat)		רבץ to lie (stretched out)	
עֵדֶר flock, herd		מָחוּץ (מִן, חוּץ) outside (§ 14. 2 b)	
רָשׁ (*ptc.*) poor		ידע to know, regard, care for	
כִּבְשָׂה *f.* ewe-lamb		שָׁאב to draw (water)　מַחֲנֶה camp	
כּוֹם *f.* cup		דמה to destroy; *Niph.* to be undone	
יַחְדָּו together		נְאֻם utterance (always in *cstr.*)	

EXERCISE.　TRANSLATE.

יְהֹוָה רֹעִי לֹא אֶחְסָר׃ 2 יֶלֶד יֻלַּד־לָנוּ בֵּן נִתַּן־לָנוּ׃ 3 נָבִיא
אָקִים לָהֶם מִקֶּרֶב אֲחֵיהֶם כָּמוֹךָ׃ 4 אִישׁ הַיָּשָׁר בְּעֵינָיו יַעֲשֶׂה׃
5 רֹעֶה הָיָה עַבְדְּךָ לְאָבִיו בַּצֹּאן וּבָא הָאֲרִי וְנָשָׂא שֶׂה מֵהָעֵדֶר
וְיָצָאתִי אַחֲרָיו וְהִכִּתִיו וְהִצַּלְתִּי מִפִּיו׃ 6 וְלָרָשׁ אֵין־כֹּל כִּי
אִם־כִּבְשָׂה אַחַת קְטַנָּה אֲשֶׁר קָנָה וַיְחַיֶּה וַתִּגְדַּל עִמּוֹ וְעִם־
בָּנָיו יַחְדָּו מִפִּתּוֹ תֹאכַל וּמִכֹּסוֹ תִשְׁתֶּה וּבְחֵיקוֹ תִשְׁכָּב וַתְּהִי־לוֹ
כְּבַת׃ 7 יוֹדֵעַ יהוה דֶּרֶךְ צַדִּיקִים וְדֶרֶךְ רְשָׁעִים תֹּאבֵד׃ 8 וַיַּרְא
וְהִנֵּה בְאֵר בַּשָּׂדֶה וְהִנֵּה־שָׁם עֶדְרֵי־צֹאן רֹבְצִים עָלֶיהָ כִּי מִן
הַבְּאֵר הַהִיא יַשְׁקוּ הָעֲדָרִים׃ 9 זאת הברית אשר אכרת
את־בית ישראל אחרי הימים ההם נאם־יהוה נתתי את־
תורתי בקרבם ועל־לבם אכתבנה והייתי להם לאלהים
והמה יהיו־לי לעם׃

The more the enemy oppressed them, the more they increased.　He used to take the tent and pitch it outside the
camp.　It is not wont to be done so in our land.　Yahweh
shall assuredly destroy the work of thy hands.　If I perish,
I perish.　Then Moses and the children of Israel sang this
song unto their God.　Whosoever shall harden his heart
and transgress my law shall be put to death.　The earth
standeth for ever.　I counsel thee, let all thy people be
gathered together.　They found maidens coming out to
draw water.　All this I give thee, if thou wilt fall down
and prostrate thyself before me.　A righteous man careth
for the life of his beast.　Evermore Yahweh supports all
who fall.　While he was yet speaking one of his servants
came and said, We are undone—all of us.

§ 47. THE ADJECTIVE. COMPARISON.

1. *Comparative Degree.*—(a) The adjective undergoes no change of termination or vocalization in comparison. The comparative degree is expressed by the positive followed by the prep. מִן, as, *Better than wine,* טוֹב מִיַּיִן, lit. *good away from,* or in distinction from, *wine; Sweeter than honey,* מָתוֹק מִדְּבַשׁ. (Cf. the modern Greek construction of ἀπό—with the accus.—after a comparative; *e.g.* καλλίτερος ἀπὸ τοὺς ἄλλους *better than the others.*) So כָּבֵד מִמְּךָ הַדָּבָר *the matter is too hard for thee.* מִן is similarly used with verbs : אֶגְדַּל מִמְּךָ *I will be greater than thou,* קָטֹנְתִּי מִכֹּל הַחֲסָדִים *I am less than* (*i.e.* too insignificant for, unworthy of) *all the mercies,* &c.

(b) The correlative comparative (e.g. *the greater—the less*) is expressed by the simple adjective with the article ; e.g. *the greater luminary* (of two), הַמָּאוֹר הַגָּדֹל ; *her younger son,* בְּנָהּ הַקָּטֹן.

2. *Superlative Degree.*—(a) The superlative is also expressed by the positive raised into a position of isolation, as, for example, by having the *Art.* prefixed, or by being distinguished by a suffix, or by being in the Gen. relation, as *He is the greatest,* הוּא הַגָּדוֹל, lit. *the great one* (among those referred to), קְטֹן בָּנָיו *the youngest of his sons (his youngest son),* מִגְּדוֹלָם וְעַד־קְטַנָּם *from the greatest of them to the least of them.*

(b) Absolute superlativeness is expressed variously, as by the word מְאֹד *very, exceedingly* (טוֹב מְאֹד *good exceedingly*), or בִּמְאֹד or עַד־מְאֹד or מְאֹד מְאֹד ; or by the repetition of the word expressing the quality, קֹדֶשׁ קָדָשִׁים[1] *holy of holies =* most holy, עֶבֶד עֲבָדִים *the most abject slave.* שִׁיר הַשִּׁירִים *the best* or *most glorious of songs:* cf. *the Book of books.*

I am taller than he	גָּבֹהַּ אָנֹכִי מִמֶּנּוּ
he is taller than his wife	,, הוּא מֵאִשְׁתּוֹ
too little to be—	קָטֹן מִהְיוֹת
his eldest son	בְּנוֹ הַגָּדוֹל
his youngest daughter	בִּתּוֹ הַקְּטַנָּה

[1] Unlike other 3rd class nouns of the 2nd declension, § 29, קֹדֶשׁ *holiness* and שֹׁרֶשׁ *a root,* form their plural not קֳ and שֳׁ but קָדָשִׁים (*qodhāshim,* not *qā*) and שָׁרָשִׁים (*sho*)—also written ″קֳ (*q°*) and ″שֳׁ, like gutturals (חֳדָשִׁים).

II

קָשֵׁב *Hiph.* to give attention

מִשְׁכָּן dwelling-place (*pl.* וֹת)

עָרוּם cunning

מַעְלָה (מַעַל with הָ loc.) upwards

חֵלֶב fat

רְכוּשׁ gain, property

דָּנִאֵל (later דָּנִיֵּאל) Daniel

עַז strong

שְׁכֶם shoulder (*suff.* שִׁכְמוֹ)

חַיָּה *f.* beast, animal

יָפֶה (*f.* יָפָה) fair

שָׁכֹל to be bereaved: *Pi.* to make childless

קֶדֶם east

EXERCISE.

קַח נַפְשִׁי כִּי לֹא־טוֹב אָנֹכִי מֵאֲבֹתָי : 2 מַה־מָּתוֹק מִדְּבַשׁ וּמֶה
עַז מֵאֲרִי : 3 אָהֵב יהוה שַׁעֲרֵי צִיּוֹן מִכֹּל מִשְׁכְּנוֹת יַעֲקֹב : 4 טוֹב
יוֹם הַמָּוֶת מִיּוֹם הִוָּלְדוֹ : 5 וְאֵין אִישׁ מִבְּנֵי יִשְׂרָאֵל טוֹב מִמֶּנּוּ
מִשִּׁכְמוֹ וָמַעְלָה גָּבֹהַּ מִכָּל־הָעָם : 6 הַיָּפָה בַּנָּשִׁים : 7 הִנֵּה
שְׁמֹעַ מִזֶּבַח טוֹב ¹לְהַקְשִׁיב מֵחֵלֶב אֵילִים : 8 כַּאֲשֶׁר שָׁכְלָה
נָשִׁים חַרְבֶּךָ כֶּן־תִּשְׁכַּל מִנָּשִׁים אִמֶּךָ : 9 וְנִבְחַר מָוֶת מֵחַיִּים
לְכֹל־הַנִּשְׁאָרִים מִן־הַמִּשְׁפָּחָה הָרָעָה הַזֹּאת : 10 וְעַתָּה יהוה
קַח־נָא אֶת־נַפְשִׁי מִמֶּנִּי כִּי טוֹב מוֹתִי מֵחַיָּי : 11 אֶעֱשֶׂה אוֹתְךָ
לְגוֹי־עָצוּם וָרָב מִמֶּנּוּ :

And the serpent was more cunning than all the beasts
(*sing.*) of the field which God had made. He has slain men
more righteous than he. Thou art wiser than Daniel. A
living dog is better than a dead lion. And that man was
greater than all the children of (the) East. And he loved
Joseph more than all his sons, for a son of old age (was) he
to him. And he lifted up his eyes and saw his brother,
the son of his mother, and he said, Is this your youngest
brother, whom ye mentioned (said) to me? And he had
two daughters, and the younger was fairer than the elder.
The greatest (men) of the city. There was not left to him
except the youngest of his sons. And their gain was too
much for dwelling together, and the land was not able to
bear them.

¹ Inf. cstr. here practically = noun : *obedience, attention.* Usually, in
this construction, without לְ (cf. here שְׁמֹעַ), sometimes with לְ (cf. לְהַקְשִׁיב).
In the statement " it is better to dwell in the corner of the housetop," &c.,
which occurs twice, Prov. 25. 24 has טוֹב שֶׁבֶת, 21. 9 has טוֹב לְשֶׁבֶת.

§ 48. THE NUMERALS.

1. *The Cardinal Numbers.*—(1) The numeral *one*, אֶחָד *m.*, אַחַת *f.*, is an adj. agreeing in gender with its noun and standing like other adjj. *after* it; as אִישׁ אֶחָד *one man*, אִשָּׁה אַחַת *one woman*.

(2) a. The number *two*, שְׁנַיִם *m.*, שְׁתַּיִם *f.* (cstr. שְׁנֵי, שְׁתֵּי), is a noun, and agrees in gender with the word which it enumerates, as שְׁנֵי אֲנָשִׁים *two men*, שְׁתֵּי נָשִׁים *two women*.

b. The curious form שְׁתַּיִם (*sh^etáyim : t*, not *th*) has perhaps been shortened from a fuller fem. form שְׁנָתַיִם or שְׁנַתַּיִם to שְׁתַּיִם, and then conformed to שְׁתֵּים on the analogy of *m.* שְׁנַיִם. Or the pronunciation may point to some such form as אֶשְׁתַּיִם (with prosthetic א; cf. אַרְבַּע *four*, from root רבע, seen in רְבִיעִי *fourth*, § 5. 5), in which case the *daghesh* is primarily *lene*, not *forte*.

(3) a. The other numerals from 3 to 10 are nouns and *disagree* in gender with the words which they enumerate, the formal fem. going with the real mas. noun and *vice versa*, as שְׁלֹשֶׁת בָּנִים *three sons*, שָׁלֹשׁ בָּנוֹת *three daughters*.

b. This curious construction is perhaps to be explained by the fact that these units were originally abstract nouns in the fem.: *three sons = a triad* (שְׁלֹשֶׁת, cstr.) *of sons*. Then the orig. construct came to be used also appositionally in the absolute, *a triad, sons,* or *sons, a triad* (שְׁלֹשָׁה בָנִים or שְׁ בָּ), *i.e.* practically adjectivally, *sons three*; and now that it was felt necessary to differentiate the genders, the already familiar fem. would be retained for use with masc. nouns, as the more important and numerous class; and a masc. would be formed to go with fem. nouns. It is also possible that the principle of dissimilation may have played some part (cf. § 35. 1 a).

(4) The *tens* are the plurals of the units (*e.g.* שָׁלֹשׁ 3, שְׁלֹשִׁים 30) except *twenty*, עֶשְׂרִים, which is the plur. of *ten*, עֶשֶׂר, there being a distinct word for *hundred*, מֵאָה. The *tens* end in *îm* alike with masc. and fem. nouns.

(5) The numerals 2–10, which are nouns, stand most commonly in the *cstr. state* before the word which they enumerate; see above, (2), (3); they may be used *in apposition* with their word, and then they stand either before or—chiefly in later style—after it; e.g. *five sons*, חֲמֵשֶׁת בָּנִים or חֲמִשָּׁה בָנִים or בָּנִים חֲמִשָּׁה. The other numerals, viz. those from 11 to

19 and the tens, are used only in apposition with their word, and stand chiefly before, though sometimes after, it; e.g. *fifteen sons*, חֲמִשָּׁה עָשָׂר בָּנִים.

(6) The units require the noun enumerated in the plural; *e.g.* תֵּשַׁע שָׁנִים *nine years*; the tens usually take the noun in the singular when they stand before it, always in the plur. when after it (Gen. **32.** 15 f.). The numbers 11 to 19 usually take the plur. except with a few common nouns like יוֹם *day*, שָׁנָה *year*, אִישׁ *man*, נֶפֶשׁ (*soul*) *person*, &c., and collectives, *e.g.* 19 *cities* (עִיר *f.*), עָרִים תְּשַׁע־עֶשְׂרֵה; but 19 *men*, תִּשְׁעָה־עָשָׂר אִישׁ.

(7) In numbers composed of tens and units such as 23, the order may be *three and twenty*, שְׁתַּיִם וְשִׁשִּׁים שָׁנָה *sixty-two years*, but also *twenty and three*, עֶשְׂרִים וְשָׁלֹשׁ שָׁנָה, and sometimes the noun is repeated with both, as *three years and twenty year* (by 6); as חָמֵשׁ שָׁנִים וְשִׁבְעִים שָׁנָה *seventy-five years*; or again, עֶשְׂרִים שָׁנָה וְשֶׁבַע שָׁנִים *twenty-seven years*.

	With the Masculine.		With the Feminine.	
	Absol.	Cstr.	Absol.	Cstr.
1	אֶחָד	אַחַד	אַחַת	אַחַת
2	שְׁנַיִם	שְׁנֵי	שְׁתַּיִם	שְׁתֵּי
3	שְׁלֹשָׁה	שְׁלֹשֶׁת	שָׁלֹשׁ	שְׁלֹשׁ
4	אַרְבָּעָה	אַרְבַּעַת	אַרְבַּע	אַרְבַּע
5	חֲמִשָּׁה	חֲמֵשֶׁת	חָמֵשׁ	חֲמֵשׁ
6	שִׁשָּׁה	שֵׁשֶׁת	שֵׁשׁ	שֵׁשׁ
7	שִׁבְעָה	שִׁבְעַת	שֶׁבַע	שְׁבַע
8	שְׁמֹנָה	שְׁמֹנַת	שְׁמֹנֶה	שְׁמֹנֶה
9	תִּשְׁעָה	תִּשְׁעַת	תֵּשַׁע	תְּשַׁע
10	עֲשָׂרָה	עֲשֶׂרֶת	עֶשֶׂר	עֶשֶׂר
11	אַחַד עָשָׂר / עַשְׁתֵּי עָשָׂר		אַחַת עֶשְׂרֵה / עַשְׁתֵּי עֶשְׂרֵה	
12	שְׁנַיִם עָשָׂר / שְׁנֵי עָשָׂר		שְׁתֵּים עֶשְׂרֵה / שְׁתֵּי עֶשְׂרֵה	
13	שְׁלֹשָׁה עָשָׂר		שְׁלֹשׁ עֶשְׂרֵה	
14	אַרְבָּעָה עָשָׂר		אַרְבַּע עֶשְׂרֵה	
	&c.		&c.	

20	עֶשְׂרִים	60	שִׁשִּׁים
30	שְׁלֹשִׁים	70	שִׁבְעִים
40	אַרְבָּעִים	80	שְׁמֹנִים
50	חֲמִשִּׁים	90	תִּשְׁעִים

100	מֵאָה *fem.*, *cstr.* מְאַת, *plur.* מֵאוֹת *hundreds.*
200	מָאתַיִם *dual* (for מִאְתַיִם).
300	שְׁלֹשׁ מֵאוֹת, 400 אַרְבַּע מֵאוֹת, &c.
1,000	אֶלֶף *masc.*
2,000	אַלְפַּיִם *dual.*
3,000	שְׁלֹשֶׁת אֲלָפִים, 4,000 אַרְבַּעַת אֲלָפִים, &c.
10,000	רְבָבָה *pl.* regular, רְבָבוֹת.
	רִבּוֹא, רִבּוֹ *pl.* רְבָאוֹת and רִבּוֹת (later forms).
20,000	רִבּוֹתַיִם *dual.*

(8) The word מֵאָה *hundred* may be used either in the *cstr.* or *abs.* in the *sing.*—most often in *abs.*: *e.g.* בֶּן־מֵאָה שָׁנָה (*son of*, i.e.) *a hundred years old* (also מְאַת); in *du.* and *plur.* only in *absol.* The word אֶלֶף *thousand* is used in the *cstr.* also, though rarely, even in the *plur.* (אַלְפֵי).

(9) The *du. fem.* of the num. is used to express repetition, שִׁבְעָתַיִם *seven times, sevenfold.* A few take suffixes שְׁנֵינוּ *we two,* שְׁלָשְׁתָּם *they three,* &c. (sh'loshtām).

2. *The Ordinal Numbers.*—The Ordinal numbers from 1 to 10 are adjectives, and construed in the ordinary way. Beyond 10 the Cardinal numbers are used also as Ordinals. The Ordinals are these:

First	רִאשׁוֹן	*fem.*	רִאשׁוֹנָה	sixth	שִׁשִּׁי
second	שֵׁנִי	„	שֵׁנִית	seventh	שְׁבִיעִי
third	שְׁלִישִׁי	„	שְׁלִישִׁית, ־יָה	eighth	שְׁמִינִי
fourth	רְבִיעִי	„	&c.	ninth	תְּשִׁיעִי
fifth	חֲמִישִׁי or חֲמִשִּׁי		„	tenth	עֲשִׂירִי

E.g. *on the seventh day,* בַּיּוֹם הַשְּׁבִיעִי; *in the eighteenth year of the king,* בִּשְׁמֹנֶה עֶשְׂרֵה שָׁנָה לַמֶּלֶךְ; or בִּשְׁנַת שְׁמֹנֶה עֶשְׂרֵה לַמֶּלֶךְ.

3. Fractions may be expressed by feminine forms of the ordinals; *e.g.* שְׁלִישִׁית *a third*; in a few cases also by segholate forms; *e.g.* רֶבַע and רֹבַע *a fourth,* חֹמֶשׁ *a fifth*; *a half* is חֲצִי. § 45. 3 b. 1 a.

עֵז *f.* she-goat ; *pl.* עִזִּים   גָּמָל camel ; *pl.* גְּמַלִּים (§ 43. 4)
כֶּלֶא imprisonment   בקע to break through
שׁאב to draw (water)   חָצֵר court (*noun*)
דּוֹר generation (*pl.* ים and oftener וֹת)

EXERCISE.   TRANSLATE.

וַיֹּאמֶר אֶל־אָבִיו אֶת־שְׁנֵי בָנַי תָּמִית אִם־לֹא אֲבִיאֶנּוּ אֵלֶיךָ׃
2 וַיִּקַּח מִנְחָה לְאָחִיו עִזִּים מָאתַיִם וְאֵילִים עֶשְׂרִים וּגְמַלִּים
מֵנִיקוֹת וּבְנֵיהֶם שְׁלֹשִׁים׃ 3 וַיְהִי בְּאַחַת וְשֵׁשׁ־מֵאוֹת שָׁנָה
לִהְיוֹת בַּחֹדֶשׁ הַשֵּׁנִי בְּשִׁבְעָה וְעֶשְׂרִים יוֹם לַחֹדֶשׁ יָבְשָׁה הָאָרֶץ׃
4 בִּשְׁלֹשִׁים וָשֶׁבַע שָׁנָה בִּשְׁנֵים עָשָׂר חֹדֶשׁ בְּעֶשְׂרִים וְשִׁבְעָה
לַחֹדֶשׁ נָשָׂא מֶלֶךְ בָּבֶל אֶת־רֹאשׁ מֶלֶךְ יְהוּדָה מִבֵּית כֶּלֶא׃[1]
5 וַיִּבְקְעוּ שְׁלֹשֶׁת הַגִּבֹּרִים בְּמַחֲנֵה הָאֹיֵב וַיִּשְׁאֲבוּ־מַיִם וַיָּבִאוּ
אֵלָיו וְלֹא אָבָה לִשְׁתּוֹתָם׃ 6 טוֹב יוֹם בַּחֲצֵרֶיךָ מֵאָלֶף׃
7 וְרָדְפוּ מִכֶּם חֲמִשָּׁה מֵאָה וּמֵאָה מִכֶּם רְבָבָה יִרְדֹּפוּ׃ 8 וַיֹּאמֶר
אֲלֵיהֶם צְאוּ שְׁלָשְׁתְּכֶם וַיֵּצְאוּ שְׁלָשְׁתָּם׃ 9 ויחי אחרי־זאת
מאה וארבעים שנה וירא את־בניו ואת־בני בניו ארבעה
דרות׃ 10 וימלך־שׁם שׁבע שׁנים וששׁה חדשׁים ושׁלשׁים
ושׁלושׁ שׁנה מלך בירושׁלם׃

His five brothers and three sisters went with him to the
house of their father.   The queen reigned sixty-four years
and died aged eighty-two : she had four sons and five
daughters ; her husband died in the forty-second year of
her life and the twenty-fourth of her reign.   And there
were born unto him three sons and seven daughters, and
his substance was six thousand sheep, and four thousand
camels, and seven hundred asses.   The days of the years
of my life have been four and seventy years.   There were
a hundred and twenty-seven cities in his land, and in one
of those cities there were a hundred and twenty thousand
people.   The half is better than the whole.   And one said
to the other, Let the two of us swear in the name of our
God ; so they sware, the two of them.

[1] יוֹם unexpressed.

§ 49. PARTICLES.

1. The particles are mostly nouns, either entire or oftener disintegrated, though some are proper interjectional or demonstrative expressions.

Being nouns they must be considered, when in relation, to be in the *construct* state, and the word following them, (or as we say, governed by them) in the Genitive. The *case* in which, being nouns, they must also stand, will vary according to many circumstances; but as the language does not mark the case endings, this is of less consequence at first.

2. 1) Some particles are so much worn down and feeble that they cannot stand in the sentence alone, but require the support of a noun or pronoun, to which they prefix themselves; while again others as the precative particle נָא are inseparable affixes. The punctuation of the important prepositional fragments בְּ, כְּ, לְ, מִן, and of the conjunction וְ, has already been given, §§ 14—15.

2) Another important inseparable prefix is the interrogative particle הֲ, the pointing of which varies:—

a) Its usual pointing is הֲ, as הֲזֶה *is this?*

b) Before simple shᵉwa it is הַ, as הַמְעַט *is it little?* occasionally followed by *Dag. forte*; otherwise it is not infrequently marked by *Methegh*.

c) Before Gutturals (except when they have ָ or ָֽ) it is also pointed הֲ, often marked by Methegh, as הַאֵלֵךְ *shall I go?*

d) Before Gutt. with ָ or ָֽ it is הֶ, as הֶחָזָק *whether it be strong?*

3. *Suffixes to Particles.* The pronominal suffixes to the particles will be found on the following pages: לְ and בְּ (p. 51) מִן (p. 53) אֶל־, עַל, עַד (p. 70) כְּ (p. 87) אֵת art. (p. 75) אֵת prep., עִם and הִנֵּה (p. 142) יֵשׁ (p. 130) אַיִן (p. 136).

Notice the fondness of particles for *ā* in suffixes, where nouns have *ē*, e. g. 2. *f. s.* and 1. *pl.,* לָךְ, לָנוּ.

4. *Adverbs.* a) In addition to the adverbs already met with in the course of the book may be mentioned the following:

אֵי, אַיֵּה, אֵי־זֶה *where?* (with suff. אַיֶּכָּה *where art thou?* אַיּוֹ *where is he?* אַיָּם). אֵיכָה, אֵיךְ, אֵי־מִזֶּה, מֵאַיִן *whence?* אָנָה *whither?* *how? how!*

b) Some advbs. directly connected with nouns, end in ם ָ, which may have been an old accus. ending: e. g. יוֹמָם *by day,* רֵיקָם *in vain* or *(with) empty (hands),* חִנָּם *for nothing* or *in vain* (from חֵן *grace*). In some words this *â* has passed into *ô* (§ 2. 2. 1): e. g. פִּתְאֹם *suddenly,* שִׁלְשֹׁם *the day before yesterday* (*three days ago,* from שָׁלֹשׁ *three*).

c) The noun סָבִיב *circuit* is mostly used as advb. and preposition *round about* (e. g. יהוה סָבִיב לְעַמּוֹ *Yahweh is round about His people*). As a preposition it always takes the plur. form, sometimes masc., e. g. סְבִיבֶיךָ *round about thee,* more often fem. סְבִיבוֹתֶיךָ.

5. a) *Conjunctions.* אִם *if;* אוֹ *or;* אוֹ ... אוֹ or אִם ... אִם *whether ... or;* גַּם *also;* גַּם ... גַּם *both ... and;* גַּם לֹא ... גַּם לֹא *neither ... nor.*

b) *But* is frequently expressed by *waw:* e. g. *But of the tree thou mayst not eat* וּמִן־הָעֵץ לֹא תֹאכַל. A stronger *but* is אוּלָם. *But* after a negative is כִּי אִם; e. g. He walks *not* in the counsel of the wicked, *but in the law of Jahweh is his delight* כִּי אִם בְּתוֹרַת יהוה חֶפְצוֹ.

c) Questions, direct and indirect, are usually introduced by the particle הֲ; disjunctive questions — (*whether*) ... *or* — by הֲ ... אִם; e. g. הֲלָנוּ אַתָּה אִם לְצָרֵינוּ (*whether*) *art thou for us or for our enemies?*

For *final* clauses, see § 23. 6 (cf. § 46. II. 5 a). לְמַעַן may also be used with *inf. cstr.:* e. g. לְמַעַן דַּעַת כָּל־עַמֵּי הָאָרֶץ *that all the peoples of the earth may know.*

d) In oaths, אִם = *certainly not,* and אִם לֹא = *certainly:* e. g. אִם־אֶעֱשֶׂה אֶת־הַדָּבָר הַזֶּה *I shall assuredly not do this thing.* (The idiom is readily explained on the assumption of an ellipse: e. g. "*cursed be I, if I do this thing*".) אִם יִהְיֶה טַל *certainly there shall not be dew.* אִם־לֹא הָאָרֶץ לְךָ תִהְיֶה לְנַחֲלָה *surely the land shall be to thee for an inheritance.* We may trace the origin of this usage in the fuller form of sentence which occasionally occurs: e. g. כֹּה יַעֲשֶׂה־לִּי אֱלֹהִים וְכֹה יוֹסִיף אִם־לֹא שַׂר־צָבָא תִהְיֶה *so shall God do to me and more also*

and so shall he add) *if thou do not become captain of the host*
(*i.e.* I swear that thou shalt become).

(e) Some prepositions become conjunctions by the addition of אֲשֶׁר; *e.g.* אַחֲרֵי אֲשֶׁר (cf. *après que*).

6. *Interjections* אָח, אֲהָהּ *ah!* אוֹי *woe!* הוֹי *ah, alas, ha!* הַס (even pl. הַסּוּ as if הַס were imper.) *hush!* מִי יִתֵּן (who will give? =) *O that! would that! e.g.* מִי יִתֵּן מוּתִי *would that I had died*, חָלִילָה *far be it!*—lit. *ad profanum!* ה loc. (as an exclamation; but also in construction, thus חָלִילָה לָּנוּ מֵעֲזֹב אֶת־יהוה *far be it from us that we should forsake Yahweh*).

עתר (*Qal*) *Hiph.* to entreat ברח to flee

שָׁאוּל Saul הגה to moan, muse, meditate

עָוֹן guilt, punishment יָעֵף to be weary, faint (§ 39. 2. 2 *a*)

יָעֵף weary, faint יָנַע, יָגַע to toil, grow weary (§ 39. 2. 2 *a*)

EXERCISE. TRANSLATE.

אָנָה אֵלֵךְ מֵרוּחֶךָ׃ 2 מֵאַיִן יָבֹא עֶזְרִי׃ 3 וַיֵּבְךְּ וְכֹה אָמַר בְּלֶכְתּוֹ מִי יִתֵּן מוּתִי אֲנִי תַחְתֶּיךָ בְּנִי׃ 4 חָלִילָה לִי יהוה מֵעֲשֹׂתִי זֹאת [1] הֲדַם הָאֲנָשִׁים הַהֹלְכִים [2] בְּנַפְשֹׁתָם׃ 5 הַעְתִּירוּ לַיהוה אֱלֹהֵיכֶם וְיָסֵר מֵעָלַי אֶת־הַמָּוֶת הַזֶּה׃ 6 אִם־לֹא אֶל־בֵּית־אָבִי תֵּלֵךְ וְלָקַחְתָּ אִשָּׁה לִבְנִי׃ 7 אִם־אֶקַּח מִכָּל־אֲשֶׁר־לָךְ׃ 8 מַה־טּוֹב לָכֶם הֲמְשֹׁל בָּכֶם שִׁבְעִים אִישׁ אִם־מְשֹׁל בָּכֶם אִישׁ אֶחָד׃ 9 וַיִּשָּׁבַע לָהּ שָׁאוּל בַּיהוה לֵאמֹר חַי־יהוה אִם־יִקְרֵךְ [3] עָוֹן בַּדָּבָר הַזֶּה וַתֹּאמֶר הָאִשָּׁה אֶת־מִי אַעֲלֶה־לָּךְ וַיֹּאמֶר אֶת־שְׁמוּאֵל הַעֲלִי־לִי וַתֵּרֶא הָאִשָּׁה אֶת־שְׁמוּאֵל וַתִּזְעַק בְּקוֹל גָּדוֹל וַיֹּאמֶר לָהּ הַמֶּלֶךְ אַל־תִּירְאִי כִּי מָה רָאִית וַתֹּאמֶר הָאִשָּׁה אֱלֹהִים רָאִיתִי עֹלִים מִן־הָאָרֶץ׃

And he said to her, My daughter, wilt thou go with this man, or wilt thou stay with me? and she said, Alas, my father, I cannot stay with thee. Whither shall I flee from

---

[1] We may assume an ellipse of *shall I drink?*

[2] Beth pretii, *at the cost* (here *risk*) *of.*

[3] קרה with suff.

thy presence?   Art thou my son or not?   O that we had died by the hand of our God in the land of Babylon, when we sat and wept by the waters thereof.   I have sworn in mine anger——ye shall not enter into my rest.   This book of the law shall not depart out of thy mouth, but thou shalt meditate therein day and night, in order that thou thyself mayst observe to do according to all that is written therein, and that thou mayst speak of it to thy children after thee, when thou sittest in thine house and when thou walkest by the way.   God never grows faint or weary: if ye believe in him, how can ye say, My way is hidden from my God? for he remembereth that we are dust, and evermore he giveth strength to the weary who put their trust in him.

VOCABULARY.

ENGLISH AND HEBREW.

A.

Abigail, אֲבִיגַיִל.

Abimelech, אֲבִימֶלֶךְ.

able, be, יָכֹל; *impf.* יוּכַל, § 39.

Abraham, אַבְרָהָם.

Abram, אַבְרָם.

abundance, הָמוֹן 1.[1]

according to, בְּ, prep.

acquire, to, קָנָה.

add, to, יָסַף, *perf.* and *ptc.* in
  Qal; other parts in *Hiph.* See
  § 39.

adversary, צַר 2. § 43.

advise. *See* counsel.

afflict, to, עָנָה, *Pi.*; affliction, עֳנִי 2.
  § 45.

after, behind, אַחֲרֵי, אַחַר; אַחֲרֵי
  after me, &c. See p. 70.

afterwards, אַחֲרֵי־כֵן אַחַר.

again, עוֹד; and she *again* bore
  וַתֹּסֶף וַתֵּלֶד, &c. See p.129 (still).

aged, vb. and adj. זָקֵן; old age,
  זְקֻנִים זִקְנָה.

alas ! אֲהָהּ אָח.

all, כֹּל 2. § 43.

allow, to, נָתַן, *acc.* and *inf.*

alone, לְבַד 2. § 43. See בד in
  Lex. *I alone,* אֲנִי לְבַדִּי, &c.

also, גַּם; both... and also, גַּם...וְגַם.

altar, מִזְבֵּחַ. *See* sacrifice.

among, amongst (midst).

and, וְ, § 15; both . . . and, וְ . . . וְ
  (also).

angel, messenger, מַלְאָךְ 1.

anger, אַף (אנף); suff. אַפִּי. § 43. 4.

angry, be, קָצַף; חרה, used im-
  pers. : he was angry, חָרָה לֹו.

anoint, to, מָשַׁח; Messiah, מָשִׁיחַ 1.

another, אַחֵר; one another . . . אִישׁ
  אָחִיו. See p. 150.

any (all); not any, none, כֹּל . . . לֹא.
  § 13. 4.

appear, to, *Niph.* of *see.*

appearance, מַרְאֶה. § 45.

approach, to (draw near).

arise, to, קוּם. § 40.

ark, תֵּבָה (*e* firm).

ark (of covenant), אֲרוֹן, with art.
  הָאָרוֹן.

arm, זְרוֹעַ, *f.* (generally); pl. *îm, ôth.*

army, חַיִל, § 41 (force).

arrow, חֵץ 2. § 43.

as, like כְּ (see p. 87); as, when כַּאֲשֶׁר.

---

[1] The figures 1, 2, 3 after nouns indicate the Declensions.

171

ascend, to (go up).

ashamed, be, בּוֹשׁ. § 40.

ashes, דֶּשֶׁן 2. *i.*

aside, turn, to, סוּר. § 40.

ask, to, יָשְׁאַל. § 36.

ass, he-ass, הֲמוֹר; she-ass, אָתוֹן 1.

assemble, קהל, *Hiph.* (gather).

assembly, עֵדָה 1, מִקְרָא, קָהָל.

atone, to, כִּפֶּר, *Pi.* § 26. 1 *a*;
pass. *Pu. ; for* עַל.

avenge, to, נָקַם; *Niph.* be avenged,
avenge oneself.

awake, to, יקין, *perf.* not in use;
impf. יָיקִין; *perf.* הֵקִין, *Hiph.*
of קוּץ.

B.

Baal, בַּעַל 2.

bad, רַע 1. § 43.

bank, שָׂפָה 1 (lip).

bark, to, נָבַח.

be, to, הָיָה. § 45.

bear a, דֹּב 2. § 43.

bear, to, carry, נָשָׂא (lift up).

bear, to, bring forth, יָלַד, § 39;
be born, *Niph.*; beget, *Hiph.*;
a boy, יֶלֶד 2; girl, יַלְדָּה 2;
kindred, מוֹלֶדֶת, § 29. 3.

beast, חַיָּה (cattle).

beauty, יְפִי 2, § 45 (fair).

bed, מִטָּה (stretch); מִשְׁכָּב 1 (lie).

befall, to, קָרָה; קָרָא, § 38. 1. 5.

before (face).

beget, to (bear).

begin, to, חלל, *Hiph.* (הֵחֵל); pass.
Hoph.; beginning תְּחִלָּה.

beguile, to, נשׁא, *Hiph.*

behind (after).

behold, הִנֵּה, הֵן 2, § 43; *behold*

I (*me*), הִנְנִי; *behold we* (*us*), הִנְנוּ.
See p. 142, note 1. Very often
followed by the *participle.*

believe, to, אמן, *Hiph.*; לְ of pers.

belly, נָחוֹן 1; בֶּטֶן 2. *i.* (womb).

beneath, instead of, תַּחַת 2; plur.
suff. תַּחְתַּי, &c., rarely sing. except תַּחְתָּם, § 36. 2.

bereaved, be, יָשְׁכֹּל, *st.*

beside, אֵצֶל, —*me*, אֶצְלִי, § 34. 4 b.

Bethel, בֵּיתְאֵל.

between, בֵּין 2, § 41; *between me
and thee,* בֵּינִי וּבֵינֶךָ; *between me
and you* וּבֵינֵיכֶם —.

beware, to, *Niph.* of *keep.*

beyond (region b.), other side,
עֵבֶר.

bind, to, saddle, חָבַשׁ; אָסַר.

bird, fowl, צִפּוֹר, עוֹף 2; pl. צִפֳּרִים.

bitter, to be, מַר, *st., impf.* יָמַר, § 42;
bitter, כִּיר 1, § 43.

bless, to, ברך, *Pi.* ; pass. *Pu.* § 36;
blessed, בָּרוּךְ; blessing, בְּרָכָה 1.

blind, עִוֵּר 3.

blood, דָּם 1; *pl.* blood shed;
with heavy suff. דְּמֵכֶם.

blot out, to, destroy, מָחָה; pass.
Niph.

boil, to, cook, בִּשֵׁל, *Pi.*

bone, עֶצֶם 2. *f.*; *pl. îm* and *ôth.*

book, סֵפֶר 2.

bosom, חֵיק 2. § 41.

both, שְׁנַיִם (two); with suff. *both of
us, we both,* שְׁנֵינוּ, &c. § 48. 1. 9.

bottle, חֵמֶת 2.

bow, a, קֶשֶׁת 2. *f.*

bow down, to, כָּרַע; trans. *Hiph.*

boy (bear).

bread, לֶחֶם 2.

broad, be, רָחַב, *st.*; broad, רָחָב 1 ; breadth, רֹחַב 2. See p. 120.

break, to, יִשְׁבֹּר; pass. *Niph.*; broken, נִשְׁבַּר; b. in pieces, *Pi.*

break down, to, פָּרַץ.

break, to (of day), עָלָה; daybreak, שַׁחַר 2.

breath, נְשָׁמָה 1.

brightness, נֹגַהּ 2.

bring, to, *Hiph.* of *come.*

bring down, to, *Hiph.* of *go down,* &c.

bring out, to, *Hiph.* of *go out.*

bring up, to, *Hiph.* of *go up.*

bring up, to = to rear, גָּדַל, *Pi.*

brook, נַחַל 2.

brother, אָח. See p. 153.

buck, he-goat, תַּיִשׁ 2. § 41.

build, to, בָּנָה. § 44.

burn, to, יִשְׂרֹף; pass. *Niph.*; with fire, בָּאֵשׁ.

burnt-offering, עֹלָה.

bury, to, קָבַר; pass. *Niph.*; grave, קֶבֶר 2. *i.*; קְבוּרָה grave, burial.

but, כִּי ; כִּי אִם, אוּלָם. § 49. 5 b.

butler, butlership, מַשְׁקֶה. § 45.

buy, to, acquire, קָנָה (possess).

buy corn, to, יִשְׁבֹּר.

by (of cause), מִן. §§ 14, 15.

by (beside), עַל, p. 70.

C.

calamity, אֵיד 2. § 41.

calf, עֵגֶל 2 ; *f.* עֶגְלָה. § 35.

call, to, cry, קָרָא, *dat.*; he called him Adam, קְרָא לוֹ אָדָם ; he called his name Adam, קְרָא אֶת־שְׁמוֹ אדם ; *he was called Adam,* נִקְרָא לוֹ אדם. § 43. 5.

captain, שַׂר (prince).

capture, to (a city), לָכַד.

carcase (corpse).

care, take, to, *Niph.* of *keep.*

cast, to, throw, יַשְׁלִךְ, *Hiph.*; pass. *Hoph.* § 27. 2.

cast lots, to. *See* fall.

cattle, בְּהֵמָה 1 ; cstr. s. 'בֶּהֱ ; cstr. pl. 'בֶּהֱ. See p. 154.

cave, מְעָרָה, 1, *â* firm.

cease, to, חָדַל, *st.*; he ceased speaking, חדל לְדַבֵּר.

cedar, אֶרֶז 2.

Chaldees, כַּשְׂדִּים.

chamber, חֶדֶר 2. *m.*

change, to, חָלַף, *Pi.*

cheek, לְחִי 2. § 45.

cherub, כְּרוּב.

child, יֶלֶד 2 ; עוֹלֵל 1 ; עוֹלָל 3 ; *children* of Israel, בְּנֵי יִשְׂרָאֵל (son).

choose, to, בָּחַר ; *acc.,* בְּ.

city, עִיר 2. *f.*; *pl.* עָרִים, p. 153.

clean, be, to, טָהֵר, *st.*; clean, טָהוֹר 1.

cleave, to, דָּבַק, *st.*; *to,* בְּ.

clothe oneself, to, put on, wear, לָבֵשׁ, *st., acc.*; *clothe* (another) *with—,* *Hiph.,* two accus. § 27. 1 d.

cloud, עָנָן 1.

cold, adj., קַר 1, § 43 ; noun, קֹר 2.

colt, עַיִר 2. § 41.

come to, come in, enter, go in, בּוֹא ; bring, *Hiph.*; pass. *Hoph.*; entrance, מָבוֹא 1.

comfort, to, נחם, *Pi.*; pass. *Pu.*

command, to, צוה *Pi.*; pass. *Pu.*;
a command, מִצְוָה 1.
commit, to, entrust (oversee).
compassion, to have, רחם *Pi.*
(pity). § 36.
conceal, to (hide).
conceive, הָרָה ; *impf.* 3 *s.f.* with
waw cons. וַתַּהַר. § 45. 1. 3.
confide, to, trust, בָּטַח ; in, בְּ.
contend, to, רִיב. § 40.
continually, תָּמִיד.
corn, דָּגָן 1, שֶׁבֶר 2.
corpse, carcase, נְבֵלָה 1.
corrupt, to, שחת, *Hiph.* (*Pi.*); pass.
Niph.
counsel, to, advise, יָעַץ, *impf.*
יִיעַץ ; deliberate, *Niph.*, *Hithp.*;
counsel, עֵצָה 1. § 39.
count, to, number, סָפַר ; מָנָה.
§ 44.
count, to, impute, reckon, חָשַׁב.
country, the (field).
court, a, חָצֵר 1. *c.*, pl. *îm* and *ôth.*
covenant, a, בְּרִית, *f.; to make a
covenant*—כָּרַת (cut); *establish,
fulfil a* —, — הֵקִים (arise).
cover, to, כסה, *Pi.*; pass. *Pu.*; a
covering, מִכְסֶה. § 45.
cow, פָּרָה (ox).
create, to, בָּרָא ; pass. *Niph.*
creep, to, רָמַשׂ, *impf.* in *o*; creeping things, רֶמֶשׂ 2, *coll.*
cross, to, pass over, by, עָבַר ;
Hiph., bring over, make go
through, &c.; a crossing, ford,
מַעֲבָר 1.
cry, to (call).
cry out, to, זָעַק, צָעַק ; a cry, צְעָקָה 1.

cultivate, to (serve).
cunning, עָרוּם 1.
curse, a, ban, חֵרֶם 2.
curse, to, אָרַר ; קלל, *Pi.*
cut down, to, cut off, cut, כָּרַת ;
pass. *Niph.*

D.

Daniel, דְּנִיֵּאל ; later דָּנִיֵּאל.
darknesss, חֹשֶׁךְ 2.
dash in pieces, רטשׁ, *Pi.*; pass. *Pu.*
daughter, בַּת 2. *i.; my d.*, בִּתִּי, &c.;
plur. בָּנוֹת 1. See p. 153.
David, דָּוִד, דָּוִיד.
dawn, daybreak, שַׁחַר 2.
day, יוֹם 2, § 41. 5; pl. יָמִים, יְמֵי.
See p. 153.
death, מָוֶת, § 41 (die).
Deborah, דְּבוֹרָה (= bee).
deceive, to (beguile).
declare, to (tell), (hear), (count).
deep, be, עָמֹק, *st.*; deep, adj. עָמֹק 1.
See § 43. 4.
deliberate, to (counsel).
delight in, to, חָפֵץ, *st.*; impf.
יַחְפֹּץ, in pause, יֶחְפָּץ.
delight, pleasure, חֵפֶץ 2. § 35;
delighting in, adj. חָפֵץ 1.
deliver, to, נצל *Hiph.*; pass. *Niph.*
depart, to, סוּר. § 40.
descend, to, יָרַד. § 39.
desert, wilderness, pasture, מִדְבָּר 1.
desire, to, חָמַד ; *impf.* יַחְמֹד, pass.
Niph.; חָפֵץ, *st.*
desolation, חָרְבָּה 2.
despise, to, קָלַל ; to be despised,
קַל (*Qal*).
destroy, to, שחת, *Hiph.* (*Pi.*);

pass. *Niph.* ; שׁמד, *Hiph.* pass. *Hoph.* (blot out).

dew, טל.

die, to, מוּת ; to kill, *Hiph.*, *Pô'l.* (מוֹתת) ; pass. *Hoph.* ; dead, מֵת *ptc.* ; death, מָוֶת 2. § 41.

disease, sickness, חֳלִי 2. § 45.

displeased, זָעֵף 1.

divide, to, בדל, *Hiph.* ; pass. *Niph.*

do, to (make).

dog, כֶּלֶב 2.

door, דֶּלֶת 2. *f.*

dove, יוֹנָה, *f.*, pl. *îm.*

draw near, to, approach, קָרַב, *st.* ; *Hiph.* bring near, offer, present ; נגשׁ, *perf.* used in *Niph.*, *impf.* in *Qal.* See § 33. *Hiph.* bring near ; near, קָרוֹב 1.

dream, to, חָלַם ; *impf.* יַחֲלֹם ; a dream, חֲלוֹם, plur. *ôth.*

drink, to, שָׁתָה ; to give to drink, water, שׁקה, *Hiph.* ; feast, מִשְׁתֶּה, § 45 ; a butler, cupbearer, מַשְׁקֶה, § 45 ; cupbearer's office, *same.*

drive out, to, גרשׁ, *Pi.*, pass. *Niph.*

drunk, be, שָׁכַר, *st.* ; strong drink, שֵׁכָר 1.

dry, be, יָבֵשׁ, *st.*, § 39 ; חָרֵב ; dry land, יַבָּשָׁה 1.

dumb, אִלֵּם 3.

dust, עָפָר 1.

dwell, to, יָשַׁב, § 39 ; שָׁכֵן, *impf.* in o (p. 80) ; *Hiph.*, to place ; tabernacle מִשְׁכָּן, pl. *ôth* (*îm*).

E.

eagle, נֶשֶׁר 2. *i.*

ear, אֹזֶן, 2. *f.*, du. ; give ear, hear-ken, הֶאֱזִין, *Hiph.*, denom. (hear).

earth, land, אֶרֶץ 2. *f.*

earthquake, רַעַשׁ (shake).

east, קֶדֶם ; *on the east of —* מִקֶּדֶם ל.

eat, to, אָכַל, § 35 ; give to eat, *Hiph.* ; meat, food (אֹכֶל 2), מַאֲכָל 2, אָכְלָה 1.

Eden, עֵדֶן.

edge, פֶּה, *with the edge of the sword* לְפִי חֶרֶב. See p. 153.

eggs, בֵּיצִים 2, pl. *f.* § 41. 4.

Egypt, מִצְרַיִם, *f.* ; Egyptian, מִצְרִי, fem. ית—. § 16. 4. 1.

Ehud, אֵהוּד.

elder, זָקֵן 1 (aged) ; elder, comp. = greater (great). § 47. 1 b.

Elijah, אֵלִיָּה (אֵלִיָּהוּ).

Elisha, אֱלִישָׁע.

embrace, to, חבק, *Pi.*

empty, רֵק (רִיק).

end, קֵץ 2, § 43 ; latter end, אַחֲרִית, *f.*

end, be ended, תַּם, *st.*, § 42 ; כָּלָה, § 44 ; to finish, complete, *Hiph.* תֵּם, *Pi.* כלה ; perfect, תָּמִים 1, תָּם 1.

enemy, אֹיֵב 3 ; enmity אֵיבָה 2.

enter, to, בּוֹא. אֶל, בְּ.

entice, *Pi.* of פָּתָה (to be simple).

entrance, מָבוֹא 1.

escape, to, מלט, *Niph.* ; rescue, *Pi.*

establish, to, *Hiph.* of קוּם *arise.*

eternity (ever).

evening, עֶרֶב 2. *c.*

ever, eternity, עוֹלָם 1, עַד ; *for ever,*

לְעוֹלָם; *eternal hills,* הֲרֵי 'עַ; never, 'לְעַ . . . לֹא.

every, כֹּל; every day, כָּל־יוֹם (all); they went *every* man to his house, הָלְכוּ אִישׁ לְבֵיתוֹ (§ 13. 4).

evil, adj. רַע 1, § 43; evil, *n.* רַע, רָעָה 2, § 43; אָוֶן 2, § 41.

except, כִּי אִם.

extinguished, be, דָּעַךְ, *st.*

eye, עַיִן 2. *f.*, § 41, du. עֵינַיִם; *pl.* עֲיָנוֹת, fountains (§ 41. 5).

Ezra, עֶזְרָא.

F.

face, faces, פָּנִים 1, *pl.*; before, formerly, לִפְנִים; *before me,* לְפָנַי, &c., p. 69; used both of *time* and *place.*

fair, beautiful, יָפֶה 1, § 45; beauty, fairness, יֳפִי 2.

fall, to, נָפַל, *impf.* in *o,* § 33; let fall, drop, cast (lots), *Hiph.*

famine (hungry).

far, to be, רָחַק, *st.*; far, adj. רָחוֹק 1.

fat, בָּרִיא 1.

father, אָב, irreg. See p. 153.

fear, to, יָרֵא, *st.*, § 39, *impf.* יִירָא; *inf.* יִרְאָה; pass. *Niph.*; terrible, *ptc.* נוֹרָא; fear, מוֹרָא 1, יִרְאָה 2, § 38; פַּחַד 2.

feast (drink).

feast, to hold a (religious), חָגַג, § 42, a (religious) feast, חַג 2, § 43 and p. 45 (near foot).

feed, to, pasture, רָעָה; shepherd, רֹעֶה.

field, שָׂדֶה 1, § 45, pl. *ôth* (*im*).

fierceness (heat), חָרוֹן.

fight, to, לָחַם, *Niph.*; *with, against,* בְּ; *for,* לְ; battle, war, מִלְחָמָה, *cstr.* מִלְחֶמֶת, § 29. 3.

fill, to (be full).

find, to, מָצָא; pass. *Niph.* § 38.

fine, thin, דַּק 1. § 43.

finish, to, כָּלָה, *Pi.*; pass. *Pu.* (be ended), also *Qal.*

fire, אֵשׁ 2. *f.* § 43.

firmament, expanse, רָקִיעַ 1.

first, former, רִאשׁוֹן (§ 35. 1 a); at first, בָּרִאשֹׁנָה.

fish, דָּג, דָּגָה 1. § 18. 3.

flame, לֶהָבָה 1.

flee, to, בָּרַח; נוּס; to put to flight, הֵנִיס (*Hiph.*); a refuge, מָנוֹס 1. § 41.

flesh, בָּשָׂר 1.

fling, to (cast).

flock, צֹאן 2; עֵדֶר 2.

flood (of Noah), מַבּוּל.

foe, אֹיֵב (enemy).

food, אָכְלָה (eat).

fool, נָבָל 1; אֱוִיל; folly, אִוֶּלֶת 2.

foot, רֶגֶל 2. *f.*

for, conj. כִּי.

force, forces, army, חַיִל 2, § 41; also wealth, valour.

ford, a, מַעֲבָר.

ford, to (to cross).

forget, to, שָׁכַח; pass. *Niph.*

fork, מַזְלֵג 3; pl. מִזְלָגוֹת.

form, to, יָצַר, § 39; *impf.*; with *waw cons.* וַיִּצֶר.

forsake, to, עָזַב (leave).

four, § 48; fourth, § 48. 2.

fowl (bird).

friend, רֵעַ. § 45.

frog, צְפַרְדֵּעַ 3. § 30.

from, out of, prep. מִן, § 14. 2, § 15. 2.

fruit, to bear, be fruitful, פָּרָה ; fruit, פְּרִי 2, § 45. 3 b.

full, be, מָלֵא, *st. ; of*, acc. ; be filled *with, Niph., acc.* ; to fill (a thing with), *Pi., two acc.,* § 38. 3 b ; fuiness, מְלֹא ; full, adj. מָלֵא.

G.

gain, to (property), רָכַשׁ ; gain, property, רְכוּשׁ.

garden, גַּן 2. § 43.

garment, בֶּגֶד 2. *i.,* suff. בִּגְדִי, &c. (not ה). שִׂמְלָה 2 and שַׂלְמָה 2 (by transposition).

gate, שַׁעַר 2.

gather, to, אָסַף, § 34 ; קבץ (*Qal*), *Pi.* ; assemble, gather themselves, and pass. *Niph.* of both vbs.

gazelle (beauty), צְבִי 2. *i.* § 45. 3.

genealogies, history, תּוֹלְדוֹת, pl. *f.* (bear).

generation, דּוֹר 2, § 41, pl. (*im*) ôth.

Gentiles, גּוֹיִם. גּוֹי nation.

Gideon, גִּדְעוֹן.

girl (bear), (lad).

give, to, נָתַן, § 33 ; *dat.* gift(s), *coll.* מַתָּן 1.

glad, be (joyful).

glorify, to, כָּבֵד, *Pi.* (be heavy) ; glory, כָּבוֹד 1.

go, to, הָלַךְ, § 39 ; walk, *Hithp.* § 26. 3 *b.*

go down, יָרַד, § 39 ; *Hiph.* bring down ; pass. *Hoph.*

go in, בּוֹא, § 40 ; bring in, *Hiph.,* pass. *Hoph.* ; followed by בְּ, אֶל, acc.

go out, יָצָא, §§ 38, 39 ; bring out, *Hiph.* ; pass. *Hoph.* ; *of* מִן, outgoing, exit מוֹצָא 1, § 38.

go up, עָלָה ; bring up, *Hiph.* ; an ascent, מַעֲלָה, § 45.

let go, to, שָׁלַח, *Pi.*

God, אֱלֹהִים, *pl.* (sing. in poetry אֱלוֹהַּ) ; with insep. prepp. 'לָא, &c. (§ 15. 1 b), but 'מֵא.

gold, זָהָב 1.

good, be, pleasing, agreeable, טוֹב, *perf. ; impf.* יִיטַב ; do good to, do right, *Hiph.* ; well, very, הֵיטֵב, inf. abs. § 39.

good, adj. טוֹב ; good things, goods, goodness, טוּב 2, the best (of), מֵיטָב (only in cstr.) 1.

govern, to, rule, *over,* מָשַׁל ב (king).

grass, דֶּשֶׁא 2 ; עֵשֶׂב 2 ; to sprout (of young grass), הִדְשִׁיא, *Hiph. denom.*

grave (bury).

great, be, grow, גָּדַל, *st.* ; bring up (a child), *Pi.* ; magnify, *Hiph.* (*Pi.*) ;—oneself, *Hithp.* ; great, גָּדוֹל 1 ; greatness, גֹּדֶל 2 ; great, רַב 1, § 43, pl. many.

grey hairs, שֵׂיבָה.

groan, to, אנח, *Niph.* § 34.

ground, אֲדָמָה 1.

grow, of grass (grass), (sprout).

grow up (be great).

guilty, be, אָשֵׁם, *st.* ; suffer, be punished (as guilty), *Niph.* ; guilt, אָשָׁם 1, עָוֹן 1.

H.

half, חֲצִי 2. § 45. 3.

halt, to, be lame, צָלַע.

hand, יָד 1. *f.*, § 18; *your —* יֶדְכֶם.

hang up, to, יקע, *Hiph.*; הוֹקִיעַ.

happen, to (befall).

hard, be, קָשָׁה; harden, *Hiph.*; hard, severe, קָשֶׁה 1 (heavy).

hate, to, שָׂנֵא, § 38; hatred, שִׂנְאָה 2.

head, רֹאשׁ, § 41. 5, pl. רָאשִׁים.

heal, רָפָא; pass. *Niph.*

hear, hearken, obey, שָׁמַע; make be heard, declare, *Hiph.* (ear); rumour, report, שֵׁמַע 2.

heart, לֵבָב 1, לֵב 2, § 43 (pl. *ôth* in both).

heaven, heavens, שָׁמַיִם 1, pl.

heavy, be, כָּבֵד, *st.*; make heavy, harden (honour, glorify), *Pi.*; heavy, כָּבֵד 1.

Hebrew, עִבְרִי, fem. עִבְרִיָּה, § 26. 4. 8.

heifer, עֶגְלָה 2.

help, to, עָזַר; help, עֵזֶר 2. § 35.

hero, mighty man, גִּבּוֹר.

hide, to, סתר, pass., reflex. *Niph.*; act. *Hiph.*; חבא, pass., reflex. *Niph.*, *Hithp.*; act. *Hiph.*

high, be, רום; lift up, *Hiph.*; high, lofty, רָם 1, *ptc.*

hill, mountain, הַר 2. § 43.

history (genealogies).

hither, here, adv. הֲלֹם.

Hittites, חִתִּים, בְּנֵי־חֵת.

ho! הוֹי.

holy, be, קָדַשׁ, *st.*; sanctify, *Pi.*; —oneself, *Hithp.*; holy, saint,

קָדוֹשׁ 1; holiness, קֹדֶשׁ 2; holy place, sanctuary, מִקְדָּשׁ, קֹדֶשׁ 1.

honey, דְּבַשׁ 2. § 29. 2.

horn, קֶרֶן 2. *f.*

horse, סוּס 2; mare, סוּסָה, *f.*

host, army, time of service, צָבָא 1, pl. *ôth.* § 38. 2.

hot, be, חַם, *st.*; hot, חַם 1, § 43; heat, חֹם 2.

house, בַּיִת 2, § 41; home, בַּיְתָה; pl. בָּתִּים, p. 153.

how! מָה, § 13. 3; אֵיךְ.

howl, to, ילל, *Hiph.* § 39. 1. 4.

hungry, be, רָעֵב, *st.*; hungry, רָעֵב; hunger, famine, רָעָב 1.

hunt, to, צוד; venison, צַיִד.

husband (man).

I.

if, אִם.

ill (evil).

image, צֶלֶם 2.

imagination, יֵצֶר 2 (form).

impute, to, reckon, חָשַׁב.

in, prep. בְּ, § 14; into, בְּ, אֶל.

increase, to (*intr.*), רָבָה.

inhabit, to, יָשַׁב, § 39. 2. 2 *b*; inhabitant, יֹשֵׁב.

inherit, to, יָרַשׁ, § 39. 2. 2 *a*, dispossess, *Hiph.*; נָחַל, give to inherit, *Hiph.*; inheritance, נַחֲלָה.

iniquity, אָוֶן 2, § 41 (evil, guilt).

innocent, נָקִי (very rarely נָקִיא).

inside, midst, heart, קֶרֶב 2. *i.*; *within the city*, בְּק׳ הָעִיר; *within me*, בְּקִרְבִּי (midst).

instead of, תַּחַת (beneath), p. 121.

Israel, יִשְׂרָאֵל.

J.

Jeroboam, יָרָבְעָם.

Jerusalem, יְרוּשָׁלַם (יְרוּשָׁלַיִם), p. 103.

Jezebel, אִיזֶבֶל.

Jonathan, יוֹנָתָן, יְהוֹנָתָן.

Jordan (the), הַיַּרְדֵּן.

Joseph, יוֹסֵף.

Joshua, יְהוֹשֻׁעַ, יֵהוֹשׁוּעַ.

journey, to, נָסַע; journey, מַסַּע 1.

joyful, be, rejoice, &c., שָׂמַח, *st.*; glad, joyful, *ptc.*; gladness, joy, שִׂמְחָה 2; also גִּיל, verb and noun, §§ 40, 41.

Judah, יְהוּדָה.

judge, to, שָׁפַט; to litigate, im-plead one another, *Niph.*; a judge, *ptc.* שֹׁפֵט; judgment, מִשְׁפָּט 1.

just, be, righteous, &c., צָדַק, *st.*; justify, *Hiph.*; — oneself, *Hithp.*; just, righteous, צַדִּיק; righteousness, צֶדֶק 2. *i.*, צְדָקָה 1.

K.

keep, to, watch, שָׁמַר; keep one-self, take care, beware, *Niph.*; watchman, *ptc.* שֹׁמֵר; watch, מִשְׁמָר 1; watch, charge, מִשְׁמֶרֶת, § 29. 3 a.

key, מַפְתֵּחַ 3 (open).

kid, גְּדִי. § 45.

kill, to, הָרַג; *Hiph.* of *die* (הֵמִית).

kindle, to, burn (*intr.*) יקד, יצת (*trans.*); *Hiph.* of יצת (הִצִּית), § 39. 3.

king, be, rule, מָלַךְ, *over*, עַל, ב; make one king, *Hiph.*; pass.

Hoph.; a king, מֶלֶךְ 2; queen, מַלְכָּה 2; kingdom, מַמְלָכָה, &c., § 29. 3 a.

kiss, to, נָשַׁק, *impf.* in *a* (also *o*); with לְ; a kiss, נְשִׁיקָה (rare).

kneel, to, בָּרַךְ, *st.*; to make (a beast) kneel, *Hiph.*; the other parts in sense of "bless"; knee, בֶּרֶךְ 2. *i.*, *f. du.* § 29, p. 101.

know, to, יָדַע, § 39. 2; impf. יֵדַע, imp. דַּע, inf. cstr. דַּעַת; pass. *Niph.*; inform, make known, *Hiph.*; pass. *Hoph.*; know-ledge, דַּעַת 2.

L.

lad, נַעַר 2; girl, damsel, *f.* נַעֲרָה 2.

ladder, סֻלָּם.

lady, mistress, גְּבֶרֶת 2. *i.* See § 29. 3 b.

lamp, נֵר.

lance, רֹמַח 2. § 37. 2.

land (earth).

last, אַחֲרוֹן (after).

law, instruction, תּוֹרָה (teach)

leaf, leafage, עָלֶה 1. § 45. 3.

lean, to, rest, press, act. סָמַךְ; one-self, *Niph.*; שָׁעַן, *Niph.*; *upon*, עַל.

learn, to, לָמַד, *st.*; make learn, teach, *Pi.*, *two acc.*

leave, to, abandon, עָזַב; pass. *Niph.*

leave off, to, stop (cease).

left (over), be, remain, שָׁאַר; to leave over, let remain, *Hiph.*; pass. *Niph.*

left (hand), שְׂמֹאול.

length (long).

leopard, נָמֵר 1.

lest, conj. פֶּן, joined with *impf.*

lick, to, לָקַק. § 42.

lie, to (speak falsely), כזב, *Pi.*; a lie, כָּזָב 1.

lie down, to, lie, יִשְׁכַּב, *st.*; a bed, מִשְׁכָּב 1; to lie down (of beasts), רָבַץ, *st.*; a stall, resting-place, מַרְבֵּץ 3. § 30.

life (live).

lift up, to, bear, נָשָׂא (high).

light, be, shine, אוֹר, *perf.* in *o*; give light, *Hiph.*, § 40; light, אוֹר 2; luminary, light, מָאוֹר 1, pl. *ôth* (*im*).

light, be, swift, קַל, *st.*, § 42; to curse, *Pi.*; lighten, *Hiph.*; light, swift, קַל 1. § 43.

like, prep. כְּ. § 14.   See p. 87.

lion, אֲרִי 2, § 45; young lion, כְּפִיר.

lip, edge, shore, שָׂפָה 1, *du.* § 17.

listen, to (hear), בְּ, אֶל.

little, be, קָטֹן, *st.*, § 22; little, קָטָן 1, קָטֹן 1, — the first form is not inflected (found only in abs., and *once* in cstr.), the second is inflected קְטַנָּה קְטַנִּים. See § 43. 4.

little, a, some, a few, מְעַט; *a little water*, *food*, &c. אֹכֶל, מַיִם כ׳ מ; *a few people*, מְתֵי כ׳ (also מְתֵי כ׳ מִסְפָּר).

live, to, חָיָה, § 45; living, חַי (from root חיי, see p. 87); life, חַיִּים; living creature, beast, חַיָּה.

lofty, be, גָּבַהּ, *st.*; lofty, high, גָּבֹהַּ 1; loftiness, height, גֹּבַהּ 2.

long, be, אָרֵךְ, *st.*; to prolong, *Hiph.*; long (אָרֵךְ) only in cstr.

אֹרֶךְ (see p. 64), אָרֹךְ 1, fem. אֲרֻכָּה (see § 43. 4); length, אֹרֶךְ 2.

look, to, נבט, *Hiph.*

lord, אָדוֹן 1; takes pl. suff., except in 1st pers. s., where it admits sing. also (prob. a later device to distinguish a human lord אֲדֹנִי from the divine אֲדֹנָי = יהוה).

lot, גּוֹרָל 1, pl. *ôth*.

Lot, לוֹט.

loud, גָּדוֹל (great).

love, to, אָהֵב, *st.*, § 34; love, אַהֲבָה (strictly *inf. cstr.*).

low, be, שָׁפֵל, *st.*; low, שָׁפָל; to bring low, *Hiph.* of שפל or כרע.

Luz, לוּז.

M.

magnify, to (be great).

maid, שִׁפְחָה 2; אָמָה 1, pl. אֲמָהוֹת, see p. 153.

make, to, do, עָשָׂה; pass. *Niph.*; to make one thing into another, *two accus.*; work, deed, מַעֲשֶׂה, § 45; פֹּעַל *poet.*; a work, פֹּעַל, p. 120.

male, זָכָר 1.

man, husband, אִישׁ; man, mankind, אָדָם.

manner, מִשְׁפָּט 1; דֶּרֶךְ 2.

mantle, מְעִיל; אַדֶּרֶת. § 29. 2.

many, be, increase, רָבָה; increase, to, act. *Hiph.*; many, רַב 1. § 43.

mare (horse).

matter (word).

measure, to, מָדַד. § 42.

meat (eat).

meditate, muse, הָגָה.

meet, to, קָרָה, קָרָא (infin. cstr. לִקְראָה); *to meet him,* לִקְרָאתוֹ, &c.

melt, to, מוּג, and *Niph.*

memory, memorial, זֵכֶר 2.

mention, to, *Hiph.* of *remember.*

merciful, to be, רחם, *Pi., acc.* חָנַן; mercy, loving-kindness, חֶסֶד.

messenger (angel).

midst, תָּוֶךְ 1, § 41; *within the house,* בְּתוֹךְ הַבַּיִת (inside).

mighty man (hero).

minister, to, שרת, *Pi.* (serve).

Miriam, מִרְיָם.

mischief, אָסוֹן (rare).

missile (send).

mistress (lady).

Moab, מוֹאָב.

month, חֹדֶשׁ 2 (new).

moon, יָרֵחַ.

more (still), עוֹד.

morning, בֹּקֶר 2.

morsel, fragment, פַּת 2. *i. f.* § 43.

Moses, מֹשֶׁה.

mother, אֵם 2. § 43.

mountain (hill).

mourn, to, סָפַד; אָבַל, *st.*; mourning, מִסְפֵּד 3.

mouth, edge, פֶּה. See p. 153.

much, רַב 1. § 43 (many).

N.

naked, עֵירֹם, pl. עֵירֻמִּים, see § 43. 4; nakedness, עֶרְוָה 2.

name, שֵׁם 3, pl. שֵׁמוֹת.

narrate, to, סִפֵּר, *Pi.*

nation, גּוֹי (people).

native land, מוֹלֶדֶת 2 (bear).

near, קָרוֹב 1 (draw near).

neck, צַוָּאר 1, *sing.* and *pl.*

new, חָדָשׁ 1.

night, לַיִל 2, § 41, usually לַיְלָה 2.

no, not, לֹא direct; אַל, with pro- hibitions, p. 83; no, none, אַיִן 2 (if with vb., vb. is in *ptc.*), p. 136, footnote.

north, צָפוֹן 1.

not to, לְבִלְתִּי, *inf.*, p. 145.

now, עַתָּה.

number, to, מָנָה (count).

nurse, מֵינֶקֶת 2. *i.* § 29. 3.

O.

oath, שְׁבוּעָה (swear).

offer, to, *Hiph.* of קרב, *draw near.*

offering, קָרְבָּן; meat (*i.e.* blood- less)—מִנְחָה; drink—נֶסֶךְ 2. *i.*; burnt—עֹלָה.

ointment, שֶׁמֶן 2.

old (elder, aged).

olive, זַיִת 2. § 41.

on, upon, בְּ, § 14. 1; עַל, p. 70.

one, § 48; one—another, p. 150 (friend), (brother).

only, רַק, אַךְ.

open, to, פָּתַח; pass. *Niph.*; door, פֶּתַח 2. *i.*; key, מַפְתֵּחַ 3; to open (of eyes), פָּקַח; pass. *Niph.*; open (of mouth), פָּצָה.

oppress, to, עָנָה, לְהַין, *Pi.*

or, אוֹ; וְאִם, אִם in interrogative or indirectly interr. sentences, —*shall we go or shall we for- bear?* הֲנֵלֵךְ—(וְאִם) אִם נֶחְדָּל; *or no, or not,* אִם לֹא, § 49. 5 c.

other, אַחֵר, pl. אֲחֵרִים.

out, out of, מִן. § 14. 2, § 15. 2.

out at, in at, בְּעַד (properly "in-terval," "distance"). See p. 96.

outside, חוּץ; *to the outside,* הַחוּצָה; *on, at, the outside of the house,* מִחוּץ לַבַּיִת, § 14. 2 b.

over, upon, עַל, p. 70.

overflow, to, overwhelm, שָׁטַף.

oversee, to, visit, פָּקַד; commit, entrust, *Hiph.*; an overseer, פָּקִיד 1.

ox, פַּר 2, § 43; שׁוֹר, § 41; cow, *fem.* פָּרָה.

P.

pain, חֳלִי 2, § 45. 3; מַכְאֹב.

palace, הֵיכָל 1, pl. *ôth* (once); cstr. הֵיכְלֵי.

palm (hand), כַּף 2. § 43.

pass by, עָבַר (cross).

passover, פֶּסַח 2.

pasture, מִדְבָּר (desert).

path, נָתִיב 1. *m.,* and נְתִיבָה, *f.*

pay, to, שִׁלֵּם, *Pi.*

people, עַם, 2. § 43.

perfect, תָּם 1, § 43; תָּמִים 1. *See* be ended.

perish, to, אָבַד, § 35; destroy, *Pi., Hiph.*

permit, to, נָתַן, *acc.* and *inf.*

Pharaoh, פַּרְעֹה.

Philistines, פְּלִשְׁתִּים.

pit, prison, בּוֹר 2, § 41; pl. *ôth.*

pity, to, רחם, *Pi.,* § 36; חָנַן, § 42.

place, to, שִׂים, שׂוּם, שִׁית, הִנִּיחַ (*Hiph.* of נוח); *Hiph.* of שׁכן. *See* set, dwell, rest.

place, a, מָקוֹם 1; pl. *ôth* (arise).

plague, נֶגַע 2; מַכָּה.

plain (*noun*), lowland, שְׁפֵלָה.

plant, to, נָטַע; a plant, נֶטַע 2. *i.*

play, to, sing, &c., זמר, *Pi.*

plead with, to, רִיב, בְּ, עִם, § 40.

plough, to, חָרַשׁ.

plunder, to, בָּזַז (spoil), (take). §42.

poor, דַּל, אֶבְיוֹן 1. § 43.

possess, to, יָרַשׁ, קָנָה; possessor, קֹנֶה; possession, מִקְנֶה, § 45.

pot, סִיר; pl. *ôth.*

pour out, שָׁפַךְ (spill).

powerful, עָצוּם 1.

prayer, תְּפִלָּה.

precept, פִּקּוּד (oversee).

presence, in p. of, לִפְנֵי (face), p. 69.

prey, מַלְקוֹחַ (take).

priest, כֹּהֵן 3.

prince, שַׂר 2. § 43.

prolong, to, *Hiph.* of אָרֵךְ, *be long.*

promise, to, אָמַר, with *infin.*

prophesy, to, נבא, *Niph.* (*Hithp.*); *concerning,* לְ, עַל; prophet, נָבִיא 1.

prove, to (try), נָסָה, בָּחַן, צָרַף, *Pi.*

proverb, מָשָׁל 1.

punished, be, *Qal, Niph.* of אָשֵׁם, *be guilty.*

pursue, to, רָדַף.

put on, wear, לָבַשׁ, *acc.*; to clothe, dress with, *Hiph.,* *two acc.,* § 27. 1 *d.* § 38. 3 b.

put, to, place, set, נָתַן. *See* place.

put out, to (the hand), שָׁלַח.

Q.

queen, מַלְכָּה 2.

quiet, שַׁאֲנָן.

quiet, become, שָׁתַק, impf. *o*.

R.

rain, מָטָר 1 ; rain, to, מָטַר, *Hiph.*

ram, אַיִל 2. § 41. 2.

ransom, כֹּפֶר 2 (atone).

read, to, קָרָא.

rebel, revolt, to, פָּשַׁע ; *against*, ב.

receive, to, לָקַח. § 33. 3 b.

redeem, to, גָּאַל, פָּדָה ; redemption, פְּדוּת ; redeemer, גֹּאֵל.

refrain, to, רָחַק, *st.* (far).

refresh, to, sustain, סָעַד.

refuge (flee), (trust).

regard, to, שָׁעָה, אֶל (look).

reign, to (king).

rejoice, to (joyful, be).

remember, to ; זָכַר ; pass. *Niph.* ; call to remembrance, mention, *Hiph.* ; memory, זֵכֶר 2.

remove, to, סוּר, intrans. ; *Hiph.* trans.

rend, to, קָרַע.

repent, to, נחם, *Niph.* נִחַם, § 36.

report, שְׁמוּעָה (hear).

rescue, to (escape), (deliver).

rest, to, שָׁבַת ; make cease, *Hiph.* ; נוח ; give rest, *Hiph.* הֵנִיחַ, *dat.* ; place, set, *Hiph.* הִנִּיחַ ; resting-place, מָנוּחַ, מְנוּחָה, § 41 ; sabbath, שַׁבָּת 1.

restore, to (return).

return, to, שׁוּב ; restore, *Hiph.*, *Pô'l.* ; return, תְּשׁוּבָה.

reveal, to, גָּלָה.

review, to, פָּקַד (oversee).

rib, side, צֵלָע, *f.* 1 ; pl. *ôth* (*îm*). See p. 114.

riches, חַיִל 2 (force) ; עֹשֶׁר 2 ; rich, עָשִׁיר.

riddle, חִידָה.

ride, to, רָכַב, *st.* ; to make ride, set on a horse, &c., *Hiph.* ; chariot, רֶכֶב 2. *i.*, מֶרְכָּבָה.

righteous, be (just).

rise, to, קוּם.

rise, to (of star, &c.), זָרַח.

rise early, to, *Hiph.* שׁכם.

river, נָהָר 1, pl. *ôth* and *îm* ; יְאֹר (mainly of *Nile* and its branches).

roll, to, גָּלַל, *Qal, Hiph.* ; pass. *Niph.*

rule over, to (govern).

rumour (report).

run, to, רוּץ ; runner, post, *ptc.* רָץ 1 ; make run, bring hastily, *Hiph.*

S.

sabbath (rest).

sacrifice, to, זָבַח ; sacrifice, זֶבַח 2. *i.* ; altar, מִזְבֵּחַ 3, pl. *ôth* (offer, offering).

saddle, to (bind).

saint (holy).

sake of, for, בַּעֲבוּר, — *of me*, בַּעֲבוּרִי, בִּגְלָלִי. *See* עבר, גלל in Lex.

salt, מֶלַח 2.

salvation (save).

Samson, שִׁמְשׁוֹן.

Samuel, שְׁמוּאֵל.

sanctify, to (holy).

sanctuary (holy).

sand, חוֹל, 2. § 41.

Sarah, שָׂרָה.

satisfied, be, שָׂבַע, *st.*, *with*, acc. ; to satisfy with, *Hiph.*, *two acc.*, § 38. 3 ; satisfied, שָׂבֵעַ 1 ; fulness, שֹׂבַע 2, שָׂבָע 1.

Saul, שָׁאוּל.

save, to, ישׁע, *Hiph.* הוֹשִׁיעַ ; pass. *Niph.*, salvation, safety, יֵשַׁע 2 ; יְשׁוּעָה.

say, to, promise, אָמַר. § 35.

scattered, be, פּוּץ (impf.) ; to scatter, *Hiph.* ; pass. *Niph.*

sceptre, tribe, rod, שֵׁבֶט 2.

scribe, סֹפֵר 3 (count).

sea, יָם 2, § 43, *cstr.* יַם־, יָם, and יָם (only in יַם־סוּף).

see, to, רָאָה, §§ 44, 45 ; pass. *Niph.* ; show, let see, *Hiph.*, *two acc.* ; seer, רֹאֶה ; sight, aspect, face, מַרְאֶה.

seed, זֶרַע 2 (sow).

seek, to, inquire at, דָּרַשׁ ; pass. *Niph.*

seek, to, בקשׁ, *Pi.*

sell, to, מָכַר ; pass. *Niph.*

send, to, שָׁלַח ; send away, loose, *Pi.* ; a missile, שֶׁלַח 2. *i.*

serpent, נָחָשׁ 1.

serve, to, till, עָבַד ; pass. *Niph.* ; enslave, *Hiph.* ; servant, עֶבֶד 2 ; service, עֲבֹדָה ; to serve = minister (mainly in sacred things), שׁרת, *Pi.*

set, to, נָתַן, שִׂים (שׂוּם), שִׁית ; כּוּן,

Hiph., *Pô'l.* (§ 40. 5) ; pass. *Niph.* (place).

seven, seventh, § 48.

shadow, צֵל 2. § 43.

shake, to, רָעַשׁ ; trans. *Hiph.* ; an earthquake, רַעַשׁ 2.

shave, to, גלח, *Pi.*, *Hithp.*

shed, to (spill).

Sheol, the underworld, שְׁאוֹל.

shepherd, herdsman, רֹעֶה (feed).

shine, to, אוֹר. § 40.

shore (lip).

short, קָצֵר 1.

shoulder, שְׁכֶם 2. *i.*

shut, to, סָגַר ; pass. *Niph.*

sick, be, to, חָלָה ; sickness, חֳלִי.

side, end (יְרֵכָה or יַרְכָה (?), (once in *sing.*—Gen. **49**. 13—with suff. יַרְכָתוֹ), *du.* יַרְכָתַיִם, *cstr.* יַרְכְּתֵי (with *dagh. l.*).

silent, be, דָּם, *st.* (*impf.* יִדֹּם), חרשׁ, *Hiph.*

silver, כֶּסֶף 2.

simple one, a, פֶּתִי 2. § 45. 3 b (3).

sin, to, חָטָא ; sin, חֵטְא 2, חַטָּאת ; sinner (sing.), חֹטֵא, *ptc.*, חַטָּא (used in plur.).

sing, to, שִׁיר ; a song, שִׁיר, and *fem.*

sister, אָחוֹת 1. See p. 153.

sit, to, dwell, יָשַׁב, § 39. 2 ; make to sit, place, *Hiph.* ; pass. *Hoph.* ; a seat, assembly, dwelling-place, מוֹשָׁב 1.

slaughter, to, שָׁחַט. § 36.

slay, to, הָרַג (die).

sleep, to, יָשֵׁן, *st.* ; sleep, slumber, נוּם ; sleep heavily, רדם, *Niph.* ; sleep, שֵׁנָה 1, תְּנוּמָה ; heavy (ecstatic) sleep, תַּרְדֵּמָה, *e* firm.

smell, to, רוח, *Hiph.*; smell, רֵיחַ 2.

smite, to, נָגַף; pass. *Niph.*; נכה, *Hiph.* הִכָּה; pass. *Hoph.* נֻגַּע; stroke, defeat, נֶגַע, מַכָּה, מַגֵּפָה 2. *i.* (The word מכה is of general use, the other two very commonly of divine plagues.)

smoke, עָשָׁן 1.

snare, פַּח 2. § 43.

sole (of foot), palm, כַּף 2. *f.* § 43.

some (a little), מִן, partitive.

son, בֵּן 3. See p. 153.

song, שִׁיר *m.* (שִׁירָה f.).

sore, רַע (bad).

sorrow, heaviness, יָגוֹן 1.

soul, נֶפֶשׁ 2. *f.*

south, נֶגֶב 2.

sow, to, זָרַע; bear seed, *Hiph.*; seed, זֶרַע 2.

speak, to, דבר, *Pi.* (pf. דִּבֶּר)—in Qal used only in *act. ptc.*; a word, thing, דָּבָר 1; *everything*, כָּל דָּבָר, *nothing*, לֹא—כָּל ד׳, or לֹא—ד׳. § 13. 4.

spill, to, שָׁפַךְ; pass. *Niph.*

spirit, wind, רוּחַ 2. *f.*

spoil, to, plunder, שָׁלַל; spoil, שָׁלָל 1.

spread, to, spread out (hands), פָּרַשׂ; יצע *Hiph.* (*impf.* יַצִּיעַ), § 39. 3.

sprout, to, צָמַח; make to sprout, *Hiph.*; sprout, branch, צֶמַח 2 *i.* (grass).

staff, מַקֵּל 3, pl. *ôth.*

stall, lair, מַרְבֵּץ 3 (lie down).

stand, to, עָמַד; set up, *Hiph.*, קום.

star, כּוֹכָב 1.

statute (command), חֹק 2, § 43, fem. חֻקָּה (precept).

steal, to, גָּנַב, *Qal* and *Pi.*; pass. *Pu.*, *Niph.*; thief, גַּנָּב.

still, yet, more, עוֹד; see p. 136 (note); *still alive*, עוֹד חַי (again).

stone, אֶבֶן 2.

stranger, sojourner, גֵּר 1, § 41; strange, foreign, נָכְרִי (*nokhri*).

street, חוּץ 2, pl. *ôth*; שׁוּק 2; רְחֹב, *f.*, pl. *ôth.*

strength (strong).

stretch, to, נָטָה, also *Hiph.* (put out); a bed, מִטָּה.

strip, to, פָּשַׁט, *Hiph.*

strong, be, חָזַק, *st.*; אָמֵץ, *st.*; strengthen, *Pi.*; עָצֵם, *st.*; strong, חָזָק, עַז, עָצוּם; strength, חֹזֶק and חָזְקָה; עֹז 2, § 43; כֹּחַ 2.

strive, to, plead, רִיב, § 40; strife, plea, מְרִיבָה 2, רִיב.

suck, to, יָנַק, § 39. 1; suckle, give suck, *Hiph.*; nurse, *ptc. Hiph.*, מֵינֶקֶת, see § 29. 3.

suffer, to, punishment (be guilty); to suffer pain, כָּאַב, *st.* (pain).

sun, שֶׁמֶשׁ 2.

swarm, to, שָׁרַץ, *with acc.*; a swarm, שֶׁרֶץ 2.

swear, to, שׁבע, *Niph.*; oath, שְׁבוּעָה.

sweat, זֵעָה, *ê* firm.

sweet, be (מָתֹק), *st.*; sweet, מָתוֹק 1, inflect. מְתוּקָה. § 41. 1 b.

sword, חֶרֶב 2. *f.*

sycamores, שִׁקְמִים.

T.

tabernacle, מִשְׁכָּן (dwell).

tablet, לוּחַ *m.*; pl. לוּחֹת.

take, to, לָקַח; pass. *Qal, Niph.,* § 33. 3 b, c; prey, plunder, מַלְקוֹחַ; take (capture in war, &c.), לָכַד; pass. *Niph.*

tall, גָּבֹהַּ (great). *Cstr.* גְּבַהּ.

tambourine, תֹּף 2. § 43.

taste, to, טָעַם; taste, sense, טַעַם 2.

teach, to, יָרה, *Hiph.,* הוֹרָה; לִמַּד (learn)*Pi.*; law, instruction, תּוֹרָה.

tell, to, נגד, *Hiph.*; pass. *Hoph.* (count), (say), (speak).

temple, הֵיכָל (palace).

tent, אֹהֶל 2; pl. אֹהָלִים (but also, with *prep.* בָּאֳהָלִים).

terrible, נוֹרָא, *Niph. ptc.* of יָרֵא (fear).

testify, to, עוּד, *Hiph.*; witness, עֵד.

that, conj. כִּי; in order that, לְמַעַן, with *infin. cstr.* (p. 168), or *imperf.* (p. 86); *that* is very often expressed by *waw consec.,* e.g. after וַיְהִי, *and it came to pass.* § 23. 3.

then, of time, אָז; *then,* of transition in thought, וֹ, simple and *consec.* § 23. 3.

thence (there).

there, שָׁם; thither, שָׁמָּה; thence, מִשָּׁם; where, whence, whither, see p. 47.

there is (was), יֵשׁ; — *water,* יֵשׁ מַיִם; *I have,* יֶשׁ־לִי, &c. (see p. 130, note 3); *there is (was) not,* אַיִן; *there is no water,* אֵין מַיִם; *suff.,* see p. 136.

therefore, עַל־כֵּן.

thief (steal).

thigh, יָרֵךְ 1; cons. יֶרֶךְ. See p. 64.

thing (speak).

thither (there).

thorn, קוֹץ 2.

thought, מַחֲשָׁבָה, § 29. 3 (count); cstr. pl. מַחְ׳.

thresh, דּוּשׁ; threshing-floor, גֹּרֶן 2, pl. ôth.

threshold, סַף 2. *i.* § 43. 1 a.

throne, seat, כִּסֵּא 3, pl. כִּסְאוֹת.

thus, כֹּה.

tidings, to bring, preach, בשׂר, *Pi.*

till, cultivate (serve).

till, until, prep. עַד; conj. עַד אֲשֶׁר, with *perf.* or *impf.* according to sense. *Suff.,* p. 70.

time, עֵת, § 43; time (*fois, mal*), פַּעַם 2, gen. *fem.,* plur. *îm* (properly *step*); twice, פַּעֲמַיִם; three times, שָׁלֹשׁ פְּעָמִים.

tingle, to, צל. § 42.

together, יַחְדָּו, יַחַד.

to-morrow, מָחָר.

tongue, לָשׁוֹן 1, gen. *fem.,* pl. ôth.

touch, to, נָגַע, ב.

tower, מִגְדָּל 1, pl. *îm* and ôth.

transgress, פָּשַׁע; *against,* ב; transgression, פֶּשַׁע 2. *i.*

tread, to, רָמַס.

tree, עֵץ 1; wood, *pl.*

tremble, to, רָגַז, *st.*

tribe (sceptre).

trust, to, to flee for refuge to, חָסָה, ב; a place of refuge, מַחֲסֶה (confide), (flee).

to try (as silver), צָרַף, בָּחַן ; to try, prove, tempt, נסה, *Pi.*

turn, to, overturn, turn into, הָפַךְ ; pass. *Niph.* (return).

turn aside, to, סוּר.

twins, תְּאֹמִים.

two, § 48; they two, both of them, שְׁנֵיהֶם, &c. § 48. 1 (9); the second time, שֵׁנִית.

U.

under (beneath).

undone, to be, דָּמָה, *Niph.*

unless, לוּלֵא, לוּלֵי (usually perf.).

until, עַד, עָדֵי, &c. (till), p. 70.

unto, אֶל, אֵלַי, &c., p. 70.

upon, עַל ; *suff.*, p. 70.

upright, יָשָׁר 1.

upwards, מֵעְלָה. *See* עַל in Lex.

Ur, אוּר.

V.

vain, empty, רֵיק, רֵק ; vanity, רִיק, שָׁוְא.

valley, גַּיְא 2, נַחַל 2, בִּקְעָה 2.

valour, חַיִל 2 (force). § 41.

vengeance, נְקָמָה 1 (avenge).

venison, צַיִד 2. § 41.

very, מְאֹד (prop. a noun).

vine, גֶּפֶן 2.

vineyard, כֶּרֶם 2 ; vinedresser, כֹּרֵם 3.

violence, wrong, חָמָס 1.

virgin, בְּתוּלָה.

vision, מַרְאָה (see).

visit, to (review), (oversee).

voice, קוֹל 2.

vow, to, נָדַר ; a vow, נֶדֶר 2.

W.

walk, to, *Hithp.* of הָלַךְ. § 26. 3 *b.*

wall, חוֹמָה.

wander, to, wave, tremble, נוּעַ ; a wanderer, נָע, *ptc.*

war (fight).

wash, to, רָחַץ ; —clothes, כִּבֵּס, *Pi.* § 26. 1 *a.*

waste, to, lay waste, שָׁמַם, *Hiph.*

waste away, to, מוּק, *Niph.* § 42.

watch, to (keep).

water, waters, מַיִם, pl.

water, to (שָׁקָה, *Hiph.*), הִשְׁקָה used as causative of שָׁתָה, p. 152.

way, manner, דֶּרֶךְ 2. *c.*

weak, דַּל 1. § 43.

wealth, חַיִל 2 (force). § 41. 2.

wean, to, גָּמַל ; pass. *Niph.*

weapon, כְּלִי, *pl.* כֵּלִים, c. כְּלֵי.

wear, to (put on).

weary, be, יָעֵף, *st.* § 39 ; weary, יָעֵף 1.

weep, to, בָּכָה. § 44, § 45. 1 (1).

weigh, to, שָׁקַל, pass. *Niph.*

well, בְּאֵר 2. *f.*

west, יָם. § 43.

what, מָה. § 13. 3.

whelp, גּוּר (lion).

when, בְּ, כְּ with inf. cstr. ; כַּאֲשֶׁר, כִּי with finite forms (p. 111).

when? how long? עַד מ', מָתַי.

whence, where, whither, p. 47.

whether ?, ?, הֲ, § 49. 2 ; אִם (or), § 49. 5 c.

who, which, אֲשֶׁר. § 13. 2.

who? מִי. § 13. 3.

whoever, whosoever, מִי. § 13. 3.

whole (all).

why? wherefore? לָמָּה (מַדּוּעַ).

wicked, רָשָׁע 1; wickedness,
רִשְׁעָה 2.

wife (woman).

wilderness (desert).

willing, to be, אָבָה. § 35.

wind (spirit).

wine, יַיִן 2. § 41.

wing, border, extremity, כָּנָף 1.
f. du. (pl. *ôth*).

wise, be, חָכַם, *st.*, impf. יֶחְכַּם;
wise, חָכָם 1; wisdom, חָכְמָה 2.

wish, to, חָפֵץ, *st.*

with, prep. עִם 2; אֵת 2. § 43.
See *suff.*, p. 142, note 1; with
of instrument, בְּ, § 14. 1 f.

withdraw, to (be far).

within (inside), (midst).

witness, עֵד 1, § 41 (testify).

wolf, זְאֵב 2, *e* firm.

woman, אִשָּׁה. See p. 153.

womb, בֶּטֶן 2. *i. f.*; רֶחֶם 2. *c.*

wood, timber (tree).

word, thing, matter, דָּבָר 1.

work, to (make).

wrestle, to, אבק, *Niph.*

write, to, כָּתַב; pass. *Niph.*
(count).

Y.

Yahweh (Jehovah), יהוה; perhaps
יַהְוֶה; usually read אֲדֹנָי, p. 41.

year, שָׁנָה 1, pl. *îm* (*ôth* poet.);
a yearling שׁ־בֶּן; 20 years old
= son of 20 years.

yoke, עֹל 2. § 43.

young, younger (little). § 47. 1.

youth, young man, נַעַר, *f.* נַעֲרָה;
time of youth, נְעוּרִים.

Z.

Zion, צִיּוֹן.

VOCABULARY.

HEBREW AND ENGLISH.

———✦———

א

אָב *a father;* cstr. אֲבִי. See p. 153.

אָבַד *to perish* (§ 35).—Impf. יֹאבַד —Hiph. הֶאֱבִיד *to destroy.*

אָבָה *to be willing* (§ 35).—Impf. יֹאבֶה.

אֲבִיגַיִל *Abigail.*

אֶבְיוֹן *m. poor.*

אֲבִימֶלֶךְ *Abimelech.*

אֶבֶן 2 *f., a stone.*

אבק Qal not in use.—Niph. נֶאֱבַק *to wrestle.*

אַבְרָהָם *Abraham.*

אַבְרָם *Abram.*

אָדָם 1 *m., man.*

אֲדָמָה 1 *f., the ground.*

אָדוֹן 1 *m., lord.*—Takes suff. of plur. noun. See *lord* in Eng.-Hebr. With prefix לַאדֹנָי &c.

אַדֶּרֶת 2 *f., a mantle.* § 29. 3.

אָהֵב *to love.*—Impf. יֶאֱהַב (1 pers. also אֹהַב). § 34 f.

אֲהָהּ *alas!*

אֵהוּד *Ehud.*

אֹהֶל 2 *m., a tent;* pl. אֹהָלִים (but בָּאֳהָלִים is found).

אָוֶן 2 *m., vanity, wickedness.* § 41.

אוֹר *to be light, shine,* (ו"ע) Perf.

אוֹר. Hiph. הֵאִיר *to give light.* § 40.

אוֹר 2 *m., light.* § 41.

מָאוֹר 1 *m., a light, luminary;* pl. *îm* and *ôth.*

אוּר *Ur.*

אָז adv. *then.*

אֹזֶן 2 *f., the ear.* § 29.

אָח *m., a brother.* See p. 153.

אֶחָד *m.,* אַחַת *f., one.* § 48.

אַחַר adv. *afterward;* prep. *after, behind;* oftener אַחֲרֵי.—אַחֲרַי *after me* &c., p. 70.

אַחֵר adj., *another;* pl. אֲחֵרִים.

אַחֲרִית *f., end, latter end.*

אֹיֵב 3 *m., an enemy.* § 30.

אֵיד 2 *m., calamity.* § 41.

אִיזֶבֶל *Jezebel.*

אֵיךְ adv. *how? how!*

אַיִן 2 (*nothing*), *there is not;* cstr. אֵין. Suff. p. 136, footnote.

אִישׁ *m., a man.* See p. 153.

אִשָּׁה *f., a woman.* See p. 153.

אָכַל *to eat* (פ"א, § 35).—Hiph. הֶאֱכִיל *to give to eat.*

אֹכֶל 2 *m., food;* אָכְלָה 2 *f., id.*

מַאֲכָל 1 *m., id.*

אַל adv. *no, not,* with *Juss.* p. 83.

אֶל prep. *unto.* Suff. p. 70.

אֱלֹהִים *pl. m., God.* (Sing. אֱלוֹהַּ used in poetry.) With prefix, לֵאלֹהִים &c., § 14. 1 c, but מֵאֱ'.

אֵלִיָּה, אֵלִיָּהוּ *Elijah.*

אֱלִישָׁע *Elisha.*

אֱלִיל *m., an idol.*

אִלֵּם 3 adj., *dumb.*

אִם adv. *if;* כִּי אִם *except.*

אֵם 2 f., *mother.* § 43.

אָמַן *to be firm.*—Hiph. הֶאֱמִין *to believe,* בְּ, לְ.

אֱמֶת 2 i. f., *truth* (contr. fr. אֲמֶנֶת). Suff. אֲמִתּוֹ.

אָמֵץ *to be strong* (st. § 23).—Pi. *to make strong.*

אָמַר *to say, to promise, intend.* § 35.

אֵמֶר, אִמְרָה *speech, word* (poetical).

אֲנִי pron. *I.* § 12.

אָסַף *to gather.*—Impf. יֶאֱסֹף, § 35. 1 b.—Niph. *to assemble.*

אַף *m., the nose, anger.*—Du. אַפַּיִם *the nostrils, face* (אנף *to breathe, be angry*). § 43. 4.

אֵצֶל 2, used as prep. *beside; beside me,* אֶצְלִי. § 34. 4 b.

אַרְבַּע *four.* § 48.

אֶרֶז 2 m., *cedar.*

אֲרִי 2 m., *a lion.* § 45. 3.

אֹרֶךְ 2 m., *length.*

אֶרֶץ 2 f., *earth, land;* pl. ôth.

אָרַר *to curse.*—Impf. יָאֹר. § 42.

אֵשׁ 2 f., *fire.* § 43.

אֲשֶׁר rel. pron. *who, which.* § 13. 2.

אַשְׁרֵי cstr. *the happinesses of* (= *happy!*). See p. 154.

אֵת *a particle placed before the* definite *acc.,* § 13. 7. Suff. § 20. 10.

אֵת prep. *with.* Suff. p. 142, note 1.

אַתָּה pron. *thou.* § 12.

אָתוֹן 1 f., *a she-ass.*

ב

בְּ prep. *in, on, among; by* of instrument. § 14. 1.

בְּאֵר 2 f., *a well;* pl. ôth.

בֶּגֶד 2 i. m., *a garment, covering.*—Suff. בִּגְדוֹ (without *dag. l.*).

בַּד 2 m. (*separation*), לְבַד *apart, alone; I alone* אֲנִי לְבַדִּי. § 43.

בדל Qal not in use.—Hiph. *to separate, divide.*—Niph. *pass.*

בְּהֵמָה 1 f., *cattle, tame beasts;* cstr. בֶּהֱמַת, cstr. pl. בַּהֲמוֹת. See p. 154.

בּוֹא *to come, go, go in* (ע״ו, ל״א).—Impf. יָבוֹא.—Hiph. הֵבִיא *to bring.* Hoph. *pass.* §§ 38, 40.

בּוֹר 2 m., *a pit;* pl. ôth. § 41.

בּוֹשׁ *to be ashamed* (ע״ו § 40).—Impf. יֵבוֹשׁ.

בָּזַז *to plunder, spoil* (§ 42).—Impf. יָבֹז.

בָּחַר *to choose* (§ 36); acc. בְּ.

בָּטַח *to trust* (§ 37); *in,* בְּ.

בֶּטֶן 2 i. f., *the womb, heart.*

בֵּין 2 (*interval*), prep. *between, among.* Repeated before the second word and usually takes the numb. of its suff.—*between me and you* בֵּינִי וּבֵינֵיכֶם.—For בֵּין . . . בֵּין also לְ . . . בֵּין.

בַּיִת 2 m., *a house.* See p. 153.

בֵּיתְאֵל *Bethel.*

בְּכֹרָה *birthright.*

בֵּן 3 *m., a son.* See p. 153.

בָּנָה *to build,* apoc. impf. וַיִּבֶן. § 45. 1.

בַּת 2 *f., a daughter.* See p. 153.

בְּעַד 2 prep. *behind, in at, out at,* ב' הַחַלּוֹן *in at, out at the window;* ב' הַחוֹמָה *over the wall.*—Suff. בַּעֲדִי § 36. 2. 2.

בָּעַל *to marry;* ptc. pass. *f.* בְּעֻלָה *married.*

בַּעַל 2 *m., lord, husband, Baal.* Suff. § 36. 2. 2.

בָּקַע *to cleave, break through.*

בֹּקֶר 2 *m., morning.*

בקשׁ Qal not in use. Pi. בִּקֵּשׁ *to seek.*

בָּרָא *to cut, fashion, to create* (§ 38).—Niph. *pass.*

בָּרִיא 1 adj. *fat.*

בְּרִית *f., a covenant;* כָּרַת ב' *to make a covenant;* הֵקִים ב' *to establish a covenant.*

בָּרַךְ *to kneel.*—Pi. בֵּרֵךְ *to bless;* Pu. *pass.* (§ 36);—*blessed* בָּרוּךְ 1 ptc. Qal.

בֶּרֶךְ 2 *i. f., the knee,* du. בִּרְכַּיִם.

בְּרָכָה 1 *f., a blessing,* cstr. בִּרְכַּת, suff. בִּרְכָתִי. § 18. 2.

בָּשָׂר 1 *m., flesh.*

בָּשַׁל *to boil.*—Pi. *to boil, seethe.*

ג

גָּאַל *to redeem.* § 36.

גָּבַר *to be strong, prevail* (st. § 22).

גִּבּוֹר *m., a hero, mighty man.*

גְּבֶרֶת, גְּבִירָה 2 *i. f., lady, mistress.* § 29. 3 b.

גְּדִי 2 *m., a kid.* § 45. 3.

גָּדַל *to be great, to grow* (st. § 22).—Pi. *to magnify, bring up* (a child).—Hithp. *to magnify oneself.*

גָּדוֹל 1 adj., *great, elder.*

גִּדְעוֹן *Gideon.*

גּוֹי *m., a nation.* Pl. גּוֹיִם, cstr. גּוֹיֵי *the gentiles.*

גָּוַע *to die, expire.* § 37.

גּוֹרָל 1 *m., lot;* pl. ôth.

גִּיל 2 *m., joy.* § 41.

גָּלָה *to uncover, reveal* (ל"ה § 44).—Niph. *pass.*—Hithp. *to uncover oneself.*

גָּלַל *to roll* (§ 42).—Impf. יָגֹל.—Hiph. הֵגֵל *to roll.* Niph. נָגֹל *to be rolled.*

גַּם adv. *also;* גַּם ... גַּם *both ... and.* § 49. 5 a.

גָּמַל *to wean; to deal fully, adequately with; recompense.* Niph. *to be weaned.*

גַּן 2 *c., garden.* § 43.

גָּנַב *to steal.*—Pi. *id.*—Pu. *pass.*

גֵּר 1 *m., a sojourner.* § 41.

גָּרַשׁ *to drive out* (§ 36); oftener Pi.—Niph. *pass.*

ד

דֹּב 2 *c., a bear.* § 43.

דְּבוֹרָה *Deborah* (= bee).

דָּבַק *to cleave* (st. § 22); *to* ב.

דבר Qal not in use except Act. ptc. דֹּבֵר *speaking.*—Pi. דִּבֵּר *to speak.*—Pu. *pass.*

דָּבָר 1 *m., a word, thing.*

דְּבַשׁ *honey,* 2 m. § 29. 2.

דָּג 1 m., *a fish* ; p. דָּגָה.

דָּוִיד, דָּוִד *David.*

דּוֹר 2 m., *generation* ; pl. (*îm* and) *ôth.* § 41.

דֶּלֶת 2 f., *a door* (door-leaf); du. דְּלָתַיִם.

דָּם 1 m., *blood, your blood* דִּמְכֶם. —דָּמִים *blood* spilt. § 18. 3.

דָּמַם *to be silent.* Impf. יִדֹּם. § 42.

דָּנִיֵּאל (later) דָּנִיֵּאל Daniel.

דַּעַת see ידע.

דֶּרֶךְ 2 c., *a way.*

דָּרַשׁ *to seek ; unto* אֶל.

דֶּשֶׁא 2 m. (young) *grass.*

דשא Qal and Hiph. each found once: *to produce grass* (denom.).

ה

ה art., *the.* § 11.

הֲ particle of interrogation. § 49. 2.

הֲלֹא *not ?*

הָדָר 1 m., *honour, majesty.*

הוּא pron. § 12.

הוֹד m., *glory, splendour.*

הָיָה *to be* (§ 45. 2).—Impf. יִהְיֶה apoc. יְהִי.—Inf. *cstr.* הֱיוֹת, לִהְיוֹת &c.

הֵיכָל 1 m., *palace, temple.*

הֻכּוֹת. See נכה.

הֲלֹם adv. *hither.*

הָלַךְ *to go.*—Impf. יֵלֵךְ.—Hiph. הוֹלִיךְ (see § 39. 2. 2 *c*).— Hithp. הִתְהַלֵּךְ *to walk, go about.* § 26. 3 *b.*

הִנֵּה, הֵן adv. *behold, lo!* Suff. p. 142, note 1.—Followed chiefly by the ptc. הִנְנִי מֵבִיא *behold I* (do, will) *bring.*

הָפַךְ *to turn, to change into* (§ 34). —Niph. נֶהְפַּךְ *pass.*

הַר 2 m., *hill, mountain.* § 43.

הָרַג *to kill, slay* (§ 34).—Niph. *pass.*

הָרָה *to conceive* (§ 44 f.).—Impf. 3 s. f. with waw cons. וַתַּהַר. § 45. 1 (3).

ר

ו conj. *and.* § 15.

ז

זְאֵב 2 m., *a wolf* (*ē* firm).

זָבַח *to sacrifice, slaughter.* § 37.

זֶבַח 2 m., *a sacrifice.*

מִזְבֵּחַ 3 m., *an altar;* pl. *ôth.* § 30.

זֶה f. זֹאת dem. pron. *this.* § 13.

זָהָב 1 m., *gold.*

זַיִת 2 m., *an olive.* § 41.

זָכַר *to remember.*—Niph. *pass.*— Hiph. *to mention, commemorate.*

זֵכֶר 2 m., *memory, memorial.*

זָכָר 1 m., *a male.*

זֵעָה 2 f., *sweat* (*ê* firm).

זָעַק *to cry out.* § 36.

זָקֵן *to be old* (st. § 22).

זָקֵן 1 adj. *old ;* noun *elder.* § 18.

זְקֻנִים m., זִקְנָה f., *old age.*

זְרוֹעַ f., *the arm ;* pl. *îm, ôth.*

זָרַח *to shine, rise* (of star). § 37.

זָרַע *to sow* (§ 37).—Hiph. הִזְרִיעַ *to yield seed.*

זֶרַע 2 m., *seed ;* cstr. זֶרַע and זְרַע.

ח

חבא Qal not in use.—Hiph. הֶחְבִּיא *to hide.*—Niph. נֶחְבָּא *to hide oneself ;* Hithp. *id.* § 34.

חָבַשׁ *to bind, bind up, saddle* (§ 34).

חָגַג *to keep a feast* (§ 42).—Impf. יָחֹג.

חַג 2 *m., a feast* (ḥajj), p. 45, § 43.

חָדַל *to cease, leave off* (st. § 22).

חָדָשׁ 1 adj. *new.*

חֹדֶשׁ 2 *m., new moon, month.* § 35.

חוֹל 2 *m., sand.* § 41.

חוֹמָה *f., a wall.*

חוּץ 2 *m., outside, street, field;* pl. ôth.—הַחוּצָה *to the outside.*—מִחוּץ לְ *on the outside of*—.

חָזַק *to be strong* (st. §§ 22, 34).

חָזָק 1 adj. *strong.*

חָטָא *to sin* (§ 34).—Hiph. הֶחֱטִיא *to condemn as sinful.*

חֹטֵא 3 (ptc.) *a sinner,* used in sing., but חַטָּא adj. used in pl.

חֵטְא 2 *m., sin.* § 38. 2.

חָיָה *to live* (§ 45. 2).

חַי *to live* (§ 42. See p. 87, note 4).

חַי 1 adj. *living, f.* חַיָּה, § 43. In oaths חַי is used of God, and חֵי (cstr. or perhaps a contracted abs.) of men: e. g. חַי יהוה וְחֵי נַפְשֶׁךָ *as J. liveth and as thy soul* (= thou) *liveth.*

חַיִּים *life.*

חַיָּה *f., a living creature, beast.*

חַיִל 2 *m., force, valour, power, army, wealth.* § 41.

חֵיק 2 *m., bosom.* § 41.

חָכָם 1 adj., *wise.* § 35.

חָכְמָה 2 *f., wisdom.* § 29.

חֵלֶב *m., fat.*

חָלָה *to be sick* (§§ 34, 44 f.).—Impf. with waw cons. וַיַּחַל.

חֳלִי 2 *m., disease, sickness.* § 45.

חָלַל—Hiph. הֵחֵל *to begin* (§ 42). —Hoph. הוּחַל *pass.*

חָלַם *to dream* (§ 34).

חֲלוֹם *m., a dream;* pl. ôth.

חָמַד *to desire* (st. § 22).—Impf. יַחְמֹד, (יֶחְמַד).—Niph. נֶחְמָד *pass.*

חֲמוֹר *m., an ass.*

חָמָס 1 *m., violence, injury.* § 35.

חָנַן *to pity* (§ 42).—Impf. יָחֹן, יְחָנְךָ = יָחָנְּךָ Gen. 43 29.

חֶסֶד 2 *m., mercy, kindness.*

חָפֵץ *to desire, wish* (st. §§ 22, 34). —Impf. יַחְפֹּץ, יֶחְפַּץ.

חָפֵץ 1 adj. *desiring,* § 35, cstr. pl. חֶפְצֵי, see § 22. 4.

חֵץ 2 *arrow.* § 43.

חָצֵר 1 *c., enclosure, court, village;* pl. îm, ôth. § 35.

חֹק 2 *m., statute.* § 43.

חָרֵב *to dry up, be waste* (st. § 22).

חֶרֶב 2 *f., sword.*

חָרָה *to be hot, angry.*—Imp. apoc. וַיִּחַר. § 45. 1.

חֶרְפָּה 2 *f., a reproach.*

חָשַׁב *to think, reckon.* — Impf. יַחְשֹׁב and יַחְ'. § 34. 2 c.

חֹשֶׁךְ 2 *m., darkness.*

חֵת *Heth;* בְּנֵי־חֵת, חִתִּים *Hittites.*

ט

טָהֵר *to be clean* (st. §§ 22, 36).— Pi. טִהַר *to cleanse.*

טָהוֹר 1 adj., *clean.*

טוֹב *to be good* (§ 40).—Perf. טוֹב. Other parts from יטב.—Impf. יִיטַב.—Hiph. הֵיטִיב. § 39. 1.

13

טוֹב 1 adj. *good.* § 41.

טוּב 2 *m., good things, goods, goodness.* § 41.

טַל *m., dew.*

טָעַם *to taste* (§ 36).

טַעַם 2 *m., taste, sense.* § 36. 2.

י

יְאֹר *m., stream* (esp. Nile).

יָבֵשׁ *to be dry* (st. §§ 22, 39).

יַבָּשָׁה 1 *f., dry land.*

יָד 1 *f., hand. Your hand* יֶדְכֶם; du. יָדַיִם, pl. יָדוֹת *hands* fig. (handles). § 16. 5.

יָדַע *to know* (פ״ו § 39).—Impf. יֵדַע.—Inf. Cstr. דֵּעַת.—Niph. נוֹדַע *pass.* — Hiph. הוֹדִיעַ *to make known.*

יְהֹוָה *Jahweh.* The vowels are those of אֲדֹנָי *lord.* With prefix לַיהֹוָה (i. e. לַאֲדֹנָי).   See § 10. 5.

יְהוּדָה *Judah.*

יְהוֹנָתָן *Jonathan.*

יְהוֹשֻׁעַ, יְהוֹשׁוּעַ *Joshua.*

יוֹם 2 *m., a day.*   See p. 153.

יוֹנָה *f., a dove;* pl. *îm.*

יוֹנָתָן *Jonathan.*

יוֹסֵף *Joseph.*

יטב see טוֹב.

יַיִן 2 *m., wine.* § 41.

יָכֹל *to be able* (§ 39).—Impf. יוּכַל.

יָלַד *to bear* (פ״ו § 39).—Impf. יֵלֵד.—Hiph. *to beget.*—Pu. *to be born.*

יֶלֶד 2 *m., a boy.* § 29.

יַלְדָּה 2 *f., a girl.*

מוֹלֶדֶת 2 *f., kindred.* § 29. 2.

יָם 2 *m., sea;* cstr. יָם *except in* יַם־סוּף *Red sea.* § 43.

יָנַק *to suck* (פ״י § 39).—Hiph. הֵינִיק *to give suck;* hence מֵינֶקֶת 2 *f., a nurse.* § 29. 2.

יָסַף Qal, and Hiph. הוֹסִיף, *to add* (פ״ו § 39. 4).

יָעַף *to be weary.* — Impf. יִיעַף. § 39. 2. 2 *a.*

יָעֵף 1 adj., *weary.*

יָעַץ *to advise, counsel* (§ 39).— Impf. יִיעַץ.—Niph. נוֹעַץ.

עֵצָה 1 *f., counsel.*

יָפֶה 1 adj., *fair.* § 45.

יָצָא *to go out* (פ״ו § 39).—Impf. יֵצֵא; inf. cstr. צֵאת (for צְאֵת). —Hiph. *to bring out.*

מוֹצָא 1 *m., an outgoing.* § 39. 3S.

יָצַג Hiph. הִצִּיג *to set, place.* (§ 39. 3).

יָצַע Hiph. הִצִּיעַ *to spread* (§ 39. 3).

יָצַר *to form* (§ 39).

יֵצֶר 2 *m., form, imagination.*

יָקַד *to burn.*—Impf. יִיקַד, יֵקַד.— Hoph. *pass.* הוּקַד. § 39. 2.

יָקַץ Qal only in Impf. יִיקַץ *to awake* (§ 39). –Perf. &c. in Hiph. הֵקִיץ.

יָרֵא *to fear* (§ 39).—Impf. יִירָא. Inf. cstr. יִרְאָה.—Niph. נוֹרָא; ptc. *terrible.*   Followed by מִן, מִפְּנֵי, and פֵּן.

יָרֵא 1 adj. *fearing.*

יָרָבְעָם *Jeroboam.*

יָרַד *to go down* (§ 39. 2. 2 *b*).— Impf. יֵרֵד &c.—Hiph. הוֹרִיד *to bring down.*—Hoph. *pass.*

הַיַּרְדֵּן *the Jordan.*

יְרוּשָׁלַם *Jerusalem.* See p. 103.

יָרֵחַ 1 *m., the moon.*

יָרֵךְ 1 *f., the thigh, side;* cstr. יֶרֶךְ. See p. 64.

יַרְכָה or יְרֵכָה ? See *side* in Eng. Hebr. 2 *f., side, end.*—Du. יַרְכְתִי, cstr. יַרְכְתַיִם.

יָרַשׁ *to inherit* (§ 39. 2).—Hiph. הוֹרִישׁ *to dispossess, destroy.* Niph. *pass.*

יֵשׁ *there is—There is water* יֵ' מַיִם. See p. 130, note 3.

יָשַׁב *to sit, dwell, inhabit* (§ 39. 2). —Impf. יֵשֵׁב.

יֹשֵׁב 3 ptc. *inhabitant.*

מוֹשָׁב 1 *m., a seat, assembly, dwelling-place.*

יָשֵׁן *to sleep* (§ 39).—Impf. יִישַׁן.

יָשַׁע Qal not in use.—Hiph. הוֹשִׁיעַ *to save.*—Niph. *pass.* § 39. 2.

יֶשַׁע 2 *m., salvation.*

יְשׁוּעָה *f., id.*

תְּשׁוּעָה *f., id.*

יָשָׁר 1 adj., *upright, righteous.*

יֶתֶר 2 i., *remnant, rest.*

כ

כְּ prep. *as, like.* § 14. Suff. p. 87, note 1. With rel. כַּאֲשֶׁר *as, when. When he kept* כַּאֲשֶׁר שָׁמַר, or בְּשָׁמְרוֹ (inf. cstr. § 31. 9 c).

כָּבֵד *to be heavy, severe* (st. § 22). —Pi. *to make heavy, harden, honour.*—Niph. *be honoured.*

כָּבֵד 1 adj., *heavy, severe, laden* (cstr. כְּבַד and כְּבֵד. See p. 64).

כָּבוֹד 1 *m., honour, glory.*

כֹּה adv. *thus.*

כֹּהֵן 3 *m., a priest.* § 36.

כּוֹכָב 1 *m., a star.*

כּוּן Qal not in use.—Hiph. הֵכִין *to set, establish.*—Pôlēl כּוֹנֵן *id.* —Niph., Pôlal, *pass.* § 40.

כִּי conj., *that, for, because;* of time *when, whenever.* כִּי אִם *except.*

כֶּלֶא 2 i. *m., a prison.* § 38.

כֶּלֶב 2 *m., a dog.*

כָּלָה *to be ended* (§ 44).—Pi. *to complete, finish.*—Pu. *pass.*

כֹּל 2 *m., all.* § 43. כָּל־דָּבָר *every-thing;* כָל־דָּבָר ... לֹא *nothing.*

כֵּן adv., *so, thus.* עַל־כֵּן *therefore.*

כָּסָה *to cover* (§ 44), Qal only in ptc. act. כֹּסֶה and pass. כָּסוּי. —Pi. כִּסָּה *to cover.*—Pu. *pass.*

מִכְסֶה 1 *m., a covering.* § 45.

כֶּסֶף 2 *m., silver, money.*

כַּף 2 *f., palm of hand, sole;* du. § 43. Pl. *ôth* (metaphorical) § 16. 5.

כָּפַר *to cover* (with pitch).—Pi. כִּפֶּר *to atone.*—Pu. *pass.*

כֹּפֶר 2 *m., bribe, ransom.*

כְּפִיר *m., young lion.*

כְּרוּב *m., cherub.*

כֶּרֶם 2 *m., vineyard.*

כַּרְמֶל *Carmel,* p. 65, note 2.

כָּרַע *to bend the knee, bow down* (§ 37).

כָּרַת *to cut off, cut down.*—Niph. *pass.* כ' בְּרִית *to make a covenant.*

כַּשְׂדִּים *Chaldeans.*

כָּתַב *to write.*—Niph. *pass.*

כָּתֵף 1 *f., shoulder;* cstr. כֶּתֶף. See p. 64.

ל

ל prep. *to, for.* See § 14. 1.

לֹא adv. *not, no.*

לֵב 2 m., *the heart,* § 43. Pl. *ôth.*

לֵבָב 1 m., id. Pl. *ôth.*

לְבַד *alone.* See בַּד.

לָבַשׁ *to put on* (clothes), *wear* (st. § 22); *acc.*—Hiph. *to clothe, put on* (another); *two acc.* § 27. 1 d, § 38. 3.

לוּז *Luz.*

לוּחַ m., *tablet;* pl. לוּחֹת.

לוֹט *Lot.*

לָחַם Niph. *to fight. With* עִם; *against* בְּ, עַל; *for* לְ. § 36.

לֶחֶם 2 c., *bread.* § 36. 2. 3.

מִלְחָמָה, מִלְחֶמֶת f., *war.* § 29. 3.

לַיִל usually לַיְלָה with *He of acc.,* 2 m., *night.* Pl. לֵילוֹת § 41.

לָכַד *to take, capture.*—Niph. *pass.*

לָמַד *to learn* (st. § 22).—Pi. לִמַּד *to teach.*

לָמָּה adv., *why?* (מָה לְ).

לְמַעַן conj., prep., *in order that, to; for the sake of,* with *infin.* and *impf.* (ענה). § 23. 6, § 49. 5.

לָקַח *to take* (§ 33. 3).—*Impf.* יִקַּח.—Inf. Cstr. קַחַת.—Niph. נִלְקַח *pass.*—(Old) pass. *pf.* לֻקַּח, *impf.* יֻקַּח. § 33. 3 c.

מַלְקוֹחַ m., *plunder.*

מֶלְקָחַיִם m. du., *tongs.*

לָקַק *to lick* (§ 42). Impf. יָלֹק.—Pi. *id.*

לָשׁוֹן 1 f., *tongue.*

מ

מְאֹד adv., *very;* also בִּמְאֹד, עַד מְ'.

מֵאָה 1 f., *hundred;* du. מָאתַיִם.

מְאוּמָה *anything* (perhaps = a *fleck*).

מָאוֹר. See אוֹר.

מַאֲכָל. See אָכַל.

מאס *to reject* (§ 36).

מַבּוּל m., *the flood* (of Noah).

מִדְבָּר 1 m., *pasture, desert.*

מָדַד *to measure* (§ 42).—Impf. יָמֹד.—Niph. *pass.*

מַדּוּעַ *wherefore?*

מָה pron. *what? whatever,* § 13. interj. *how! how?*

מוֹאָב *Moab.*

מוּג *to melt* (§ 40).—Niph. *pass.*

מוֹלֶדֶת. See יָלַד.

מוֹצָא. See יָצָא.

מוּת *to die* (§ 40). Perf. מֵת.—Impf. יָמוּת.—Hiph. הֵמִית *to kill.*—Pô'lēl מוֹתֵת *id.*—Hoph. *pass.*

מֵת 1 ptc., *dead.*

מָתַי *when?*

מְתִים cstr. מְתֵי (in a few phrases) *males, men.*

מָוֶת 2 m., *death* (§ 41).

מִזְבֵּחַ. See זָבַח.

מָחָה *to blot out, destroy* (§ 44).

מַחֲנֶה *camp.*

מָחָר 1 *to-morrow.*

מִטָּה. See נָטָה.

מָטַר Qal not in use.—Hiph. *to rain.*

מָטָר 1 m., *rain.*

מִי, מָה pron. *who? whoever, who-*

soever; what? whatsoever. § 13.
With prep. בַּמֶּה *how? by what?*
(בַּמֶּה in *p.* and bef. א).—מִי יִתֵּן
Oh that! with Impf. &c. § 49. 6.

מַיִם pl. *m., water.* See p. 57.

מֵינֶקֶת. See יָנַק.

מִכְסֶה. See כסה.

מָכַר *to sell.*—Niph. *pass.*

מָלֵא *to be full* (st. § 22, 38); *of,*
acc.—Niph. *to be filled.*—Pi.
to fill; with *two acc.* § 38. 3.

מָלֵא 1 adj. *full.*

מַלְאָךְ 1 *m., angel, messenger.*

מְלָאכָה *f., work;* cstr. מְלֶאכֶת.
§ 29. 3.

מלט Qal not in use.—Niph. *to*
escape.—Pi. *to rescue, deliver.*

מִלְחָמָה. See לָחַם.

מָלַךְ *to rule, be king;* over, בְּ, עַל.
—Hiph. *to make one king.*—
Hoph. *pass.*

מֶלֶךְ 2 *m., a king.*

מַלְכָּה 2 *f., a queen.*

מַמְלֶכֶת, מַמְלָכָה *a kingdom.* § 29. 3.

מֶלְקָחַיִם. See לָקַח.

מִן. prep. (§ 14), *out of, from,*
away from; hence *of cause*
by, on account of. Suff. § 15. 2.
Compar. degree § 47.

מָנָה *to count, number,* § 44.—
Niph. *pass.*

מָנוֹחַ. See נוּחַ.

מִנְחָה 2 *f., an offering, present.*

מַסַּע *a journeying* (from נָסַע).
§ 33. 4.

מִסְפֵּד 3 *m., mourning.* § 30.

מִסְפָּר. See סָפַר.

מַעֲבָר. See עָבַר.

מְעַט 2 *m., a little, some, a few.*

מַעְלָה *upwards.* See p. 162.

מַעֲלָל 2 *m., deed, practice* (only in
plur., and usually in bad
sense).

מַעֲשֶׂה. See עָשָׂה.

מָצָא *to find* (§ 38).—Niph. *pass.*

מִצְוָה. See צָוָה.

מִצְרַיִם *Egypt.*

מָקוֹם. See קוּם.

מַקֵּל 3 *m., a staff,* § 30. Pl. ôth.

מקק Qal not in use. (§ 42).—
Niph. *to melt away.*

מִקְרָא. See קָרָא.

מַרְאֶה. See רָאָה.

מָרַר *to be bitter* (§ 42. 3).—Imp.
יֵמַר.—Hiph. הֵמַר *to make bitter.*

מַר 1 adj., *bitter;* מָרָא Aramaic
form of *fem.* מָרָה.

מְרִיבָה. See רִיב.

מִרְיָם *Miriam.*

מֹשֶׁה *Moses.*

מוֹשָׁב. See שָׁבַן.

מָשַׁל *to rule;* over, בְּ.

מָשָׁל 1 *m., a proverb.*

מִשְׁמָר. See שָׁמַר.

מִשְׁפָּט. See שָׁפַט.

מִשְׁפָּחָה 2 *f., clan,* § 29. 3.

מָתַק *to be sweet* (st. § 22).

מָתוֹק 1 adj., *sweet; f.* מְתוּקָה.
§ 41. 1.

נ

נָא *enclitic particle of entreaty;*
אַל־נָא *dissuasive.*

נבא Qal not in use (§ 38).—Niph.
to prophesy.—Hithp. *id.; also to*

act like an (ecstatic) prophet, to rave.

נָבִיא 1 *m., a prophet.*

נָבַח *to bark* (§ 37).

נבט Qal not in use (§ 33).— Hiph. הִבִּיט *to look.*

נְבֵלָה 1 *f., a corpse, carcase.*

נָבַע *to bubble up ;* Hiph. הִבִּיעַ *to pour forth* (§ 33).

נגד Qal not in use (§ 33).—Hiph. הִגִּיד *to tell, shew.*—Hoph. *pass.*

נֶגֶד 2 prep., *before, in presence of.* Suff. נֶגְדִּי.

נָגַע *to touch, smite* (§ 33, 37).— Pi. *id.*—Hiph. *make to touch, reach to,* בְּ.

נֶגַע 2 *i. m., a stroke, plague.*

נָגַף *to smite, defeat* (§ 33).— Impf. יִגֹּף.—Niph. *pass.*

נגשׁ Perf. Qal not in use.—Impf. יִגַּשׁ.—Perf. in use Niph. נִגַּשׁ *to draw near.*—Hiph. *to bring near* (§ 33).

נָד 1 *m., a fugitive* (ptc. of נוד *to wander*).

נָדַר *to vow* (§ 33).

נֵדֶר, נֶדֶר 2 *m., a vow.*

נָהָר 1 *m., a river* (§ 36). Pl. *îm and ôth.*

נוּחַ *to rest* (§ 40).—Hiph. הֵנִיחַ *to give rest to* (לְ of person); and הִנִּיחַ *to set down, deposit, place ;* with *waw* וַתַּנַח.

מָנוֹחַ 1 *m., resting-place.* § 41.

נוּס *to flee* (§ 40).

נוּעַ *to move about* (§ 40) ; ptc. נָע *a wanderer.*

נָחַל *to inherit, possess.*—Hiph.

to give, to inherit. — Hoph. *pass.*

נַחֲלָה *f., inheritance.*

נַחַל 2 *m., torrent, torrent-valley, wady.*

נחם Qal not in use.—Niph. נִחַם *to repent, to pity* (§ 33. 1 d). —Pi. נִחַם *to comfort* (§ 36).

נָחָשׁ 1 *m., a serpent.*

נָטָה *to bend, incline, stretch* (§ 33, 44).—Impf. יִטֶּה, apoc. יֵט.— Hiph. *id.* הִטָּה, impf. יַטֶּה, apoc. יֵט.

מִטָּה *f., a bed.*

נָטַע *to plant* (§ 33, 37).—Impf. יִטַּע.

נכה Qal not in use (§ 33, 44). —Hiph. הִכָּה, *to smite ;* impf. apoc. יַךְ.—Hoph. *pass.*

מַכָּה *f., a stroke.*

נָמֵר 1 *m., a leopard.*

נָסַךְ *to pour out, found ; set, esta blish* (from different roots).

נֶסֶךְ 2 *i. m., a drink-offering.*

נָע. See נוּעַ.

נַעַל 2 *f., sandal, shoe.* § 36. 2.

נַעַר 2 *m , a lad,* § 36. 2 ; *f.* נַעֲרָה *a girl.*

נָפַל *to fall* (§ 33). Impf. יִפֹּל.— Hiph. הִפִּיל *to make fall, cast.*

נֶפֶשׁ 2 *f., breath, soul.* Pl. *ôth.*

נצב Qal not in use. (§ 33).— Hiph. הִצִּיב *to set, place.*— Hoph. *pass.*—Niph. *reflex.* and *pass.*

נצל Qal not in use (§ 33).— Hiph. הִצִּיל *to deliver.*—Hoph. *pass.*

נָקִי, (very rarely נָקִיא) 1 adj., *innocent.*

נְקָמָה 1 *f., vengeance.*

נֵר *m., lamp.*

נשׁא Qal not in use (§§ 33, 38).—Hiph. הִשִּׁיא *to deceive, beguile.*

נָשַׁק *to kiss* (§ 33).—Impf. יִשַׁק (לְ of person).

נָשָׂא *to lift up, take up, raise* (§§ 33, 38). Impf. יִשָּׂא. Inf. cstr. שְׂאֵת (לָשֵׂאת). Niph. *pass.*

נָתִיב 1 *m.,* and נְתִיבָה *f., path.*

נָתַן *to give, put, account* (33. 3 a). Perf. נָתַתִּי &c. Impf. יִתֵּן. Inf. cstr. תֵּת, תִּתִּי, &c.

ס

סָבַב *to turn, turn away* (§ 42).—Hiph. *to turn* (act.).

סָגַר *to shut.*—Niph. *pass.*

סוּס 2 *m., a horse;* סוּסָה *f. mare.*

סוּר *to turn aside, remove, depart* (§ 40).—Hiph. *to remove, take away.*

סֻלָּם 1 *m., a ladder.*

סָמַךְ *to lean, press upon.*—Niph. *reflex. to lean.*

סָעַד *to sustain, refresh* (§ 36).

סָפַר *to count, write.*—Pi. סִפֵּר *to recount, declare.*

סֹפֵר 3 *m., ptc. scribe.*

סֵפֶר 2 *m., a book.*

מִסְפָּר 1 *m., number.*

סָתַר chiefly in Hiph. *to hide.*—Niph. *reflex.* and *pass.,* Hithp. *reflex.*

ע

עָבַד *to labour, till, serve* (§ 34). Niph. *pass.*

עֶבֶד 2 *m., a servant* (§ 35).

עָבַר *to pass, pass over, cross* (§ 34).—Hiph. *to bring over, make pass.*

עֵבֶר 2 *m., the other side;* בְּעֵבֶר *beyond.*

מַעְבָּר (or מַעֲבָר) 1, 3 *m., a ford* (only in cstr. מַעְבַּר).

עֲבוּר 1 *m.,* cstr., with בְּ as prep., *on account of;* בַּעֲבוּרִי *for my sake.*

עֵגֶל 2 *m.,* and עֶגְלָה 2 *f., calf, heifer* (§ 35).

עוּד Hiph., הֵעִיד *to testify, bear witness, protest* (§ 40).

עֵד 1 *m., a witness.*

עַד *prep. until, till.* Suff. p. 70.

עֵדֶן *Eden.*

עוֹד *adv., still, yet, again* (encore). Suff. see p. 136 footnote.

עָוֹן 1 *m., guilt, sin, punishment.* Pl. ôth.

עוֹלָם 1 *m., age, eternity;* מֵעוֹלָם *from of old;* עַד לְעֹ׳, עַד עֹ׳ *for ever.*

עוּף *to fly* (§ 40).

עוֹף 2 *m., a bird, fowl.*

עִוֵּר 3 *adj., blind.*

עֵז *f., she-goat,* pl. עִזִּים. § 43. 4.

עֹז 2 *m., strength* (§ 43).

עָזַב *to leave, forsake* (§ 34).—Niph. *pass.*

עָזַר *to help* (§ 34).

עֵזֶר 2 *m., help.* Suff. עֶזְרִי. § 34. 4 b.

עֶזְרָא *Ezra.*

עֲטָרָה *f.*, cstr. עֲטֶרֶת *crown.*

עַיִן 2 *f., the eye, du.* עֵינַיִם. § 41. Pl. עֲיָנוֹת *wells.*

עִיר 2 *f., a city.* Pl. עָרִים, cstr. עָרֵי.

עָלָה *to go up, break* (of day) (§ 34, 44).—Impf. יַעֲלֶה, apoc. יַעַל.—Hiph. *bring up, offer up.*

עַל prep., *upon, over.* Suff. p. 70.

עִם prep., *with, along with.* Suff. p. 142, note 1.

עַם 2 *m., people.* § 43.

עָמַד *to stand* (§ 34).—Hiph. *set, place.*

עָנָה *to be low, afflicted* (§ 44).—Pi. *to afflict.*

עֳנִי 2 *m., affliction.* § 45.

עָנָה *to answer, witness* (§ 44); *against* ב.

מַעֲנֶה *m., answer;* מַעַן *purpose, intent;* used only with ל in לְמַעַן (i) as prep., *on account of, for the sake of;* (ii) as conj. followed by (a) inf. cstr., *to the intent that, in order to,* or (b) impf., with or without אֲשֶׁר, *to the intent that, in order that.* § 23. 6, § 49. 5 c.

עָנָן 1 *m., a cloud.*

עָנַן Qal not in use.—Pi. *to cloud, to bring on clouds;* inf. cstr. with Suff. עֲנְנִי for עֲנְנִי. § 3. 3, § 7. 5.

עָפָר 1 *m., dust.* § 35.

עֵץ 1 *m., tree.* § 18. 3.

עֵצָה. See יָעַץ.

עָצַם *to become strong, numerous.*

עֶצֶם 2 *f., a bone.* Pl. *îm, ôth.*

עֶרֶב 2 *m., evening.*

עָשַׁק *to oppress, injure* (§ 34).

עָשָׂה *to do, work, make* (§ 34, 44).—Impf. apoc. יַעַשׂ.—Niph. נַעֲשָׂה *pass.,* but *fem.* נֶעֶשְׂתָה.

מַעֲשֶׂה *m., a work.* § 45.

עָשַׁן *to smoke.* § 34.

עֵת 2 *c., time.* Pl. *îm, ôth.* § 43. 4.

עַתָּה adv., *now.*

עָתַר Qal and Hiph. *to pray, entreat.*

פ

פֶּה *m., mouth.* See p. 153.

עַל־פִּי *according to.* See p. 129.

לְפִי חֶרֶב *with the edge of the sword.*

פַּח 2 *m., snare.* § 43.

פֶּלֶא 2 i. *m., a wonder.*

פְּלִשְׁתִּים *Philistines.*

פָּנִים 1 *m.,* pl. *face, faces.* לְפָנִים *formerly,* לִפְנֵי *before,* לְפָנַי *before me;* p. 69.

פֶּן conj., *lest,* with *impf.*

פָּעַל *to do* (§ 36); ptc. פֹּעַל *a worker.*

פֹּעַל 2 *m., a work.* § 36.

פָּצָה *to open* (mouth).

פָּקַד *to visit, inspect, review.*—Niph. *pass.*—Hiph. *to commit to.*

פָּקִיד 1 *m., an overseer.*

פִּקּוּד *m., a precept.*

פָּקַח *to open* (of eyes &c.) (§ 37). Niph. *pass.*

פַּר 1 *m., an ox;* f. פָּרָה *a cow,* p. 57, footnote. § 43.

פָּרָה *to be fruitful, bear fruit* (§ 44).

פְּרִי 2 *m.*, *fruit.* § 45.

פַּרְעֹה *Pharaoh.*

פָּשַׁע *to rebel; against,* בְּ.

פֶּשַׁע 2 *i. m.*, *rebellion, transgression.*

פַּת 2 *i. m.*, *a morsel, bit.* Suff. פִּתִּי. § 43. 1.

פָּתָה *to be open* (§ 44).—Pi. *to entice.*—Hiph. *to make open, to enlarge;* impf. apoc. יֶפְתְּ.

פֶּתִי 2 *m.*, *simple.* § 45. 3.

פָּתַח *to open.* § 37.

פֶּתַח 2 *i. m.*, *an opening, door.*

מַפְתֵּחַ 3 *m.*, *a key, an opening;* cstr. מִפְתַּח. § 30.

צ

צֹאן 2 *c.*, *a flock* (small cattle).

צָבָא 1 *m.*, *a host, time of service.* Pl. ôth. § 38. 2.

צָדַק *to be righteous, just* (st. § 22). —Hiph. (Pi.) *to justify.*— Hithp. *to justify oneself.*

צֶדֶק 2 *i. m.*, *righteousness.* § 29. 1 b.

צְדָקָה 1 *f.*, *id.*

צַדִּיק *righteous, just;* only *mas.*

צוּד *to hunt* (§ 40).

צוה Qal not in use. Pi. צִוָּה *to command, charge.* Impf. apoc. יְצַו, *imp.* צַו.—Pu. *pass.* § 44.

מִצְוָה *f.*, *a command.*

צִיּוֹן *Zion.*

צֵל 2 *m.*, *a shadow.* § 43.

צֶלֶם 2 *m.*, *an image, likeness.*

צָלַע *to halt, limp* (§ 37).

צֵלָע 1 *f.*, *side, rib;* cstr. צֶלַע. See p. 114.

צָמַח *to sprout* (§ 37).—Hiph. *to make sprout.*

צֶמַח 2 *i. m.*, *a sprout, branch.*

צָעַק *to cry out.* § 36.

צָפַן *to hide, lay up.*

צָפוֹן 1 *m.*, *the north.*

צְפַרְדֵּעַ 3 *f.* coll. *frogs* (pl. *îm*).

צַר 1 adj., *adversary.* § 43.

ק

קָבַב *to curse* (§ 42).

קָבַץ *to collect, gather.*—Pi. *id.*

קָבַר *to bury.*—Niph. *pass.*

קֶבֶר 2 *i. m.*, *a grave.*

קָדַשׁ *to be holy, sacred* (st. § 22). —Pi. *to hallow, sanctify.*— Hiph. *id.*—Niph., Hithp. *reflexive.*

קָדוֹשׁ 1 adj., *holy.*

קֹדֶשׁ 2 *m.*, *holiness, sanctuary.*

מִקְדָּשׁ 1 *m.*, *sanctuary.*

קוֹל 2 *m.*, *voice, sound.* § 41.

קוּם *to arise, stand* (§ 40, Parad.). —Hiph. *to set up, establish.*

קָם 1 ptc., *standing.* § 41.

מָקוֹם 1 *c.*, *a place.* Pl. ôth.

קוֹץ 2 *m.*, *thornbush, thorn.* § 41.

קָטֹן *to be little* (st. § 22, Parad.).

קָטֹן 1 adj., *little* (not inflected but very common).

קָטָן 1 adj., *little,* f. קְטַנָּה (inflected form). See § 43. 4.

קָלַל *to be light, despised* (§ 42, Parad.).—Pi. *to make light of, to curse.*—Hiph. *to lighten of.*

קַל 1 adj., *light, swift.* § 43.

קָנָה *to acquire, buy, possess.* § 44.

מִקְנֶה *m., possession, property, cattle.* § 45.

קֵץ 2 *m., end.* § 43.

קָצַף *to be angry.*

קָצֵר 1 *adj., short.*

קָרָא *to call, cry, read.*—Pu. *pass,* קָרָא לוֹ קַיִן *he called him Cain;* נִקְרָא לוֹ *he was called.* See p. 142.

מִקְרָא 1 *m., convocation, an assembly.* § 38.

קָרָה and קָרָא *to befall, acc.* § 38. 1. 5. Inf. cstr. *f.* קִרְאָה, with prep. לִקְרָאתִי *to meet me;* לִקְרַאת הָאִישׁ *to meet (against) the man.*

קָרַב *to draw near, come near* (st. § 22).—Hiph. *to bring near, to offer.*

קָרוֹב 1 *adj., near, neighbour, relative.*

קֶרֶב 2 *i. m., inside, heart.* בְּקִרְבִּי *within me;* בְּקֶרֶב הָעִיר *within, in the midst of, the city.* § 29. 1b.

קֶרֶן 2 *f., horn.*

קָרַע *to tear, rend* (§ 37).

קָשַׁב Hiph. *to attend, give attention.*

קֶשֶׁת 2 *f., a bow.*

ר

רָאָה *to see* (§ 44).—Impf. יִרְאֶה, apoc. יֵרֶא, תֵּרֶא &c., but וַיַּרְא 3 *m.,* 3 *f.,* וַתֵּרֶא.—Niph. *pass., to appear.*—Hiph. *to shew, two acc.*

מַרְאֶה *m., a sight, appearance, face.* § 45.

רֹאשׁ 2 *m., head;* pl. רָאשִׁים. § 41. 5.

רִאשׁוֹן *adj., first, former.* § 48. 2.

רָבַב *to be many* (§ 42), used only in Perf. and Inf. cstr.

רַב 1 *adj., great, much;* pl. *many.* § 43.

רָבָה *to increase, multiply* (§ 44); impf. apoc. יֵרֶב and יִרֶב.—Hiph. *to multiply, cause to increase.*—Inf. abs. הַרְבֵּה; הַרְבָּה *adv., much.*

רְבִיעִי *adj., fourth.* § 48.

רָבַץ *to lie down* (of beasts) (st. § 22).

מַרְבֵּץ 3 *m., a stall, lair;* cstr. מִרְבַּץ. § 30.

רָגַל *to slander.*

רֶגֶל 2 *f., a foot,* du., p. 101.

רָדַף *to pursue.*—Pi. *id.*

רוּחַ 2 *c., breath, wind, spirit.* Pl. ôth.

רוּם *to be high, to rise up* (§ 40).—Hiph. *to lift up.* Ex. 40.—Hoph. *pass.*

רָם 1 *adj., high, lofty.* § 41.

מָרוֹם 1 *m., height, high place.*

רוּץ *to run* (§ 40).

רָחַב *to be broad, wide* (st. § 22).

רֹחַב 2 *m., breadth.*

רְחֹב 2 *f., broadway, street.* Pl. ôth.

רָחַם *to love* (§ 36).—Pi. רִחַם *to have pity, compassion, on.* Pu. *pass.*

רָחַץ *to wash* (§ 36).

רָחַק *to be distant, to withdraw* (§ 36).

רָחוֹק 1 *adj., distant.*

רִיב *to plead, contend* (§ 40).

רִיב 2 *m., contention, strife.* § 41.

מְרִיבָה *f., id.*

רִיק 2 *m., emptiness, vanity.*

רֵק (רִיק) *empty.*

רָכַב *to ride* (st. § 33).—Hiph. *to set upon* a beast.

רֹמַח 2 *m., a lance, spear.*

רָמַס *to tread.*

רָמַשׂ *to creep.*

רֶמֶשׂ 2 *m., creeping things,* coll.

רִנָּה 2 *f., a ringing cry, complaint.*

רָעֵב *to be hungry* (st. § 22).

רָעֵב 1 *adj., hungry, famished.*

רָעָב 1 *m., hunger, famine.*

רָעָה *to feed, tend* (§ 44).—Ptc. רֹעֶה *a shepherd.*

רֵעֶה *m., a friend;* אִישׁ ... רֵעֵהוּ *one ... another.* § 45. 4.

רָעַע *to be evil* (§ 42, st.).—Hiph. הֵרַע *to afflict, injure.*

רַע 1 *adj., evil;* f. רָעָה *an evil.*

רָעַשׁ *to quake* (§ 36).—Hiph. *to shake.*

רַעַשׁ 2 *m., earthquake.*

רָפָא *to heal* (§ 38).—Niph. *pass.*

רִצְפָּה 2 *f., a coal, hot stone.*

רָקַב *to rot* (st. § 22).

רָקִיעַ 1 *m., firmament.*

רָשָׁע 1 *adj., wicked.*

שׁ

שָׁאַב *to draw* (water). § 36.

שָׁאַל *to ask* (§ 36); לְ *in reference to.*

שְׁאוֹל *c., Sheol, the underworld.*

שָׁאוּל *Saul.*

שָׁאַר *to be left over, to remain* (Qal rare).—Hiph. *to leave over.*—Niph. *pass.*

שָׁבָה § 44 f., *to take captive.*

שֵׁבֶט 2 *m., rod, sceptre, tribe.*

שֶׁבַע 2 *seven;* שְׁבִיעִי *seventh.* § 48.

שבע Qal not in use.—Niph. *to swear* (§ 37).

שָׁבַר *to break.*—Niph. *pass.* Ptc. נִשְׁבָּר *broken.*—Pi. *to break in pieces.*

שֶׁבֶר 2 *i.,* and שֵׁבֶר 1 *m., breach.*

שָׁבַר *to buy or sell corn.*

שֶׁבֶר 2 *m., grain, corn.*

שָׁבַת *to rest, cease.*—Hiph. *to finish.*

שַׁבָּת 1 *c., rest, sabbath.*

שַׁדַּי *m., almighty* (?) generally with אֵל *God.*

שׁוּב *to turn, return* (§ 40).—Hiph. *to restore, bring back.*

שׁוֹפָר 1 *c., a trumpet.* Pl. ôth.

שׁוּק 2 *m., street.* Pl. שְׁוָקִים. § 41.

שׁוֹר 2 *m., ox.* Pl. שְׁוָרִים. § 41.

שָׁחַט *to slay, slaughter* (§ 36, Parad.).

שַׁחַר 2 *m., dawn.*

שחת Qal not in use.—Pi. שִׁחֵת *to destroy* (§ 36).—Hiph. *id.; to act corruptly, to corrupt.*—Niph. *pass.*

שִׁיר 2 *m., a song;* f. *id.* § 41.

שִׁית *to set, place* (§ 40).

שָׁכַב *to lie down* (st. § 22).

שָׁכַח *to forget* (§ 37). — Niph. *pass.*

שָׁכַל *to be bereaved* (of children) (st. § 22).

שְׁכֶם *m., shoulder.* Suff. שִׁכְמוֹ.

שָׁכַן *to dwell.*—Impf. יִשְׁכֹּן (§ 22. 2). Hiph. *to cause to dwell, place.*

מִשְׁכָּן 1 m., *dwelling, tabernacle.*

שָׁכַר *to be drunken* (st. § 22).

שָׁלַח *to send, stretch out.*—Pi. *send away; let go.*

שֻׁלְחָן 2 c., *a table.*

שׁלך Qal not in use.—Hiph. *to cast, cast off.*—Hoph. *pass.*

שָׁלֵם *to be whole, sound* (st. § 22). —Pi. *to complete, perform, pay.*

שָׁלֵם 1 adj., *whole, sound.*

שָׁלוֹם 1 m., *soundness, health, peace.*

שָׁלֹשׁ 1 adj., *three.* § 48.

שָׁם adv., *there;* שָׁמָּה *thither;* מִשָּׁם *from there, thence.*

שֵׁם 3 m., *a name.* Pl. שֵׁמוֹת. § 30. 2.

שׁמד Qal not in use.—Hiph. *to destroy.*—Niph. *pass.*

שְׁמוּאֵל *Samuel.*

שָׁמַיִם 1 pl., *heaven, heavens.* § 16. 5.

שָׁמֵם *to be desolate* (§ 42). Impf. יִשֹּׁם, יְשֹׁם and יֵשַׁם.—Hiph. *to desolate.*—Niph. *pass.*

שָׁמַע *to hear, listen to,* אל, ל, ב (§ 22).—Niph. *pass.*

שֵׁמַע 2 m., *a report.*

שָׁמַר *to keep, watch.*—Niph. *to take heed, beware.*—Hithp. *to keep oneself.*

שֹׁמֵר 3 ptc., *watchman.*

מִשְׁמָר 1 m., and מִשְׁמֶרֶת f., *ward, watch, observance.* § 29. 3.

שֶׁמֶשׁ 2 c., *the sun.*

שִׁמְשׁוֹן *Samson.*

שָׁנָה 1 f., *a year.* Pl. שָׁנִים (Poet. *ôth*).

שְׁנַיִם du., *two.* § 48.

שֵׁנִי 1 adj., *second.* § 48.

שׁען Qal not in use.—Niph. *to lean, rest on.*

שַׁעַר 2 c., *a gate.*

שִׁפְחָה 2 f., *handmaid.*

שָׁפַט *to judge.*—Niph. *to litigate.*

שֹׁפֵט 3 ptc., *a judge.*

מִשְׁפָּט 1 m., *judgment.*

שָׁפַךְ *to pour out, spill.*—Niph. *pass.*

שָׁפֵל *to be low, abased* (st. § 22).

שָׁקַל *to weigh.*—Niph. *pass.*

שָׁרַץ *to swarm; with acc.*

שֶׁרֶץ 2 m., *creeping things.*

שׁרת Qal not in use.—Pi. שֵׁרֵת *to serve, minister* (§ 36).

שׁקה See next word.

שָׁתָה *to drink* (§ 44).—Impf. apoc. יֵשְׁתְּ.— Niph. *pass.*— Hiph. הִשְׁקָה *to give drink, to water.*

מַשְׁקֶה m. ptc., *a cupbearer, butler;* also *butlership.*

מִשְׁתֶּה m., *a feast.*

שׂ

שָׂבַע *to be sated, satisfied* (st. § 37); *with, acc.*—Hiph. *to satisfy; one with—, two acc.*

שָׂדֶה (שָׂדַי poet.) 1 m., *a field.* § 45. 3.

שָׂחַק *to laugh* (§ 36); Pi. *to play, sport.*

שִׂיחָה f., *meditation.*

שִׂים *to set, place* (§ 40).

שֵׂכֶל 2 i. m., *understanding.*

שָׂמַח, שָׂמֵחַ *to rejoice, be glad* (§ 37).

שָׂמֵחַ adj., *glad, joyful.*

שָׂנֵא *to hate* (§ 38. st.).

שָׂפָה 1 f., *lip, edge, bank;* du. שְׂפָתַיִם. pp. 68 f.

שָׂרָה *Sarah.*

שָׂרַף *to burn.*—Niph. *pass.*

שָׂרָף 1 m., *a seraph.*

שַׂר 1 m., *a prince, captain.* § 43.

ת

תֵּבָה 1 f., *ark* (ē firm).

תָּוֶךְ 2 m., *midst;* cstr. תּוֹךְ, § 41. בְּתוֹכִי *within me.*

תּוֹלְדוֹת pl. f., *generations, history* (see יָלַד).

תּוֹרָה f., *instruction, law* (ירה).

תַּחַת prep., *under, beneath, instead of.*—Suff. תַּחְתִּי. § 36. 2.

תָּמַם *to be complete, ended* (§ 42)—Impf. יִתֹּם.—Hiph. *to complete, finish.*

תָּם 1 adj., *complete, perfect* (§ 43).

תָּמִים 1 adj., *id.*

תָּמִיד adv., *continually.*

תֹּמֶר 2 m., *a palm tree.*

תִּפְאָרָה and תִּפְאֶרֶת 2 f., *glory.*

תְּפִלָּה *prayer.*

תָּקַע *to strike, blow* (a trumpet).

תַּרְדֵּמָה f., *a deep sleep* (רדם).

תְּשׁוּעָה. See ישע.

PARADIGMS OF VERBS AND NOUNS

THE REGULAR

	Qal act.	Qal stat.		Niph'al
Perf. Sing. 3 m.	קָטַל	כָּבֵד	קָטֹן	נִקְטַל
3 f.	קָטְלָה	כָּבְדָה	קָטְנָה	נִקְטְלָה
2 m.	קָטַלְתָּ	כָּבַדְתָּ	קָטֹנְתָּ	נִקְטַלְתָּ
2 f.	קָטַלְתְּ	כָּבַדְתְּ	קָטֹנְתְּ	נִקְטַלְתְּ
1 c.	קָטַלְתִּי	כָּבַדְתִּי	קָטֹנְתִּי	נִקְטַלְתִּי
Plur. 3 c.	קָטְלוּ	כָּבְדוּ	קָטְנוּ	נִקְטְלוּ
2 m.	קְטַלְתֶּם	כְּבַדְתֶּם	קְטָנְתֶּם	נִקְטַלְתֶּם
2 f.	קְטַלְתֶּן	כְּבַדְתֶּן	קְטָנְתֶּן	נִקְטַלְתֶּן
1 c.	קָטַלְנוּ	כָּבַדְנוּ	קָטֹנּוּ	נִקְטַלְנוּ
Impf. Sing. 3 m.	יִקְטֹל	יִכְבַּד	יִקְטַן	יִקָּטֵל
3 f.	תִּקְטֹל	תִּכְבַּד		תִּקָּטֵל
2 m.	תִּקְטֹל	תִּכְבַּד		תִּקָּטֵל
2 f.	תִּקְטְלִי (ין)	תִּכְבְּדִי		תִּקָּטְלִי
1 c.	אֶקְטֹל	אֶכְבַּד		אֶקָּטֵל (אִקָּטֵל)
Plur. 3 m.	יִקְטְלוּ (וּן)	יִכְבְּדוּ		יִקָּטְלוּ
3 f.	תִּקְטֹלְנָה	תִּכְבַּדְנָה		תִּקָּטַלְנָה
2 m.	תִּקְטְלוּ (וּן)	תִּכְבְּדוּ		תִּקָּטְלוּ
2 f.	תִּקְטֹלְנָה	תִּכְבַּדְנָה		תִּקָּטַלְנָה
1 c.	נִקְטֹל	נִכְבַּד		נִקָּטֵל
Imp. Sing. 2 m.	קְטֹל (קָטְלָה)	כְּבַד (כִּבְדָה)		הִקָּטֵל (הִקָּטֵל)
2 f.	קִטְלִי (קָטְלִי)	כִּבְדִי		הִקָּטְלִי
Plur. 2 m.	קִטְלוּ	כִּבְדוּ		הִקָּטְלוּ
2 f.	קְטֹלְנָה	כְּבַדְנָה		הִקָּטַלְנָה
Jussive 3 sing.	יִקְטֹל	יִכְבַּד		יִקָּטֵל (יִקָּטֵל)
waw cons. impf.	וַיִּקְטֹל	וַיִּכְבַּד		וַיִּקָּטֵל (וַיִּקָּטֵל)
Cohortative 1 sing.	אֶקְטְלָה	אֶכְבְּדָה		אֶקָּטְלָה
waw cons. perf.	וְקָטַלְתָּ	&c.		
Inf. cstr.	קְטֹל	כְּבַד (כְּבֹד)		הִקָּטֵל
absol.	קָטוֹל	כָּבוֹד		הִקָּטֹל, נִקְטֹל
Part. act.	קֹטֵל	כָּבֵד	קָטֹן	
pass.	קָטוּל			נִקְטָל

VERB. §§ 20—28.

Piël	Puäl	Hithpaël	Hiphïl	Hophäl
קִטֵּל (קַטֵּל)	קֻטַּל	הִתְקַטֵּל (יִתְקַטֵּל)	הִקְטִיל	הָקְטַל
קִטְּלָה	קֻטְּלָה	הִתְקַטְּלָה	הִקְטִילָה	הָקְטְלָה
קִטַּלְתָּ	קֻטַּלְתָּ	הִתְקַטַּלְתָּ	הִקְטַלְתָּ	הָקְטַלְתָּ
קִטַּלְתְּ	קֻטַּלְתְּ	הִתְקַטַּלְתְּ	הִקְטַלְתְּ	הָקְטַלְתְּ
קִטַּלְתִּי	קֻטַּלְתִּי	הִתְקַטַּלְתִּי	הִקְטַלְתִּי	הָקְטַלְתִּי
קִטְּלוּ	קֻטְּלוּ	הִתְקַטְּלוּ	הִקְטִילוּ	הָקְטְלוּ
קִטַּלְתֶּם	קֻטַּלְתֶּם	הִתְקַטַּלְתֶּם	הִקְטַלְתֶּם	הָקְטַלְתֶּם
קִטַּלְתֶּן	קֻטַּלְתֶּן	הִתְקַטַּלְתֶּן	הִקְטַלְתֶּן	הָקְטַלְתֶּן
קִטַּלְנוּ	קֻטַּלְנוּ	הִתְקַטַּלְנוּ	הִקְטַלְנוּ	הָקְטַלְנוּ
יְקַטֵּל	יְקֻטַּל	יִתְקַטֵּל	יַקְטִיל	יָקְטַל
תְּקַטֵּל	תְּקֻטַּל	תִּתְקַטֵּל	תַּקְטִיל	תָּקְטַל
תְּקַטֵּל	תְּקֻטַּל	תִּתְקַטֵּל	תַּקְטִיל	תָּקְטַל
תְּקַטְּלִי	תְּקֻטְּלִי	תִּתְקַטְּלִי	תַּקְטִילִי	תָּקְטְלִי
אֲקַטֵּל	אֲקֻטַּל	אֶתְקַטֵּל	אַקְטִיל	אָקְטַל
יְקַטְּלוּ	יְקֻטְּלוּ	יִתְקַטְּלוּ	יַקְטִילוּ	יָקְטְלוּ
תְּקַטֵּלְנָה	תְּקֻטַּלְנָה	תִּתְקַטֵּלְנָה	תַּקְטֵלְנָה	תָּקְטַלְנָה
תְּקַטְּלוּ	תְּקֻטְּלוּ	תִּתְקַטְּלוּ	תַּקְטִילוּ	תָּקְטְלוּ
תְּקַטֵּלְנָה	תְּקֻטַּלְנָה	תִּתְקַטֵּלְנָה	תַּקְטֵלְנָה	תָּקְטַלְנָה
נְקַטֵּל	נְקֻטַּל	נִתְקַטֵּל	נַקְטִיל	נָקְטַל
קַטֵּל		הִתְקַטֵּל	הַקְטֵל	
קַטְּלִי		הִתְקַטְּלִי	הַקְטִילִי	
קַטְּלוּ	wanting	הִתְקַטְּלוּ	הַקְטִילוּ	wanting
קַטֵּלְנָה		הִתְקַטֵּלְנָה	הַקְטֵלְנָה	
יְקַטֵּל	יְקֻטַּל	יִתְקַטֵּל	יַקְטֵל	&c.
וַיְקַטֵּל	וַיְקֻטַּל	וַיִּתְקַטֵּל	וַיַּקְטֵל	
אֲקַטְּלָה		אֶתְקַטְּלָה	אַקְטִילָה	
קַטֵּל	(קֻטַּל)	הִתְקַטֵּל	הַקְטִיל	(הָקְטֵל)
קַטֹּל, קַטֵּל	קֻטֹּל	(הִתְקַטֵּל)	הַקְטֵל	(הָקְטֵל)
מְקַטֵּל		מִתְקַטֵּל	מַקְטִיל	
	מְקֻטָּל			מָקְטָל

THE VERBAL SUFFIXES

See also suffixes to

Qal

Perf.	**3** *s. m.*	**3** *s. f.*	**2** *s. m.*	**2** *s. f.*
Suff.	קָטַל כָּבֵד	קְטָלָה	קְטַלְתָּ	קְטַלְתְּ
s. 1 c.	קְטָלַנִי כְּבֵד'	קְטָלַתְנִי כְּבֵד'	קְטַלְתַּנִי	קְטַלְתִּינִי [1]
2 m.	קְטָלְךָ כְּבֵדְךָ	קְטָלַתְךָ	—	—
2 f.	קְטָלֵךְ &c. ‑ָךְ	קְטָלָתֶךְ	—	—
3 m.	קְטָלוֹ	קְטָלַתְהוּ —תּוּ תָּ‑הוּ	קְטַלְתּוֹ	קְטַלְתִּיהוּ
3 f.	קְטָלָהּ	קְטָלַתָּה	קְטַלְתָּהּ	קְטַלְתִּיהָ
pl. 1 c.	קְטָלָנוּ	קְטָלַתְנוּ	קְטַלְתָּנוּ	קְטַלְתִּינוּ
2 m.	קְטָלְכֶם כְּבֵד'	—	—	—
2 f.	קְטָלְכֶן	—	—	—
3 m.	קְטָלָם	קְטָלָתַם	קְטַלְתָּם	קְטַלְתִּים
3 f.	קְטָלָן	קְטָלָתַן	קְטַלְתָּן	קְטַלְתִּין

Impf.	**3** *s. m.*	**3** *pl. m.*	*Imper. s.*	*pl.*
Suff.	יִקְטֹל יִכְבַּד	יִקְטְלוּ	קְטֹל כְּבַד	קִטְלוּ
s. 1 c.	יִקְטְלֵנִי יִכְבְּדֵנִי	יִקְטְלוּנִי יִכְבָּד'	קָטְלֵנִי [2] כְּבָד'	קִטְלוּנִי כְּבָד'
2 m.	יִקְטָלְךָ יִכְבָּדְךָ	יִקְטְלוּךָ	—	—
2 f.	יִקְטְלֵךְ &c.	יִקְטְלוּךְ	—	—
3 m.	יִקְטְלֵהוּ	יִקְטְלוּהוּ	קָטְלֵהוּ	&c.
3 f.	יִקְטְלֶהָ (‑ָהּ)	יִקְטְלוּהָ	קָטְלֶהָ (‑ָהּ)	as in
pl. 1 c.	יִקְטְלֵנוּ	יִקְטְלֵנוּ	קָטְלֵנוּ	imperf.
2 m.	יִקְטָלְכֶם יִכְבָּד'	יִקְטְלוּכֶם יִכְב'	—	plural
2 f.	יִקְטָלְכֶן	יִקְטְלוּכֶן	—	
3 m.	יִקְטְלֵם	יִקְטְלוּם	קָטְלֵם	
3 f.	יִקְטְלֵן	יִקְטְלוּן	קָטְלֵן	

And so all parts of impf. ending in a Consonant,

So 2 *pl. m.,* and 2, 3 *pl. f.* which becomes תִּקְטְלוּ.

[1] This column may be also written defectively, e.g. קְטַלְתִּנִי, &c.   [2] The first syll. throughout imperative is half-open, e.g. כָּתְבֵנִי.

REGULAR VERB.   § 31.

Lamedh He verbs, p. 229.

	Qal			Pi‘ēl
1 s. c.	*3 pl. c.*	*2 pl. c.*	*1 pl. c.*	*3 s. m.*
קְטַלְתִּי	קְטָלוּ	קְטַלְתֶּם	קְטַלְנוּ	קִטֵּל
—	קְטָלוּנִי כָּבֵד'	קְטַלְתּוּנִי	—	קִטְּלַנִי
קְטַלְתִּיךָ	קְטָלוּךָ	—	קְטַלְנוּךָ	קִטֶּלְךָ
קְטַלְתִּיךְ	קְטָלוּךְ	—	&c.	קִטְּלֶךְ
—יד	קְטַלְתִּיהוּ	&c.	as 3 *pl.*	קִטְּלוֹ
קְטַלְתִּיהָ	קְטָלוּהָ	as 3 *pl.*		קִטְּלָהּ
—	קְטָלוּנוּ		—	קִטְּלָנוּ
קְטַלְתִּיכֶם		—		קִטֶּלְכֶם
קְטַלְתִּיכֶן		—		קִטֶּלְכֶן
קְטַלְתִּים	קְטָלוּם			קִטְּלָם
קְטַלְתִּין	קְטָלוּן			קִטְּלָן

Impf. and imper. with nûn energ.		*Infin. cstr.*		
		קְטֹל	כְּבֹד	יְקַטֵּל
יַקְטְלֶנִּי יִקְבְּ'	קְטָלֵנִּי כָּבְ'	קָטְלִי (ֶנִי)	כְּבְדִי	יְקַטְּלֵנִי
יִקְטְלֶךָ		קָטְלְךָ קָטְלֶךָ	כְּבָדְךָ	יְקַטֶּלְךָ
—		קָטְלֵךְ	כְּבָדֵךְ	יְקַטְּלֶךָ
יִקְטְלֶנּוּ	קְטָלֵנּוּ	קָטְלוֹ (ֶהוּ) &c.		יְקַטְּלֵהוּ
יִקְטְלֶנָּה	קְטָלֶנָּה	קָטְלָהּ		יְקַטְּלָהּ
		קָטְלֵנוּ		יְקַטְּלֵנוּ
		קָטְלְכֶם	כְּבָדְ'	יְקַטְּלֵכֶם
		קָטְלְכֶן		יְקַטְּלְכֶן
		קָטְלָם		יְקַטְּלֵם
		קָטְלָן		יְקַטְּלֵן

For the use and meaning of these suff.
see § 31. 9 a.

The first syll. is half-open: e.g. כְּתְבוּ,
except before ךָ and כֶם, where it is closed,
e.g. כִּבְדְּךָ, כְּתָבְךָ ; cf. § 31. 3 c.

PE NUN VERB. § 33.

	Qal		Niph.	Hiph.	Hoph.
Perf. Sing. 3 m.	(נָגַשׁ)	נָפַל	נִגַּשׁ	הִגִּישׁ	הֻגַּשׁ
3 f.			נִגְּשָׁה	הִגִּישָׁה	הֻגְּשָׁה
2 m.			נִגַּשְׁתָּ	הִגַּשְׁתָּ	הֻגַּשְׁתָּ
Impf. Sing. 3 m.	יִגַּשׁ	יִפֹּל	יִנָּגֵשׁ	יַגִּישׁ	יֻגַּשׁ
3 f.	תִּגַּשׁ	תִּפֹּל	&c.	תַּגִּישׁ	
2 m.	תִּגַּשׁ	תִּפֹּל		תַּגִּישׁ	
2 f.	תִּגְּשִׁי	תִּפְּלִי		תַּגִּישִׁי	
1 c.	אֶגַּשׁ	אֶפֹּל		אַגִּישׁ	
Plur. 3 m.	יִגְּשׁוּ	יִפְּלוּ		יַגִּישׁוּ	
3 f.	תִּגַּשְׁנָה	תִּפֹּלְנָה		תַּגֵּשְׁנָה	
2 m.	תִּגְּשׁוּ	תִּפְּלוּ		תַּגִּישׁוּ	
2 f.	תִּגַּשְׁנָה	תִּפֹּלְנָה		תַּגֵּשְׁנָה	
1 c.	נִגַּשׁ	נִפֹּל		נַגִּישׁ	
Imp. Sing. 2 m.	גַּשׁ (גְּשָׁה)	נְפֹל	הִנָּגֵשׁ	הַגֵּשׁ	
2 f.	גְּשִׁי	נִפְלִי	הִנָּגְשִׁי	הַגִּישִׁי	
Plur. 2 m.	גְּשׁוּ	נִפְלוּ	הִנָּגְשׁוּ	הַגִּישׁוּ	wanting
2 f.	גַּשְׁנָה	נְפֹלְנָה	הִנָּגַשְׁנָה	הַגֵּשְׁנָה	
Juss. 3 sing.				יַגֵּשׁ	
waw cons. impf.				וַיַּגֵּשׁ	
Cohort. 1 sing.	אֶגְּשָׁה			אַגִּישָׁה	
waw cons. perf.	וְנִגַּשְׁתָּ				
Inf. cstr.	גֶּשֶׁת	נְפֹל	הִנָּגֵשׁ	הַגִּישׁ	הֻגַּשׁ
absol.	נָגוֹשׁ	נָפוֹל	הִנָּגֵשׁ	הַגֵּשׁ	הֻגֵּשׁ
Part. act.	נֹגֵשׁ	נֹפֵל	נִגָּשׁ	מַגִּישׁ	
pass.	נָגוּשׁ	—			מֻגָּשׁ

PE NUN VERB. § 33.

	Qal		Niph.	Pass. Qal
Perf. Sing. 3 m.	נָתַן	לָקַח	נִלְקַח, נִתַּן	לֻקַּח
3 f.	נָתְנָה	לָקְחָה		
2 m.	נָתַתָּ, נָתַתָּה	לָקַחְתָּ		
2 f.	נָתַתְּ	&c.		
1 c.	נָתַתִּי			
Plur. 3 c.	נָתְנוּ			
2 m.	נְתַתֶּם			
2 f.				
1 c.	נָתַנּוּ			
impf. Sing. 3 m.	יִתֵּן	יִקַּח	יִקַּח, יִנָּתֵן	יֻקַּח, יֻתַּן, יֻלְקַח
3 f.	תִּתֵּן	תִּקַּח		
2 m.	תִּתֵּן	תִּקַּח		
2 f.	תִּתְּנִי	תִּקְּחִי		
1 c.	אֶתֵּן, אֶתְּנָה	אֶקַּח		
Plur. 3 m.	יִתְּנוּ	יִקְּחוּ		
3 f.				
2 m.	תִּתְּנוּ	תִּקְּחוּ		
2 f.				
1 c.	נִתֵּן	נִקַּח		
Imp. Sing. 2 m.	תֵּן, תְּנָה	קַח, קְחָה		
2 f.	תְּנִי	קְחִי		
Plur. 2 m.	תְּנוּ	קְחוּ		
2 f.				
Juss. 3 *sing.*	יִתֵּן	יִקַּח		
waw cons. impf.	וַיִּתֵּן	וַיִּקַּח		
Inf. cstr.	תֵּת, תִּתִּי (נְתֹן)	לָקַחַת, קַחְתִּי	הִלָּקַח, הִנָּתֵן	
abs.	נָתוֹן	לָקוֹחַ	הִנָּתֹן	
Part. act.	נֹתֵן	לֹקֵחַ		
pass.	נָתוּן	לָקוּחַ	נִתָּן	

PE GUTTURAL

	Qal		Niph.
	act.	stat.	
Perf. Sing. 3 m.	עָמַד חָתַם	חָזַק חָכַם	נֶעֱמַד נֶחְתַּם
3 f.	עָמְדָה		נֶעֶמְדָה
2 m.	עָמַדְתָּ		נֶעֱמַדְתָּ
2 f.	עָמַדְתְּ		נֶעֱמַדְתְּ
1 c.	עָמַדְתִּי		נֶעֱמַדְתִּי
Plur. 3 c.	עָמְדוּ		נֶעֶמְדוּ
2 m.	עֲמַדְתֶּם		נֶעֱמַדְתֶּם
2 f.	עֲמַדְתֶּן		נֶעֱמַדְתֶּן
1 c.	עָמַדְנוּ		נֶעֱמַדְנוּ
Impf. Sing. 3 m.	יַעֲמֹד יַחְתֹּם	יֶחֱזַק יֶחְכַּם	יֵעָמֵד
3 f.	תַּעֲמֹד	תֶּחֱזַק	תֵּעָמֵד
2 m.	תַּעֲמֹד	תֶּחֱזַק	תֵּעָמֵד
2 f.	תַּעַמְדִי	תֶּחֶזְקִי	תֵּעָמְדִי
1 c.	אֶעֱמֹד	אֶחֱזַק	אֵעָמֵד
Plur. 3 m.	יַעַמְדוּ	יֶחֶזְקוּ	יֵעָמְדוּ
3 f.	תַּעֲמֹדְנָה	תֶּחֱזַקְנָה	תֵּעָמַדְנָה
2 m.	תַּעַמְדוּ	תֶּחֶזְקוּ	תֵּעָמְדוּ
2 f.	תַּעֲמֹדְנָה	תֶּחֱזַקְנָה	תֵּעָמַדְנָה
1 c.	נַעֲמֹד	נֶחֱזַק	נֵעָמֵד
Imp. Sing. 2 m.	עֲמֹד	חֲזַק	הֵעָמֵד
2 f.	עִמְדִי	חִזְקִי	הֵעָמְדִי
Plur. 2 m.	עִמְדוּ	חִזְקוּ	הֵעָמְדוּ
2 f.	עֲמֹדְנָה	חֲזַקְנָה	הֵעָמַדְנָה
Juss. 3 sing.			
waw cons. impf.	וַיַּעֲמֹד	וַיֶּחֱזַק	
Cohort. 1 sing.	אֶעֶמְדָה		
waw cons. perf.	וְעָמַדְתָּ		
Inf. cstr.	עֲמֹד		הֵעָמֵד
absol.	עָמוֹד		נַעֲמוֹד נַחְתּוֹם
Part. act.	עֹמֵד		נֶעֱמָד נֶחְתָּם
pass.	עָמוּד		

VERB. § 34.		PE ’ALEPH. § 35.
Hiph.	**Hoph.**	**Qal**
הֶעֱמִיד הָחְתִּים	הָעֳמַד הָחְתַּם	אָכַל
הֶעֱמִידָה	הָעֳמְדָה	
הֶעֱמַדְתָּ	הָעֳמַדְתָּ	
הֶעֱמַדְתְּ	הָעֳמַדְתְּ	
הֶעֱמַדְתִּי	הָעֳמַדְתִּי	
הֶעֱמִידוּ	הָעֳמְדוּ	
הֶעֱמַדְתֶּם	הָעֳמַדְתֶּם	
הֶעֱמַדְתֶּן	הָעֳמַדְתֶּן	
הֶעֱמַדְנוּ	הָעֳמַדְנוּ	
יַעֲמִיד	יָעֳמַד	יֹאכַל
תַּעֲמִיד	תָּעֳמַד	תֹּאכַל
תַּעֲמִיד	תָּעֳמַד	תֹּאכַל
תַּעֲמִידִי	תָּעֳמְדִי	תֹּאכְלִי
אַעֲמִיד	אָעֳמַד	אֹכַל
יַעֲמִידוּ	יָעֳמְדוּ	יֹאכְלוּ
תַּעֲמֵדְנָה	תָּעֳמַדְנָה	תֹּאכַלְנָה
תַּעֲמִידוּ	תָּעֳמְדוּ	תֹּאכְלוּ
תַּעֲמֵדְנָה	תָּעֳמַדְנָה	תֹּאכַלְנָה
נַעֲמִיד	נָעֳמַד	נֹאכַל
הַעֲמֵד		אֱכֹל
הַעֲמִידִי		אִכְלִי
הַעֲמִידוּ	wanting	אִכְלוּ
הַעֲמֵדְנָה		אֱכֹלְנָה
יַעֲמֵד		
וַיַּעֲמֵד		וַיֹּאכַל (וַיֹּאמֶר)
אַעֲמִידָה		אָכְלָה
וְהַעֲמַדְתָּ		
הַעֲמִיד &c.		אֹכֵל
הָעֲמֵד	הָעֳמֵד &c.	אָכוֹל
מַעֲמִיד &c.	מָעֳמָד &c.	אֹכֵל
		אָכוּל

'AYIN GUTTURAL

	Qal	Niph'al	
Perf. Sing. 3 m.	(נָחַם) שָׁחַט	נִשְׁחַט	נָחַם
3 f.	שָׁחֲטָה	נִשְׁחֲטָה	
2 m.	שָׁחַטְתָּ	נִשְׁחַטְתָּ	
2 f.	שָׁחַטְתְּ	נִשְׁחַטְתְּ	
1 c.	שָׁחַטְתִּי	נִשְׁחַטְתִּי	
Plur. 3 c.	שָׁחֲטוּ	נִשְׁחֲטוּ	
2 m.	שְׁחַטְתֶּם	נִשְׁחַטְתֶּם	
2 f.	שְׁחַטְתֶּן	נִשְׁחַטְתֶּן	
1 c.	שָׁחַטְנוּ	נִשְׁחַטְנוּ	
Impf. Sing. 3 m.	יִשְׁחַט	יִשָּׁחֵט	יִנָּחֵם
3 f.	תִּשְׁחַט	תִּשָּׁחֵט	
2 m.	תִּשְׁחַט	תִּשָּׁחֵט	
2 f.	תִּשְׁחֲטִי	תִּשָּׁחֲטִי	
1 c.	אֶשְׁחַט	אֶשָּׁחֵט	
Plur. 3 m.	יִשְׁחֲטוּ	יִשָּׁחֲטוּ	
3 f.	תִּשְׁחַטְנָה	תִּשָּׁחַטְנָה	
2 m.	תִּשְׁחֲטוּ	תִּשָּׁחֲטוּ	
2 f.	תִּשְׁחַטְנָה	תִּשָּׁחַטְנָה	
1 c.	נִשְׁחַט	נִשָּׁחֵט	
Imp. Sing. 2 m.	שְׁחַט	הִשָּׁחֵט	הִנָּחֵם
2 f.	שַׁחֲטִי	הִשָּׁחֲטִי	
Plur. 2 m.	שַׁחֲטוּ	הִשָּׁחֲטוּ	
2 f.	שְׁחַטְנָה	הִשָּׁחַטְנָה	
Juss. 3 sing.	יִשְׁחַט	&c.	
waw cons. impf.	וַיִּשְׁחַט	&c.	
impf. with suff.	יִשְׁחָטֵנִי	&c.	
Inf. cstr.	שְׁחֹט	הִשָּׁחֵט	הִנָּחֵם
absol.	שָׁחוֹט	נִשְׁחוֹט	
Part. act.	שֹׁחֵט	נִשְׁחָט	נֶחָם
pass.	שָׁחוּט		

VERBS. § 36.

Pi'ēl		Pu'al		Hithp.
נֵחַם	בֵּרַךְ	נֻחַם	בֹּרַךְ	הִתְבָּרַךְ הִתְנַחֵם
	בֵּרְכָה		בֹּרְכָה	הִתְבָּרְכָה
	בֵּרַ֫כְתָּ		בֹּרַ֫כְתָּ	הִתְבָּרַ֫כְתָּ
	בֵּרַכְתְּ		בֹּרַכְתְּ	הִתְבָּרַכְתְּ
	בֵּרַ֫כְתִּי		בֹּרַ֫כְתִּי	הִתְבָּרַ֫כְתִּי
	בֵּרְכוּ		בֹּרְכוּ	הִתְבָּרְכוּ
	בֵּרַכְתֶּם		בֹּרַכְתֶּם	הִתְבָּרַכְתֶּם
	בֵּרַכְתֶּן		בֹּרַכְתֶּן	הִתְבָּרַכְתֶּן
	בֵּרַ֫כְנוּ		בֹּרַ֫כְנוּ	הִתְבָּרַ֫כְנוּ
יְנַחֵם	יְבָרֵךְ	יְנֻחַם	יְבֹרַךְ	יִתְנַחֵם יִתְבָּרֵךְ
	תְּבָרֵךְ		תְּבֹרַךְ	תִּתְבָּרֵךְ
	תְּבָרֵךְ		תְּבֹרַךְ	תִּתְבָּרֵךְ
	תְּבָרְכִי		תְּבֹרְכִי	תִּתְבָּרְכִי
	אֲבָרֵךְ		אֲבֹרַךְ	אֶתְבָּרֵךְ
	יְבָרְכוּ		יְבֹרְכוּ	יִתְבָּרְכוּ
	תְּבָרֵ֫כְנָה		תְּבֹרַ֫כְנָה	תִּתְבָּרַ֫כְנָה
	תְּבָרְכוּ		תְּבֹרְכוּ	תִּתְבָּרְכוּ
	תְּבָרֵ֫כְנָה		תְּבֹרַ֫כְנָה	תִּתְבָּרַ֫כְנָה
	נְבָרֵךְ		נְבֹרַךְ	נִתְבָּרֵךְ
נַחֵם	בָּרֵךְ			הִתְנַחֵם הִתְבָּרֵךְ
	בָּרְכִי			הִתְבָּרְכִי
	בָּרְכוּ			הִתְבָּרְכוּ
	בָּרֵ֫כְנָה			הִתְבָּרֵ֫כְנָה
נַחֵם בָּרֵךְ		נֻחַם בֹּרַךְ		הִתְנַחֵם הִתְבָּרֵךְ
בָּרֵךְ				
מְנַחֵם מְבָרֵךְ		מְנֻחָם מְבֹרָךְ		מִתְנַחֵם מִתְבָּרֵךְ
		מְנֻחָם מְבֹרָךְ		

LAMEDH GUTTURAL

	Qal	Niph.	Pi'el
Perf. Sing. 3 *m.*	שָׁלַח	נִשְׁלַח	שִׁלַּח
3 *f.*	שָׁלְחָה	נִשְׁלְחָה	שִׁלְּחָה
2 *m.*	שָׁלַחְתָּ	נִשְׁלַחְתָּ	שִׁלַּחְתָּ
2 *f.*	שָׁלַחַתְּ	נִשְׁלַחַתְּ	שִׁלַּחַתְּ
1 *c.*	שָׁלַחְתִּי	&c.	&c.
Plur. 3 *c.*	שָׁלְחוּ		
2 *m.*	שְׁלַחְתֶּם		
2 *f.*	שְׁלַחְתֶּן		
1 *c.*	שָׁלַחְנוּ		
Impf. Sing. 3 *m.*	יִשְׁלַח	יִשָּׁלַח	יְשַׁלַּח
3 *f.*	תִּשְׁלַח	תִּשָּׁלַח	תְּשַׁלַּח
2 *m.*	תִּשְׁלַח	תִּשָּׁלַח	תְּשַׁלַּח
2 *f.*	תִּשְׁלְחִי	תִּשָּׁלְחִי	תְּשַׁלְּחִי
1 *c.*	אֶשְׁלַח	אֶשָּׁלַח	אֲשַׁלַּח
Plur. 3 *m.*	יִשְׁלְחוּ	יִשָּׁלְחוּ	יְשַׁלְּחוּ
3 *f.*	תִּשְׁלַחְנָה	תִּשָּׁלַחְנָה	תְּשַׁלַּחְנָה
2 *m.*	תִּשְׁלְחוּ	תִּשָּׁלְחוּ	תְּשַׁלְּחוּ
2 *f.*	תִּשְׁלַחְנָה	תִּשָּׁלַחְנָה	תְּשַׁלַּחְנָה
1 *c.*	נִשְׁלַח	נִשָּׁלַח	נְשַׁלַּח
Imp. Sing. 2 *m.*	שְׁלַח	הִשָּׁלַח	שַׁלַּח
2 *f.*	שִׁלְחִי	הִשָּׁלְחִי	
Plur. 2 *m.*	שִׁלְחוּ	הִשָּׁלְחוּ	
2 *f.*	שְׁלַחְנָה	הִשָּׁלַחְנָה	
Juss. 3 *sing.*			
waw cons. impf.			
impf. with suff.	יִשְׁלָחֵנִי	&c.	
Inf. cstr.	שְׁלֹחַ	הִשָּׁלַח	שַׁלַּח
absol.	שָׁלוֹחַ	נִשְׁלֹחַ	שַׁלֵּחַ
Part. act.	שֹׁלֵחַ	נִשְׁלָח	מְשַׁלֵּחַ
pass.	שָׁלוּחַ		

VERBS. § 37.

Pu'al	Hithp.	Hiph.	Hoph.
שֻׁלַּח	הִשְׁתַּלַּח	הִשְׁלִיחַ	הָשְׁלַח
שֻׁלְּחָה	הִשְׁתַּלְּחָה	הִשְׁלִיחָה	הָשְׁלְחָה
שֻׁלַּחְתָּ	הִשְׁתַּלַּחְתָּ	הִשְׁלַחְתָּ	הָשְׁלַחְתָּ
שֻׁלַּחַתְּ	הִשְׁתַּלַּחַתְּ	הִשְׁלַחַתְּ	הָשְׁלַחַתְּ
&c.	&c.	הִשְׁלַחְתִּי	&c.
		הִשְׁלִיחוּ	
		הִשְׁלַחְתֶּם	
		הִשְׁלַחְתֶּן	
		הִשְׁלַחְנוּ	
יְשֻׁלַּח	יִשְׁתַּלַּח	יַשְׁלִיחַ	יָשְׁלַח
		תַּשְׁלִיחַ	
		תַּשְׁלִיחַ	
		תַּשְׁלִיחִי	
		אַשְׁלִיחַ	
		יַשְׁלִיחוּ	
		תַּשְׁלַחְנָה	
		תַּשְׁלִיחוּ	
		תַּשְׁלַחְנָה	
		נַשְׁלִיחַ	
	הִשְׁתַּלַּח	הַשְׁלַח	
wanting		הַשְׁלִיחִי	wanting
		הַשְׁלִיחוּ	
		הַשְׁלַחְנָה	
		יַשְׁלַח	
		וַיַּשְׁלַח	
	הִשְׁתַּלֵּחַ	הַשְׁלִיחַ	
		הַשְׁלֵחַ	הָשְׁלֵחַ
	מִשְׁתַּלֵּחַ	מַשְׁלִיחַ	
מְשֻׁלָּח			מָשְׁלָח

LAMEDH 'ALEPH

	Qal		Niph.
Perf. Sing. 3 *m.*	מָצָא	מָלֵא	נִמְצָא
3 *f.*	מָצְאָה	מָלְאָה	נִמְצְאָה
2 *m.*	מָצָאתָ	מָלֵאתָ	נִמְצֵאתָ
2 *f.*	מָצָאת	מָלֵאת	נִמְצֵאת
1 *c.*	מָצָאתִי	מָלֵאתִי	נִמְצֵאתִי
Plur. 3 *c.*	מָצְאוּ	מָלְאוּ	נִמְצְאוּ
2 *m.*	מְצָאתֶם	מְלֵאתֶם	נִמְצֵאתֶם
2 *f.*	מְצָאתֶן	מְלֵאתֶן	נִמְצֵאתֶן
1 *c.*	מָצָאנוּ	מָלֵאנוּ	נִמְצֵאנוּ
Impf. Sing. 3 *m.*	יִמְצָא	&c.	יִמָּצֵא
3 *f.*	תִּמְצָא		תִּמָּצֵא
2 *m.*	תִּמְצָא		תִּמָּצֵא
2 *f.*	תִּמְצְאִי		תִּמָּצְאִי
1 *c.*	אֶמְצָא		אֶמָּצֵא
Plur. 3 *m.*	יִמְצְאוּ		יִמָּצְאוּ
3 *f.*	תִּמְצֶאנָה		תִּמָּצֶאנָה
2 *m.*	תִּמְצְאוּ		תִּמָּצְאוּ
2 *f.*	תִּמְצֶאנָה		תִּמָּצֶאנָה
1 *c.*	נִמְצָא		נִמָּצֵא
Imp. Sing. 2 *m.*	מְצָא		הִמָּצֵא
2 *f.*	מִצְאִי		הִמָּצְאִי
Plur. 2 *m.*	מִצְאוּ		הִמָּצְאוּ
2 *f.*	מְצֶאנָה		הִמָּצֶאנָה
Juss. 3 *sing.*			
waw cons. impf.			
waw cons. perf.	וּמָצָאתָ		&c.
impf. with suff.	יִמְצָאֵנִי		
Inf. cstr.	מְצֹא		הִמָּצֵא
absol.	מָצוֹא		נִמְצֹא
Part. act.	מֹצֵא	מָלֵא	נִמְצָא
pass.	מָצוּא		

VERBS.　§ 38.

Pi'ēl	Pu'al	Hithp.	Hiph.	Hoph.
מִצֵּא	מֻצָּא	הִתְמַצֵּא	הִמְצִיא	הֻמְצָא
מִצֵּאָה	מֻצָּאָה	as	הִמְצִיאָה	הֻמְצָאָה
מִצֵּאתָ	מֻצֵּאתָ[1]	Pi.	הִמְצֵאתָ	הֻמְלֵאתָ[1]
&c.	&c.		הִמְצֵאת	as
			הִמְצֵאתִי	Pu.
			הִמְצִיאוּ	
			הִמְצֵאתֶם	
			הִמְצֵאתֶן	
			הִמְצֵאנוּ	
יְמַצֵּא	יְמֻצָּא	יִתְמַצֵּא	יַמְצִיא	יֻמְצָא
as	as	as	תַּמְצִיא	as
Niph.	Qal	Niph.	תַּמְצִיא	Qal
			תַּמְצִיאִי	
			אַמְצִיא	
			יַמְצִיאוּ	
			תַּמְצֶאנָה	
			תַּמְצִיאוּ	
			תַּמְצֶאנָה	
			נַמְצִיא	
מַצֵּא		הִתְמַצֵּא	הַמְצֵא	
	wanting		הַמְצִיאִי	wanting
			הַמְצִיאוּ	
			הַמְצֶאנָה	
			יַמְצֵא	
			וַיַּמְצֵא	
			יַמְצִיאֵנִי	
מַצֵּא		הִתְמַצֵּא	הַמְצִיא	הֻמְצָא
נִמְצָא			הֻמְצָא	
כְּמַצֵּא		כְּהִתְמַצֵּא	מַמְצִיא	
	מְמֻצָּא			מֻמְצָא

---

[1] Or possibly הֻמְצָאתָ, מֻצָּאתָ, &c. The only existing example of a pf. pass.
inflected in a manner to indicate its vowel, is pointed $\bar a$ not $\bar e$. (Ez. 40. 4.)

PE YODH AND PE

Verbs פ"ו.

	Qal			Niph.
Perf. Sing. 3 m.	יָשַׁב	יָרֵא	יָרַשׁ	נוֹשַׁב
3 f.				נוֹשְׁבָה
2 m.				נוֹשַׁבְתָּ
2 f.				&c.
1 c.				
Plur. 3 c.				
2 m.				
2 f.				
1 c.				
Impf. Sing. 3 m.	יֵשֵׁב	יִירָא	יִירַשׁ	יִוָּשֵׁב
3 f.	תֵּשֵׁב			תִּוָּשֵׁב
2 m.	תֵּשֵׁב			תִּוָּשֵׁב
2 f.	תֵּשְׁבִי			תִּוָּשְׁבִי
1 c.	אֵשֵׁב			אִוָּשֵׁב
Plur. 3 m.	יֵשְׁבוּ			יִוָּשְׁבוּ
3 f.	תֵּשַׁבְנָה			תִּוָּשַׁבְנָה
2 m.	תֵּשְׁבוּ			תִּוָּשְׁבוּ
2 f.	תֵּשַׁבְנָה			תִּוָּשַׁבְנָה
1 c.	נֵשֵׁב			נִוָּשֵׁב
Imp. Sing. 2 m.	שֵׁב (שְׁבָה)	יְרָא	רַשׁ (רֵשׁ)	הִוָּשֵׁב
2 f.	שְׁבִי			הִוָּשְׁבִי
Plur. 2 m.	שְׁבוּ			הִוָּשְׁבוּ
2 f.	שֵׁבְנָה			הִוָּשַׁבְנָה
Juss. 3 sing.				
waw cons. impf.	וַיֵּשֶׁב		וַיִּירַשׁ	
Cohort. 1 sing.	אֵשְׁבָה			
Impf. in a with suff.	יְדָעֵנִי	Imper. דָּעֵהוּ		
Infin. cstr.	שֶׁבֶת	יִרְאָה[1]	רֶשֶׁת	הִוָּשֵׁב
absol.	יָשׁוֹב		יָרוֹשׁ	
Part. act.	יֹשֵׁב	יָרֵא	יֹרֵשׁ	נוֹשָׁב
pass.	יָשׁוּב		יָרוּשׁ	

[1] Very rarely יִרָא.

WAW VERBS. § 39.

Group headings, left to right: **WAW VERBS. § 39.** (Hiph., Hoph.) | **Verbs פ״י.** (Qal, Hiph.) | **Verbs assimilating.** (Qal, Niph., Hiph)

Hiph.	Hoph.	Qal	Hiph.	Qal	Niph.	Hiph
הוֹשִׁיב	הוּשַׁב	יָנַק	הֵינִיק	יָצַת	נִצַּת	הִצִּית
הוֹשִׁיבָה	הוּשְׁבָה		הֵינִיקָה	יָצֹק		
הוֹשַׁבְתָּ	הוּשַׁבְתָּ		הֵינַקְתָּ			
&c.	&c.		&c.			
יוֹשִׁיב	יוּשַׁב	יִינַק	יֵינִיק	יִצַּת		יַצִּית
תּוֹשִׁיב		תִּינַק	תֵּינִיק	יִצֹּק		
תּוֹשִׁיב		תִּינַק	תֵּינִיק			
תּוֹשִׁיבִי		תִּינְקִי	תֵּינִיקִי			
&c.		אִינַק	אֵינִיק			
		יִינְקוּ	יֵינִיקוּ			
		תִּינַקְנָה	תֵּינִקְנָה			
		תִּינְקוּ	תֵּינִיקוּ			
		תִּינַקְנָה	תֵּינִקְנָה			
		נִינַק	נֵינִיק			
הוֹשֵׁב			הֵינֵק			
הוֹשִׁיבִי			הֵינִיקִי			
הוֹשִׁיבוּ			הֵינִיקוּ			
הוֹשֵׁבְנָה			הֵינֵקְנָה			
יוֹשֵׁב			יֵינֵק			יַצֵּת
וַיּוֹשֵׁב			וַיֵּינֶק			
הוֹשִׁיב	הוּשַׁב		הֵינִיק			
הוֹשֵׁב	הוּשַׁב		הֵינֵק			
מוֹשִׁיב	מוּשָׁב	יוֹנֵק	מֵינִיק			מַצִּית
	מוּשָׁב	יָנוּק				

'AYIN WAW AND

Qal

	act.	stat.	stat.	
Perf. Sing. 3 m.	קָם	מֵת	בּוֹשׁ	בִּינָה
3 f.	קָמָה	מֵתָה	בּוֹשָׁה	בַּנְתָּ
2 m.	קַמְתָּ	מַתָּה	בֹּשְׁתָּ	&c.
2 f.	קַמְתְּ	מַתְּ	בֹּשְׁתְּ	
1 c.	קַמְתִּי	מַתִּי	בֹּשְׁתִּי	
Plur. 3 c.	קָמוּ	מֵתוּ	בּוֹשׁוּ	
2 m.	קַמְתֶּם	מַתֶּם	בָּשְׁתֶּם	
2 f.	קַמְתֶּן	מַתֶּן	בָּשְׁתֶּן	
1 c.	קַמְנוּ	מַתְנוּ	בֹּשְׁנוּ	
Impf. Sing. 3 m.	יָקוּם	יָמוּת	יֵבוֹשׁ	יָבִין
3 f.	תָּקוּם		תֵּבוֹשׁ	תָּבִין
2 m.	תָּקוּם		תֵּבוֹשׁ	תָּבִין
2 f.	תָּקוּמִי		תֵּבוֹשִׁי	תָּבִינִי
1 c.	אָקוּם		אֵבוֹשׁ	אָבִין
Plur. 3 m.	יָקוּמוּ		יֵבוֹשׁוּ	יָבִינוּ
3 f.	תְּקוּמֶינָה		תֵּבוֹשְׁנָה	תְּבִינֶינָה
2 m.	תָּקוּמוּ		תֵּבוֹשׁוּ	תָּבִינוּ
2 f.	תְּקוּמֶינָה		תֵּבוֹשְׁנָה	תְּבִינֶינָה
1 c.	נָקוּם		נֵבוֹשׁ	נָבִין
Imp. Sing. 2 m.	קוּם קוּמָה	מוּת	בּוֹשׁ	בִּין
2 f.	קוּמִי		בּוֹשִׁי	בִּינִי
Plur. 2 m.	קוּמוּ		בּוֹשׁוּ	בִּינוּ
2 f.	קֹמְנָה		בֹּשְׁנָה	
Juss. 3 sing.	יָקֹם			יָבֵן
waw cons. impf.	וַיָּקָם			וַיָּבֶן
Cohort. 1 sing.	אָקוּמָה			אָבִינָה
waw cons. perf.	וְקַמְתָּ			וּבַנְתָּ
Inf. cstr.	קוּם	מוּת	בּוֹשׁ	בִּין
absol.	קוֹם	מוֹת	בּוֹשׁ	בּוֹן
Part. act.	קָם קָמָה	מֵת	בּוֹשׁ	בָּן
pass.	קוּם קוּמָה			(בּוֹן בִּין)

YODH VERBS. § 40.

Niph.	Hiph.	Hoph.
נָקוֹם	הֵקִים	הוּקַם
נָק֫וֹמָה	הֵקִ֫ימָה	הוּקְמָה
נְקוּמֹ֫תָ	הֲקִימֹ֫תָ	הוּקַ֫מְתָּ
נְקוּמֹת	הֲקִימֹת	הוּקַמְתְּ
נְקוּמֹ֫תִי	הֲקִימֹ֫תִי	הוּקַ֫מְתִּי
נָק֫וֹמוּ	הֵקִ֫ימוּ	הוּקְמוּ
נְקוּמֹתֶם[1]	הֲקִימֹתֶם	הוּקַמְתֶּם
נְקוּמֹתֶן	הֲקִימֹתֶן	הוּקַמְתֶּן
נְקוּמֹ֫נוּ	הֲקִימֹ֫נוּ	הוּקַ֫מְנוּ
יִקּוֹם	יָקִים	יוּקַם
תִּקּוֹם	תָּקִים	תּוּקַם
תִּקּוֹם	תָּקִים	תּוּקַם
תִּקּ֫וֹמִי	תָּקִ֫ימִי	תּוּקְמִי
אֶקּוֹם	אָקִים	אוּקַם
יִקּ֫וֹמוּ	יָקִ֫ימוּ	יוּקְמוּ
	תְּקוּמֶ֫ינָה, תָּקֵ֫מְנָה	תּוּקַ֫מְנָה
תִּקּ֫וֹמוּ	תָּקִ֫ימוּ	תּוּקְמוּ
	תָּקֵ֫מְנָה	תּוּקַ֫מְנָה
נוּקַם	נָקֵם	נוּקַם
הִקּוֹם	הָקֵם, הָקִ֫ימָה	
הִקּ֫וֹמִי	הָקִ֫ימִי	
הִקּ֫וֹמוּ	הָקִ֫ימוּ	
הִקֹּ֫מְנָה	הָקֵ֫מְנָה	
	יָקֵם	
	וַיָּ֫קֶם	
	אָקִ֫ימָה	
	וַהֲקִימֹת	
הִקּוֹם	הָקִים	הוּקַם
הָקוֹם, נָקוֹם	הָקֵם	
נָקוֹם	מֵקִים	מוּקָם
f. נְקוֹמָה	f. מְקִימָה	מוּקָם

Forms of Intens.

Act.	Pass.	Reflex.
קֹמֵם		הִתְקֹמֵם
קוֹמֵם	קוֹמַם	הִתְקוֹמֵם
קִמְקֵם	קָמְקַם	הִתְקַמְקֵם

like *Pi'ēl* &c. of the
Regular Verb.

---

[1] The only examples of 2 *pl.* have *ó*, not *û*.

VERBS DOUBLE

Qal

	act.		stat.	
Perf. Sing. 3 m.	(סֹב) סָבַב		קַל	בֵּל
3 f.	(סַבָּה) סָבְבָה		קַלָּה	&c.
2 m.	סַבֹּ֫ותָ		קַלֹּ֫ותָ	
2 f.	סַבֹּות		קַלֹּות	
1 c.	סַבֹּ֫ותִי		קַלֹּ֫ותִי	
Plur. 3 c.	(סַבּוּ) סָבְבוּ		קַלּוּ	
2 m.	סַבֹּותֶם		קַלֹּותֶם	
2 f.	סַבֹּותֶן		קַלֹּותֶן	
1 c.	סַבֹּ֫ונוּ		קַלֹּונוּ	
Impf. Sing. 3 m.	יָסֹב	יִסֹּב	יֵקַל	יִמַּל
3 f.	תָּסֹב	תִּסֹּב	תֵּקַל	תִּמַּל
2 m.	תָּסֹב	תִּסֹּב	תֵּקַל	תִּמַּל
2 f.	תָּסֹ֫בִּי	תִּסֹּ֫בִּי	תֵּקַ֫לִּי	תִּמְּלִי
1 c.	אָסֹב	אֶסֹּב	אֵקַל	אֶמַּל
Plur. 3 m.	יָסֹ֫בּוּ	יִסֹּבוּ	יֵקַ֫לּוּ	יִמַּלוּ
3 f.	תְּסֻבֶּ֫ינָה	תִּסֹּבְנָה	תִּקַלֶּ֫ינָה	תִּמַּלְנָה
2 m.	תָּסֹ֫בּוּ	תִּסֹּבוּ	תֵּקַ֫לּוּ	תִּמְּלוּ
2 f.	תְּסֻבֶּ֫ינָה	תִּסֹּבְנָה	תִּקַלֶּ֫ינָה	תִּמַּלְנָה
1 c.	נָסֹב	נִסֹּב	נֵקַל	נִמַּל
Imp. Sing. 2 m.	סֹב			
2 f.	סֹ֫בִּי			
Plur. 2 m.	סֹ֫בּוּ			
2 f.	סֻבֶּ֫ינָה			
Juss. 3 sing.	יָסֹב	יִסֹּב	יֵקַל	&c.
waw cons. impf.	וַיָּ֫סָב	וַיִּסֹּב	וַיֵּקַל	
Cohort. 1 sing.	אָסֹ֫בָּה	אֶסֹּבָה	&c.	
waw cons. perf.	וְסַבֹּותָ			
Inf. cstr.	סֹב		קֹל קַל	
absol.	סָבֹוב		קָלֹול	
Part. act.	סֹובֵב		קַל קָלֶה	
pass.	סָבוּב			

'AYIN. § 42.

Niph.	Hiph.	Hoph.	Forms of Intens. Act.	Pass.	Reflex.
נָסַב	הֵסֵב	הוּסַב	קֹלֵל	קֹלַל	הִתְקֹלֵל
נָסַבָּה	הֵסַבָּה	הוּסַבָּה	קוֹלֵל	קוֹלַל	הִתְקוֹלֵל
נְסַבּוֹת	הֲסִבּוֹתָ	הוּסַבּוֹתָ	קֹלְקֵל	קָלְקַל	הִתְקַלְקֵל
נְסַבּוֹת	הֲסִבּוֹת	&c.	like *Pi'ēl* &c. in the Regular Verb.		
נְסַבּוֹתִי	הֲסִבּוֹתִי				
נָסַבּוּ	הֵסַבּוּ				
נְסַבּוֹתֶם	הֲסִבּוֹתֶם				
נְסַבּוֹתֶן	הֲסִבּוֹתֶן				
נְסַבּוֹנוּ	הֲסִבּוֹנוּ				
יִסַּב	יָסֵב יָסֹב יָסַב	יוּסַב			
תִּסַּב	תָּסֵב	&c.			
תִּסַּב	תָּסֵב				
תִּסַּבִּי	תָּסֵבִּי				
אֶסַּב	אָסֵב				
יִסַּבּוּ	יָסֵבּוּ				
תִּסַּבֶּינָה	תְּסִבֶּינָה				
תִּסַּבּוּ	תָּסֵבּוּ				
תִּסַּבֶּינָה	תְּסִבֶּינָה				
נָסַב	נָסֵב				
הִסַּב	הָסֵב				
הִסַּבִּי	הָסֵבִּי				
הִסַּבּוּ	הָסֵבּוּ				
הִסַּבֶּינָה	הָסֵבֶּינָה				
	יָסֵב				
	וַיָּסֶב				
הָסֵב	הָסֵב	הוּסַב			
הִסּוֹב	הָסֵב				
מֵסַב מְסִבָּה נָסָ— ; נְסַבָּה		מוּסַב			

LAMEDH HE (LAM. YODH

	Qal	Niph.	Pi'ēl	Pu'al
Perf. Sing. **3** *m.*	גָּלָה	נִגְלָה	גִּלָּה	גֻּלָּה
3 *f.*	גָּלְתָה	נִגְלְתָה	גִּלְּתָה	גֻּלְּתָה
2 *m.*	גָּלִיתָ	נִגְלֵיתָ	גִּלִּיתָ ‑ֵיתָ[2]	גֻּלֵּיתָ
2 *f.*	גָּלִית	נִגְלֵית &c.	&c.	&c.
1 *c.*	גָּלִיתִי	נִגְלֵיתִי		
Plur. **3** *c.*	גָּלוּ	נִגְלוּ		
2 *m.*	גְּלִיתֶם	נִגְלֵיתֶם		
2 *f.*	גְּלִיתֶן	נִגְלֵיתֶן		
1 *c.*	גָּלִינוּ	נִגְלֵינוּ[1]		
Impf. Sing. **3** *m.*	יִגְלֶה	יִגָּלֶה	יְגַלֶּה	יְגֻלֶּה
3 *f.*	תִּגְלֶה	תִּגָּלֶה		
2 *m.*	תִּגְלֶה	תִּגָּלֶה		
2 *f.*	תִּגְלִי	תִּגָּלִי		
1 *c.*	אֶגְלֶה	אֶגָּלֶה		
Plur. **3** *m.*	יִגְלוּ	יִגָּלוּ		
3 *f.*	תִּגְלֶינָה	תִּגָּלֶינָה		
2 *m.*	תִּגְלוּ	תִּגָּלוּ		
2 *f.*	תִּגְלֶינָה	תִּגָּלֶינָה		
1 *c.*	נִגְלֶה	נִגָּלֶה		
Imp. Sing. **2** *m.*	גְּלֵה	הִגָּלֵה הִגָּל	גַּלֵּה גַּל	—
2 *f.*	גְּלִי	הִגָּלִי		
Plur. **2** *m.*	גְּלוּ	הִגָּלוּ		
2 *f.*	גְּלֶינָה	הִגָּלֶינָה		
Juss. **3** *sing. m.*	&c. יִגֶל	יִגָּל	יְגַל	
waw cons. impf.	&c. וַיִּגֶל			
waw cons. perf.	וְגָלִיתָ	וְנִגְלֵיתָ		
Inf. cstr.	גְּלוֹת	הִגָּלוֹת	גַּלּוֹת	גֻּלּוֹת
absol.	גָּלֹה	נִגְלֹה	גַּלֵּה	גֻּלֹּה
Part. act.	גֹּלֶה —לֶה	נִגְלֶה	מְגַלֶּה	
pass.	גָּלוּי גְּלוּיָה			מְגֻלֶּה
stat.	קָשֶׁה —שֶׁה			

---

[1] 1 pl. Niph. always *i*.

AND WAW VERBS.   § 44.

Hithp.	Hiph.	Hoph.	Suffixes.
			Perf. Sing. 1 c. גָּלַנִי ‑ֵ‑נִי
הִתְגַּלָּה	הִגְלָה	הָגְלָה	2 m. גָּלְךָ
הִתְגַּלְּתָה	הִגְלְתָה	הָגְלְתָה	2 f. גָּלֵךְ
הִתְגַּלִּיתָ ‑ֵ‑יתָ	הִגְלִיתָ [2] ‑ֵ‑יתָ	הָגְלֵיתָ ‑ֵ‑יתָ	3 m. גָּלָהוּ
			3 f. גָּלָהּ
			Plur. 1 c. גָּלָנוּ
			2 m.
			2 f.
			3 m. גָּלָם
			3 f.
יִתְגַּלֶּה	יַגְלֶה	יָגְלֶה	*Impf. Sing.* 1 c. יִגְלֵנִי
			2 m. יִגְלְךָ
			2 f. יִגְלֵךְ
			3 m. יִגְלֵהוּ
			3 f. יִגְלֶהָ
			Plur. 1 c. יִגְלֵנוּ
			2 m.
			2 f.
			3 m. יִגְלֵם
הִתְגַּלֵּה הִגָּל — גָּל	הַגְלֵה הֶגֶל	—	3 f.
			Imp. Sing. 1 c. גָּלֵנִי
יִתְגַּל	הֶגֶל וַיֶּגֶל		3 m. גָּלֵהוּ
			3 f. גָּלֶהָ
			Plur. 1 c. גָּלֵנוּ
			3 m. גָּלֵם
הִתְגַּלּוֹת	הַגְלוֹת	הָגְלוֹת	
הִתְגַּלֵּה	הַגְלֵה	הָגְלֵה	
מִתְגַּלֶּה	מַגְלֶה	מָגְלֶה	
		מֻגְלֶה	

---

[2] 1 sing. Pi. Hiph. Hithp. usually *é*, probably to avoid the threefold *i*; e. g. גִּלֵּיתִי.

THE ACCENTS.

1. Of the accentual *signs* some stand above, and some below the word ; when above, the sign stands upon the initial cons. of the accented syll., as מַיִם ; when below, it stands after the vowel of the syll., as מַיִם, except in the case of *ḥolem* and *shureq*, when it is placed under the conson., as יוֹם, רוּחַ. When the accented syll. begins with two conss. the sign is put on the second. A few signs are restricted to particular positions, such as the initial or final letter of a word, and do not indicate the Tone syll.

2. *The Accentual system.*[1] The Accentual system is very intricate and in some parts obscure. A brief outline of its uses as a means of inter-punction will here suffice :—

a) The text is broken into verses, *P^sûqîm*, and the end of each *Pāsûq* is marked by the sign :, called *Sôph pasuq* (end of the verse). The accent on the final word is called *Sillûq*, its sign being like Methegh.

הָאָרֶץ: . . . . Gen. I. 1.

b) The greatest logical pause within the verse is indicated by a sign called *'Athnāh* "breathing," or "rest."

הָאָרֶץ: . . . . אֱלֹהִים . . . . Gen. I. 1.

c) If there be two great pauses in the verse the greatest or one next the end of the verse is marked by 'Athnah, and the one nearer the beginning of the verse by sign ⸶ called *S^gôltâ*, as,

כֵּן . . . . לָרְקִיעַ . . . . הָרְקִיעַ . . . . Gen. I. 7.

d) If the clause of words lying between Ṣilluq and 'Athnah, or between 'Athnah and Ṣegolta, or between 'Athnah and the beginning of the verse, Ṣegolta being absent, requires to be divided by a pretty large pause, this is in all these cases marked by a sign ⸱ called *Zāqēph qāṭôn*, resembling simple sh^ewa placed over the word,[2] as,

לַמַּיִם: . . . . . . מַבְדִּיל . . . . . . הַמַּיִם . . . . . . אֱלֹהִים . . . . . . Gen. I. 6.

---

[1] The accents described in a)—f) are known as disjunctives.

[2] The sign ⸴ called *z. gādhôl*, of the same distinctive power, is used when its word is the only word in the accentual clause : as לְהַבְדִּיל Gen. I. 14.

e) *R*e*bhîa'*, in appearance like *hôlem*, but standing higher, often indicates subdivisions within *zāqēph* sections : as,

וַיֹּאמֶר אֱלֹהִים . . . הַשָּׁמַיִם . . . . הַלַּיְלָה: . . . Gen. I. 14.

f) A distinctive of less power than Zakeph is *Tiphḥâ*, which marks a pause which the rhythm *requires* as a preliminary to the great pauses indicated by Ṣilluq and 'Athnaḥ. Its sign ֖ is a line bent backwards, as,

בְּרֵאשִׁית . . . . אֱלֹהִים . . . . הַשָּׁמַיִם . . . . הָאָרֶץ: . . . Gen. I. 1.

g) These are the main distinctive accents, and by stopping at them, as at the points in modern languages, the reader will do justice to the sense. Very roughly (*a*) may be said to correspond to our full stop (.), (*b*) to our colon (:), (*c*), (*d*) and (*e*) to our semi-colon (;), and (*e*) to our comma (,).

There are several more distinctives of lesser force. There is also a number of conjunctive accents or *Servants*, as they are called, to the disjunctives, accents which are placed on the words that stand immediately before and in close relation with those on which distinctives are placed. It would seem to follow from the variety of the conjunctive signs that they had musical significance, otherwise one connective might have served all distinctives alike. The two most common *conjunctives* are *Mêr*e*khâ* ֥, which serves Ṣilluq and *Tiphḥa*, and *Mûnāḥ* ֣, which serves 'Athnaḥ and *Zaqeph*. See Gen. I. 1. 2.

h) The books *Job*, *Proverbs* and *Psalms* have an accentuation in some respects different from that of the other books, called the *Poetical*. The end of the verse is marked as in Prose by Ṣilluq and Ṣoph paṣuq ; also the great distinction next the end by 'Athnaḥ ; but this is not the greatest distinction in the verse, which is that next the beginning, marked by a sign ֫ *'Ôlé w*e*yôrēdh* (sometimes wrongly called *Mêr*e*khâ Mahpākh* or *M*e*huppākh*), thus :

רְשָׁעִים . . . . עָמַד . . . . יָשָׁב: . . . . Ps. I. I.

INDEX OF SUBJECTS.